THE RHINE AS
MUSICAL METAPHOR

MUSIC ADVISOR TO
NORTHEASTERN UNIVERSITY PRESS
GUNTHER SCHULLER

THE RHINE
AS MUSICAL
METAPHOR

CULTURAL IDENTITY
IN GERMAN
ROMANTIC MUSIC

CECELIA HOPKINS PORTER

NORTHEASTERN UNIVERSITY PRESS
BOSTON

Northeastern University Press

Library of Congress Cataloging-in-Publication Data

Porter, Cecelia Hopkins.
The Rhine as musical metaphor : cultural identity in German
romantic music / Cecelia Hopkins Porter.
p.   cm.
Includes bibliographical references (p.   ) and index.
ISBN 1-55553-284-5 (cl : alk. paper)
1. Symbolism in music.   2. Rhine River.   3. Music
and society.   4. Music—Germany—19th century—
History and criticism.   I. Title
ML3838.P67   1996
781.5'6—dc20   96-14967
MN

Designed by Janice Wheeler

Composed in Centaur by Coghill Composition, Richmond,
Virginia. Printed and bound by the Maple Press, York,
Pennsylvania. The paper is Perfection Eggshell, an acid-free stock.

MANUFACTURED IN THE UNITED STATES OF AMERICA
00   99   98   97   96   5   4   3   2   1

TO
GORDON KIRSCHNER
WITH ADMIRATION
AND LOVE

AND TO THE MEMORY OF
PAUL HENRY LANG,
JACK M. STEIN,
DONALD M. McCORKLE,
YOKO WATANABE MITANI,
AND MY PARENTS

CONTENTS

ILLUSTRATIONS

LIST OF FIGURES

LIST OF MUSICAL EXAMPLES

ACKNOWLEDGMENTS

Much time has elapsed and several major discoveries have been made since I launched this project with a doctoral dissertation. As the years unfolded in the wake of that study, I continued to ponder the image of a river and music as my subject. This quest entailed summoning the Rhine as a metaphor for certain facets, some already formulated and some less obvious, of German Romantic music in that important *Vormärz* decade leading to the Revolution of 1848, the midpoint of the nineteenth century. Periods of doubt and scepticism not infrequently seemed to cloud the horizon, as they should for all scholars. Each wave of uncertainty, however, resulted in my acquisition of further data that in amount and significance served ultimately to reaffirm my underlying assumption. On every such occasion that process led to rethinking and ultimately reshaping my story.

Thus this book was born, after a lengthy gestation period that incurred my considerable indebtedness to scholarly peers, friends, and family members for their abiding support, ferreting of information, and thoughtful comments. I owe perhaps the most long-standing and decisive debt to the late Prof. Jack M. Stein, chairman of the German Department of Harvard University when I was his student. He urged me to continue my study of music in Germany, and so, with the aid of a German government fellowship, I was on my way to Berlin for a year. Until his untimely death, Prof. Stein encouraged me in my pursuit of German music and its history. The late Prof. Paul Henry Lang at Columbia University offered me valuable suggestions as I assumed the career of musical scholar and critic. I also profited greatly from seminars on the German lied and Franz Schubert given by Prof. Walter Wiora at Columbia. The late Prof. Donald M.

McCorkle offered sage advice and enthusiasm as I honed my topic and undertook the initial research for my project.

I wish to express my deep gratitude also to Prof. John Rink at the University of Surrey in England and to the British Academy, which awarded me a grant to pursue the most recent phase of my work at the International Conference on Nineteenth-Century Music held at the university in July 1994.

There are many others to name: Prof. E. Eugene Helm, my dissertation adviser at the University of Maryland; Maryland professors Lawrence Moss and George Jones; Dr. Paul Kast, of the Heinrich-Heine-Institut in Düsseldorf; Dr. Peter Ostwald, of the University of California; William Parsons, of the Music Division in the Library of Congress, who generously devoted much time in my quest for musical and pictorial sources; the late Edward Waters and Elmer Booze, also of the Library; Prof. Dale H. Porter (my brother-in-law) of Western Michigan University; the perspicacious critic of my manuscript, Prof. John J. Daverio, of Boston University; Dr. Gerd Nauhaus, director of the Schumann-Haus in Zwickau; Iris Golumbeck, of the German Historical Institute in Washington, D.C.; and Dr. Knut Dorn of Wiesbaden.

I would also like to underline the sometimes unique advantages of being an independent scholar often working without the full resources of official academia. For years my friends Klaus and Elizabeth Brand (and on occasion Klaus's colleagues at Volkswagen of America) provided me with support and contributions of valuable information from and about Germany. "For my inspiration," the Brands also personally siphoned and bottled a 1972 *Spät Lese* (singularly captioned *Echtes Schmutzwasser aus dem deutschen Rhein [Aqua Rhenus Pollutus]*) from the left bank of the river at Boppard. To this day, my rare, custom-bottled vintage continues to age handsomely in my study. My attorney friend Elizabeth Chase also made contributions of recordings and scholarly material. My parents never faltered in their untold hours of helping me care for my four progeny as the arrival of each one expanded the Porter household during my doctoral work. One day, moreover, my father proudly divulged that, as a child in the St. Louis public school system, he and his classmates had sung Carl Wilhelm's setting of "Die Wacht am Rhein" in English daily as part of ritualistic opening exercises in the pre–World War I era. Each of my children contributed much to the writing of this book: Rebecca was a top-notch editor; Elizabeth gave reams of psychological support; Bartholomew congratulated me as each stage of the project was completed; and Lawrence patiently answered all my cries of help when my word processor refused to cooperate. My husband, Douglas, has always been my chief source of inspiration and courage—the true alpha and omega of it all.

To all these benefactors, both named and unnamed, go my endless gratitude and recognition, for they are all part of the Rhenish mystique.

THE RHINE AS
MUSICAL METAPHOR

INTRODUCTION

*A*t a West Coast aquarium a docent once explained that a sea otter's fur consists of over 800 million hairs that keep the animal waterproof and warm. In preening this coat, the guide continued, a sea otter requires assistance from a fellow member of the species, supporting social interdependence among individual animals in the group. The necessity for grooming assistance by a sea otter "valet" provides the foundation for the complex structure of sea otter society.

In itself, the existence of 800 million hairs per sea otter is only an astonishing but arcane statistic. That this phenomenon underlies the essence of sea otter civilization as an essential link in the global food chain, however, contributes useful information to the store of human knowledge.

So it is with historical scholarship in general and the history of music in particular. The phenomenon that around four hundred German lieder concerning the Rhine River and its associations were published during the *Vormärz* could simply exhaust, rather than stimulate, further music-historical thought. If we are also aware, however, that other songs published during that turbulent decade preceding the Revolution of 1848—songs referring to the Danube or Elbe—number only twenty at most, there is ample justification for investigating the historical significance of the four hundred Rheinlieder. The study of this rich lode of musical literature, in fact, should contribute to our knowledge of musical life and issues in German Romantic society.

BACKGROUND OF THE RHINE CRISIS

In June 1839 a fleet of the Ottoman Empire raced from the Dardanelles under the command of its Capitan-Pasha, Ahmed Fevzi, only to alter course in midvoyage. Veering away from their assigned Syrian port, where they were to buttress the Turks' determined collection of tribute from Pasha Muhammad 'Ali, the mutinous crew docked instead at Alexandria and into the welcoming arms of the Ottomans' rebellious vassal himself. This momentous scene formed part of a larger drama taking place on a vast stage extending from the Near East to Western Europe. The Egyptians' revolt endangered the integrity of the Ottoman Empire, the fate of which was crucial to the European balance of power vis-à-vis control of the eastern Mediterranean.

France sympathized with Muhammad 'Ali's insurrection while incurring the wrath of Britain, Austria, Russia, and Prussia. These four allies of the Ottomans retaliated against the French with the London Treaty of 15 July 1840, a clandestine ultimatum designed to quell the revolt of France's protégé against the Turkish realm. The indignant French, led by Prime Minister Adolphe Thiers, threatened to take their "natural frontier of the Rhine," thereby provoking no small measure of angst among Germans, for whom the Rhine had become a vital cultural and national symbol in their struggles toward nationhood. Thus the likelihood of war on the Mediterranean posed a similar prospect in Europe, along the Rhenish and Alpine border areas. Within days the Rhinelands had shifted into central focus on the high altar of German nationalistic spirit as multitudinous Rhine poems, ranging from the lofty to the garish, saturated the popular press in defiance of French saber rattling. Almost four hundred musical settings of this poetry were published or selected for republication in response to the Rhine crisis of 1840, continuing through the decade that opened with Schumann's "song year" (during which eight of his nine Rheinlieder were composed) and concluded while Wagner was gestating the poem of his massive Rhine tetralogy, *Der Ring des Nibelungen*.[1]

THE RHINE AS METAPHOR

One of the choicest dividends of scholarship during the antediluvian precomputer era was the chance discovery of unsolicited but enticing data that fell one's way in pursuit of a topic in library card catalogues. Such was the case years ago in the Library of Congress Music Division, when, during a random perusal through the voluminous pages of Adolph Hofmeister's three-volume (plus supplement) edition of *C. F. Whistling's Handbuch der musikalischen Literatur* (hereafter referred to as the Hofmeister catalogues), listing after listing of German lieder referring to the Rhine caught my attention. All the examples were published during the 1840s decade.[2]

The wealth of implications and associations subsumed in the Rhine as metaphor became evident only in gradual stages during the writing of this book, as did the necessity for a cross-disciplinary approach. Despite diversity of vocabulary and materials, the investigation of "extramusical" developments from the earlier to the mid-nineteenth century confirmed my initial suspicion that the Rhine image had imbedded itself, as an element of both comfort and inspiration, deeply within the German Romantics' heart and soul. And it did so with much of the force and sense of provocation wrought by the presence of the Berlin Wall in the minds of their twentieth-century descendants.

The metaphor of the Rhine cannot be replaced with that of any other river. Throughout history, human beings have invested rivers with magical powers in that they not only separate and hence define one culture as opposed to another but also, as arteries of commerce and communication, unite diverse populations. One could certainly make a case for seeking the character of America's Middle West by "exploring" the Ohio or striving to recapture the essence of medieval Florence through a study of the Po. Yet important as the Ohio and Po are, they simply do not have the same ring to them that the Rhine does. That is possibly the overwhelming difference between the Rhine and these other two rivers. For the soul of the Germans' Rhine is the resonance of the Nibelungs and the echoes of the Loreley. One simply cannot conceive of a Germany encapsulated in a musicless silence.

Nor does the Rhine image convey the essence of German music in the eighteenth or twentieth century as well as it does the nineteenth. The ancient *Vater Rhein*, its rushing currents for eons providing the lifeblood of European civilization, became a central object of aesthetic appreciation only with the coming of a singularly pictorial epoch, that of German Romanticism. This era, one dominated by landscape art and nature poetry, was also one of shattering dissonances ensuing from the pressures of a burgeoning industrialization and commercialism, demographic upheavals, and tumultuous political realignments. These profound social and economic changes also overturned the socioeconomic foundation of music, restructuring the interrelationships of performance, patronage, and aesthetic ideals.

The conjunction of these massive forces, while undermining the dominion of the old order, furnished the context from which the Germans launched their grueling struggle to forge a national identity. The process was set into motion with Prussia's acquisition of the Rhineland at the close of the Wars of Liberation in 1815. The resulting alliance of Berlin and Düsseldorf—the capitals, respectively, of Prussia and of its new Rhine Province—brought together Germans long separated by the Protestantism of the east and the Catholicism of the west. This new political alliance, moreover, joined the Prussians of Germany's "outlands" with the increasingly affluent, urbanizing Rhine corridor. As a consequence, this union intensified artistic and other cultural bonds between these two important cities, not the least significant outcome of which was a reinforcing of musical ties.

The Rheinlieder published in the decade of the *Vormärz* gave voice to a far-reaching constellation of forces marking European, and especially German, culture of the time. The image of the Rhine River, both real and idealized, played a central role in all these currents of thought. The quest for a national identity, in both its political and cultural aspects, engaged the German mind. Germans sought a geographical line of demarcation defining their territory. The Rhine, which had divided Latin from Germanic civilization for millennia, also provided a boundary against the equally nationalistic French. As we have seen, Prussia, already seeking control over Germans as a whole, had established its hegemony on this river in 1815. This accomplishment marked the end of inroads into German lands by a Napoleonic France. The Rhine, moreover, furnished the Germans with a major focus for their dreams of nationhood at a time when nature had captivated a scientific world embracing the evolutionary concept of all life as an organic continuum. This notion strengthened the German Romantics' faith in familial roots connecting them with each other and with their distant but common past. The Rhine as a supreme manifestation of nature served to incarnate all these feelings of connectedness.

The Romantic era was also one of seismic economic and social change moving toward a new order in which a developing mercantile, materialistic society was beginning to view geographical and other property as a moral right. In fact, that same France that considered its Rhine claim justified by nature had become England's chief imperialist rival, as the London Treaty of 1840 verified.

The Rhine had been a critical artery of commerce and communication since ancient times. The dawn of the Industrial Age further reinforced its role as a critical factor in the social, economic, and political coming of age among the European middle classes. This was particularly true in the musical life of such Rhine cities as Düsseldorf and in the growing institution of the Lower Rhine Music Festivals. In these events, as sharply reflected in Düsseldorf, the middle-class acquisition of continually growing economic resources was beginning to position this segment of society at the reins not only of industry and commerce but also of music and the other arts. The middle classes were assuming control of the previously aristocratically governed arts establishment and were becoming the new patrons, public, and entrepreneurs of music. Nowhere was this more evident than in Düsseldorf, the capital of Prussia's Rhine Province, and in the province's Lower Rhine Music Festivals.

As for the arts, the Rhine as a majestic image of nature was coming to be idealized for its beauty to a degree hitherto unknown. By the mid-nineteenth century, landscape painting had become a truly independent genre. This was exemplified by the frescoes of the Nazarenes, a group of German artists in Rome, which included scenes from the *Nibelungenlied*, the entire first half of which takes place on the Rhine. In poetry and prose as well, nature had become a new object of aesthetic veneration, with the Rhine as a chief subject. It was no wonder that with the Rhine crisis of 1840 a multitude of poets expressed this veneration in terms of the Rhine and its old mythological and historical associations.

Thus the examination of the four hundred Rheinlieder published in the 1840s offers us a window into nineteenth-century Germany, a pivotal culture in European Romanticism as a whole. The majority of these songs were second-rate music, but they show us the world in which Schumann wrote his *Dichterliebe*, his Festival Overture with Chorus on the "Rheinweinlied," and his Third ("Rhenish") Symphony; in which Mendelssohn produced his opera fragment *Lorelei*; and in which Wagner created *Der Ring der Nibelungen*. After leaving Paris in the spring of 1842, in fact, Wagner confessed, "For the first time I saw the Rhine—with hot tears in my eyes, I, poor artist, swore eternal fidelity to my German fatherland."[3]

THE APPROACH

This study of German Romantic music rests on basic data culled from the Hofmeister catalogues and the music itself: the specific stylistic and formal characteristics of the songs, their composers and performers, their publication, the poetic and geographical symbolism on which the music is based, and the place of these songs in the temporal context of nineteenth-century cultural, socioeconomic, and political history.

The music has been approached not only chronologically but analytically through the aesthetic device of a metaphor: the conglomerate of concepts and feelings evoked by an ancient, storied river elevated by the German Romantics to ethereal realms as the all-pervasive apotheosis of nature's beauty. The Greek *metaphérein* derives from *meta*, denoting motion or the process of change. *Phore* denotes a bearer of something. Thus a metaphor signifies a bearer of change and hence an instrument of transferred meaning. The use of the Rhine as a metaphor for German Romantic music offers a kinetic image for an era in which the newly heightened appreciation of visual beauty was paired with ideals of motion in the process of longing (*Sehnsucht*), becoming (*Werden*), and the joy of wayfaring (*Wanderlust*).

A metaphor can be applied to, or be made to stand for, an object or concept with which it is not ordinarily associated in order to suggest comparison with another object or concept. The latter is thereby endowed with a new, more specific meaning. Thus the Rhine image represents German Romantic music and musical life. Both, like this river, were centered on nature's beauty, its kinetic and perpetual process of becoming, its human feelings, its folklike grace and accessibility to all humankind, and its unifying force in a familial sense—to name but a few attributes.

The Rhine metaphor refers both to the river itself—with its tangible physical, political, commercial, and aesthetic attributes accumulated over the centuries—and to the Romantics' idealization of the river. It provides a timely symbol for an epoch when the decentralizing forces of centuries-old German particularism were having to yield to a growing mutual sense of national, over regional, identity. The Rhine as symbol offered a supreme common denominator, even a *Weltgeist* uniting the multifarious spheres of a specific culture's musical *Weltanschauung*. The concept of the Rhine as a sublime image of nature unveils a heretofore obscured element of unity (perhaps what Joseph Kerman means by "insight into music as aesthetic experience") in the historical panorama of an era so frequently characterized as antithetical.[4]

Central to this *Weltanschauung* is the peculiarly German Romantic theme of yearning for identity with the Rhine, as the apotheosis of Germanness, and yearning for escape from devastating feelings of isolation and abandonment. Yet underlying such urges was a dread of beauty's fatal allure, as represented so powerfully by the Rhine image.[5] These themes were voiced not only in the desolate landscapes of the painter Caspar David Friedrich but also in other realms poised on the verge of forsaking the old securities: in music, the waning of definable tonality in the face of an apparently rudderless dissonance; in religion, the eroding of established beliefs against the onslaught of existential doubt and despair; and in society, the weakening of regional and ethnic bonds with the encroachment of an anonymous national and eventually global population. All these forces were propelling time-honored practices inexorably into oblivion. For music, this meant the demise of the small-scaled world where, for example, more intimate channels of communication within the more exclusive circles of aristocratic music making were to vanish.

I make no apology for the follow-one's-nose approach in the process of unearthing the Rhine image as a central element in defining German Romantic music. This process entailed allowing the songs listed in the Hofmeister catalogues and lieder anthologies to pinpoint both concrete historical events and the mind-set of mid-nineteenth-century Germany. As Barbara Tuchman and Gertrude Himmelfarb profess, the historian must suspend the imposition of personal bias on the material at hand in order to preserve the social reality and moral imagination of those he or she seeks to evaluate.[6]

The approach used in this study also owes something to the now-orthodox "new history," whereby the realignment of chronologically ordered narrative ("history from above") furnishes the context for the analysis of the subject at hand, here the Rheinlieder, as quantifiable information ("history from below"). These two historiographical outlooks have been joined in assessing the place of the Rheinlieder in music history. For both the songs and their cultural context reveal a central concern with humankind's past and with the essence of nature. This is also evident in several extramusical areas in the nineteenth century. The biological sciences dealt with the primeval eons of the universe and its various life forms. The psychological sciences tended to focus on the human past by means of individual entities. And the nascent socioanthropological sciences confronted the history of humankind collectively. All these disciplines took wing with the onset of the Romantic era.

The opening chapter exposes the various facets of German Romantic *Volkstümlichkeit* (the ideal of the folklike, the popular, and hence the German) that furnished the ideological setting for the Rheinlieder. This German Romantic ideal subsumed in music both a characteristic style and modes of performance practice. The exploration of *Volkstümlichkeit* particularly helps define aspects of a developing nineteenth-century German cultural national- ism and its relationship to the glorification of nature. In doing so, this process brings to light such active movements as the growth of an amateur choral tradition, its patriotic foundation, and the origins of Rhine Roman- ticism, especially among German literati.

The first part of chapter 2 summarizes the international machinations endangering the already tenuous balance of power in western Europe vis-à- vis the crumbling Ottoman Empire. The complications involved in this situation provoked France into threatening to take the Rhine River. The resulting German alarm over this matter, especially in the light of Napo- leon's earlier occupation of Rhine territories now controlled by Prussia, stirred a minor Rhenish functionary, Nikolaus Becker, to compose a poem defending the Rhine as Germany's own. The ardor of his verses, equaled only by their triviality of expression, inspired a heated polemic both within French and German intellectual circles and between the two peoples them- selves. It also prompted at least 111 composers to set Becker's poem to music and gave rise to contests to determine the "best" version.

The second part of this chapter reviews the mixed reception of these settings and other Rheinlieder by leading critics in professional German music journals. In offering their judgments, these writers laid bare then- current aesthetic concerns, some of the most prominent issues being those of middle-class philistinism and commercialism in music.

After considering common notions in nineteenth-century natural science, historiography, and psychology, chapter 3 discusses related themes in the poems of the Rheinlieder. These themes include those of *Sehnsucht* (longing), *Werden* (becoming), *Wanderlust* (the joy of wayfaring), and *Weltschmerz*. All these share related motives. Another group of poems pays homage to a golden German past, represented especially by its military heroes, as well as supporting a more generalized political and cultural sense of identity. The chapter concludes with an examination of the Rheinlieder texts based on the Loreley and Nibelung images. The historical evolution of these figures serves to illumine such German Romantic topics as animism, longing, love entwined with death, and related mythical notions.

Chapter 4 describes the *volkstümlich* musical style of the Rheinlieder, ranging from the simplest examples to the lieder of major German Romantic composers that endeavor, to varying degrees, to capture the essence of folksong style within the context of the art song.

The last chapter considers the practice of music in the Rhineland in the light of *Volkstümlichkeit:* the *Volk* and their involvement in performance. As seen through the examples of Düsseldorf, the Prussian Rhineland capital, and the Lower Rhine Music Festivals, several prominent nineteenth-century issues are documented. They include dilettantism in choral performance and musical entrepreneurship, the competing rise of professionalism in orchestral playing, and Rhine nationalism. These were the same issues brought to light by the Rheinlieder and their historical milieu.

In the final analysis, this book attempts to assess a body of music, the Rheinlieder, in order to deepen our understanding of that culture known as German Romanticism. It is hoped that this view of nineteenth century music will provide a reasoned response to Dale H. Porter's challenge that the historian strive to evoke "imaginative reconstructions of past experience. This evocation has as its purposes the enrichment of the present, through integration with forms of experience based on other conditions and assumptions than one's own [and] the corollary critique of present-mindedness based on an increased sense of perspective."[7]

. 1 .

VOLKSTÜMLICHKEIT AND CULTURAL NATIONALISM: THE HISTORICAL CONTEXT OF THE GERMAN ROMANTIC LIED

*I*n a review of the celebrated lied "The Watch on the Rhine," the eminent Viennese critic Eduard Hanslick remarked, "Musical worth has nothing to do with what makes a song popular and elevates it to historical significance."[1] The Rheinlieder phenomenon of the 1840s precisely illustrates Hanslick's dictum. Apart from their intrinsic artistic worth, the popularity of these songs toward midcentury derived chiefly, in this case, from their success as the timely German *volkstümlich*, or popular, folklike, expression of a national cause. At this particular time, moreover, the Germans' national cause was symbolized to an extraordinary degree by the image of the Rhine.

The nineteenth-century definition of *Volkstümlichkeit* combined the quality of direct, folklike simplicity, in imitation of folksong style, with contemporary overtones of cultural nationalism that specifically evoked the notion of the German folk. For a lied fully to express the quality of musical *Volkstum*, the *Neue Zeitschrift für Musik* critic Gottschalk Wedel (the pseudonym of Anton Wilhelm Florentin von Zuccalmaglio [1803–69]) argued, "Melody . . . as well as meter must be written completely from the people's heart, must be completely fit for the mouth of the folk. The word must awaken great remembrances or inspire great thoughts."[2] Four days later he discussed national German implications of Handel's "See, the Conquering Hero Comes" from *Judas Maccabaeus*, which, he noted, "breathes the deep seriousness of the German spirit and expresses the most joyful *volkstümlich* enthusiasm. . . . In this work, the melodic flow . . . is noticeable, which, side by side with noble worth, corresponds to the musical spirit of the German people."[3]

At least as early as 1767, the philosopher-poet Johann Gottfried von Herder (1744–1803) had regarded *das Volk* as defined by its own peculiar national and cultural character.[4] Herder maintained that every *Volk* truly manifested a universal divine force, each equally favored by God. He repudiated any implication that any single people merited a position superior to any other. In his *Deutsches Volkstum* of 1810, however, the Prussian Friedrich Ludwig Jahn (1778–1852), known as "Vater Jahn," declared the German *Volk*, above all the Prussians, a primordially ordained force representing humanity's holy people.[5] He conceived *Volkstum* as a mystical power and the essence of the *Volk*, or the Reich. In fact, Jahn even considered the Rhine as the symbol of this essence, the river uniting all German *Volk* from the Netherlands to Switzerland.

In their combined notions of the "popular" (i.e., "of the people") and the "national," the German Romantics also exalted such philosophers as Georg Wilhelm Friedrich Hegel (1770–1831). With his concept of dialectic, he extended the pairing of nature and nation with eternal, paradivine mystical forces. Among these the abiding *Volksgeist* was supreme. Hegel viewed his pantheistic synthesis of God, the *Weltgeist*, reason, history, and nature as the foundation of the national state. And he emphasized a "natural," or organic, "dialectic evolution" of the nation-state whereby the thrust of a world force on each *Volk* would bestow on it a characteristic spirit and goal.[6]

By the nineteenth century, the middle classes in western Europe were seeking to obtain absolute political power in the nation, no longer conceived as the realm of a single ruling monarch. The nineteenth-century ideal for propertied citizens was to belong to a common territory, to share representation in a common administration, and to be collectively conscious of a genuine or supposed legacy.[7]

The notion of German Romantic *Volkstümlichkeit* included the assumption that patriotic feelings had evolved organically from "the people" and hence had derived quintessentially from nature. The sense of a community of national feeling, moreover, also reflected the parallel notion of group interest, particularly that of a family, a "natural" social unit.[8]

As nationalism gradually intensified throughout post-Napoleonic Europe, the Germans' version of patriotism acquired a distinctly metaphysical and biological cast. The philosopher-poet Friedrich von Schlegel (1772–1829) had elevated the "Teutonic" nationalistic dream to mystical heights. Even the German Romantics' Francophobia can be traced to their entrenched conviction that their homeland had originated as a sanctified primordial entity of nature. Indeed, as Hans Kohn observes, whereas French nationalism had derived from a rational societal outlook, German nationalism had evolved from "the 'natural' fact of a community, held together . . . by traditional ties of kinship and status. . . . German nationalism substituted for the legal and rational concept of 'citizenship' the infinitely vaguer concept of 'folk,' which . . . was fully developed by Herder and the German romanticists."[9]

The ardent Wars of Liberation poet Ernst Moritz Arndt (1769–1860) likewise regarded the German "nation" as evidence of a single common blood and language, or undefiled *Ursprache*. In his view, these elements formed the basis for the familial designation "folk." Similarly, the Rhenish journalist Jakob Venedey expressed his faith in the essentially biological essence of a nation. He argued that "ethnic [national] peculiarity is . . . indivisible like an organism and . . . therefore no people of a province will ever . . . have the right to separate themselves . . . from their mother race."[10] Nowhere else at that time could one find such an absolute distinction between the French and German concepts of nationalism and nationhood.

NATIONAL AND LIBERAL CONSCIOUSNESS IN THE RHINELANDS: A CONCATENATION OF ALLEGIANCES

The Wars of Liberation dissolved official connections between the Rhinelanders and the French, thereby realigning a nascent sense of Rhenish identity within the context of potential pan-German unity. This reversal of allegiances stimulated a consolidation of German liberal and national forces that reached dramatic dimensions in the Rhinelands. Encouraged by Napoleon's defeat, the Rhenish bourgeois merchants dedicated themselves to championing the cause of liberal rights and institutions. At the same time, they advocated an ideal of national unification. This ideal, they believed, would help dissolve the ancient divisive forces of particularism on which the fortunes of separatist-minded German princes depended.

THE JULY REVOLUTION OF 1830

On 27 July 1830 Paris republicans forced their Bourbon King Charles X to abdicate in favor of the duke of Orleans, who, as Louis-Philippe, ascended the throne two weeks later.[11] On the one hand, the July Revolution visibly advanced the status of the French upper bourgeoisie. And it directly encouraged liberal Rhenish political journalists to promote a merger of local and national patriotism based on a common constitution.[12] On the other hand, this uprising served only to heighten the anxiety of Prussia and Bavaria that their satellites, the Prussian Rhine Province and Bavarian Rhine Palatinate respectively, might now prefer local autonomy over allegiance to their ruler state.[13]

The Rhinelanders, however, supported liberal plans of their own. Those in the French-oriented Palatinate and Baden (in southwest Germany) favored local constitutional government in conjunction with pan-German allegiance.[14] The Prussian Rhine Province, however, supported local autonomy within a Berlin-controlled government.

Although concurring in the fundamental goal of constitutionalism, German liberals of the *Vormärz* disagreed as to the means deemed necessary for its realization. The "dualistic" approach combined democracy with monarchy, the former providing a check against possible encroachments by the latter. The "moderates" supported the French pacifist ideal of pan-Europeanism while simultaneously defending the territorial realignments established by the Vienna Congress in 1815. The Bonn University curator Joseph von Rehfues, for example, insisted that the Rhine's left bank belonged to the German Federation, while the Prussian Rhineland naturally would give obeisance to Berlin as its administrative authority.[15]

In like manner, the liberal press of the Prussian Rhine Province—as represented by the *Düsseldorfer Zeitung*, for example—largely approved of a Prussian-led national German state.[16] Adding to the already complicated polemic, the German Viscount Gustave de Failly proposed another version of "moderate" liberal pacifism. Since Catholicism, he argued, linked France with the Rhinelanders, the French should abandon thoughts of wresting political control of the Rhine from the Germans. Instead, he contended, France could preserve its own integrity simply by noninterference with the Germans' struggle for unification under a constitutional government.

TOWARD A TURNING POINT

The anxieties provoked by the events of 1830, together with the French Rhine threat of July 1840, clearly had developed into the broader issue of German nationalism. Meanwhile, as the liberalism of the 1840s began to pervade Europe, antiroyalist French rebels drove Louis-Philippe from the throne and proclaimed the Second Republic. The successful Paris Revolution of 1848 inspired in turn an outbreak of popular reformist demonstrations among the Germans. The governments of Baden, Hesse, and Württemberg soon yielded to pressures for a parliamentary system and free press. On 13 March riots erupting into pitched battles shook Berlin. The reign of Metternich collapsed. A week later King Ludwig I of Bavaria abdicated as Munich spurned his "Lolamontanism." On 21 March the Prussian monarch, Friedrich Wilhelm IV, yielded to the people's demand for the way to be opened for liberal government and a unified German state.

Presumably the Germans' millennium was at hand. The intellectuals and other contingents of the middle classes now pressed for representative government. By mid-March 1848 the Frankfurt Parliament, or German National Assembly, had convened. By the following January delegates from the various German states had drafted a national constitution. In the interim, however, reactionary forces were stifling the efforts of liberals and democrats, whose effectiveness had already been weakened by bitter factional strife. By autumn 1848 both royalty and the military had regained much of their former control, and the succeeding June witnessed the dissolution of the Assembly.

Das Volk nevertheless had spoken, and thenceforth the unity of the German states had become the wrenching issue for monarchs and masses alike.

VOLKSTÜMLICHKEIT AND MUSICAL STYLE: THE ROMANTICS' APPROPRIATION OF THE FOLKSONG IDIOM

The notion of the *Volk* also played a crucial role in the music of the *Vormärz*. Whether for simple amusement or for more serious occasions, the Rheinlieder adhered, in varying degrees, to a *volkstümlich* musical style. Inheriting the eighteenth-century legacy of C. G. Krause, C. P. E. Bach, J. F. Reichardt, J. A. P. Schulz, and C. F. Zelter, the songs of their nineteenth-century counterparts were intended to be "accessible." Cast either in an unaccompanied format or with simple guitar or piano support, they were easily singable with their modest range, melodic writing, harmony, and rhythm.[17]

The Rheinlieder of Schumann, Liszt, Franz, Cornelius, Loewe, and a few other composers fulfilled the requirements of true art songs while also

betraying certain lighter aspects of *Volkstümlichkeit*. Alongside the more perva-
sively *volkstümlich* Rheinlieder and art songs inclining toward that style, the
Hofmeister catalogues covering the 1840s list a number of traditional "folk
songs" with Rhine associations.

The *Volkstümlichkeit* ideal in songs paralleled the German Romantics' enthusiastic revival of old folk traditions and literature. Achim von Arnim
(1781–1831) and Clemens Brentano's (1778–1842) *Des Knaben Wunderhorn*
(The boy's magic horn) of 1805–8 included both traditional and the editors'
newly composed folk poems, offering a rich source of *volkstümlich* models
simple in their content and expression, with the music consistently repeated
through all verses. Walter Wiora describes this famous collection as an
"idea landscape" of historical and Romantically glorified notions that in
turn inspired new concepts or repoeticization.[18]

Although folksong style visibly influenced the poetry of Eichendorff,
Heine, Uhland, Mörike, and other German Romantics, folk tradition for a
time made little direct impact on the musical style of the lied. For the
amassing of folksong melodies in the Romantic period remained far behind
that of the texts. *Wunderhorn* had no musical counterpart, because Romantic
composers, unlike the poets, had not yet formally pursued the conscious
acquisition and compilation of folksong material. Hence composers had
few or no such melodies available to them in printed collections earlier
than the 1830s and 1840s.[19] Instead, Schubert and other composers, Wiora
has observed, relied on the immediate experience of listening to folk melodies.

The absence of notated folksong models obscures the extent to which
folk song influenced the music of the Romantic lied. Only a handful of
nineteenth-century German composers—such as Beethoven, Weber, Silcher, and Brahms—arranged or cited specific folk songs in their works.
More often, they resorted to the use of folksong types in the composition
of new songs. Romantic composers, unlike their poet contemporaries, were
thus restricted to the direct and indirect use of the intangibilities of oral
tradition. In addition to relying on folksong types or styles rather than on
specific melodies, Romantic lied composers absorbed folk traditions that
appealed to them as strange or old, such as the relatively atypical use of
minor keys.[20]

In addition to their strictly musical characteristics, the melodic types and
styles appropriated by Romantic composers from folk songs evidenced a
transmusical significance and background. They symbolized various aspects

of the poetic life: the notions of the forest, the hunt, roaming, pilgrimages, and other images that the Romantics musically "poeticized or repoeticized." For that purpose, both the poetic and musical legacy of the folk song offered a wealth of means. "Spheres of life and realms of the musical language," Wiora remarks, "are related to one another, and Romantic and neo-Romantic music cannot be understood at all without this connection."[21] One could view the nineteenth-century use of "natural" instrumental timbres, such as that of the *Waldhorn*, in a similar way. For the Romantics, the manipulation of sound quality revealed an ideal of music as a cosmic force guarding the secrets of the universe.[22] The infusion of the folksong idiom into the lied was a chief factor in the German Romantic revival of the song, just as it was later in the songs of Moussorgsky, Dvořák, Bartók, and others.

The borrowing of the folksong idiom became an issue in itself. The music historian August Reissmann (1825–1903), for instance, distinguished between the folk song proper and the lied showing *volkstümlich* characteristics. The *volkstümlich* lied, he contended, could never attain the degree of *Volksgemüth* (folk spirit) conveyed by the folk song, except to a degree when the musical setting accorded with the integrity of the text. This would mean restricting the setting to basic harmonies, plain melodies and rhythms, and modest keyboard accompaniments. For Reissmann, the *volkstümlich* lied "stands . . . between the folk song proper and the art song. From the latter it has the rounded-off, smooth form; from the former the universality, the easy comprehensibility . . . of its content."[23]

THE EXTENSION OF THE TERM
VOLKSTÜMLICH

According to Reissmann, the concept of the *volkstümlich* lied applied to the music of J. A. P. Schulz (1747–1800), Handel, Haydn, Mozart, and even to that of Schubert and Mendelssohn. The *volkstümlich* lied expressed the essence of the folk and was, therefore, universally comprehensible. Some dramatic national event such as the threat of war could furnish particularly suitable subject matter for the composition of a *volkstümlich* lied. (The Rheinlieder phenomenon of the 1840s forcefully demonstrated Reissmann's pronouncement.) The historian viewed the "artless melodies" described in Schulz's *Lieder im Volkston bey dem Klavier zu singen* (Berlin, 1782–90) as more "folklike than artlike," enabling any amateur singer to easily perform and remember them.[24]

Reissmann singled out specific composers of the *volkstümlich* lied, whom he praised for successfully incorporating folksong style within the bounds of the art song. His concept was a broad one. From the eighteenth century he chose Johann Adam Hiller's (1728–1804) *liederartig* (liederlike) singspiel melodies. These, the historian claimed, suited amateur singers and public taste in their simplicity of words and music. Schulz's settings of folksong-like poems by such groups as the Göttinger Hain (see p. 32), Reissmann maintained, offered truly *volksbildend* (instructive for the folk) material. The melodies of Peter Winter (1754–1825) and Joseph Weigl (1766–1846) were extolled for their pleasing integration of German *Volksempfinden* (feeling for the folk) and Italian opera elements. Equally noteworthy were the *volkstümlich* songs of Johann André (1774–1842), including his setting of Matthias Claudius's (1740–1815) well-known "Rheinweinlied," published in the mid-1770s.[25]

Reissmann additionally cited certain works of Weber as quintessentially *volkstümlich*, such as his opera *Der Freischütz* and his patriotic Wars of Liberation lieder. Their German *Gemüthleben* (sensibility), he said, was skillfully paired with "dreamy [Romantic] inwardness." Reissmann particularly admired Weber's famous Rheinlied "Lützows wilde Jagd," based on a poem from Theodor Körner's (1791–1813) *Leyer und Schwert*. It expressed truly *volkstümlich*-patriotic fervor, he noted, through its harmonic brilliance. In Reissmann's view, this phase of the *volkstümlich* lied had concluded with the "sweetly harmonious melody" of Schubert's and Mendelssohn's songs; for they captured "the old naïveté of the original folk song," making them comprehensible to the entire nation.

This writer even categorized certain Handel oratorios as admirably *volkstümlich*. Their "consciousness of the folk," he wrote, was amazingly coupled with both the highest art and ready comprehensibility. Reissmann went on to applaud Hiller and Schulz for musically transforming into art that "which already rings in the folk." With equal ardor he commended Handel, Haydn, Mozart, and Mendelssohn for awakening folk spirit to an unprecedented degree.

Reissmann admitted that the *volkstümlich* origins, the inner folk spirit, of the *Männerchor* (male chorus) had advanced public music making and music education. Yet he belittled the multitude of *Männerchor* composers (specifically the Rheinlied composer Conradin Kreutzer) for exploiting mere sound for its own sake, thereby diluting the essential Germanness of its *Volkstümlichkeit*. As a result, he lamented, the *Männergesangverein* (men's song

society) had degenerated into pure dilettantism. Yet Carl Loewe and Mendelssohn, he noted, had attempted to restore true German spirit into the
Männergesang, thereby achieving a *volkstümlich* fusion of the art song with the
folk song. Such admirable male choruses, he remarked, included the Rheinlieder "Die Lorelei" of Silcher, "Was ist des deutschen Vaterland?" of
Gustav Reichardt, and "Es klingt ein heller Klang" of Nägeli.[26]

THE BIEDERMEIER: *VOLKSTÜMLICHE HAUSMUSIK*

Hans Joachim Moser's much later but still cogent view of music in the
German *Vormärz* singled out *volkstümlich* lieder refined by shades of the Biedermeier. In his view, the Biedermeier style signified a modification of sheer
Volkstümlichkeit by exalting the particular folk virtues of complacency and
domesticity.

The term *Biedermeier* originated in 1852 with Ludwig Eichrodt's (1827–92)
parody of a village schoolmaster's poem. Romantic writers adopted the
expression as a means of ridiculing what they saw as the conventional and
superficial pathos of German middle-class petit bourgeois life. In this sense,
the term approached Schumann's notion of the philistine. By the turn of
the nineteenth century, however, the expression Biedermeier had acquired a
more positive meaning. It now referred to *Vormärz* furniture and painting
reflecting the modest inclinations of a humble family-oriented society no
longer threatened by Napoleon's troops.

Among painters such as Carl Spitzweg (1808–85), Schubert's intimate
friend Moritz von Schwind (1804–71), Adrian Ludwig Richter (1803–84),
and Alfred Rethel (1816–59), the Biedermeier outlook implied a sentimental
escape to a safety zone. Its fairy-tale aura of "delicate melodies" represented
"an interregnum of mitigated Romanticism."[27]

In 1937 Moser summarized his concept of the Biedermeier in music: "As
Weber, a leading Romantic in the realm of opera, yet remained almost pre-
Romantic in the lied, so too Spohr and Marschner, the progressive masters
of Romantic opera, oratorio, and chamber music, also confined themselves
to a somewhat Biedermeier quality in the lied. Nevertheless, we must view
the rather ironic style designation 'Biedermeier' without censure." Moser
contrasts "the homey, the idyllic" paintings and engravings of L. Richter,
Schwind, Spitzweg, and P. O. Runge with the "daemonic," "fantastic," the
"truly Romantic" landscapes of their contemporary Caspar David Friedrich

(see pp. 85–86). The works of the former artists, he continued, belonged to the miniature world of Weber's lieder. By contrast, he claimed, Friedrich's art is comparable to the works of Schubert.[28]

Moser classified the lieder of the Biedermeier as unadorned "home-baked *Hausmusik*." They were the art of the ordinary, the folksong-like, the consciously restrained, with a limited number of verses, strophic form (the music repeated for each stanza), and an unassuming piano part. Biedermeier also encompassed the "spontaneous"—sung in the open air without written music and perhaps with a guitar—and the sometimes melancholic, or the unadventurous as opposed to the fantastic. Moser's definition of Biedermeier music also comprised hunting songs and student songs for chorus.[29] Both types are well represented by Rheinlieder.

As Ernst Bücken, another historian, expressed it, the Biedermeier in music represented "the true art of the miniature that enchants us in a bourgeois landscape and idyll." This style, he said, remained outside the stylistic mainstream of the Romantic lied. The Rheinlieder of Robert Franz (1815–92), for example, epitomized Bücken's notion of a Biedermeier world, a restricted realm where one merely "complains about fate" rather than, like Schumann, "titanically defying" it. Although tending toward the Romantic with mystical, idealized landscapes of nature and the past, Franz's lieder, Bücken continued, evidenced genuine Biedermeier qualities in their spare melodies, avoidance of tone painting (moderation in the musical expression of the text), and spare harmony. Yet Bücken clearly distinguished Franz's works from the prevailing shallow, trite lieder production of his day. Liszt, this historian recalled, admired Franz's Eichendorff settings, while contrasting their earthy realism and freshness of rhythm and form with Schumann's, steeped in a Romantic "haze." Bücken similarly appraised Heinrich Marschner's (1795–1861) lieder as pure Biedermeier in their "unruffled and uninspired sobriety." These songs, he remarked, diverged, though not unfavorably, from the more Romantic tendencies of Marschner's opera *Hans Heiling*.[30]

As the Biedermeier epoch faded toward midcentury, the German cultural historian Wilhelm Heinrich Riehl (1823–97) gave his definition of the "homey" Biedermeier lied:

> If one would sing these lieder in the salon, one would profane them and bore the salon [audience]. Only in the sanctuary of the house and with and before the friends of the house should they be sung. They are not at all calculated [to

display] the shimmer of external effect; above all, in fact, the composer hopes that their inner effect might be deeply felt. A lied should ... resemble a painter's pencil sketch: ... only an outline, not a finished picture. Here lies the essential character of a lied. Like lyric poetry, our best lieder almost always are only contours and sketches.[31]

In sum, Biedermeier music represented the *volkstümlich* at its most innocent. For the most part, moreover, this version of *Volkstümlichkeit* harbored no military or political inferences.

PATRIOTIC *VOLKSTÜMLICHKEIT*

From its eighteenth century beginnings, Richard Kötzschke maintained, "the *Männergesang* ... became a truly *volkstümlich* art only when the Wars of Liberation deeply excited the entire thinking and feeling of the Germans and patriotic sentiment had been kindled to the highest degree. It is not at all conceivable whether and how the *Männergesang* would have developed without the Wars of Liberation, and one can confidently maintain that the art song for male chorus, in its nineteenth-century form, was a product of the Wars of Liberation."[32]

During the postwar period, veterans themselves formed choral groups in order to continue singing their *Kriegslieder* (war songs). The *Turner* (members of patriotic gymnast associations) of this era likewise enthusiastically engaged in choral singing. *Turnvater* Jahn, their leader, had once remarked that "song is the breath of life and of love."[33] Indeed, that same patriotic élan that informed the singing of lieder in organized groups during these years also thrived within family groups and other small, informal social circles. *Volkstümlichkeit* thus embraced sheer conviviality as well as the more specific purposes of patriotism and conscious artlessness.

Amateur choral groups, principally the all-male organizations, dedicated much of their repertoire to *Kriegslieder* that expressed the *vaterländisch* (patriotic) side of *Volkstümlichkeit*. Good examples of such *volkstümlich* music were the *Sechs deutsche Kriegslieder*, from 1813 and 1814, by Albert Methfessel (1785–1869), a Rheinlied composer and founder of the Hamburg *Liedertafel* in 1823. In fact, two of these songs were Rheinlieder (see pp. 163–64). This nationalistic type of lied originated at a time when Germans were struggling to emerge from the despair of the Napoleonic times, as Methfessel's foreword to the first edition of his *Kriegslieder* explained:

In this exalted time, where the flame of courage and heroic enthusiasm kindles hearts, the arts too must attest to their splendid effects. . . . With love for my German fatherland, and with the consciousness of having willed something good, I bequeath these songs to my contemporaries. And even if only one of these resounds in the multitude of German men and warms German hearts, how very much am I rewarded! Let connoisseurs judge what was accomplished by me in regard to art. My main endeavor was to be noble and simple, for that is the mark of all those songs which, chosen by the great voice of the folk, resound loudly and enthusiastically everywhere. Modestly I sent these songs out into the storm-tossed world. They were received with great interest, and already the first edition is sold out. I am being pressed to prepare a second. . . . Soon the clangor of war will yield to the gentle songs of peace. Then the returning warrior shall lay these songs next to his fame-wreathed weapons, and to all may they be memories of a great era.[34]

THE *KOMMERSGESANG*

The *Kommersgesang*, or student song, combined the humor and complacency of the Biedermeier with the emotional overtones of a patriotic *Volkstümlichkeit*. This subgenre of song reached its apogee during Schubert's lifetime, a period when German university life revolved around the student club. In many of these student songs, the Rhine provided the focus for venting feelings of pride and comradeship within the German student community.[35] The momentous Jena *Burschentag* (students' rally) in March 1818 was marked by the fervid singing of freedom songs in an outburst of patriotism. A large number of the more popular student songs, including the Rheinlied "Bekränzt mit Laub" (for Schumann's *Fest-Ouverture* on this lied, see p. 194), soon entered the repertoire of German family singing circles, confirming the expansion of this nationalistic-musical zeal beyond the confines of academia.[36]

In addition to manifesting *vaterländisch* sentiments, *Kommerslied* texts dealt with love, mythological notions, humorous adventures—often presented parodistically—or outright communal pleasure. Several important poets and composers, as well as numerous lesser figures, contributed to this rich body of literature, much of which originated in the German universities of the southwest. Rheinlied poets who wrote student songs included Joseph Victor von Scheffel, who sentimentalized over his happy days as a Heidelberg student. The Tübingen University music director Friedrich Silcher and the North German Albert Methfessel, called "the singer of the German *Kommersbuch*" by Riehl, also composed student songs.

The melodies of the German student songs, as with those of established folk songs, gradually underwent the process of alteration in the course of frequent performance. Thus a single song can appear in a number of melodically and rhythmically inconsistent versions depending on the geographical area and singing tradition involved. Some students fashioned parodies by composing new texts to existing melodies. These accounted for a large number of Rheinlieder, as shown by the song books of the 1840s and later decades.

INFORMAL, "AD HOC" SINGING

The Rheinlieder, like other mid-nineteenth-century German songs, were performed and propagated in two different atmospheres, one informal, one organized. The prefaces to two major collections of these songs divulge much concerning the informal manner in which Germans in the 1840s performed them. Franz Samans, the editor of *365 fröhliche Guitarrlieder*, stated that he intended his collection to be sung "outside in free nature."[37] For those, however, who desired to enjoy them at home with the piano, guitar, or even the harmonica, he added letters indicating the chords for accompaniment. In the preface to the 1843 edition of his song book, Carl Hase explains that these "good, worldly songs" had been designed especially for singing at home on winter evenings after the day's labor, not for historical, scholarly purposes.[38]

Hase's lieder collection consists nevertheless of folk songs assembled by such "historical" and "scholarly" personages as Arnim, Brentano, and Erk. It also contains songs from the editor's own circle of friends: lieder glorifying youthful days, their homes, and their *Wanderschaft* (wayfaring). The Rheinlieder appearing in these and similar sources from the 1840s were undoubtedly designed for enjoyment by "the folk" in the most informal way.

An earnest and amusingly chauvinistic writer for the *Neue Zeitschrift für Musik* enthusiastically described the spontaneity of *volkstümlich* lieder singing along the Rhine in 1842. As he and his guide ascended the Siebengebirge[39] one pleasant day,

> two brightly clothed hikers appeared and broke into a textless two-part song. A third traveler joined them, then a passing horseman as the fourth, the resulting quartet thereupon taking up a familiar folk song. To the writer's surprise,

the newly formed ensemble of complete strangers performed skillfully in four parts as if having done so all their lives. They had been brought together by accident, had remained in each other's company for some time through the power of this song, and had dispersed again after singing; not one of them had learned the song artificially, but each performed it according to an unconscious instinct, somewhat as the bird sings his melody, filling out his part in harmony in the way Mother Nature had shown him. Not always, my guide said, would it be so fortunate that singers of all voice ranges would find themselves together. But it would often be even better that small clubs are formed in which every melody is performed in parts according to this method.

The chronicler then makes a startling claim:

Thus I had new proof that music for many voices, that song in parts, from which the more recent music—I might say, music in general—originated, had its cradle in Germany; that the spring still bubbles forth on the Lower Rhine, out of which at one time Ockeghem, Willaert, and von Muer—still earlier, Hucbald, Franco, and Hermannus Contractus—created.[40]

ORGANIZED SINGING: THE LIEDERTAFEL, MALE CHORUS, AND GERMAN PATRIOTISM

Apart from spontaneous singing, the performance of volkstümlich Rhine songs also assumed a more structured character. As we shall see in chapter 4, the Rheinlieder as a whole, whether solo or part-songs and whether serious or light in intent, exhibited a volkstümlich musical style that well served the propagation of German political and cultural nationalism. A substantial number of these lieder, which voiced patriotic ideals, were designed for male choruses and often were dedicated to a specific Männergesangverein or Liedertafel (an organized group devoted to male choral singing).

The Development of the Volkstümliche Liedertafel   The first Männergesangverein of consequence in the nineteenth-century sense was the Liedertafel established in Berlin during late 1808 by the influential composer and teacher Karl Friedrich Zelter (1758–1832). Envisioned as the reincarnation of King Arthur's round table, the group evolved from a professional base consisting entirely of illustrious Berlin Singakademie members. These composers, poets, and paid singers convened monthly under the full moon to partake of the pleasures of song. In addition to its social and artistic exclusivity, this first Berlin *Liedertafel* contributed through some of its repertoire toward the support of anti-Napoleon sentiment in that city.[41]

Zelter's *Liedertafel* furnished the model for similar societies in Frankfurt an der Oder and in Leipzig (both were organized in 1815), as well as in Magdeburg, Dessau, Münster, Danzig, Koblenz, and elsewhere among the Germans.[42] Memories of the Wars of Liberation continued to influence the repertoire of these groups. Meanwhile, under the aegis of the writer and composer Hans Georg Nägeli (1773–1836), a number of song clubs had appeared in Switzerland between 1805 and 1812, though with a purpose somewhat differing from that of the North German *Liedertafel*. With the lied as his tool, Nägeli endeavored to present music as the universal legacy of the folk at large. Accordingly, under the influence of Johann Heinrich Pestalozzi's (1746–1827) new educational theories, he advocated the *volkstümlich* development of singing, with particular emphasis on the *Männergesang*.[43] Singing societies based on Nägeli's close-to-the-folk model soon spread over Switzerland and into South Germany, where they were known as *Liederkränze*. During the 1820s *Liederkränze* appeared in Stuttgart, Karlsruhe, Munich, Ulm, Reutlingen, Nürnberg, Frankfurt am Main, and in other Rhine locations as well as in many other German-speaking areas. The number of such organizations, whose repertoire not infrequently included Rheinlieder, increased steadily up to the decade of the 1840s.[44]

Gradually, however, the North German *Liedertafeln* abandoned Zelter's requirement of total professional membership and admitted amateurs into their societies in compliance with the ideal that the folk as a whole should be represented. Eventually this policy eliminated the crucial difference between North and South German song clubs.

Liedertafeln, now more *volkstümlich* in character, spread throughout North Germany. By the 1830s *Männergesangvereine* flourished in all middle- to large-sized cities and in some smaller urban centers. In these organizations social and artistic purposes were combined with an intensifying patriotism as the birth pangs of a nation were making themselves increasingly obvious. On the Lower Rhine alone, twenty-eight *Liedertafeln* were established between 1840 and 1848, a phenomenon clearly coinciding with the publication of hundreds of Rheinlieder during that decade.[45]

Rhineland Singing Societies   The number of exclusively male and occasionally female *Gesangvereine* increased throughout Germany, spawning the proliferation of part-songs and an ever-expanding number of major festivals during the 1820s, 1830s, and 1840s.[46] Along the Rhine these song clubs and

the festivals they sponsored intentionally cultivated a sense of both local
Rhenish and pan-German identity. The Rheinlieder filled a significant proportion of concert programs. Interestingly enough, each event usually also
brought performances of oratorios by Handel, Mozart overtures, and Italian arias.[47]

The growth of *Liedertafeln* ushered in a new sense of German camaraderie,
particularly striking in Rhenish areas during the post-Napoleonic decades.
The very nature of choral performance, of course, signifies a group experience.[48] Unlike the more accomplished, individualistic, and competitive demands of orchestral playing, the minimal formal training required in
choruses afforded a broad all-inclusive membership. Pride in common middle-class ideals, moreover—for chorus members were drawn mostly from
the middle classes—further intensified the sense of group identity and loyalty, as in Düsseldorf's Choral Society. By the 1830s, furthermore, large-
scale choral institutions in developing urban centers, though retaining their
dilettante level of performance, began to undertake formal public concerts.
Their new prominence added even greater esteem for mass involvement in
music. This collective expression, particularly of national consciousness,
was most conspicuously provoked in the choral organizations proliferating
along the Rhine. The group-oriented Rheinlieder of the 1840s performed
by the Rhineland's active choral institutions helped reinforce the Rhine's
image as the nucleus of nationalistic concerns, implanted into the very
marrow of German Romantic music.

The amateur nature of these German Romantic choral societies raises
some interesting questions about the social uses of music at that time. Did
the rising number of *Liedertafeln,* with their social, democratic orientation,
absorb the very dilettantes now being excluded from the more organized
and regulated orchestral and choral institutions by the increasing proportion of professional musicians? Did professionalism thus indirectly lend
support to the nationalism nurtured in these organizations by forcing the
displaced dilettantes to assemble under the convenient guise of "Germanness"?

An unnamed writer for the *Allgemeine musikalische Zeitung* of January 1844
complained that during the 1830s *Liedertafeln* had neglected patriotic songs,
which, he said, should have been uppermost in their repertoires. The journalist also lamented what he considered a drastic reduction in lieder festivals. He claimed that only the advent of Becker's Rhine poem in 1840, set
by hundreds of composers and sung by thousands, had brought a revival

of the *Männergesang*. On the wings of this renewed patriotism, the writer commented, other "national anthems" had gained or regained popularity: Arndt's Rheinlied poem "Was ist des deutschen Vaterland?" particularly popular in Gustav Reichardt's setting; Hoffmann von Fallersleben's "Deutschland, Deutschland über alles," set to Haydn's "Gott, erhalte Franz den Kaiser" (also set to music by Methfessel); and Liszt's version of Herwegh's "Rheinweinlied" (also set by Mendelssohn, Franz, Marschner, and thirteen other composers).

The inception and proliferation of the *Liedertafeln* thus coincided with and heightened the burgeoning of German nationalism.[49] "After the Rheinlied period," the *Zeitung* critic added, "the number of composers was legion—every *Liedertafel* conductor prepared material for singing."[50]

Controversy nevertheless ensued over the aesthetic value of *Liedertafel* music. In 1845, for example, an unnamed writer for the *Neue Zeitschrift für Musik* lamented: "What is the reason for today's Liedertafelmania; how has such a thing raged so shockingly until now? How has it happened that these *Liedertafeln* have won so much power over all dilettante musical activity, so that only with difficulty can one hold together the larger mixed-chorus song clubs for the performance of greater, better music—namely, religious works and oratorios?"[51]

After quoting this comment, F. M. Gredy, a writer for the journal *Caecilia*, retorted passionately, denying that the song clubs had initiated the decline "of better and more noble music."[52] Because *Caecilia* was published in the Rhine city of Mainz, Gredy not surprisingly defended the city's *Liedertafel*. Organized circa 1831, the group, he claimed, had always sought "a higher idea, not simple amusement, as its main task."[53] The club, Gredy insisted, sang not only the finest "Tafel- und Gesellschafts-Lieder," but also oratorios and other works for male voices by recognized composers. In fact, even a *Damen-gesangverein* (ladies' song club) had been established to perform pieces for women's voices alone and works for mixed chorus. "Always connected with a humane, religious, or patriotic purpose," Gredy boasted, the expanded Mainz *Liedertafel* had fulfilled such civic responsibilities as the presentation of public concerts to benefit such charitable causes as the erection of the Beethoven and Gutenberg monuments in Mainz. The song clubs had also inaugurated music festivals.[54] The Mainz *Liedertafel*, Gredy additionally proclaimed, owed much to the propitious circumstance that it belonged "to a city that through its fortunate situation on the splendid Rhine stream, and particularly through the taste of its inhabitants, who are receptive to everything good and beautiful, . . . incontestably is one of the most blessed in Germany."[55]

Gredy passionately championed four-part compositions for male voices, which he esteemed as "a truly indigenous product of the German muse" and a type of music that inspired civic or national pride—the popular Rheinlied "Was ist des deutschen Vaterland?" for example. He added that *Liedertafeln*, in fact, were contributing toward the ennobling of the human spirit and social dialogue. These groups, Gredy continued, also introduced such moral benefits as disdain for "vulgar inn visits," "the suppression of [merely] ordinary lieder," the improvement of church singing, and thereby a beneficial influence on the church service itself. "Where would be found . . . a stronger dam against the swell of modish cling-clang streaming here from outside," he asked, "against the extravagant admiration of modern virtuoso capers, than here? Our *Liedertafeln* do not need to be spurred on to *Volkstümlichkeit*; their most intrinsic element is the *volkstümlich*, and their effect will certainly be spread increasingly and ever more blessedly over the entire people."[56]

For purposes of historical perspective in the light of Gredy's bias, it should be noted that important composers, almost all of whom wrote Rheinlieder, contributed to the literature of the *Liedertafel*. These included Michael Haydn, Weber, Schubert, Silcher, Konradin Kreutzer, Cornelius, Liszt, Loewe, Marschner, Franz and Vincenz Lachner, Mangold, Türk, Spohr, Wagner, Robert Schumann, Mendelssohn, Methfessel, Rietz, and numerous others.[57]

VOLKSTÜMLICHKEIT IN NATURE: RHINE ROMANTICISM

As the visual splendors of nature came to dominate the attention of German Romantic artists, so also the aesthetic, alongside the commercial and strategic, value of the Rhine moved onto center stage as a subject of landscape painting. From its first stirrings in the later seventeenth and eighteenth centuries, the aesthetic appreciation of the Rhine's natural beauty came into full flower only with the advent of German Romanticism. Painters and poets sought to fuse humankind and the beauties of the natural world in a new union, as René Wellek notes, "to overcome the split between subject and object, the self and the world, the conscious and the unconscious."[58]

From Distant Times   The sphere of meaning in the term *Volkstümlichkeit* dealing with humanity's affinity to nature took resplendent form in a feeling for the Rhine's beauty, a feeling rooted in ancient history. Scattered references from the ancient past and through the centuries paid tribute to the omnipotence and beauty of the Rhine. The ancient Romans apotheosized the river as *deus rhenus*. The first-century Roman historian Cornelius Tacitus rigorously documented the maneuvers of the Roman legions, Gauls, and Germanic tribes as they crisscrossed the Rhine for territorial purposes.[59]

In the early fourteenth century, a Rhineland contemporary of the mastersinger Frauenlob (Heinrich von Meissen) poetically recounted:

> Umb singens willen wollt ich ziehen an den Rin;
> Mir wart geseit, wie hie die besten senger sin.

> (I wished to go to the Rhine to hear the singing;
> I saw that here are the best singers.)[60]

A "Rheinweinlied" has been attributed to a mid-fifteenth-century German nun, Clara Hätzlerin:

> Wein, Wein von dem Rhein,
> Lauter, klar und fein,
> Deine Farb' gibt gar lichten Schein
> Wie Krystall und Rubeln.

> (Wine, wine from the Rhine,
> true, clear, and lovely,
> your color illuminates
> like crystal and rubies.)

The physician Hieronymus Münzer extolled the Rhine in 1495 as "the river of Paradise."[61]

Several sixteenth-century poets paid anthropomorphic homage to the Rhine as conjugally linked to the Danube. For example, the poet Pistorius wrote:

> Aller Wasser König der Rhein,
> Die Donau soll seine Gemahlin sein

> (The Rhine, king of all waters,
> the Danube shall be his consort.)

The Marquis Freher likewise wrote:

> Ister cunctorum fluviorum iure vocatur conjux,
> cui Rhenus iure Maritus erit
> (If the Danube should be the wife of all waters,
> So should, with all rights, the Rhine be her husband.)

Another poet of that century, Schede-Melissus, exalted the Rhine as "father of nymphs."[62]

The seventeenth-century Rhine poetry of Johann Angelus Silesius [Johannes Scheffler] (1624–77) and Friedrich von Spee (1591–1635) voiced a mystical love of nature. After the devastation of the Thirty Years' War (1618–48), embryonic literary references depicted the Rhine as an idyllic landscape rich in Roman castle ruins—a prelude to the Romantic glorification of the many medieval fortresses on the river. The feeling for landscape is also evident at this time in the copper engraved urban panoramas of Matthäus Merian (1593–1650).

The poets of the Göttinger Hain, formed in September 1772 in homage to Friedrich Gottlieb Klopstock (1724–1803), exalted the Rhine as nature's crowning glory, sanctified for its aesthetic appeal as a landscape and for its revivifying wine. The Hain group apostrophized the river, personifying Vater Rhein as a giver of wine. With the Hain, Rhine wine poetry rose to a subgenre that continued far into the nineteenth century.[63] Hölty addressed Vater Rhein as resident in Paradise; Voss exclaimed, "Hail to thee, Rhine wine! . . . Health, youth, kiss, song, and dance flame in thee." Claudius's poem "Bekränzt mit Laub den lieben, vollen Becher" (Bedeck with wreaths the lovely, brimming glass) and "Am Rhein, am Rhein, da wachsen unsre Reben" (On the Rhine, on the Rhine, there grow our vines) gained much popularity, as did Klopstock's ode "Der Rheinwein."

Nature's Beauty Published: Rhine Travel Literature   In the later eighteenth century, multitudes of tourists from the burgeoning middle classes, taking advantage of their new wealth and leisure, flocked to Europe's picturesque vistas. The Rhine was a favored destination (see figure 1.1). The new appreciation of nature's beauty, coupled with the modish yearning to be at one with it and with its past, contributed to an "acting out" of the themes of *Wanderlust* and *Sehnsucht*. Rhine journals and steel engravings, replacing the more expensive ones of copper, proliferated as art works. The *Bibliotheca geographica*, a survey published in 1858 of German travel books appearing between 1750 and 1856, listed 120 Rhine publications, excluding maps and

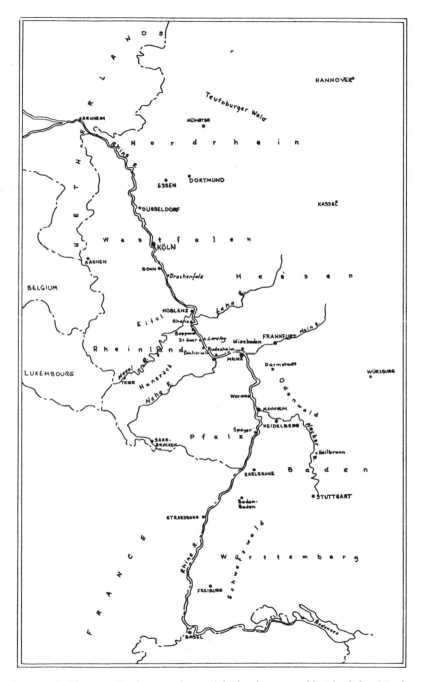

Fig. 1.1. *The Rhine from Basel to Rotterdam, with landmarks represented by Rheinlieder. (Map by Douglas R. Porter.)*

panoramas, as opposed to 40 for the Danube, 25 for the Elbe, 6 for the Weser, and only 2 each for the Oder and Weichsel.[64]

German poets and other writers virtually transformed their Rhine impressions into a literary genre. The native Rhinelander Johann Wolfgang von Goethe's (1749–1832) Rhine excursions of 1774 and 1814–15 abound in descriptive reminiscences. Goethe conveyed these thoughts subjectively in pantheistic poetic imagery. This imagery reflected his *Naturgefühl* (feeling for nature) experienced during pilgrimages and festivals along the Rhine. His journeys drew scores of literati to "salons" addressing the river's beauty in an expanding corpus of Rhine literature. These gatherings included Stolberg, Matthisson, Alexander von Humboldt, Hölderlin, Ludwig Tieck, Wackenroder, Heinrich von Kleist, Körner, and Brentano.[65]

Friedrich von Matthisson's (1761–1831) personification of the Rhine extended to aural dimensions:

> High on the Nektar's mountains,
> Where the vintager maiden
> Sings songs of bliss,
> Even the winepresses creak
> In harmony and jubilation,
> Roar on, thou silver waves, O Rhine.

In another animistic, or personifying, Rhine description, Matthisson proclaimed:

> King of German rivers art thou, O Rhine!
> How splendidly is Mainz wreathed by the Nektar's hills,
> And Bacharach's and Bingen's mossy stones
> Are mirrored in thy verdant crystal!

(See chapter 3 for a discussion of German Romantic Rhine animism.)

Heinrich von Kleist (1777–1811) expressed obvious nature animism after his Rhine trip in July 1801: "Ah, . . . that is an area like a poet's dream, . . . this Rhine valley, which now opens, now closes, now blooms, now is desolate, now laughs, now alarms." Ludwig Tieck's (1773–1853) fate tragedy *Genoveva*, of 1799, similarly personified the Rhine:

> . . . There the Rhine begins to smack its banks.
> What can they tell each other, the two,
> The old Rhine and these old oaks?[66]

From Heidelberg to Cologne   From 1805 a circle of poets and other literary figures assembled at the ruined Heidelberg castle (see figure 1.2). This gathering marked the opening phase of Rhine Romanticism. With it came a new coalescence: the merger of an escalating glorification of landscape beauty with the ascendancy of German lyric poetry. René Wellek has called the latter genre a quintessentially Romantic incarnation of nature as a unified organic continuum encapsulating the emerging unconscious. German lyric poetry, Wellek maintains, "suggests immediacy of personal experience, even inspiration, . . . [and] unconscious solitary speaking. . . . It is a poetry of the famous *Gemüt*, of the cultivation of the soul. . . . It comes near to the Romantic ideal of an identification of subject and object, man and Nature, self and the world."[67]

The Heidelberg Romantics included Johann Heinrich Voss (1751–1826), the jurist-aesthetician Anton Friedrich Thibaut (1772–1840), Ludwig Achim Freiherr von Arnim, Clemens Brentano, the journalist Joseph von Görres (1776–1848), Joseph Freiherr von Eichendorff (1788–1857), and the Rhinelander Friedrich Hölderlin (1770–1843).[68] The latter's subjective, protracted poem "Der Rhein" of 1801 had, in fact, ushered in mainstream

Fig. 1.2. Carl Philipp Fohr, Heidelburg Castle ("metaphorical landscape"). Pen and watercolor, 1813–14. Courtesy of Hessisches Landesmuseum Darmstadt.

Rhine Romanticism. The poem assigned "the free-born Rhine," its voice being that "of the noblest of rivers," to "the race of the demigod." Thus the epic breadth and metaphor of neoclassicism was conjoined with Romantic nature animism.[69]

At the dawn of the nineteenth century, Heidelberg literati also entered upon the rediscovery and restoration of Germanic folklore, collecting *Märchen* (fairy tales), *Legenden* (legends), and *Sagen* (sagas). In addition, this group virtually launched a new body of literature extending and recreating the old. Here, as with the German Romantic exploration of ancient myths and medieval epics, the restoration process helped resurrect the historic national past. This process served, especially through the fairy tale and its reincarnation in the imagery of nature animism, to recover mankind's past with the symbols of childhood. In this way, the Germans were awakened to a new national self-consciousness. This phase of the German Romantic restoration movement concerned the acquisition of a cultural and corporate identity. It also represented the fulfillment of a pivotal nineteenth-century concept: the notion of an individual's ascent from the unconscious to the conscious, as explained in greater length in chapter 3. This ascent formed part of an organic process in nature corresponding to that being considered in nineteenth-century natural science, psychology, philosophy, history, and other fields.

By the 1820s Rhine Romanticism had reached Cologne, where enclaves of intellectuals conceived and published metaphorical idealizations of the river in numerous journals. The Cologne "network," which had also dedicated its efforts toward the Cologne Cathedral project, included the art scholars and brothers Melchior and Sulpiz Boisserée and Heinrich Heine's colleague, the political journalist Joseph von Görres. It soon attracted the extraordinarily influential Friedrich Schlegel. His compelling poeticization of the Rhine landscape continually evidenced sheer nature animism. In his personification of the coursing Rhine, Schlegel reflected, "As he [the Rhine] plummets down with gigantic force in a colossal plunge over the cliffs, he then rolls mightily in his broad waves through the most fertile lowland plains, to lose himself at last in the level countryside; thus is he the only too faithful image of our fatherland, of our history, and of our character."[70]

The outpouring of Rhine Romanticism issuing from the Cologne circle also engulfed such Wars of Liberation poets as Maximilian von Schenkendorf and Ernst Moritz Arndt. Their verses humanizing the Rhine's quintessential Germanness ultimately were set to music published during the Rhine crisis decade of the 1840s. Literary coteries in nearby Bonn and Düsseldorf soon swelled the ranks of the Rhine Romantics. The aesthetic idealization of this river in German literature and landscape art was now coming full circle with such figures as the Nazarene painter Peter von Cornelius (1783–1867, uncle of the composer Peter Cornelius), the Prussian scholar and professor Wilhelm von Humboldt (1767–1835), August Wilhelm von Schlegel (1767–1845), and the *Maikäferbund* poets Karl Simrock (1802–76), Wolfgang Müller von Königswinter (fl. 1830–60), and others.[71]

2

MUSIC OF CRISIS

The Rhineland had nothing to do with Egypt and Syria,
but then there is no connection either between militant
attitudes and reason.[1]

FROM THE NILE TO THE RHINE

*T*he fateful *Vormärz* years, which began with Schumann's "song year," closed as the poem of
Wagner's *Ring* was taking shape, and gave rise to
hundreds of Rheinlieder, marked a turbulent period
of upheaval in European society. The reader is asked therefore to indulge
the accounting of the complex and interrelated extramusical forces constituting the historical matrix of the Rheinlieder. Perhaps these songs had to
compensate in directness and fervency for the shifting uncertainties of the
times in which they were written and published.

The political machinations resulting in the London Treaty rekindled the
whole Eastern Question and its implications for the status of the several
European nations. The Ottoman Empire was disintegrating within and
steadily losing control over its vassal states without. For the dissipation of
Turkish rule posed a serious threat to the Concert of Europe, a concept
that had been idealistically proclaimed by the forces opposing Napoleon.
Pasha Muhammad 'Ali's revolt, however, exposed the illusiveness of Ottoman unity and jarred the Concert in its provokation of additional tension
between Britain and France. The latter nation, moreover, felt justified in
elevating Muhammad 'Ali's insurrection into a national cause.[2]

Through his advancement of Egyptian economic, military, and political resources, the pasha had assured his realm imperial standing both within the Ottoman Empire and in the eyes of the European powers. Among the latter, Britain would profit most from assuring Egypt's virtual self-containment under firm Turkish suzerainty, since the establishment of French or any other competing European government in the Levant would have imperiled the security of Britain's route to India.[3]

THE LONDON TREATY AND
THE FRENCH

Led by Foreign Minister Lord Palmerston, Britain nevertheless entered into a covert agreement with Russia, Austria, and Prussia in London on 15 July 1840. This pact offered Muhammad the hereditary pashalik of Egypt and the lifetime rule of southern Syria in return for surrendering control of Crete, the rest of Syria, certain Arabian territories, and the commandeered Turkish fleet. Indignant over this subterfuge maneuvered by the London Treaty signatories, France's prime minister, Adolphe Thiers, launched a series of deft diplomatic moves calculated to restore France's prestige in the European political theater. Buoyed by neo-Napoleonic nationalism, Thiers viewed the London Treaty as good reason to reinforce his nation's ancient claim to the Rhine. The French public and press immediately aligned themselves with their prime minister, condemning their country's exclusion from the London accord in the hope that by protecting their sphere of influence in the Mediterranean they would also safeguard their Rhenish and Alpine frontiers.[4]

The *Revue des deux mondes* of 14 August 1840 affirmed the French sense of betrayal by the London Treaty allies: "There is . . . a perfect agreement, . . . that [France's] honor, her dignity, her dearest interests have been injured." In mid-September, the *Revue* continued: "With the actuality of the 15 July treaty, there is not one Frenchman . . . who could imagine leaving France disarmed. There is not one Frenchman who would not demand that the prime minister put our fleets, our armies, our fortifications, our magazines, the whole military state of the country, on a formidable footing to prepare us equally for defense and offense."[5]

An additional factor swayed French public opinion. A messianic cult of Napoleon had solidified in the months immediately preceding the London agreement and had begun to encourage French feelings of national disgrace over the treaties of 1815. Plays, prose, and verse contributed substantially to the faddish romanticization of the Napoleonic legend in the hope of restoring the country's past glory. Though a pacifist, the poet-statesman Alphonse de Lamartine (1790–1869) evoked this spectral Napoleonism to justify French claims for the Rhine and Alps as France's "natural" frontiers.[6] Addressing the French Chamber of Deputies on 11 January 1840, he declared "rivers and mountains as the eternal and immobile" boundaries set by nature, as though "unwritten treaties among peoples." "Mention the Rhine and the Alps, and you are understood [by France] before you have finished. Its glory has remained there, her spirit is there again."[7]

Louis-Philippe initially supported his prime minister's call for general mobilization to recapture the Rhine frontier.[8] Thiers gave an impassioned speech before parliament on 29 October 1840, urging that body to declare war in light of the Rhine issue. But the French monarch eventually quelled his countrymen's fears over the London Treaty as insufficient reason for such an extreme measure. He therefore forced Thiers to resign, at last silencing French calls for a Rhine war.

GERMAN ALARM ON THE RHINE

Meanwhile, however, the Germans of the Prussian, Bavarian, and Baden Rhinelands had mobilized for a "war of deliverance," reinstating that patriotic spirit that had sustained them through the Wars of Liberation. French diplomats stationed along the Rhine reported that German war fervor had escalated alarmingly since the signing of the London Treaty and the ensuing French threat.[9]

From July to September 1840 the *Augsburger allgemeine Zeitung* published a series of pro-German articles entitled "Über den Rhein" by the Cologne judge Christian Josef Friedrich Matzerath. The writer refuted the French concern that German Rhinelanders wanted Paris as much as they wanted Berlin in order to survive politically and economically. He threatened, in fact, a German war in response to French mobilization.[10]

By late October 1840 the *British and Continental Examiner* of Leipzig had declared: "The sacred name of liberty is the shibboleth of the invading Gauls. Is not the sacred name of liberty dishonoured, when assumed as a war-cry by those who at the same time lay claim to the provinces of the Rhine, and would rob Germany of her fairest and most fertile lands? . . .

Let France pause ere she rouse a noble and highminded people by accumulations of insults and wrongs."[11]

Blown in on the gusts of injudicious belligerency, the clouds of war darkening the European autumn of 1840 thus seemed to have vanished by the year's end. Nevertheless, the reversal of French foreign policy, as evidenced by Thiers's forced resignation, occurred too late to allay German fears over losing the Rhine. The initial French reaction to the London Treaty continued to reverberate into the autumn of 1840 from the shores of the eastern Mediterranean to the cliff of the Loreley, reactivating the age-old forces of Latin-Germanic antipathy.

DEUS RHENUS AND VATER RHEIN

From ancient times, the strategic value of the Rhine in defining territorial boundaries and providing a crucial link for commercial traffic between East and West had fomented an endless succession of political-military confrontations and alignments. As noted earlier, in the first century C.E. the Latin historian Cornelius Tacitus described the maneuvers of the Roman legions, Gauls, and Germanic tribes as they crisscrossed the Rhine, gaining victory or defeat at the hands of their antagonists. The medieval *Nibelungenlied* and its earlier sources and later versions documented century upon century of strife in defense of dominions bordering the Rhine from the Alps to the Lowlands (see chapter 4).

Between 1792 and 1794 the French army wrought repeated devastation in the Rhinelands, capturing Speyer, Worms, Mainz, Frankfurt, Cologne, Bonn, and Coblenz. At the Peace of Basel and of Campo Fermio, concluded in April 1795 and October 1797, respectively, France gained the entire left bank of the Rhine except for Prussian territories there. These measures soon prompted the gradual organization of resistance on the Rhine by the various German states. Adding to the complexities of the situation was the tangled mass of ever-fluctuating alliances continually altering Franco-German relationships. We have seen that, at the same time, the Germans had become increasingly involved in the interrelated issues of an actively gestating liberalism and its goal of constitutional government. These matters went hand in hand with the even more emotionally intense quest for a national identity. The shattering social and political upheavals marking the mid-nineteenth century were swelling the forces of discord, resounding further in the Rhinelands up to the Revolution of 1848 and beyond.

NAPOLEON'S RHINE

By the turn of the century, the French had organized a redistribution of Rhineland territories to compensate German princes for the states the latter had lost on the river's left bank. This arrangement helped define the new German "middle" states that had been brought under Napoleon's control in 1805 by the Peace of Pressburg. In July 1806 Napoleon established the sixteen-state Rhenish Confederation, including Bavaria, Württemberg, Baden, Hesse-Darmstadt, Westphalia, and Berg.[12] With Napoleon as its self-proclaimed protector, the Rhenish Confederation thus owed allegiance to the French Empire. The Rhinelanders now faced the demise of the centuries-old German system of multiple-state particularism based on a firmly entrenched adherence to individual sovereignty (see figure 2.1).

With his victory at the Battle of Jena in October 1806, moreover, Napoleon had occupied Berlin and gained all of Prussia's territories west of the Elbe. As a result, this state was forced to sever all federative ties with other German areas. In July 1807 Russia and France signed the Peace of Tilsit, establishing a four-part division of the former German Empire. The entire left bank of the Rhine thus became an integral part of France, with the main regions of Germany making up the Rhenish Confederation. The do-

Fig. 2.1. Napoleonic Europe, 1812. (Map by Douglas R. Porter.)

minions of both Austria and Prussia were respectively restricted to the Germans' southeastern and northeastern border regions.

Many currents of French cultural and political ideology consequently streamed into German territories, chiefly affecting the Rhinelanders, who were closest to France. The reorganization of the Rhine's left bank into seven *départements* also imposed French administrative reforms. The Rhinelanders acquired Napoleon's *code civil*—with its principle of egalitarian society—along with his economic concepts, particularly those of potential benefit to future industrial expansion. The French presence thus tended to restrict the growth of German national sentiment to small nodes of intellectuals, while the promulgation of German nationalism stood to gain from the easing and expansion of cultural exchanges now rendered possible.[13]

THE FADING OF THE FRENCH PRESENCE: VIENNA TO BERLIN

The rise to power of the Francophobic Prince Metternich, appointed Austrian foreign minister in 1809, however, would eventually eliminate German subjugation to a Napoleonic France. In October 1813 the Battle of Leipzig ended French domination over all Germans east of the Rhine. The Treaty of Ried forced Bavaria's withdrawal from Napoleon's Rhenish Confederation, consequently dissolving the Confederation itself. On New Year's Day 1814 Prussian troops led by Marschall Gebhard Leberecht Blücher crossed the central Rhine, spearheading the invasion of France.[14]

The Wars of Liberation concluded with the Congress of Vienna, which, convening from September 1814 to June 1815, established the Germanic Confederation (see figure 2.2). While not a true national state, this amorphous conglomeration of thirty-five monarchical states and four city republics did offer incentives to the growth of German patriotic feeling by delimiting German boundaries and bolstering internal peace. These measures served to discourage foreign invasions, thereby strengthening nascent sentiments of German unity. Yet the age-old tradition of German particularism, born of the lingering dreams to restore ancient dynasties, persisted still. The survival of this ancient German *Weltanschauung* promised, at least for a while longer, that each individual state could retain its own basic autonomy and its own political, social, and hence cultural identity.[15]

The Vienna Congress realigned French and Prussian holdings in the Rhinelands. France retained most of Alsace and all its pre-Revolutionary

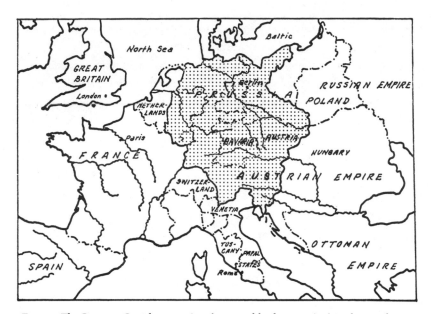

Fig. 2.2. The Germanic Confederation, 1815 (represented by dot pattern). (Map by Douglas R. Porter.)

enclaves along the Upper Rhine's left bank and gained Saarlouis and the south shores of the Saar River. The Congress awarded Prussia the Rhine Province, which now reached north to the Netherlands, west from the Rhine to Aachen and the Luxembourg border, south to the Lorraine boundary and the Bavarian Palatinate, and along the remainder of the left bank of the Rhine adjacent to Lorraine. (The significance of Prussia's new acquisition provides the raison d'être for chapter 5, which discusses the role of Düsseldorf and the Lower Rhine Music Festivals vis-à-vis Rhine Romanticism.) With its population now more than doubled and its territories reaching across the entire North German plain from the Nieman to the Rhine, Prussia became the strongest power on the Rhine and now controlled the crucial link between North and South Germany in both peace and war. The expansion of Prussia, furthermore, established even closer political, socioeconomic, and musical relationships between its capital, Berlin, and that of its new Rhine Province, Düsseldorf, as explained later.[16]

THE ALIEN FRENCH

In March 1815 Napoleon returned from exile on Elba and in June met defeat at Waterloo. His reappearance resurrected the Germans' ancient Francophobia, as witnessed, for example, by the influential *Rheinischer Merkur*, the political journal published from 1814 to 1816 at Coblenz by Josef Görres, an advocate for the Germans' annexation of the Rhine's left bank. The growing sense of German identity also prompted the organization of several patriotic associations concentrated in Rhine areas, notably in southwest Germany. These groups were founded on their dedication to German national feeling.

As nationalistic sensitivities gradually intensified throughout post-Napoleonic Europe, the Germans' version of patriotism acquired a distinctly metaphysical and biological cast. Above all, German intellectuals sought to dispel the ghost of France, identified by them with Enlightenment antiquarianism and hence rejected as alien. Disdaining the eighteenth-century French ideals of universal peace and glorification of the individual, these German Romantic nationalists, Hans Kohn contends, based "their concept of regeneration upon the self-willed and self-contained national group . . . [and on] the regenerative power of war."[17] The withdrawal of French occupation forces, in fact, unleashed among Germans a profound and enduring resentment of French, equated with Western, civilization.[18] As the nineteenth century opened, for example, Friedrich Schlegel assessed the French spirit of rational universalism as merely an attempt to subsume the national yearnings of other peoples within a dominant Gallic culture.[19]

One must also bear in mind that the German Romantics had inherited from their forebears a deeply rooted sense of isolation from the West. This outlook had engendered an ambivalent emotional mixture of both pride and anxiety, based on feelings of biological kinship as the basis of a community or nation. This was the Germans' ancient notion of *das Volk*, a notion that diametrically opposed the rational French concept of "citizenship." The ardent Wars of Liberation and Rheinlieder poet Ernst Moritz Arndt, for example, defined the German "nation" as representative of a single common blood and language, or undefiled *Ursprache*. These elements formed the basis for the familial metaphor *Volk*, the heart of the German Romantic *Volkstümlichkeit* ideal.[20]

THE BECKER POEM AND ITS AFTERMATH

Any new claims to an ancient, majestic river flowing through the European heartland directly imperiled existing political, economic, and cultural relationships among a legion of nations. This was especially true of those peoples astride its shores. The French Rhine threat of July 1840 had assaulted the German soul. Amid the torrent of anti-French outcries uttered by German pamphleteers and journalists, the Rhenish jurist Nikolaus Becker (1809–45) aroused his compatriots' nationalistic feelings perhaps most dramatically with a persuasive bit of doggerel. His poem "Der deutsche Rhein" first appeared in the *Trierische Zeitung* on 18 September 1840 and had been published in most German newspapers by mid-autumn.[21] The immediate popularity of Becker's poem belied its banality, as unmistakable in the original German as in translation:

> They shall not have the Rhine
> The free German Rhine, Though, like greedy ravens
> They hoarsely cry for it, So long as calmly flowing
> It wears its garment green, So long as oars resounding
> Can beat upon its wave.
>
> They shall not have the Rhine
> The free German Rhine, So long as hearts take pleasure
> In its fiery wine. So long as by its stream
> The cliffs steadfast still stand, So long as it reflects
> The lofty domes o'erhead.
>
> They shall not have the Rhine
> The free German Rhine, So long as daring youths
> Woo slender maidens there. So long as in its depths
> A fish can freely swim, So long as song is heard
> Within its singers' mouths.
>
> They shall not have the Rhine
> The free German Rhine, Until its flood engulfs
> The last man's every bone![22]

Becker had composed his poem in late July 1840, immediately after the French had threatened to take the Rhine. He had read a series of articles entitled "Über den Rhein," in defense of German rights to the Rhine, by the influential liberal Christian Joseph Matzerath. In August Becker sent his verses to Matzerath, who recited them to his friends, the well-known poets Ferdinand Freiligrath and Karl Simrock (see chapter 3). The latter two then published "Der deutsche Rhein" the following spring in their *Rheinisches Jahrbuch für Kunst und Poesie.*[23]

On 15 October 1840 Cologne paid tribute to the new Prussian monarch, Friedrich Wilhelm IV, with a performance of Becker's poem set to music by Conradin Kreutzer (1780–1849). The audience at the Cölner Theater even joined in for an encore (see example 4.3). The citizens of Cologne, part of the Prussian Rhine Province, christened the lied the "Colognaise." This sobriquet clearly indicated the Germans' longing for a national anthem equal in status to the "Marseillaise" of their arch-competitor for the Rhine.[24]

After the extravagant reception given Kreutzer's setting, Becker enjoyed a flood of official accolades and costly gifts from Friedrich Wilhelm, Bavaria's Ludwig I, and citizens representing the Rhine towns of Mainz and Carlsruhe. Various other patriotically inclined souls fêted the poet at further celebration banquets. No political pamphlet or journal, not even Joseph von Görres's *Rheinischer Merkur*, could arouse a popular response comparable in intensity to that created by the rhymes of this otherwise obscure Rhenish jurist. His poem gave expression to an urgent sense of national honor that concerned not only the issue of the Rhine but also that of pan-German unity. An inscription on the crystal wine glass presented to Becker by the city of Mainz extolled him as the "author of the German national anthem."[25]

PRUSSIA AND ITS RHINE PROVINCE

Friedrich Wilhelm IV ascended the Prussian throne barely three months after the signing of the London Treaty. His succession temporarily rejuvenated German hopes for liberalism and nationalism. The new monarch sought at first to ameliorate certain policies inherited from his father's repressive regime. He worked to reduce the tensions between Protestant Prussians and Catholic Germans and attempted to introduce liberalizing measures regarding censorship and freedom of speech.[26]

In September 1842 the king laid the cornerstone of the Cologne Cathedral to mark the undertaking of both its completion and restoration (see figure 2.3). This example of Prussian tolerance in acknowledging the significance of a historic Rhine landmark briefly raised the hopes of German nationalists. As he participated in the ceremony, the Prussian monarch boasted: "The spirit that builds these portals is the same that broke our

Fig. 2.3. Unfinished Cologne Cathedral, after a German tourist map, 1842. (Pen and ink by Cecelia H. Porter.)

chains twenty-nine years ago; it eliminated both an insult to the fatherland [and] the alienation of this Rhine bank. . . . This spirit is that of German unity and power. May the the portals of the Cologne Cathedral become gates of a most splendid triumph!"[27]

For a while, the pan-German patriotism emanating from Berlin and the Rhinelanders alike soared on the hope that Prussia's military forces could stave off the French "war dragon." The growth of industrialization, more-over, encouraged Prussians and Rhinelanders together to envision reciprocal economic advantages as a result of their symbiotic political union.

NATIONAL CONTESTS

Although hundreds of Rheinlieder flooded Germany in the 1840s, Becker's poem outdistanced them all in the number of musical settings it inspired, its sensational reception, and the extent of its immediate influence. From late 1840 through the following spring, German music journals, hoping to expand readership, publicized a national competition to determine the "best" setting of Becker's Rhine poem. There were nearly two hundred entries.[28] Several local and regional contests were instituted to determine the finest composition of "Der deutsche Rhein." Robert Schumann, Conradin

Kreutzer, Heinrich Marschner, Carl Gottlieb Reissiger, Jean J. H. Verhulst, Julius Becker, and Gustav Kunze entered their settings in the widely advertised Leipzig *Concurrenz-Concert* of 7 December 1840. The audience granted Kunze's composition the prize (see example 4.5).[29]

Joseph Lenz won both the local Breslau contest and a regional competition among the award-winning composers of the Becker poem from Breslau, Leipzig, and Berlin. The Breslau firm of F. Ernst Christoph Leuckart, who published Lenz's setting, proclaimed:

> The shining victory that this lied has won—as much over the best local [Breslau] Rheinlied compositions as also over the Leipzig and Berlin prize compositions at the competition concerts especially instituted for that purpose—is certainly the most conclusive evidence for the excellence of the same. Not only among the Rheinlied melodies but among all modern vocal compositions, Lenz's lied is the most successful of the more recent publications, according to the assurance of the most esteemed musical notables. Now the German national wish to be able to sing the Rheinlied to only one melody can be fulfilled; the innumerable pretenders have all been removed from the field.[30]

During all the excitement, issue after issue of the *Allgemeine musikalische Zeitung* and the *Neue Zeitschrift*, both published in Leipzig, displayed many competitive advertisements. These represented individual publishers announcing the latest settings of Becker's verses available at their houses. Robert Friese's notices of his publication of Schumann's composition predominated, of course, among announcements in the *Neue Zeitschrift*, for Friese also published Schumann's journal. In November 1840 this publisher announced his third printing of the Schumann setting. The following January brought the seventh printing.[31]

Even as late as 3 March 1841 Gottfried Wilhelm Fink, the editor and critic for the *Allgemeine musikalische Zeitung*, observed, "Almost every city and nearly every music circle has a special melody [for Becker's poem] of its own that particularly pleases it."[32]

Felix Mendelssohn's letter on 18 November to his friend Karl Klingemann in London reveals, however, that the Rheinlied commotion only served to generate the composer's Berlinesque sarcasm:

> This entire city [Leipzig] rings with a song that has a political tendency against the French and that the journals, with all their forces, want to make popular. With the lack of any other public concern, they succeed, and everyone talks

about the "Rheinlied" or the "Colognaise," as they accurately designate it. . . .
The verses begin: "Sie sollen ihn nicht haben, den freien deutschen Rhein"
(They shall not have it, the free German Rhine), . . . repeated at the beginning
of every strophe. As if such words made the least sense! If [the poem] at least
said: "We intend to keep it!" But "sie sollen ihn nicht haben" appears to me
too fruitless, too useless, too juvenile. If I possess something solidly and surely,
what is the point of singing that it should belong to no one else? It is now sung
at the court in Berlin and in the casinos and clubs here, and naturally the
musicians pounce on it as if they are crazy and are composing it for their own
immortality. The Leipzig composers have set no fewer than three melodies to
it, and every day something about this lied appears in the paper. Yesterday . . .
it was even announced that I, too, had made a setting of this poem, whereas
never even in a dream would I have thought to set such defensive enthusiasm
to music.[33]

Two days later Mendelssohn urged his brother Paul to attend a Leipzig
concert including his own *Lobgesang* (Hymn of praise) and Kreutzer's setting
of Becker's Rheinlied. He lamented:

I could write you a long complaint about this said Rheinlied. You have no idea
what kind of hullabaloo they make of it here, and how this journalistic enthusiasm is so repugnant to me. . . . Young men and faint-hearted people may scream
about it, but true men do not make anything of what they already possess, for
having it is good enough. I am angered that, among other things, the newspapers
have even printed—besides the four settings of these splendid words that Leipzig has delivered—one by me and [have announced] that it would now be
published with my full name; and I can therefore lie to no one, because in
public I am speechless. At the same time, my publisher, Härtel, has told me
that, if I set it, he will sell six thousand copies in two months. No, Paul—that
I will not do![34]

Even in late February 1841 Becker's Rhine poem continued to arouse
German patriotic sentiment. The public craved more settings. The pain
suffered by Mendelssohn over the Rheinlied phenomenon likewise persisted, as his letter from Leipzig to the pastor Julius Schubring in Dessau
on 27 February indicated:

Now for my critical spectacles, and a reply concerning your Becker "Rheinlied."
I like it very much; it is well written, and sounds joyous and exhilarating, but
(for a *but* must of course be uttered by every critic) the whole poem is quite

unsuitable for composition, and essentially unmusical. I am well aware that in saying this, I am rashly throwing the gauntlet down to you and to many of my colleagues in Germany; but such is my opinion, and the worst part of it is that I am confirmed in this by most of the compositions that I know. (For Heaven's sake, let this remain a secret between us, otherwise, as journalists publish every trifle nowadays, I may possibly be conveyed someday across the frontiers as a Frenchman.) But, jesting apart, I can only imagine music when I can realize the mood from which it emanates; merely artistically correct tones suiting the rhythm of the poetry, becoming *forte* when the words are vehement, and *piano* when they are meek, sounding very pretty, but expressing nothing—I never yet could comprehend; and still such is the only music I can discover for this poem. Neither forcible, nor effective, nor poetical, but only supplementary, collateral, musical music. The latter, however, I do not choose to write. . . . Besides, I consider the poem to be neither bold nor cautious, neither enthusiastic nor stoical, but only very positive, very practical, very suitable indeed for many at the present time; however, I cannot even momentarily interest myself in any object of which I can perceive [only] the momentary nature, and from which I can expect no durability. . . . Forgive the whole diatribe, which is uncivil besides, because you composed the song yourself. But as you have an immense majority of musicians on your side, you will not, I think, be offended by my dissentient protestation, but probably rather disposed to laugh at it. I could not help coming out with what I thought.[35]

According to the *Allgemeine musikalische Zeitung*, the audience at a Leipzig competition concert offered by the *Musikverein Euterpe* on 6 December 1840 demanded that the chorus and orchestra presenting Jean J. H. Verhulst's (1816–91) setting of Becker's poem repeat the performance. The *Zeitung* praised this work as "natural and easily comprehensible" and its instrumental writing as quite "well crafted and calculated." The publication added that the Germans' enthusiastic reception of Becker's verses "wherever and with whatever settings it is sung" merits commendation. The journal nevertheless offered this caveat: "Unfortunately, however, among the excessively large number of settings of ['Der deutsche Rhein'], of which we know almost all that have appeared in print, there is hardly one that would give reason to hope for general popularity or exclusively greater longevity. Even Herr Verhulst's setting . . . still has too little originality to be able to grip one powerfully and to produce a lasting effect."[36]

Five days after the Leipzig contest, the *Neue Zeitschrift* announced that forty settings of the Becker poem already had been published. The writer also suggested that, despite Kunze's triumph, only the passage of time would determine which melody, but certainly not the winning composition, would prevail over the others. One week after the Leipzig competition, Schuberth placed a double-column advertisement in the *Neue Zeitschrift* broadcasting his firm's publication of settings of "Der deutsche Rhein" by Kunze and Julius Becker. The publisher offered free copies to any German song club requesting them directly from him. In late January 1841 the *Allgemeine musikalische Zeitung* reported on a concert given in Berlin's Königsstädter Theater. At this event, the publication noted, "Die Rheinländer," a patriotic occasional work by an unnamed composer, caused a "sensation." The concert also introduced a setting of Becker's poem for male solo voice, chorus, and orchestra by the theater kapellmeister, Franz Gläser.[37] In February the *Neue Zeitschrift* announced the publication of three more versions of "Der deutsche Rhein." By May the *Allgemeine musikalische Zeitung* noted that more than one hundred settings of Becker's poem had been published and that on 15 April eight of these (some unaccompanied, some with brass instruments added) had been performed by a one-hundred-voice male chorus at a Berlin benefit concert.[38]

This array of reports suggests that composers, as well as music publishers, cities, and regions, contended with each other in the contests for settings of "Der deutsche Rhein." These competitions clearly bolstered personal and national pride, as the prolific number of compositions based on Becker's verses demonstrates. Thus an exceedingly mediocre poem inspired at least two hundred musical settings by everyone from celebrated composers to the most obscure dilettantes. These settings, along with the fierce competitions, prolific publication, and heady advertising surrounding them, demonstrated that at the onset of the 1840s the Rhine had unquestionably become a pan-German nationalistic symbol even in the musical arena. Perhaps, even more significantly, the vigor of these events implied that, with the Rhine as a journalistic "commodity," a patriotic cause had been linked with the commercial spirit. Thus the role of the press in this affair confirmed a strong capitalistic element in German Romanticism.

PARODIES AND CRITICISMS

The popularity of Becker's "Der deutsche Rhein" also spawned a distinctive new body of Rhine literature in the form of impassioned prose and gushing poetic parodies, twenty-eight being responses to Becker's verses. Not all of the poetic rejoinders, however, had a parodistic intent. A larger number of them, in fact, echoed the solemnity of Becker's patriotism, such as Max von Schneckenburger's (1819–49) spirited "Die Wacht am Rhein" (The watch on the Rhine), dating from late November 1840 (see figure 2.4). This poem, set to Carl Wilhelm's (1815–73) music in 1854, eventually far surpassed Becker's in popularity (see p. 165). The first of Schneckenburger's six strophes begins:

> A call rings like thunder's sound,
> Like clashing of swords and surging of waves;
> To the Rhine, to the Rhine, to the German Rhine,
> Who will be the river's guardian?
> Dear fatherland, have no fear,
> The watch on the Rhine stands fast and true.

The poem reaches perhaps its most intense ardor with the penultimate verse:

Fig. 2.4. "Die Wacht am Rhein" by Carl Wilhelm (Leipzig and Berlin: C. F. Peters, n.d.), cover ("Frau Germania") and music.

> So long as a droplet of blood still glows,
> And as a fist still draws the sword,
> And an arm still cocks the rifle,
> No Frenchman shall set foot on thy shores.
> Dear fatherland, have no fear,
> The watch on the Rhine stands fast and true.

In "Das Lied vom Rhein an Niklas Becker," also written in 1840, the Wars of Liberation poet Ernst Moritz Arndt directly addressed Becker's poem with even more ecstatic imagery:

> A song of the Rhine sounded,
> A song from a German mouth,
> And quickly like a blaze of lightning
> It flew widely all round,
> And hot like a blaze of lightning
> It flashed through every breast
> With the agony of old birth pains,
> With the pleasure of young joys.
> From the south away to the north
> Its bright echo
> Has become like a song of arms
> Of the fatherland.
> Now roar joyfully, Rhine:
> Never shall a Frenchman
> Be watchman over my treasure!
> On and on may that resound.[39]

Becker's rhymes, however, also gave rise to pointed satire, lampooning what the political writer and Rhinelander Karl Ferdinand Gutzkow (1811–78) considered Becker's political naïveté and the "Rheinlied epidemic" that followed. In his poem "Rheinlied und Rheinleid" (Rhine song and Rhine sorrow), written and published in 1840, August Heinrich Hoffmann von Fallersleben (1798–1874) mercilessly derided the popularity of Becker's Rheinlied. This author of the later German national anthem "Deutschland, Deutschland über alles" (which appeared only one year after this satire) complained:

> In every house a terrible piano,
> In every house a voice and hand,

In every house you hear enthusiasts
For the dear German fatherland.
And the enthusiasm knows no end,
It makes a way for itself by day and night,
It surges forward through doors, cupboards, and walls
So that people even awaken out of their sleep.
You stand up, you lie down,
You hear of "the free German Rhine,"
You wake up, and again
The screaming about "the free German Rhine."
You may rest now, go, away!
You hear in a thousand melodies
"They shall, shall not have it!"
Scream from the Tilsit to the Wesel.
All Germany sings—and meanwhile,
The dear free German Rhine!
There the blind Hessians fling
Bricks thither into its bed.[40]

Two pamphlets published anonymously in Prussia's Rhine Province in May 1844 parodied in poetry the failed attempts made until then to realize the vision of the Rhineland, Prussia, and other German states joined in a common drive to abolish absolutism. In "Am Rheine liegt eine kleines Land" (On the Rhine lies a little land), an anonymous poet mocked the seemingly infinite deluge of musical settings inspired by Becker's Rhine poem:

Recently stupid lads sang
To a thousand melodies:
"They shall not have it,
The free German Rhine."
Now the glow fades,
No barrel-organ grinder
Will earn another groschen
If he sings the Rheinlied.
Recently when they laid the stone
For the cathedral in Cologne on the Rhine,
We gladly nurtured the hope
Of being a happy people.
Now the dream has disappeared,

It was a farce
Of a few short hours;
We are not yet at the goal.[41]

In January 1844 the poet Heinrich Heine (1797–1856) ridiculed "Der deutsche Rhein" with penetrating wit:

And when I came to the Rhine bridge,
Well onto the harbor bulwark,
There I saw Father Rhine flowing
In the quiet moonlight.

"I greet thee, my Father Rhine,
How have things gone with thee?
I have often thought of thee
With longing and desire."

Thus I spoke, and there I heard deep in the water
Quite strange, morose sounds,
Like the coughing of an old man,
A grumbling and weak groaning . . . ,
"At Biberich I swallowed stones,
Truly, they did not taste nice!
Yet more heavily in my stomach lie
The verses of Niklas Becker.
. . . When I hear it, the stupid song,
Then I would like to tear off
My white beard, indeed I would like
To drown me in myself!"

. . . Thus lamented poor Father Rhine. . . .
I spoke to him many a consoling word . . . ,
"O fear not, my Father Rhine,
The jeering jest of the French;
They are no longer the old French. . . .
They sing no more, they spring no more,
They sink their heads pensively.

They philosophize and speak now
Of Kant, of Fichte, and Hegel. . . .
They will become Philistines just like us. . . .

Calm thyself, Father Rhine,
Think not of bad songs,
Thou shalt soon hear a better song—
Farewell, we shall meet again."[42]

Robert E. Prutz's (1816–72) ponderous "Der Rhein," completed in early December 1840, however, idealizes Becker's verses as an example of the freedoms desperately needed for Germany and its Rhine to unite in nationhood:

The German Rhine! How powerfully the word resounds!
Already we see it, the golden green river,
With bright cities, castles proud and splendid,
The Loreley there, and there the Cologne Cathedral!
The free Rhine! Memory of our victories,
Thou, baptized with the blood of those most noble,
Fame of our fathers, who bought thee with
Swords, not with songs, in the holy war!

Who now has the right to speak and sing
Of "the free Rhine," the free German son?
O these songs that resound so bravely,
By the eternal God, they seem like an insult to me. . . .

This does not mean you [Becker], who first sang
The proud word of "the free German Rhine"
The song has swelled out of your full breast. . . .
It flies forth free, whither the winds will it. . . .

My call concerns you, you princes and vassals,
In whose hands lies our fate!
It concerns you Germans, near and far, you all. . . .
You must begin the fight first with yourselves!
. . . The troubled Rhine's wave should flow.
Then be yourselves first German and free! . . .

Free speech, you bards, on your thrones! . . .
The press free! . . .
And if in future days
Proud France longs for our Rhine,

Then we will endure it with our hands on the sword.
For then we will succeed in holding
[the Rhine] free forever. . . .
Then it will be worthwhile to fight unto death,
Then, German and free, then
It will remain our Rhine![43]

In his commentary to the Rhine poems of both Becker and Prutz, the influential German journalist Arnold Ruge pronounced "Der deutsche Rhein" inadequate inspiration for overcoming German political indifference and dissension. These qualities, he remarked, contrasted sharply with the patriotism buoying up Germans during the Wars of Liberation. To the contrary, the London Treaty crisis, Ruge stipulated, required a degree of nationalistic fervor equaling that of Germans in their campaigns against Napoleon.[44] In a similar vein, Nikolaus Müller (1770–1851), a patriotic songbook editor in Mainz, charged that Becker's poem should have voiced a German claim for the entire Rhineland area, even the ever-disputed Alsace, which the French retained after the Vienna Congress.[45]

Similarly, in his 1841 poem "Protest" the poet Georg Herwegh (1817–75) faulted Becker's "Der deutsche Rhein" for implying that Germany would be liberated merely by establishing a Rhine blockade against the French:

So long as I am still a Protestant,
I, too, want to protest.
And every German musician
Shall spread [the German cause] by making music!
If all the world sings "the *free* Rhine,"
Yet I shall sing no, you gentlemen!
The Rhine, the Rhine could be freer—
Thus I want to protest. . . .
From the Rhine to the ocean,
If there are no free men thereon,
Then I want to protest. . . .
And if the world sings
"The *free* Rhine!" . . .
The Rhine, the Rhine could be freer,
We must protest.[46]

Karl Gutzkow, the poet and theater director Franz Freiherr von Dingelstedt (1814–81), and Friedrich Theodor Vischer (1807–87), the proposer of

a Nibelungen drama, concurred in condemning Becker's Rheinlied for woe-
fully insufficient zeal. An anonymous "North German" likewise disparaged
the popularity of Becker's Rheinlied as only a modish phenomenon among
the nonthinking philistine masses. The latter, he complained, would sing
any of the poem's various melodies, regardless of quality, if these "performances" were simply hosted in a German drinking establishment. To the
contrary, he wrote, the causes of freedom and nationalism could be advanced only with the Germans' elimination of political oppression and
divisive attitudes.[47]

The political author Friedrich Engels (1820–95)—the famous associate
of the Rhinelander Karl Marx—complained that the Germans' sense of
Volkstum (nationhood) characteristically emerged only under the threat of
foreign oppression.[18] Gutzkow, their colleague, quite literally parodied
Becker's Rheinlied in his poem "An die neuen Franzosenfresser" (To the
French gluttons), written in late 1840:

> "They shall not have it,
> The free German Rhine!"
> Yet you must not, like boys,
> Cry yourself hoarse over it!
> You do not want
> To give up the Rhine?
> Or give up
> A free German life,
> A free German house?[49]

FRENCH POLEMIC VERSE

On reading Becker's Rheinlied in mid-May 1841, the French poet-statesman
Alphonse de Lamartine immediately penned his own interminable poetic
response, "La Marseillaise de la paix, réponse à M. Becker, auteur du 'Rhin
allemand,'" published in the Paris *Revue des deux mondes* on 1 June of that
year. On 11 January 1840, six months before the London Treaty crisis, Lamartine had appeared before his colleagues in the French parliament to
question the validity of the Vienna Congress boundary treaties imposed on
France by the victorious powers. His "Marseillaise" espoused the cause of
"Europe ideology" in an eloquent appeal for universal peace, regardless of
individual nations' boundary claims:

Flow free and superb between thy great banks,
O Rhine, Nile of the Occident, fount of nations! . . .
Flow free and magnificent through our ruins,
River of Arminius, of the Gaul, of the German!
Charlemagne and Caesar, camped on thy hills, . . .

And why hate each other, and place between the races
These boundaries or these
Waters that the eye of God abhors?
Do we see any traces of frontiers in heaven? . . .

Egoism and hate alone have a country;
Fraternity does not have any!
Flow free and royal among all of us, O river!
And ask not, in thy fertile course,
If those whom thy wave carries or whom thy urn waters,
Beheld on thy banks the dawn or the West.

It is no longer seas, degrees, or rivers
That circumscribe the legacy of humanity.
The limits of souls are their only frontiers;
The world, in becoming enlightened, rises toward unity.

My country is wheresoever France shines,
Where her genius breaks forth
Before dazzled eyes!

. . . Flow freely to those seas where
The Euphrates goes to die,
Entwine the web of the globe's arteries;
Render the herb and the fleece to this ungrateful land.
Let men be one people, and the rivers one water![50]

Upon reading Lamartine's "Marseillaise" in the *Revue des deux mondes*, the renowned French Romantic poet Alfred de Musset (1810–57) rejoined with his defiant poem "Le Rhin allemand, réponse à la chanson de Becker." It was first published (under his nom de plume, "Vicomte de Launay") simultaneously in both *La Presse* and the *Revue de Paris* on 6 June 1841. Musset's verses directly reflected the French chauvinist, or anti-German, factions active in the Paris salon of Madame Émile (Delphine Gay) de Girardin

(1804–85). Musset's "Le Rhin," an impatient retort against Lamartine's fraternal pacifism, instead addressed Becker's Rheinlied as the words of merely an insolent *provocateur*:

> We already have your "German Rhine" [Becker's poem],
> It has remained in our glass,
> A verse that one sings better;
> Does it remove the proud trace
> Of our horses' hooves marked in your blood? . . .
>
> What were your German virtues doing
> When our Caesar, all-powerful,
> Covered your plains with his shadow?
> Where, then, has he fallen, these "last remains"!
>
> . . . If you forget your history,
> Your young maidens surely
> Preserved our memory;
> They poured out your humble white wine for us.
>
> Let it flow in peace, your German Rhine—
> That our Gothic cathedrals
> Be modestly reflected in it;
> But be fearful lest your drunken airs
> Awaken the dead from their bloody repose.[51]

Lamartine dismissed Musset's poetic rejoinder to Becker as shallow. The author of "La Marseillaise de la paix," however, resented Musset's apparent success in persuading the French to support his antagonistic, militaristic attitude.[52] Thus Lamartine claimed:

Becker came to publish a popular and patriotic song that resounded in every heart and mouth on both banks of the Rhine. . . . Musset responds to these ardent and fiery strophes with jeering and prosaic verses to which the national spirit (I mean stupidity) responds with immense applause—with that prodigal craze for its favorite of the day, a craze that proves only one thing: that patriotism was not more poetic than it was politic in France at this time. I avow that [Musset's verses] appear to me to be beneath the dignity, as well as below the genius, of France. . . . At the tribunal (in parliament) and with all my forces, I fought both the coalition, calling itself parliamentary, and the universal war for the sake of a parvenu pasha. In an hour of inspiration, I wrote the "Marseillaise de la paix," the only response to make, in my opinion, to a Germany justifiably offended by our threats. . . . I was declared a dreamer and [Musset] a national poet; the "Marseillaise [de la paix]" rose again only after the fall of the parliamentary coalition [Thiers's fall from power]. They wished for a refrain of the barracks; they scoffed at the note of peace.[53]

France as a whole nevertheless sided with the views expressed in Musset's militaristic poem. And, not surprisingly, the Germans acclaimed Lamartine's poem of peace and denounced the brazen innuendos of Musset's "Le Rhin." The German historian Karl Biedermann recalled in 1881:

The little Thiers, convinced—as the chief creator of the Napoleonic myth—that he had a general of Napoleonic genius in his belly, opened his big mouth and screamed angrily with his thin, reedy voice for the Rhine, that is, for the German Rhinelands. To this effrontery the Germans gave a bad poem, Becker's Rheinlied, as an answer, to which the French set a still worse one that Alfred de Musset had perpetrated over the absinthe flask. The good Lamartine made an end to this German-French war luckily conducted only in bad verses, presenting us with the sugar-water goblet of his "Marseillaise de la paix."[54]

Not to be outdone by French eloquence, however, the famous German patriotic lyricist Ferdinand Freiligrath (1810–76) translated Lamartine's "Marseillaise" into German. Several other Germans chose it as the model for additional verses of their own. On 19 July 1841 the Athenäum: Zeitschrift für das gebildete Deutschland further praised Lamartine's peaceful response to Becker's Rheinlied:

Lamartine—that same Lamartine who made the Rhine again the catchword of the French on the political podium—knew, as soon as he assumed the poetic point of view, to answer Becker's Rheinlied with a poem, to bring an infinitely higher viewpoint to light; in his "Marseillaise de la Paix" he offers the hand of peace to Becker's one-sided crying of shibboleths; he says the word "nation" is a barbarism, as soon as it gives occasion to isolate itself, to oppose other nations.[55]

A few days later the Athenäum reminded its readers that it had already published Musset's poem on 19 June, though only with the intention of exposing what it considered the vapidity of his assertions:

If Napoleon had wanted to make the Rhine Province French, this injury to our nationality has avenged itself heavily on him. Therefore the scales weigh equally on both sides; neither of the two nations can lift itself above the other, but each ought, in a reasonable way, to be concerned about peace and about the necessity for a reciprocal balance between both. "Sie sollen ihn nicht haben"— that is, they should have not a foot of the ground—that goes without saying; that is implied in the simple meaning of nationality, and will continue to be; but we too should avoid becoming greedy devourers of the French.[56]

The polemic aroused by Becker's Rhine poem, however, was not over.

THE "RHEINLIEDER" CRITICS

Anticipating the event orientation of the modern press, even professional German music journals soon entered into the controversy occasioned by the Rheinlieder. These contributions thereby afford us further insight into the position of music among the Germans toward the mid-nineteenth century.[57] The *Allgemeine musikalische Zeitung*, the *Neue Zeitschrift für Musik*, and *Iris im Gebiete der Tonkunst* provide a good sampling of the most cogent contemporary comment on these songs. All these publications had reached a zenith of their development, wielded wide influence, and between them represented a variety of individual and collective editorial opinions.[58]

Rheinlieder reviews and other articles pertaining to this music confirmed that most critics, to varying degrees, viewed the Rheinlieder as appropriately patriotic. They nevertheless continued to apply traditional aesthetic criteria to this body of music, remaining ever alert in the campaign against philistinism. German music at this time, moreover, tended to invite almost universal interest, buoyed by the burgeoning middle classes and their commercial spirit. Hence the pages of the journals, courting public taste, clearly reflected elements of this universalism and commercialization, particularly evident in their treatment of music as "news."

These publications and their critics additionally display a singular reciprocity between music, the lied, and one of the most salient aspects of German Romanticism: an emerging nationalism of which the Rhine was a supreme symbol.

GERMAN MUSIC JOURNALS OF THE NINETEENTH CENTURY

The loquacious Rheinlieder reviews and advertisements announcing a profusion of Becker Rhine poem settings opened a new chapter in the historical role of professional German music journals. This chapter was to reveal the transformation in purpose, outlook, and scope undergone by such publications from the time of their inception in the seventeenth century. Originally conceived as theoretical expositions oriented exclusively toward the musically erudite, journals had gradually broadened to include consideration of contemporary works and other topics attractive to a more comprehensive, educated readership.[59]

By the early nineteenth century, the Enlightenment term *kritisch* (critical) had yielded to *allgemein* (universal or general), as indicated in the titles of German periodicals. The new musical publications thus sought to present a comprehensive selection of subjects to attract the attention of an increasingly broad and diverse public, a significant factor in the enlarged spectrum of public musical life.[60] The *Allgemeine musikalische Zeitung,* founded in 1798, pioneered this new trend toward informing the educated readership at large, as well as the more limited circle of professional musicians. As a result, its circulation soon exceeded that of earlier musical publications.

As they terminated the first stage in the evolution of the *Allgemeine musikalische Zeitung* on 28 December 1848, its editors reviewed the original purpose of their journal, "founded at the time of the richest and noblest productivity in music; Mozart had just died, Haydn was still engaged in full artistic activity, Beethoven was at the beginning of his career. The task [of the *Allgemeine musikalische Zeitung*] was to disseminate the products of such a time among the connoisseurs and amateurs of music, to work in an enlightening way for their understanding and their appreciation, [and] to form their public."[61]

In addition to its appeal as *allgemein,* the *Allgemeine musikalische Zeitung* in its role as a *Zeitung* represented a shift in journalistic outlook toward a "news magazine" or "newspaper."[62] In contrast to the *Zeitschrift* or "journal" (Schumann's publication, for example), which typically remained general, abstract, and critical, the *Zeitung* tended to promulgate the more immediate communication of current events. As a rule, this attitude has continued to dominate the arts sections and the coverage of "newsworthy" musical events in the daily American press.

As the nineteenth century unfolded, the terms *Zeitung* and *Zeitschrift,* though not totally distinguishable, gradually came to signify a division among the various musical journals in objectives, modes of thought, and readership. The *Allgemeine musikalische Zeitung* established standards of coverage followed by similar German publications through the nineteenth century. It evolved a format consisting of biography, reviews (of theoretical works, books on music, and compositions), commentary on recently invented or "improved" instruments, and reports from foreign correspondents.[63] Ultimately, during G. W. Fink's reign, the journal could not be adapted to the exigencies of changing times or to the competition presented by Schumann's *Neue Zeitschrift*.

The latter was joined by Berlin's *Iris im Gebiete der Tonkunst* in devoting much space to the Rheinlieder polemic. *Iris*, founded in 1830 by the witty Berlin critic Heinrich Friedrich Ludwig Rellstab (1799–1860), endeavored to provide a comprehensive commentary on the overall state of music, in addition to a routine accounting of current musical events.[64]

Schumann founded the *Neue Zeitschrift* in 1834 in collaboration with his future father-in-law, Friedrich Wieck (1785–1873), along with Ludwig Schunke (1810–34) and Julius Knorr (1807–61). Editor until 1844, the composer idealistically envisioned the *Neue Zeitschrift* as a means for overcoming "that unartistic period just past, and to hasten a new, poetic era." This era was to be no longer burdened by the dilettantish scourge of the "talentless," the "commonplace talents," and the "talented ones who wrote too much."[65] The founders of the *Neue Zeitschrift* consequently initiated a new journalistic policy of including articles highly receptive to contemporary working artists and reviews introducing their compositions to the public. As the voice of the "New German School," the *Neue Zeitschrift* had thus developed by the 1850s into a determined partisan, even political, influence in musical life.[66]

Under Schumann's rigorous control, both the general format of the *Zeitschrift's* criticisms and its consistent emphasis on reviews of published music, rather than manuscripts, continued practices similar to those of the *Allgemeine musikalische Zeitung*. As in the early years of the latter, the *Neue Zeitschrift* distinguished between what it viewed as the best, the merely mediocre, and poor music by the amount of space allotted to the particular composition.[67]

Most reviews of Rheinlieder appearing during the 1840s in the *Neue Zeitschrift*, the *Allgemeine musikalische Zeitung*, and *Iris* were assigned generous space on the page. The treatment of music in these journals nevertheless disclosed important shades of difference in approach. Although they shared an orientation toward professional musicians or the seriously interested layman, they consciously ignored the *Allgemeine musikalische Zeitung's* concentration on presenting a broad general public with "news" of recent musical events.

The *Neue Zeitschrift*, however, far exceeded the other two journals in focusing on the purely musical aspects of compositions and, as the voice of Romanticism, on their cultural and national content. This was particularly true in the reviews of the Rheinlieder.[68] Both the *Allgemeine musikalische Zeitung* and *Iris*, though quite divergent in tone, tended to treat Rheinlieder publication more as a newsworthy phenomenon than as material for technical appraisal.[69] The reviews of these songs in the *Neue Zeitschrift*, and in *Iris* to some extent, disclosed what the "professionals" valued. Those in the *Allgemeine musikalische Zeitung* tended to center on the interests of the musical public at large.

RHEINLIEDER IN THE
NEUE ZEITSCHRIFT

The most radical advocacy of musical nationalism among these journals occupied the pages of Schumann's *Neue Zeitschrift für Musik* between February and mid-August 1841. This publication devoted an imposing series of six lengthy articles to the Becker poem and its settings, the most sizable body of comment on this subject. The author was Carl Kossmaly (1812–93), a lieder composer, lexicographer, and regular critic for this journal.[70]

Kossmaly's views reflected the *Neue Zeitschrift*'s serious, abstract tone and educational intent.[71] He saw compensation for the Germans' lack of a national political identity in the unity of the German spirit in "art and learning," that is, in cultural nationalism. "In the realm of ideas," he observed, "in short, in everything concerning intelligence and spiritual capacity, not only inner unity and national independence but also a decided superiority must be granted to the Germans." Kossmaly claimed German supremacy and national identity particularly in music, "the most *volkstümlich*, . . . the most sublime . . . of all arts." He specifically cited the lied in this respect because of its "peculiar mixture—combining soul [*Gemüth*] and melancholy—in the German character" and because of the Germans' propensity for the subjective single-mindedness needed for lied composition.[72]

Kossmaly took special pains to laud the *Volkslied* as the glorification of a nation's spiritual and historical past and as the echo of a people's peculiar character and sentiment. Its text was to conform to "the spirit, the prototype of the people," and the entire nation was to be able to identify completely with its *Volksweise* (folk melody). Deploring the current and crucial lack of a genuine German *Volkslied*, he rebuked the critics who, he thought, wrongly caviled at the superficiality of Becker's "Der deutsche Rhein." He instead acclaimed this poem as an estimable *Volkslied* text, one that voiced the prevalent German nationalistic sentiment recently heightened by the Rhine crisis. In short, he contended, Becker's verses fully realized the ideal of *Volkstümlichkeit*. Kossmaly broadened this term by joining the notion of national patriotic expression with its previous, more limited meaning: the conscious cultivation of simplicity and naturalness that marked the strophic lied of early Classicism.

Kossmaly measured the *Volkstümlichkeit* of each Rheinlied he surveyed. The music had to communicate the poem's patriotic élan and the essence of the *Volk*. With obvious bias he extolled Schumann's setting of the Becker poem (see example 4.14) for its "steely melody, full of German power and gentleness. In this proud, noble rhythm, courage, inspiration, and noble anger are announced in the most highly significant way. Here rules the spirit of Arminius, and at the entrance of the full chorus, one supposes unconsciously that he hears the German oaks rustle. Incontestably one of the most excellent compositions of Becker's poem, to which is due the most universal esteem."[72]

For similar reasons Kossmaly equally commended the compositions of "Der deutsche Rhein" by August Schäffer, Carl Langrock, and Carl Mangold. He betrayed a certain naïveté, however, in applauding Carl F. Weisheit for translating the poem's "tame and sociable patriotism" through a "truly patriarchal harmony" consisting of only tonic and dominant chords; for matching what he deemed the frenzied seriousness of the final strophe by means of a "tragic, hair-bristling change of key," appropriately accompanied by a trumpetlike figure; and for ingeniously characterizing the "indeterminate political physiognomy of Germany" through a key that ambivalently fluctuated between C major and A minor. Kreutzer's celebrated melody was considered too graceful for such a patriotic text. Gustav Kunze's prize composition was judged merely ostentatious. And Joseph Lenz's award-winning piece (see p. 49) was described as "a musical distortion of the poetic meter, weakening the poem's declamatory spirit."[74]

IRIS IM GEBIETE DER TONKUNST

Nothing contrasted more with Kossmaly's solemn, resolute encouragement of musical patriotism than the Rheinlieder reviews of Heinrich Friedrich Ludwig Rellstab, the scrupulous, droll Berliner and editor of *Iris im Gebiete der Tonkunst*. From January through July 1841 he ceaselessly bewailed his martyrdom to the cause of Rheinlieder, particularly the deluge based on Becker's verses. "We would sincerely wish that the German," Rellstab confessed, "would manifest his love of fatherland and enthusiasm otherwise than in such provocative poems, which truly are not less premature than the French screams for the Rhine."[75] Perhaps he revealed his Berlin prejudice, or cosmopolitanism, in protesting against François Hünten's setting of another Rhine poem, which annoyed Rellstab because the poet "claim[s] the three stars of cheerfulness, of lieder, and of wine exclusively for the Rhine. They shine also on the Main, on the Spree, on the Danube—only not, perhaps, on the Neva and Weichsel."[76]

By mid-March 1841 satire had overtaken a weary Rellstab, who almost daily continued to discard a new setting of Becker's poem into the wastepaper basket. The situation was redeemed, however, by the arrival of Friedrich von Drieberg's *Sie sollen ihn nicht haben, den freien deutschen Rhein: Eine Kanonade von 100 Componisten für vier Singstimmen*, a canonic burlesque of the excess of compositions based on Becker's lines. Rellstab proclaimed "finally, for once, a first-rate composition of [Becker's] Rheinlied! And why? Because it is a parody, not of the poem, not of the patriotism in it, not even of the overclimaxed, artificially manufactured enthusiasm for it, but only of the hundred—no, of the hundred thousand compositions of it!"[77]

In April, Rellstab launched a small fusillade of irony and metaphorical wit against another barrage of settings of "Der deutsche Rhein," this time by Eduard Salleneuve, S. T. Steinbrunn, Gustav Reichardt, Carl F. Seyffert, Moritz Ernemann, Mangold, and Lenz:

> Here the readers of *Iris* have seven compositions of the circa seventy that have forced open the editor's house. All seven are unsurpassable, except that one excels the others in approximately the way Münchhausen's fierce lions ate each other up to the tails. We can lack nothing more after all these demonstrations of heroism; we shall drive the French over the Rhine if they show themselves on this side; nay, we shall drive the Rhine over them! Should, however, the old father [the Rhine] move, because of the pain of his stones, . . . out of his banks, with these bales of compositions one might easily make a dam from Basel to Rotterdam that will avert all danger. For this purpose I recommend, if necessary, all the compositions of the Rheinlied; meanwhile, until this *casus necessitatis* occurs, may we sing them all.[78]

Though less fervent than Kossmaly, Rellstab did seriously measure the expression of *Volkstümlichkeit* in these songs. He complained that Sigismund

Neukomm's composition of "Der deutsche Rhein" relied on the use of large choruses and a sizable orchestra simply for outward display. The piece, he regretted, "will not be accepted by the people, for it lacks naturalness and, above all, simplicity of melody."[79] Thus Rellstab emphasized the older meaning of *Volkstümlichkeit* in the lied, that is, folklike naturalness and simplicity. He had no special regard for nationalism, especially Rhenish.

In their numerous reviews of Rheinlieder the critics for the *Allgemeine musikalische Zeitung* earnestly weighed how effectively the composer had translated nationalistic intent into music. But they exhibited neither the degree of abstraction nor the extent of nationalistic zeal found in Schumann's *Zeitschrift*. An unnamed writer for the *Allgemeine musikalische Zeitung* thoroughly analyzed the patriotic effectiveness of a Liszt Rheinlied, a setting of Ernst Moritz Arndt's popular "Das deutsche Vaterland." While admiring Liszt's individualistic spirit in this "heaven-storming song" for four-part male chorus and a large orchestra, the critic nevertheless lamented that in this beautiful "hymn to the German fatherland" the composer's excessive outbursts of French revolutionary intensity generated too much passion and length for a genuine German *Volkslied*. Worse, the writer observed, Liszt even weakened the poet's call for national unity through the naïve differentiation of each German-speaking region. The verse about Austria, for example, was composed in a "genial $3/4$ meter," while "Prussia progresses in proud B-flat major and in *forte*." But "the good Swabia must be satisfied with B-flat minor in *piano*." Liszt was also chastised for his disorganized plethora of striking key changes, melodic "unrest," disruptive accents confusing the meter, and forbidden operatic exclamations of *nein* and *ja*. As opposed to this example, the writer concluded, the power of a genuinely *volkstümlich* lied should evidence simplicity of execution and effect.[80]

Gottfried Wilhelm Fink (1783–1846), the editor and one of the principal critics for the *Allgemeine musikalische Zeitung*, succinctly expressed another view after examining one hundred settings of Becker's poem. Their patriotic zeal, he remarked, could serve, in fact, to alarm the French and Germans sufficiently to avert any actual military confrontation over the Rhine at all.[81]

THE PHILISTINE PRESENCE

As well as the issue of nationalism, these critics discussed the artistic merits of Rheinlieder at every level from high art to mediocrity. In this way they disclosed a thorough intermingling of popular fare and serious composition that one associates today with much of the American press.

While the critics did endeavor to assess songs of any artistic level, they nevertheless were quick to denounce poor technical skill, faulty text-music relationships, and any symptoms of philistine influence. They weighed the degree of originality, ridiculed embarrassing sentimentality, deplored the superabundance of songs, and debated the *Männerchor* vogue. In so doing, these writers and their journals attested to the vigor of the German musical establishment, the universality of musical life, and the pervading influence of the commercial spirit.

Every critic discussed a composer's sheer compositional proficiency and his treatment of the text. Kossmaly pronounced a lied to be of the greatest merit if the musical setting intensified or even re-created the poetic content, for "there is . . . a transcendental, secret, unexplainable something embodied" in the music that the text alone cannot convey. Lieder of this sort, he concluded, "stand above their texts, which should serve only as an external point to lean against, as the earthly bearer of the idea-become-music."[82] Kossmaly meticulously observed the musical fulfillment of the poem's meter, structure, and emotional tone. From the settings of the Becker poem, for example, he singled out August Schäffer's melody "in steel and iron, juicy and powerful, which we unconditionally count among the fortunate interpretations of the poem." He rejoiced in "the patriotic élan" of Carl Mangold's setting. Yet he chided the tranquil versions of Heinrich Carl Breidenstein and others for denying the passion of Becker's inflamed verses. He accused Lenz of needlessly lengthening the poem by repeating lines and of distorting the poem's meter and hence its declamatory force. Kossmaly also faulted compositions containing monotonous, weak, awkward, or incorrect harmony, melody, and counterpoint, as in the setting by Julius Becker.[83]

But it was this same Becker who as a critic revealed a similar concern for preserving the poetic declamation. In this respect, he praised Emanuel Klietzsch's setting of Heine's "Lorelei" text.[84] Rellstab in *Iris* and the critics for the *Allgemeine musikalische Zeitung* (except for Fink, who dismissed the settings of Becker's Rheinlied as unworthy of aesthetic judgment) likewise examined text-music correspondence and compositional skill without, however, the *Neue Zeitschrift*'s explicit detail.

The scourge of philistinism caused universal concern in these journals. Schumann's publication, of course, never missed a chance for lofty discourse on this subject. Kossmaly deplored the dilettantism particularly endangering the lied (a genre, he claimed, allowing easy success and requiring little artistically). He warned against the tidal wave of superficial songs threatening to engulf "all true creation founded on study and learning in the whirlpools of a whining, feeble, monotonous sentimentality." With every Rheinlied, Kossmaly looked for that originality, character, enthusiasm, feeling (*Empfindung*), and inspiration that Schumann and his associates so eloquently upheld as their ideal. Kossmaly, for instance, snickered at an uninventive composition of Becker's poem (the composer was unnamed), one so mechanical and tame in melody that it suited only "such a humble, submissive, and patient nation as the German nation." Yet he delighted in the melodic originality of Carl Leibl's setting of the same verses and favored the setting by C. Bernhard Breuer as a piece that "without any ostentation . . . nevertheless in no way lapses into triviality and the commonplace."[85]

"Philistine" was Kossmaly's favorite epithet, applied to anything smacking of the operatic, which he equated with the banal or sentimental, the Italian opera composer Vincenzo Bellini (1801–35) being the common whipping boy. He denounced Conradin Kreutzer's celebrated composition of "Der deutsche Rhein," the piece that had electrified the Cölner Theater audience in October 1840: "The melody, although kept flowing and singable—that is taken for granted with Kreutzer—is lost too much in certain phrases that have become stereotyped, in banal operatic commonplaces; that is, it lacks that characteristic individuality, that original peculiarity, without which a genuine *Volksmelodie* cannot indeed be thought of."[86]

Kossmaly's opinions on this subject reached perhaps their most sarcastic zenith when he condemned Gustav Kunze's prizewinning setting of the Becker Rheinlied as a pompous work recalling "certain apples glowing splendidly on the outside, but rotten and wormy on the inside. . . . If only the dullest prose and the home-baked commonplace become the main ingredients of the German character, then this so-called prize composition, which reproduces the boring sobriety of our true citizens and Philistines in masterly strokes, may be greeted as . . . a genuine German *Volksmelodie*, with which the dear German nation can . . . drink much beer and vigorously talk political nonsense!"[87]

The philistine menace inspired similar taunts from other writers. Julius Becker contemptuously remarked that Friedrich Christian Ehrlich's lied "Sehnsucht nach dem Rheine" (Longing for the Rhine) was one of those merely pleasing songs that "stir one just as deeply as is the custom in the salons, where one serves ice cream in summer and tea in winter. . . . They soar . . . to that proper passion which, at its loftiest, only reaches the highpoint of an excusably harried and rumpled maker of sentiment."[88] Antiphilistine satire, it seems, had its Daumiers among the music critics.

These writers also registered their discomfort over the sheer profusion of lieder. Their views on this subject, as well as other articles in these journals, attested not only to the vigor of German musical life at this time but also to the perils of its universality, at least in song. Time and again the music critics of the 1840s warned that a proliferation of lieder had resulted in quantity at the expense of excellence. Kossmaly, pointing an accusing finger at the profusion of *Liedertafeln*, continually bemoaned the "enormous sum of superficial, empty, and colorless lieder compositions" flooding Germany.[89] Rellstab's concern about the prodigious number of songs and of song composers equaled Kossmaly's. One might attribute this particular musical manifestation of popular culture to the possible circumstance that most of these song composers, with some major exceptions, were merely zealous amateurs. This, however, was not the case, at least with the Rheinlieder composers. Virtually all of them had received serious, thorough musical educations from respected teachers and institutions and had served in one or more professional musical capacities such as that of kapellmeister, conductor or director of music festivals, composer, teacher, or author of books on musical subjects.

MUSIC AS "NEWS"

Behind the reviews of Rheinlieder one can sense the same event orientation that compels the modern press, which is out to win and maintain a broadly based readership. The creators of the Rheinlieder "literature," so amply represented in the journals, correctly assumed a current, engrossing interest on the part of the general populace, both readers of these publications and consumers of the "product." For these songs voiced the timely nationalistic impulses that had so immediately gripped the German mind of the 1840s. The journals could not overlook music of such topical concern. As we have seen, these publications, through critical commentary and advertisements, had even publicized the national competition to determine the "best" setting of Becker's poem. In this way, they broadcast an event that captured the public imagination and, of course, proved lucrative to the music publishers. Through their critics and advertisements, these music journals helped foster the commercial spirit in the wooing of general public taste. From their pages we learn that compositions of Becker's "Der deutsche Rhein" brought not only composers but publishers and cities into active rivalry and that these contests probably further stimulated the pan-German mass production of works based on this poem. The journals were decidedly attuned to this popular event, and such an orientation clearly betrayed a susceptibility to the commercialization of music.[90]

Thus we see that, at a crucial point in the emergence of German national consciousness, patriotic sentiments broke into song and drew the attention of professional music critics, who could not remain immune to public pressures. In its handling of Rheinlieder as both art and "news," the musical journalism of the day articulated several of the main themes of mid-nineteenth-century German life.

THE RHEINLIEDER
TEXTS AND THE
NINETEENTH-CENTURY
GERMAN WORLD

*T*he Rheinlieder texts bring into high focus many of the notions and tendencies previously discussed in this study. Images such as Vater Rhein, knights, wayfarers, pilgrimage towns, and elves or water sprites confirm that the Rhine, with all its historic and poetic ramifications, stands as a meaningful symbol of German Romantic cultural and national identity. The humanoid figures of the Loreley and Nibelung, two of the most visible examples of the Rhine metaphor, represent nature in the animistic, that is, personified, terms of a new mythology. Together, all these poeticized Rhine symbols, in fact, make manifest how comprehensive was the German Romantics' idealization of historic and mythic events, sites, and heroes representing their common ancestral past, both real and imagined. The resulting collections of myths, epics, and legendary lore prodded a national collective identity into consciousness, offering profound truths regarding the Germans' very origins. Georg Wilhelm Friedrich Hegel, likening Germanic to Greek mythology, emphasized the unconscious meaning of classical allegory: "Those peoples, at the time when they composed their myths, lived in a state altogether poetic; they expressed their most secret and most profound sentiments, not by abstract formulae, but by the forms of the imagination."[1]

In its glorification of the past, the new Germanic mythology brought together all that was German, thereby fulfilling the dream of a culturally unified nationhood. In his essay "On Poland" of 1822, for example, Heinrich Heine exalted the *Nibelungenlied* as the apogee of medieval Germanness. Caustically complaining against existing remnants of Enlightenment neoclassicism, he even advised: "May the time soon come when no learned schoolboy draws a comparison between the Cologne Cathedral and the Pantheon, between the *Nibelungenlied* and the *Odyssey*, when one recognizes the splendors of the Middle Ages in their organic context, compares them only with themselves, and calls the *Nibelungenlied* a versified cathedral and the Cologne Cathedral a stony *Nibelungenlied*."[2]

The Germans' new mythology merging nationalistic and aesthetic concerns was also giving rise to an expanding body of lyric poetry. Thus poets and dramatists, some of whose works were set to music, as well as other writers and painters, heightened a growing cultural and national sense of identity through newly created animistic mermaids and dwarfs in a corporate reenactment of the organic ascent to consciousness. This notion of ascent was a principal tenet of nineteenth-century German thought.

NINETEENTH-CENTURY CONCEPTS AND THE RHEINLIEDER TEXTS: NATURAL SCIENCE, HISTORIOGRAPHY, PSYCHOLOGY AND PSYCHIATRY, NATURE PHILOSOPHY, LANDSCAPE ART

In his *Childe Harold's Pilgrimage* of 1816, George Gordon, Lord Byron, memorialized his visit to the Drachenfels, a rocky promontory overlooking the Rhine near Bonn. This English Romantic poet, like his German counterparts, described the Rhine in anthropomorphic terms. Such anthropomorphism could perhaps be viewed as a poetic version of the *Volkstümlichkeit* ideal in its exaltation of the folklike. The second verse contains this encomium:

> The castled crag of Drachenfels
> Frowns o'er the wide and winding Rhine,
> Whose breast of waters broadly swells
> Between the banks which bear the vine;
> And hills all rich with blossom'd trees,
> And fields which promise corn and wine. . . .
> The river nobly foams and flows;
> The charm of this enchanted ground,
> And all its thousand turns disclose
> Some fresher beauty varying round:
> The haughtiest breast its wish might bound

Through life to swell delighted here;
Nor could on earth a spot be found
To nature and to me so dear,
Could thy dear eyes in following mine
Still sweeten more these banks of Rhine![3]

Byron's celebration of the Rhine at the Drachenfels, in addition to the specific anthropomorphic features and emotions attributed to the river, reflects many of the themes pervading the Rheinlieder of the 1840s: unrequited love, a sense of oneness with nature's beauty and enchantment, and a feeling of the river's perpetuity.

The texts of the German Romantic Rheinlieder likewise form a rich complex of these and additional motives, which parallel important developing notions in nineteenth-century natural science, historiography, psychology and psychiatry, nature philosophy, and art. The biological concept of nature as engaged in a perpetual process of change and development was echoed in the teleological argument proposed by historians and nature philosophers that the passage of time is generative and goal-directed. This notion also underlay the ever-present Rheinlieder theme of the river in a state of eternal flow.

The nineteenth-century biological principle of an organism's totality in its emotional, intellectual, and physical spheres was bolstered by a growing psychological belief in the total interaction between psychological and physical phenomena in humans. This coincided with the views of German Romantic historians and nature philosophers, moreover, who conceived of the totality of the nation as a "natural" association, an outlook also present in Rheinlieder themes. It followed then that the Rhine, a supreme manifestation of both nature and common familial roots, was the "natural" emblem of a unified state of Germanness.

Contemporary with the German Romantic study of the mind, of history, and of the essence of the universe, moreover, were the poetic formulations of human disillusionment: unfulfilled longing, alienation, and irrationality. These were translated into the perpetual shadows of angst and the desire to escape the world. The uncertainty of these feelings underlay the psychological concept, central to German Romanticism, of the hidden unconscious. And this notion was reflected in the Rheinlieder poems that dealt with the reality and unreality of magic, dreams, and other mysterious properties ascribed to the Rhine and its accumulated associations. In this poetry one finds the related philosophical and psychological notion of *Werden* (becoming), the unconscious striving toward the conscious. This gave the Rheinlieder an added dimension in which a multiplicity of emotions were transformed into visual humanoid figures such as Loreleys and Nibelungs, giving full witness to the animistic inclinations of German Romantic thought.

NATURAL SCIENCE AND THE ROMANTICS

The Romantic fascination with nature assumed explicit form in the prodigious development of natural science. This science was replacing the previously absolute authority of physics, mathematics, and astronomy (mechanical materialism) and of reason structured according to these disciplines.[4] Thus the ancient concept of nature as fixed and immutable yielded to the notion of perpetual change offered by a genuine science of biology liberated from past metaphysical and theological constraints.

Undertaking the systematic study of the phenomena of life, nineteenth-century biologists affirmed the perpetual evolution and the fundamental organic unity (in both structure and function) of the animal and plant worlds. These ideas now applied as well to the cosmos. Developments in organic chemistry confirmed the biological premise that the primary reality lay with the total individual, his emotions and intellectual processes of the mind as well as his physical being. From the 1820s successful syntheses of organic compounds and numerous physiological discoveries, such as those in cellular pathology, further corroborated the concept of universal organic structure by demonstrating the application of the conservation-of-energy principle to living organisms.[5] This "biological revolution," moreover, opened up the fields of psychology and psychiatry to probe the inherent unity of mind and body. Emotions now became a subject for scientific investigation.

Among the nineteenth-century notions supporting that of the organic unity of the universe were those of nature's evolutionary process, conjectured since ancient times and nurtured through centuries of cosmological, anatomical, geological, and philosophical speculation. The notion of evolution survived as a working hypothesis with Bacon, Descartes, Leibnitz, and Kant until science could substantiate it through data amassed from observation and experiment. In his *Histoire naturelle* of 1749, the celebrated French naturalist Georges Louis Leclerc, Comte de Buffon (1707–88) presented his concept of nature as a single entity, extending Newton's reduction of the inanimate world to a unifying system of law including biological phenomena. Buffon rejected the traditional concept of the immutability of species in favor of a belief in the perpetual development of vegetable and animal life in time. As the earth passed through succeeding epochs, he contended, many species were "perfected or degenerated . . . by the favours or disfavours of Nature." Maintaining the connection of the plant with the animal kingdom, Buffon approached Gottfried Wilhelm Leibnitz's (1646–1716) concepts of "monads," that every living object consisted of a mass of minute particles, each a pattern of the whole individual. The French scientist thus accounted for the origin of life without a special act of creation, introducing instead a view of humankind as integral with all nature.[6]

Methodological advances in plant hybridization and animal breeding further contributed to the rejection of the old notion of the immutability of species in favor of the view of nature as progressing to some higher purpose. Charles Bonnet, another important eighteenth-century French naturalist, envisioned a continuous gradation from minerals, plants, and animals up to humankind itself. He even anticipated Romantic nature allegory, postulating "that on some of the heavenly bodies the evolution might have advanced farther than anything which had been seen on the earth itself— the stones having an organic structure, the plants possessing feelings, the animals being able to talk and the men behaving like angels." Bonnet's concept influenced early nineteenth-century naturalists investigating the earth's geological past. Jean Baptiste de Monet, known as Lamarck (1744–1829), for example, cited fossil data as indicating that, through the earth's continuous history, all creatures had developed linearly in a single comprehensive evolutionary process.[7] Scientific investigation had therefore determined the cumulative series of environmental modifications as a primarily organic mechanism of evolution. From 1750 on, moreover, the systematic exploration of the globe advanced physical geography and meteorology, tracing the earth's history from newly acquired evidence and disproving biblical cosmogonies of the earth's past such as its cataclysmic origins by water or fire.[8]

Charles Darwin's (1809–82) Beagle voyages represent perhaps the culmination of this global exploration. By the 1830s his evolutionary theory, with its organic postulate, had been formulated except for the concept of the struggle for existence. Its theoretical support, the role of the environment in evolution, was soon furnished by the English economist Thomas Malthus (1766–1834) and other economist-writers of the Industrial Revolution.[9] The publication of Darwin's *The Origin of Species by Means of Natural Selection* in 1859 admitted into biology the laws of change and probability guiding the physical sciences. This gave wide acceptance to Darwin's theory of organic evolution through natural selection, buttressed by the earlier work of Joseph Hooker and T. H. Huxley. Darwin's ideas directly influenced the development of psychology and psychiatry, sociology, philosophy, political theory, economics, and other fields. Their inherent processes were newly conceived as organically unified stages of development determined by an environment ever in flux.

THE NEW HISTORICAL ATTITUDE

The nineteenth-century biologists' developing notion of all nature as a continuum and organic whole paralleled a similar outlook among historians. As Herbert Butterfield observes, the Romantics indeed attempted "to embrace the whole course of things in time and to relate the successive epochs to one another—the transition to the view that time is actually aiming at something, that temporal succession has meaning and that the passage of ages is generative. . . . The survey became wider than that of human history, and the mind gradually came to see geology, pre-history and history in due succession to one another."[10]

The historians' new notions of progress and man's inherent perfectibility, fortified by the rise of industrialization, supported the scientists' comprehensive notion of evolution. By the late seventeenth century, the old cataclysmic view that foresaw the necessity of a scientific revolution to change the course of history had begun to yield to the new historical attitude that change would resemble a growth occurring in nature. With his emerging new sense of power over material things, man began to consider Providence a force in his own hands rather than a capricious interference with nature's laws. Such historical enterprises as Fontenelle's examination of myths, Vico's investigation of primitive societies, and the study of the development of human reason furthered man's belief in his own innate gift of rationality and perfectibility.[11] As the study of science and history converged to advance the concept that all nature was proceeding slowly but inexorably to a higher goal, the entire universe was gradually conceived in terms of historical process.

The organic concept of nature and its process of becoming also coincided with developing ideas of German Romantic nationalism. In his *Ideen zur Philosophie der Geschichte*, written between 1784 and 1791, Johann Gottfried von Herder viewed history as the development of the various potentialities inherent in human nature. For the statesmen and pamphleteers of the French Revolution and the Germans resisting Napoleon, such as Joseph von Görres and Johann Gottlieb Fichte (1762–1814), *la loi naturelle* and *Naturtrieb* philosophically justified the existence, even the primary significance, of patriotism. Görres maintained that it was "purely instinctual that a people thus contained precisely and clearly within its natural boundaries would seek to collect itself from a state of dispersion to one of unity."[12] The German historian Heinrich von Treitschke (1834–96) considered the "political capacity innate in man" and the consequent "inherently necessary" unity of a people, referring particularly to Prussia, as inborn in nature.[13] This "natural" process justified the exercise of state power to forge the nation-state and its national character.[14] The German philosopher Friedrich Wilhelm von Schelling (1775–1854) viewed humanity, like nature, as a single unified organism, a concept he acknowledged had originated with Herder.

GERMAN ROMANTIC *WERDEN:* PSYCHOLOGY AND THE PURSUIT OF CONSCIOUSNESS

The view of nineteenth-century biologists and historians that life had evolved in an organic continuum had further parallels in the developing contemporary sciences dealing with the human mind. Enlightenment philosophers had attempted to forge a new society on the rational and mechanistic axioms used to further human knowledge of the physical universe. By the nineteenth century, however, rationalist optimism had yielded to disillusionment. Similarly, the rediscovery of human irrationality had overthrown the reign of reason in favor of emotion and faith, as exemplified by the *Weltschmerz* of Goethe's Werther and the psychopathological plays of Heinrich von Kleist.

The resistance launched against the rationalists' detached objectivity had been anticipated, like many other Romantic attitudes, by Jean Jacques Rousseau (1712–78) in his *Lettres morales*, in which he had affirmed, "Exister, pour nous, c'est sentir; et notre sensibilité est incontestablement antérieure à notre raison."[15]

As interest in the study of the mind assumed an increased significance in the nineteenth century, the investigation of the psyche joined with the new biology and the new history in affirming the unity of life, that of mind and body.[16] Although the French psychiatrist Étienne Dominique Esquirol (1772–1840) and his disciples did not yet fully comprehend the concept of emotions and ideas as part of a dynamic process (the principle of psychological causality inherent in motivational psychology), they established the basis of clinical psychiatry through their methodical approach to the classification and description of mental symptoms.[17] An Esquirol follower, J. Moreau de Tours (1804–84), however, concluded that mental symptoms indicated disturbances of the whole personality. Along with his German contemporaries, he sought to study the irrational, emotional, and unknown forces of the mind. In true Romantic fashion he viewed the diseased person as a whole, including the hidden psychological design behind the illness. In this, Moreau anticipated psychoanalytic thinking and closely approached the concept of the unconscious. As he observed: "It appears then that two modes of existence—two kinds of life—are given to man. The first one results from our communication with the external world, with the universe. The second one is but the reflection of the self and is fed from its own distinct internal sources. The dream is a kind of in-between land where the external life ends and the internal life begins."[18]

Moreau's concept of psychosis as a manifestation of the total personality, rather than as an isolated, "partial" aberration, typified the dynamic, integrative tendency also prevalent among some German psychiatrists. The psychiatrist Johann Christian Heinroth (1773–1843), for example, first used the term *psychosomatic*, viewing the external body and internal psyche as inseparable within the self. Schooled in strict Lutheranism, he ascribed mental disturbance to sin, thereby expressing in religious-moralistic language the central concepts of modern psychiatry, that of inner conflict and "conscience" (*Gewissen*), or the sense of guilt. Psychiatrists contemporary with Heinroth similarly argued that personality functions were based in humans' instinctual and volitional forces. In this way they maintained the thoroughly biological outlook that the psychological life manifested in an organism should be viewed as a psychobiological entity.

It can be seen, therefore, that mid-nineteenth-century psychiatrists contributed to German Romantic thought a dynamic orientation, that is, an integrative view of the whole person and a recognition of the biological basis of psychological forces. The Germans' emerging scientific approach

to the mind would soon begin to replace the mystical belief in a preestab-
lished vital force governing living organisms. In their new concern for the
nature of the psyche, the Romantics had positioned psychiatry at the
threshold of modern concepts and methodologies.

GERMAN ROMANTIC NATURE PHILOSOPHY

The overriding themes pervading the poetry of the Rheinlieder, as of German Romantic poetry in general, also mirrored those basic not only to
German Romantic psychological and psychiatric thought but also to contemporary nature philosophy. Central to these themes was the notion of
self-consciousness, meaning consciousness of self. Peter Rudnytsky calls the
period from Friedrich von Schiller (1759–1805) to Sigmund Freud (1856–
1939) an "age of Oedipus," when the German Romantics "took [Sophocles']
Oedipus the King as a paradigm for their own obsession with self-consciousness."[19] Schiller, Rudnytsky believes, categorized both Goethe and the ancient Greeks as "naïve" and himself as the "sentimental" or reflective
modern poet. Schiller viewed the latter as an alienated individual who saw
"in irrational nature only a happier sister who remained in our mother's
house, out of which we fled abroad in the arrogance of our freedom."
This statement, Rudnytsky believes, "with its imagery of the male poet
ambivalently seeking to sever his attachment to his 'happier sister' nature
and escape his 'mother's house,' fuses oedipal motifs with the typical Romantic concern with the burdens of self-consciousness. . . . Schiller adum-
brates psychoanalysis in recognizing that our love for nature is closely
related to the feeling with which we mourn the lost age of childhood."[20]

Similarly, Hegel likened Adam's fall to the odyssey of Oedipus, positing
that "the step into opposition, the awakening of consciousness, follows
from the very nature of man." Closely associated with Hegel, the lyric poet
Friedrich Hölderlin saw in Oedipus "the despairing struggle to come to
himself, the roughshod, almost shameless striving to become master of his
own, the foolish-wild searching after a consciousness."[21]

In *The Phenomenology of Mind* of 1807, Hegel recognized a sphere within
the mind not directly available to consciousness, contending that "what is
'familiarly known' (*das Bekannte*) is not properly known (*erkannt*), just for the
reason that it is 'familiar.' "[22] The distinction between these two forms of
knowledge became a cornerstone of German Romantic philosophy. The

goal of the oedipal odysseys of consciousness, later the essence of psycho-analysis, demanded a process of reaching toward the "properly known," that is, transforming the unconscious (Hegel's *das Unbewusste*) into the conscious (*erkannt*).

The parallels between German Romantic philosophy and psychology-psychiatry, on the one hand, and the literature of this era, on the other, offer a rich spectrum of common motives. In varying ways aspects of artistic creativity were linked with the oedipal odyssey. Schelling, like Novalis (Friedrich von Hardenberg [1772–1801]), equated nature and humanity as a single mighty, unified organism. Schelling's view of nature as a gradual process of assumption of consciousness interjected a human element into nature. Schelling saw aesthetic creativity as an interaction between the conscious and unconscious mind beyond the scope of rational analysis. The study of dreams and other irrational phenomena, moreover, coincided with, rather than reflected, the study of artistic creation, "which attempted to break through the barrier of the five senses and explore the relationship between the worlds of the psyche and the soma, visionary perception and physical reality."[23]

In his lectures on the philosophy of art, given between 1802 and 1805, Schelling offered a view of music as that art "which to the greatest degree divests itself of corporeality and is borne upon invisible, almost spiritual wings." This concept evolved into the notion that true, ideal music is supra-sensuous rather than sensuous.[24] Fichte's notion of the intellectual perception of the self's consciousness heightened the position of the conscious, self-directing creative artist. The physician-philosopher Gotthilf Heinrich von Schubert's *Ahnungen einer allgemeinen Geschichte des Lebens* (Ideas on a general history of life) of 1821 and his *Geschichte der Seele* (History of the soul) of 1830 dealt with the subconscious basis of psychological phenomena. Walzel calls this "the unintelligible concatenation of conscious and subconscious activity which seemed to consign the human soul to a place on the unstable fringe of the world of Nature and of reason."[25] Much influenced by Schelling, Schubert's study of psychological problems, *Ansichten von der Nachtseite der Naturwissenschaft* (*Views on the Night Side of Natural Science*), ca. 1806, probed the seemingly irrational phenomena discovered, but not fully understood, by eighteenth-century scientific investigators.

The perpetual state of motion inherent in the concept of the oedipal odyssey, moreover, reflected the kinetic Romantic concepts of *Wanderlust* (the joy of wayfaring), *Werden* (becoming), and *Sehnsucht* (longing). As

August Wilhelm von Schlegel observed in his Romantically melancholic view of Christianity: "Such a religion must waken the vague foreboding, which slumbers in every feeling heart, into a distinct consciousness that the happiness for which we are here striving is unattainable; that no external object can ever entirely fill our souls; and that all earthly enjoyment is but a fleeting and momentary illusion."[26]

In fact, as so evident in German Romantic literature, the chief representative figure of the *Sehnsucht* quest is the hero-wanderer, the archetypal symbol of the human potential for becoming and the personification of his yearning. The wanderer always prevails within an anthropocentric universe.

Thus by means of a vocabulary (verbs, verbal nouns, and adverbs) and syntax (parallel and paratactic constructions) connoting motion, by the use of kinetic images of light, color, sound, and space, finally by the inclusion of natural motion imagery (wind, cloud, water, and bird images) and that of human design (mill wheels and fountains), the Romanticists created a world in flux harmoniously reflecting and encouraging the wanderer's peripatetic existence.[27]

The multitude of German Romantic lieder suffused with barcarole and other "wave" musical motives, as with figures depicting wanderers and the aura of mills and fountains (as in Schubert's *Die schöne Müllerin*) expressed the kinetic themes of *Wandern, Werden,* and *Sehnsucht.* These applied with great force to the Rheinlieder of the 1840s, as they did to Wagner's Rhine-pervaded *Ring.*

GERMAN ROMANTIC
LANDSCAPE ART

Likewise, German Romantic landscapists relied heavily on kinetic images to forge organically unified works of art. Schiller, with Hegel and Fichte, asserted that the self-directing artist could express himself only through a forward-moving process of striving for unity with nature, as opposed to the retrospective repose of the Classical landscape idyll. The painter and nature philosopher Carl Gustav Carus (1789–1869) perceived landscape art as the symbolic depiction of the recondite force, ever pressing forward, that binds external nature to human feelings in an organic unity. The philosopher and poet Johann Gottfried von Herder affirmed that everything in nature has a beauty of its own that is the resulting expression of its own greatest content. The pioneer geographer Alexander von Humboldt directed the Romantics' attention increasingly to the myriad impressions engendered by natural phenomena always in flux.

For the philosophers Friedrich von Schlegel and Arthur Schopenhauer (1788–1860), the organic concept implied the artistic expression developed from humanity's pantheistic, subjective identification with nature. Human feelings were similarly ascribed to nature. The Rhine likewise aroused human feelings toward nature's beauty. Nature's sublimity was expressible ultimately only through poetic allegory, as exemplified animistically in the Loreley and Nibelung figures of the Rheinlieder.

Humankind's emotional preoccupation with nature's beauty was transposed perhaps most palpably into Romantic landscapes, many with Rhine subjects. Not until seventeenth- and eighteenth-century Classicism had landscape art evolved into a distinctly independent genre. Some seventeenth-century landscape artists anticipated the Romantic contributions to their genre. The paintings of Rembrandt van Rijn (1606–69) conveyed a penetrating sense of mystery and unrest, those of Jacob van Ruisdael (1628–82) a melancholy consciousness of humanity's solitude and insignificance in confrontation with nature. Among the French contemporaries of these Lowlanders, Nicolas Poussin (1593–1665) and Claude Lorrain (1600–1682) developed a landscape art with nature envisioned "as the fount of ideal beauty and of poetry reflecting the emotions and actions of men."[28] The landscapes of eighteenth-century Classicism ranged from the colorist representations of Antoine Watteau (1684–1721) to the light-sensitive, transparent views of Canaletto (Giovanni Antonio Canal the Younger [1697–1768]) and the deeply dramatic fantasies of Thomas Gainsborough (1727–88).

While Classical painters idealized the natural beauty of the outside world, Romantic artists went so far as to abandon the studio to record the phenomena of nature immediately through the innumerable, ever-changing effects of movement, color, shadow, and light. The Classical artists expressed the boundlessness of landscape through an abundance of particulars arranged in a tranquil, orderly panorama of objective nature representation. Romantic landscapists, however, simplified the given expanse, conveying the subjective merging of humankind with nature's infinity in a commonality of feeling equaling that expressed in the lyric poems of Goethe, Eichendorff, and Heine.

The German Romantic landscapist Caspar David Friedrich (1774–1840) affirmed that "Des Künstlers Gefühl ist sein Gesetz" (the artist's feeling is his law).[29] Thus he sought to express both human feelings aroused by nature, such as melancholy, and those transposed to nature itself. He conveyed these feelings through a subjective iconography derived from conventional religion but metamorphosed into supernatural symbols from the natural world, such as ominously intermingling stormy seas and cloudy skies. With the Romantics' new consciousness of the value of human irrationality and emotions, music, art, and literature came to be regarded not simply as echoes of reality or the realizations of a fixed, rationally constructed ideal. Instead they provided both an introduction into the inner life of things and comfort against the instability and vast oppression of an enigmatic, even unfathomable, universe.

The Aristotelian concept of art as mimesis had finally yielded to the concept of art as a means of expression. In his observations on a new Romantic aesthetic replacing the Aristotelian principle of *imitatio naturae*, Croce cites the Abbé Batteux's *The Fine Arts Reduced to a Single Principle* (1746). The task of art, Batteux insisted, was to "select the most beautiful parts of Nature in order to frame them into an exquisite whole which shall be more beautiful than Nature's self, without ceasing to be natural."[30] Friedrich, for example, subjectively suffused his play on the traditional emblematic associations of plants and trees with melancholy and anxiety. All nature became "the hieroglyphic language of God." He created a feeling of intimate communion with nature's most intangible phenomena—light, color, and atmosphere. He thereby reduced the landscape to the manifestation of a hidden divinity.[31]

Despite their obvious differences, the works of Friedrich and his radical German contemporary Philipp Otto Runge (1777–1810) exemplified Friedrich Schlegel's contention that "because they are inexpressible, the highest things can only be said allegorically." For Runge, then, the art of *Landschafterei* (landscape painting) could express cosmic feelings.[32] His animistic images, like Friedrich's, signified the transsensual exploration of feelings.

RHEINLIEDER POEMS: *SEHNSUCHT, WANDERLUST, WERDEN, WELTSCHMERZ*

The themes of *Sehnsucht, Wanderlust, Werden,* and *Weltschmerz* pervaded and joined the German Romantic fields of natural science, history, psychology, nature philosophy, and landscape art, among others. They were equally powerful motives coursing through the poetry of the Rheinlieder. As we examine the primary notions at the heart of these poems, we can identify basic assumptions common to all these fields. The songs of *Sehnsucht, Wanderlust, Werden,* and *Weltschmerz* conveyed emotional confrontations with life as an existence of painful perpetual change (*Werden*) proceeding to an as-yet-unfathomable end. They also conveyed the overwhelming force of human irrationality and emotions, unconscious yearnings, and striving for consciousness of self. All these were subsumed as essential factors in the unity of life, of humankind both in itself and in its relation to nature, as symbolized by the Rhine. Emotions and consciousness of self also underlay works of art that translated nature's beauty and humanity's sense of that beauty into allegorical terms such as the Rhine's Loreley and Nibelung.

Sehnsucht   One of the most predominant human feelings present in the Rheinlieder texts is that of *Sehnsucht,* the longing for an unrequited love, a golden German past, or the beauties of a particular Rhineland area. This longing was permeated with aching *Weltschmerz* and a deep sense of loss. Two melancholic Rheinlieder poems evoke the historical ambience of the *Königsstuhl,* a mammoth pulpitlike throne surveying the Rhine landscape above the unassuming village of Rhens, south of Coblenz. This towering octagonal structure of gray stone was erected by the fourteenth-century Emperor Karl IV. At this site the three elector archbishops of Cologne, Trier, and Mainz traditionally convened in the open air to elect emperors, publish decrees, and sign treaties.

In the Rhine crisis year of 1840 the Coblenz citizenry established a project to reconstruct the throne, destroyed by French forces in the devastations of 1794. According to the *Allgemeine musikalische Zeitung* of 3 March 1841, considerable revenue for the restoration efforts had been obtained the previous January through a public music festival of local Rhine music societies held at Mühlheim on the river.[33]

Two Rheinlieder poems of the 1840s betray a longing to restore the Königsstuhl's glorious past: Aloys Schreiber's (ca. 1761–1841) "Der Königsstuhl bei Rhense" and E. G. Drimborn's (fl. 1820–50) "Kaiser Wenzel." Schreiber's verses, written in 1810, resound with patriotic fervor. No trace of this sacred throne has survived, he bemoans, for "the free German land" has succumbed to the ravages wrought by "children's mischief."[34] Schreiber continues: "On the Rhine, on the Rhine, there bloom our vines no more, the castles of our princes stand there desolate and empty."[35] He concludes, "Let the Rhine be the river of Germany. Germany's scepter shall come into the hand of no stranger!"

Drimborn's poem, concerning the Emperor Wenzel (or Wenzeslaus), parodies the true historical reason for this monarch's loss of the imperial crown at the Königsstuhl. Before an assembly of German princes gathered around the venerated throne, Wenzel proclaims his preference for wine over the splendor and anxieties of royal responsibilities. Consequently he accepts Kurfürst (Elector) Ruprecht von der Pfalz's proposal to exchange his authority for the lesser prince's red Assmannshausen wine. As the concluding moral of this tale, Wenzel declares that "wine is worth more than crowns."

A number of Rheinlieder express yearning for the Rhineland's beauties, such as those of the Odenwald, a wooded mountain district between Darmstadt, Heidelberg, and the Main River. "Der Baum im Odenwald" (The tree in the Odenwald), from *Des Knaben Wunderhorn*, contrasts the reality of the despondent lover caught in a snowy Switzerland with his longing for the forest and birds of his Odenwald homeland. Two other examples from *Wunderhorn*, "Der unerbittliche Hauptmann" (The pitiless captain) and "Zu Strassburg auf der Schanz" (At the Strassburg bulwark) voice homesickness for a Rhine birthplace. The first is directed toward Rhenish Switzerland, the second toward the sad beauty of Strassburg, where a multitude of slain soldiers lie buried. The two poems include detailed descriptions, even of such prosaic elements as the Rhine's fish, which evoke painful *Weltschmerz*.

Another Rheinlied poem pervaded by a longing for the Rhine landscape is Max von Oër's (1806–46) "Die Glocken zu Speier" (The bells at Speyer). These verses were historically based on the fate of the Holy Roman Emperor Heinrich IV (d. 1106), the excommunicated monarch who made a celebrated pilgrimage of penance to Pope Gregory VII at Canossa (see figure 3.1). They also concern the emperor's son Heinrich V (d. 1126), who terminated the divisive Investiture Dispute by decreeing the Worms Concordat. Von Oër's poem relates the traditional account of Speyer's enigmatic *Kaiserglocke* (imperial bell): in response to the death of the saintly, but destitute, Heinrich IV, the bell miraculously broke a long silence, summoning all the city bells to sound together with its own peals. At the demise of Heinrich V, however, the great bells failed to toll, for, unlike that of his pious father, the son's worth consisted only in his amassed golden treasure.

In "Mutterseelen allein" (All alone), the poet Karl Christian Tenner (1791–1866) etches a nature scene of tranquil repose: a nightingale gently circling in the silent moonlight over a quiescent Rhine. This setting reinforces the young fisherman's sense of isolation. Peter Cornelius (1824–74), the poet-composer of "Botschaft" (Message), identifies the Rhine shore as

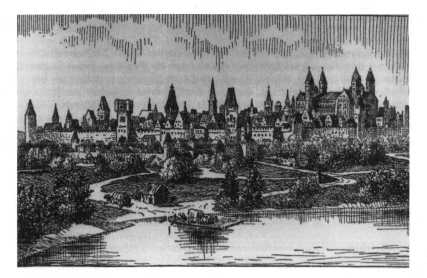

Fig. 3.1. Speyer, after a painting by Franz Ulm. From Georg Hölscher, Das Buch vom Rhein (Cologne: Hoursch & Bechstedt, 1927), p. 191.

"the most beautiful place" but also as the site where he directs his song of longing for a love unfulfilled. The anonymous poet of "Sehnsucht nach dem Rhein" wistfully yearns for a host of Rhine-associated visions: moss-enshrouded castle ruins, cloisters concealed in the mist, vintners' songs, and echoes resounding from cliffs, vaguely alluding to the Loreley. The poet also dreams of "the lovely lays of gray antiquity, joining fantasy and reality to fairy-tale magic," part of the rich legacy of sagas and songs bringing memories of knightly Rhineland heroes.

Weltschmerz All of Heinrich Heine's five Rheinlieder poems published with musical settings in the 1840s (discussed in detail in chapter 4) virtually exude *Weltschmerz* of the most potent kind. The common denominator underlying all the texts is this native Rhinelander's piercing emotional ambiguity regarding his German identity. His poem "Anno 1839," dating from the year prior to the Rhine crisis, discloses his conflicting feelings of affection and alienation toward his German homeland. As the opening lines indicate, Heine could never resist sarcasm:

> O, Germany, my distant love,
> Whenever I remember thee,
> I weep—almost![36]

As an exile in Paris, Heine expressed both sides of his love-hate attraction to the Germans: his longing for them, but also his ridicule of their provincial tendencies such as pride in their complying womenfolk. Yet in the final verse he confessed his yearning for the German oak grove, a recurring symbol in German Romantic poetry.

At various times, however, Heine admitted feelings of genuine national loyalty, as he wrote in March 1824: "I know that I am one of the most German animals that exists; I know only too well that German is to me what water is to the fish. . . . At heart I love that which is German more than anything else in the world; therein I have my delight and joy, and my breast is an archive of German feeling."[37]

The Rhine crisis of 1840 brought Heine a sense of conflicting patriotic allegiances. In 1841 as the preface to *Germany: A Winter's Tale*, he wrote:

> I love the fatherland as well as you. Because of this love I have spent thirteen years of my life in exile, and because of this love I return to exile, perhaps forever. I am the friend of all men if they are reasonable and good men, and because I myself am not so stupid or so evil as to wish that my own Germans and the French, both the chosen peoples of humanity, should break each others' necks to the advantage of England and Russia . . . I will never yield the Rhine to the French for the very simple reason that the Rhine belongs to me. Yes, it belongs to me by my inalienable birthright. I am the far freer son of the free Rhine [a reference to Becker's Rhine poem]; my cradle stood upon its banks, and I see no reason why the Rhine should belong to anyone other than the children of its own country.[38]

At times Rheinlieder poets exalt the Rhine's splendors somewhat naïvely rather than in tones of *Weltschmerz*. An anonymous "Rheinlied" fraternally summons fellow Germans to delight merely in the river's waves of green and silver, its "mirror brightness, wreathed round by cliff and forest," and its spirit that lifts one "gently on the wings of inspiration." The Rhine imagery even extends to animistic dimensions:

> See there how [the Rhine] so paternally embraces mountains of full vines!
> See how his strong arm, full of power and life, rings with the wild cliffs!
> Grown old, they stand there, the proud ruins on unmeasured heights!
> [The Rhine] rises, he sinks, he streams, he rests never, he remains
> eternally young and beautiful.

(The sources of this poem and succeeding poems discussed in this chapter can be found in the Index of Rheinlieder under the poet's name [or, in the case of an "anonymous" listing, under the title of the poem]. Abbreviated source titles are given in complete form on pp. 225–28 of this Index.)

Similarly, Countess Ida Hahn-Hahn's (1805–80) "Am Rheinfall" (At the Rhine waterfall) simply and briefly counterposes the image of a precipitous, raging waterfall and the fear it engenders with the immediate assurance of "protection from danger" through the loved one's presence.

Fantasy and Escape   Although a large number of Rheinlieder poems touch on fantasy in one way or another, two examples illustrate this theme with singular force. Arthur Lütze's "Der Drachenfels" (The Dragon's Rock) recounts a grisly drama enacted high above the Rhine near Bonn, where a jutting outcrop commands a splendid panorama downstream toward the Cologne Cathedral (see figure 3.2). A variation on Siegfried's slaying of the dragon, the ballad chronicles an encounter between a golden haired virgin and a fang-gnashing, hissing creature. When she is offered as a sacrifice to the monster, she resourcefully flashes her crucifix, dispatching him abruptly downward into "the gaping grave" of the Rhine.[39] Another poem, the anonymously authored "Romanze vom Wolfsbrunnen," refers to the Hei-

Fig. 3.2. The Drachenfels, after an engraving by Matthäus Merian, 1640. From Hölscher, Das Buch vom Rhein, p. 337.

delberg reservoir at Wolfsbrunnen, where, according to legend, a mysterious enchantress fell victim to a wolf, hence the name.

Two-thirds of the way north from Heidelberg to Darmstadt lie the ruins of Rodenstein castle. According to a variation on an ancient Germanic folk legend, a wild huntsman and his entourage dashed away from the fortress at the prospect of imminent battle. "With fearful din," they took refuge in the nearby castle of Schnellerts.[40] Joseph Victor von Scheffel's (1826–86) six poems (subsequently set to music) on the ghostly figure of Rodenstein recount the unlikely adventures of this wine-loving knightly rogue. In "Rodensteins Auszug" (Rodenstein's departure) the hero, driven from his Odenwald grave by a threatening Rhine wind, reenacts his age-old ride in honor of the lamentably defunct Holy Roman Empire. Entreating a smithy to polish his sword, he then searches for a successor to assume command of his nocturnal tours of duty.

Escape from the sufferings of life through intoxication is another central theme in the Rheinlieder poems of the 1840s. Absurd exploits in intoxication provide the basic narratives in the remaining Rodenstein poems, for example. In one poem, the nocturnal huntsmen raid the vicar's wine cellar, leaving him resigned that Satan (one of Rodenstein's guises) has absconded with his entire wine supply. Ironically, the cleric chooses to ride off with the devilish old knight's "infernal choir" itself. Yearning to impede Rodenstein's course of action, the innkeeper of another poem orders the intruder disrobed as the latter readies his hunting-horn goblet to enjoy the contents of the wine cellar. The undaunted knight nevertheless continues to imbibe, with a whimsical retort that drinking in underclothes merely renders the act a more comfortable experience.

A further Rodenstein example divulges why this ghostly figure must "hunt" for wine into eternity. According to the tolling of an ancient bell, the earth would never receive his grave until he had satisfied his thirst—a purposely impossible stipulation. In a variation on this quest, the master of Frankenstein castle hospitably welcomes the huntsman with wine proffered in Charlemagne's sacred drinking horn. On another occasion, Rodenstein, entering a Darmstadt inn, mocks his chief trumpeter for quaffing beer instead of wine.

Scheffel's poem "Perkêo" parodies the tale of a historical jester in the court of the early eighteenth-century Palatine Elector Carl Philipp. The jester is depicted as the shrewd, wine-thirsting dwarf of Heidelberg castle. In biblical metaphors, Scheffel identifies Perkêo, who "conquered a giant thirst" after fifteen years of draining the mighty Heidelberg vat, with "little David, who once succeeded against Goliath." "The truth lies in wine," so the poem goes. The dwarf, buried in a cellar grave adjoining the now depleted vat, is then transformed into yet another ghostly image who nightly and perpetually ravages the city's wine supplies.

An anonymous poet's "Der rheinische Wein" maintains anatomical exactitude in extolling the salutary effects of Rhine wine on the body, mind, and mood. He even personifies one vintage as a caressable beloved. A further unattributed example, "Vor dem Königsschusse" (Before the best shot), portrays German marksmen on the Lower Rhine drinking to obliterate melancholia and indulge only in joyful fellowship. Similarly, August Mahlmann's (1771–1826) "Weinlied" goes to exuberantly detailed lengths to credit wine from "the great vat at Heidelberg" as the instigator of convivial, song-filled merrymaking. According to this panegyric, the miraculous beverage of Bacchus sustains downtrodden souls when "the times are bad"; one should, in fact, emulate the Heidelberg senators in enlisting burgundy or champagne to heal "the sick times," for Rhine wine soothes tempers and erases class distinctions in "the new Reich."

Gottfried August Bürger's (1747–94) poem "Bacchus" offers encomia to Rhine wine through classical Greco-Roman allusions. Humorously the poet declares Bacchus's wine "happier music" than that made by Apollo's lyre, emphasizing: "Before all else, we will bring the great Heidelberg vat full of Niersteiner [wine] to Parnassus. . . . Instead of laurel trees, we will plant vine stocks there and dance easily, like the Bacchantes around full casks. Until now people have lived there according to the old custom, all too soberly; on that account the nine virgins, too, forever remained too shy." The poet advises, in addition, that the value of Bacchus's nectar also lay in its aphrodisiac potential.

In "Doppeltes Vaterland" (Double fatherland), the poet C. Wilhelm Müller (1794–1827) admits two conflicting allegiances: while the banks of the Elbe mark his birthplace, his "throat is at home on the Rhine, for it thirsts only after wine."[41] Song-accompanied wine drinking not only fortifies a sense of brotherhood but also banishes all misery; "what pleases the spirit does the body no harm" for, in fact, the genuinely health-conscious should elect to "die on wine rather than on pills."

According to Müller's second poem, "Die Arche Noah" (Noah's ark), "wine and joyous songs" restore to us "what Adam once lost through his wicked bite." In a nineteenth-century allegory of the biblical event, the poet exalts Noah, "the planter of noble vines," for resisting the temptations of debauchery and sin and for surviving the flood by removing his family to the great Heidelberg vat. Transubstantiated into the ark, the vat remained on the Heidelberg mountain as a memorial to "holy wine," leaving its cultivation to be restored by Noah's new vines planted after the deluge had subsided.

Rather than dwelling on Rhine wine as a means of avoiding life, some of the "songs of intoxication" praise the pleasure created by its transcendent attributes, which are considered distinctly German: the astonishing potency of Rhine wine or the experiences associated with it such as love, song, and camaraderie. Interestingly, the poets preserve the vintners' categories of wine according to the specific Rhineland regions of each type. "Zur gold-nen Bremm" (At golden Bremm) acclaims a medieval town on the middle Mosel, a tributary of the Rhine. Here, legend has it, the first grapevines of the Rhineland were planted. "Saarbrücken" pays poetic homage to this venerated town on the Saar. (Both these poems are anonymous.) Scheffel's "Lied für die Krone: Der Pfarr' von Assmannshausen Sprach" (Song for the crown: The priest of Assmannshausen spoke) focuses on the modest Rhine town of Assmannshausen, renowned for its unusual red wine.

The anonymous poet of "Rüdesheim" idealizes this picturesque hamlet on the Rhine's right bank, a site fabled for its "Rüdesheimer Riesling." The poet intersperses his narrative with ample exaggeration. Spurned by a vintner's handsome daughter, a richly endowed count of Rüdesheim de-votes the remainder of his life to self-consolation in "noble" wine, the subject of the folksong-like refrain. The count eventually even forfeits his castle and submits to servitude, all for the sake of wine.

The anonymous poet of the Rheinlied poem "Coblenz" honors the old Roman city overlooking the confluence of the Mosel and the Rhine. An unattributed seventeenth-century Rheinlied republished in the 1840s, "Zu Miltenberg am Maine," lauds this ancient eastern Odenwald town for its excellent wine, which engenders song and comradeship.

A pair of Scheffel poems pay tribute to historic Heidelberg, the centu-ries-long Palatinate capital and university town bordering on the Odenwald at the intersection of the Neckar and the Rhine. Likening the city to his bride, the poet of "Alt Heidelberg" blissfully exults in thoughts of love, wine, and beautiful spring flowers associated with this site.

VALHALLA: IDEALIZING THE
GERMAN PAST

Unlike the Rheinlieder texts that center on various shades of German Romantic feelings, cherished traditions, and hallowed landmarks, those of another substantial group reflect a different sense of cultural identity. This
body of Rheinlieder deals more directly with a patriotism based on political
and, at times, military themes associated with the Rhine. These poems
comprise both the newly composed revolutionary lyrics of that decade and
a resurgence of the patriotic poetry written in response to the travails
wrought by the Wars of Liberation. Adhering to the *volkstümlich* ideal of
immediate singability, the Wars of Liberation poets patterned their lyrics,
typically to be sung in unison, chiefly to the melodies of existing soldier,
folk, or student songs, and even to ancient chorales. As Oskar Walzel
observed, "the poets of the Liberation created no new lyric form; purposely
and effectively they poured new wine into old skins."[42] Thus they contributed another chapter to the literature of contrafacta.

Between the revolutions of 1830 and 1848, the movement known as *Das
junge Deutschland* (Young Germany) injected a strain of zealous, if not fanatic,
political commitment into the literary world. Originating in direct response
to the July Revolution, Rheinlieder poets sought to rally German nationalistic spirit. Numbering among its main supporters were the writers Heinrich Heine, Karl Gutzkow, Ludwig Börne (1786–1837), Heinrich Laube
(1806–84), Ludolf Wienbarg (1802–72), and Theodor Mundt (1801–61).
Their liberal-democratic goals encompassed the emancipation of the individual, women, and Jews. They also advocated freedom of the press.

The Rhine crisis decade of 1840, however, altered the aims and methods
of political literature, transforming the rather vague idealism of the Young
Germans into the more substantial revolutionary aspirations that emerged
from the spirit of the *Vormärz*. In the aftermath of the sensation caused by
Becker's Rheinlied, Herwegh led the revolutionary lyricists in the production of political poetry that had reached a peak by the end of 1841. This
reinvigorated political zeal failed, however, to inspire lyrics of the highest
literary worth or originality.

A number of Rheinlieder passively reflect the longing to preserve and
cherish what is German rather than pledge actively to retrieve what may
not be. These more contemplative Rhine songs demonstrate that many

Germans responding to the French Rhine threat of 1840 guarded and idealized this river more by reason of territorial definition, in the sense of the Rhine as a buffer, than as a frontier gateway to westward expansion.

The anonymous "Hebt an den Chor" (Raise up the chorus) quite innocuously exalts the Rhine, for example, as the means of protecting the German fatherland against foreign intrusion. The list of those innate virtues making up a common German legacy to be merely protected includes the by now expected conglomeration of references to holy Rhine wine, the German language, blood relationships, songs, oaks, rivers, love, and eagles. The authors of these poems identify two attributes of Germanness. First, one needs German wives to steadfastly tend the home and assure continual occupancy of the cradle. Second, one must maintain the inborn German temperament, particularly loyalty and the ability to indulge in merrymaking at the appropriate times.

By way of contrast and a smidgen of irony, two remaining Rhine poems deserve consideration in this discussion of culturally inclined political nationalism in German Romantic song. In refreshing opposition to the nearly universal claim that the Rhine alone signifies the essence of the German, Arndt's oft-quoted "Was ist des deutschen Vaterland?" (What is the German fatherland?), from 1813, actually questions whether the Rhine, "where the vine glows" (another reference to Claudius's "Rheinweinlied"), or even Prussia or Swabia, merits elevation as the supreme symbol of the quintessentially German. The notion of this fatherland, to the contrary, implies a totality greater than any of its individual regions. It extends "as far as the German tongue resounds and God in heaven sings songs!" The most renowned patriotic song for two generations until replaced in popular esteem by the equally anti-French "Die Wacht am Rhein," Arndt's verses limited the concept of the German nation simply to the advocacy of steadfast German friendship and enmity toward the French.

The texts of some of the Rheinlieder of the 1840s simply express a patriotism inspired by the image of the Rhine. In general they voice a common allegiance to the fatherland and at times even advocate an immediate call to war.

A few poems vaunt the power of Prussian leadership as it tightened its grasp on the Rhineland, acquired in 1815. Ludwig Uhland's (1787–1862) "Vorwärts" (Forward) exhorts all German-speaking peoples of the year 1813 to accept Prussian guidance in ridding the Rhineland of the French.

Two further examples, referring to 1840, confirm the critical value of the Prussian presence on the Rhine. The anonymous "Rheinpreussens Loblied zum 15. Oktober" (Rhenish-Prussian song of praise for 15 October) commemorates Friedrich Wilhelm IV's coronation in 1840, an event already shown to have coincided conveniently with the Rhine crisis at its acme. The poem presents the Rhenish Prussians as the most fortunate folk on the earth, for a tolerant, worthy monarch "honors a foreign law in his own land—our law." In the mind of this poet, in fact, the Rhenish Prussians could not justify complaints against Prussian rule since, under a Berlin administration, they were now enjoying religious freedom, the many economic advantages of a flourishing river commerce, and the means with which to produce and enjoy fine wine. "Praise the king and honor the Rhine!" the unknown author declares, adding "long live the good Prussian on the Rhine!" Also from 1840, Hermann von Boyen's (1771–1848) "Preussens Losung" (Prussia's watchword) similarly boasts of the Prussian virtues that "joined the Memel with the Rhine" and the Prussian sword that protects "throne and hearth." The poet—himself a Prussian field marshal, army reformer, and associate of Scharnhorst—concludes that the Rhinelanders owe their enjoyment of equitable and reasonable laws, as well as religious and social equality, to Prussian rule.

SONGS OF THE FATHERLAND: CULTURAL PATRIOTISM

A chief recurring subtheme in this poetry is praise for the power of Rhine wine to forge fraternal allegiance to an envisioned united and liberated German fatherland. Another is its capability to reinforce patriotism through inspiring intimations of a golden national past resplendent with countless castles and knights.

In Johann Martin Miller's (1750–1814) "Auf, ihr meine deutschen Brüder" (Up, my German brothers), only those who love "the Rhine's gift" deserve membership in the German fatherland. Admittance into the latter assures Germans the attainment of "all the beautiful things" that they have always cherished: steadfast friendships, family bonds, virtue, the preservation of revered customs, and the mother tongue "so reviled" by the French. In "Unser Berather" (Our adviser), the poet Göttling (fl. 1820) pronounces the Germans' "drink of freedom" as the means of preserving their liberty, which will continue to flourish "as long as vines still bloom on the Rhine."

Three poems entitled "Rheinweinlied" enjoyed exceptional popularity: Johann Heinrich Voss's "Mit Eichenlaub den Hut bekränzt!" (With leaves of oak the hat bewreathe!), written ca. 1780; Matthias Claudius's "Bekränzt mit Laub" (Bewreathed with leaves) from 1775; and Georg Herwegh's "Wo solch ein Feuer noch gedeiht" (Where such a fire thrives), dating from the Rhine crisis period of October 1840. Voss exalts Vater Rhein's fragrant, sparkling wine as the appealing symbol of a victorious German fatherland liberated from a tyrannical France. Claudius revels in the singularity and magical powers of Rhine wine, for it alone grants Germans a full measure of patriotic courage and élan: "On the Rhine, on the Rhine, there grow our vines; blessed be the Rhine!"[43] In his poem Herwegh, one of the most famous political lyricists of the 1840s, pledges that even if wine were the only issue, the Rhine would still "remain German" on both banks. Only the defender of the Rhine merits possession of its noble golden wine and a German home.

IDEALIZING THE GERMAN PAST: HEROES

The decided prominence of German military heroes in the texts of the Rheinlieder testifies to that surge of national messianism that from early in the nineteenth century had impassioned many peoples of Europe. Immediately prior to the Rhine crisis of July 1840, for example, the British historian Thomas Carlyle (1795–1881) presented Londoners with his lectures *Heroes, Hero-Worship and the Heroic in History.* In the opening oration, offered in May 1840, Carlyle proclaimed: "And now if worship even of a star had some meaning in it, how much more might that of a Hero! . . . No nobler feeling than this of admiration for one higher than himself dwells in the breast of man. It is to this hour, and at all hours, the vivifying influence in man's life. Religions, I find, stand upon it; not Paganism only, but far higher and truer religions—all religion hitherto known.[44] In that same year, the French indulged in their own display of national messianism by the removal of Napoleon's remains to Paris, where, at Les Invalides, they could worship their glorious emperor.

Rheinlieder poets at times summoned the ghosts of such historical German religious figures as Martin Luther or the mythical Nordic deity Odin, the sky father corresponding to the Greek Zeus. They also called on the spirits of illustrious writers and statesmen. But above all, as the object of their national zeal they favored past military heroes, immortalized in their associations with the Rhine. Perhaps most important of all, these champions of their historical and mythical past gave mid-nineteenth-century Germans a focus for their sense of common ancestry and hence deep justification for their dreams of nationhood.

Hermann   The ancient Germanic hero Hermann (Latin: Arminius) provided poets with a subject for nearly two dozen Rheinlieder texts (see figure 3.3). This leader of the Cheruscan tribe vanquished the Roman legions under Varus in 9 c.e. at the battle of the Teutoburger Forest (the *Hermannsschlacht*), east of the Rhine near Münster. Hermann's victory symbolized the permanent removal of the Roman threat to the Germanic peoples' visions of future hegemony. In 1689 a work of Danish writer Daniel Casper von Lohenstein (1635–83), *Grossmütiger Feldherr Arminius*, was published, glorifying Hermann's preservation of the German fatherland.[45] During the course of the ensuing century, Johann Elias Schlegel (1719–49), Justus Möser (1720–94), and Friedrich Gottlieb Klopstock fashioned the theme of Hermann into dramatic works.[46]

The growing opposition to Napoleon's European advances impelled Heinrich von Kleist to compose his celebrated play *Die Hermannsschlacht*, completed in 1808 and published in 1821. Offering a historical parallel be-

Fig. 3.3. Hermann Monument in the Teutoburger Forest, bronze and stone. Engraving, 1841, from Hermanns Taschenbuch für 1842 (Minden and Leipzig: Ferdinand Essmann). From Ernst Volkman, ed., Um Einheit und Freiheit (Leipzig: Philipp Reclam jun., 1936), p. 20.

tween the Germans' political situation at the Battle of the Teutoburger Forest and their lot during the Napoleonic period, this epic tragedy, in Walzel's words, displays "the illustrious past as in a mirror and proclaims what the Germans once were and what they ought to become again."[47] Kleist transformed the ancient Romans and Cheruscans into the nineteenth-century French and Germans, respectively. Another German national-historical dramatist, Christian Dietrich Grabbe (1801–36), likewise entitled his Hermann play of 1835 *Die Hermannsschlacht.*

In the same fashion, the largest single group of Rheinlieder idealize the storied Hermann as the symbolic inspiration sustaining Germans of later eras in their efforts to define and preserve a common national identity. Above all, this struggle was aimed at French threats directed to the Rhine.[48] These texts deify the image of Hermann as the warrior-savior to be reincarnated for the political and military purposes of the present.

Extending this religious metaphor, many other Rheinlieder poets refer in various ways to the Germans' "holy wars" against the French over the centuries. During the French devastation of Rhine areas in the later seventeenth century, for example, Assmann Freiherr von Abschatz's (d. 1699) poem "An die Deutschen" summoned a sanctified contemporary Hermann to liberate "the Germans' Rhine" by driving the French back "to the Rhône and Seine."

A number of Rheinlieder texts liken the Wars of Liberation to the Hermannsschlacht, the contemplation of which their authors immediately associate with the sacred Rhine or the blessed oaks and eagles of the Teutoburger Forest. Zacharias Werner's (1768–1823) "Kriegslied" (war song) exhorts the Germans, as "Hermann's descendants," to unite in a "holy," "just" war to reclaim their Rhine, thereby removing "foreign disgrace" from the shores of the German nation. The poet, rising to an even loftier cause, envisions the Germans' battle not merely as a defense of family, home, and crown, but also as a potential means "to save humanity at large," presently trampled beneath Napoleon's wicked heel.

Further texts depicting the Wars of Liberation as the sacred embodiment of Hermann's campaign against the Romans ascribe a certain immortality to the Germans' Rhine claims. Gustav Salchow's (1779–1829) "Morgenlied der schwarzen Freischaar, 1813" (Morning song of the black volunteer corps, 1813) invokes the souls of Hermann's Cheruscan tribe, proclaiming that "the German Reich shall endure" forever. In 1812, one year before the onset of the Wars of Liberation, Ernst Moritz Arndt, perhaps the most eloquent poetic spokesman for the German cause during that conflict, vowed in "Der Freiheit Schlachtruf" (Freedom's battle cry), "O Germany, holy fatherland! O German love and loyalty! Thou high land! Thou beautiful land! . . . And we shall have our revenge!"

Other Rheinlieder poems portrayed the French Rhine threat of 1840 as another opportunity to renew that German sense of identity inherited from Hermann's ancient victory. These include Ludwig Uhland's "Die sterben-den Helden" (The dying heroes). In his verses Uhland reflects on soldiers dying on the battlefield, reassuring themselves that the savior Hermann will reward their heroic deaths for the fatherland with a welcoming wine-filled feast. In "Die Teutoburger Schlacht," von Scheffel reconstructs Hermann's redemption of German honor to underscore the immortal link joining that deed with the national aspirations of the 1840s.

A few Rheinlieder texts reincarnate Hermann as another hero of the past, one always connected, regardless of historical accuracy, with the Ger-man national cause. Franz Anton Zuccarini's (1754–1823) "Es schlingt sich die Kunde, es kreist der Pokal" (The circle turns, the cup is passed round) favorably likens King Arthur to the fabled Hermann. For Germans should emulate the Knights of the Round Table in their virtuous, courageous pro-tection of their "holy" brotherly allegiance to the fatherland. Friedrich David Gräter's (1768–1830) "Ein Hoch dem Schütz Armin und Berthold Schwarz" (A toast to the marksman Arminius and Berthold Schwarz) praises Hermann as the spiritual ancestor of Berthold Schwarz, the four-teenth-century German monk who allegedly preceded even the Chinese in the invention of gunpowder. Thus the poet envisions the figure of Schwarz as the paternal progenitor of the family to which all German marksmen in the service of their homeland belong. For like Hermann, "the savior of Germany," Schwarz in his discovery had fortified the Germans' defense against future foreign threats.

In "Scharnhorst der Ehrenbote" (Scharnhorst, the messenger of honor), Arndt reincarnates Hermann in the figure of Gerhard von Scharnhorst (1755–1813), who died a martyr from the wounds of battle against Napoleon. Resorting to religious terms, like many other Rheinlieder authors of politi-cally nationalistic texts, the poet likens the memory of the "immortal" Wars of Liberation hero to "a holy sign [indicating] . . . that shame will vanish from the fatherland of green oaks, from the German fatherland."

While the majority of Rheinlieder poets recall the memory of Hermann in order to inflame German fortitude against potential foreign intrusion,

Leopold Haupt's (1808–74) "Weh dir, mein Vaterland!" (Woe to thee, my fatherland!) warns of evils at work within the German *Volk* itself. This poem, written in 1819, summons Hermann's descendants (again with the understood metaphor of the national "family") to restore the time-honored German virtues of loyalty and honesty obliterated by certain "wicked persons" in the fatherland of "holy oaks." "All the brave who are descended from Hermann," as the poet relates, "seek the bright day of our freedom in the destruction of despotism and of lies. It was written in our hearts with fire: to protect virtue and law and justice, to love the fatherland more than ourselves, to be free men."

A few Rhine songs conjure up the vision of this historical-legendary patriot more to laud national drinking habits than to urge the German brotherhood to battle. From this perspective, they incline more closely to cultural, rather than to directly political, nationalistic expression. In his "Rheinweinlied," Karl Göttling entreats his fellow Germans to "drink Rhine wine only out of *Römerbecher*."[49] Enshrine in German memories, he implores, that "our fathers drank wine out of Roman skulls; be it Romans, be it Frenchmen—whoever comes to steal freedom—his head shall be the festive, happy goblet of German grapes. Raise up the green *Römer!* Long live Hermann!"

Rather circuitously, this same poem also exalts Martin Luther, a considerably later German "savior," who followed Hermann's example through a later liberation of the fatherland from the Roman yoke. In a similar vein, Voss's "Rheinweinlied" (see p. 98) enjoins his fellow countrymen to partake of the fragrant, sparkling wine bestowed on them by Vater Rhein, for this "noble drink," like the spirit of Hermann and Luther, belongs to them, not to tyrannical France.[50]

Blücher   Nine Rheinlieder poems envision the distinguished Prussian field marshal Gebhard Leberecht von Blücher (1742–1819) as the Hermann of the Wars of Liberation. This warrior's victories had included a triumphal crossing of the Rhine at Kaub on New Year's Day 1814, an accomplishment resulting in his subsequent defeat of Napoleon at La Rothière (about thirty kilometers east of Troyes) and Laon, battles occurring from February to March 1814. Like other Rheinlieder poems eulogizing military heroes, the Blücher texts further confirm a revival of German anti-Napoleonic feeling that accompanied the Rhine crisis of the *Vormärz*. The Rheinlieder poems based on Blücher's exploits represent a well-documented compendium of the marshal's achievements and noteworthy character traits. Though in his seventies during the campaigns, the silvery-haired "Marshal Forward" nevertheless stalwartly accumulated victory after victory, escorting the French all the way from the Oder to the left bank of the Rhine for the sake of "the holy German Empire." His achievements also gave prominent visual witness to the ever-intensifying force of Prussia in the Rhineland, the tremendous implications of which are discussed in chapter 5.

Arndt, the Wars of Liberation poet par excellence, composed three of the earliest Blücher poems: "Feldmarschall Blücher," "Zur Feier des 18 Oktobers 1814" ("At the celebration of 18 October 1814"), and "Victoria." The well-known lyric poet Friedrich Rückert (1788–1866) contributed the poem "Marschall Vorwärts" at this time. August Kopisch's (1799–1853) "Blücher am Rhein" and Adelheid von Stolterfoth's (1800–1875) "Blüchers Rheinübergang" (Blücher's Rhine crossing) date from the late 1830s and focus on the Prussian field marshal's Rhine triumph as an opening to the German invasion of France. Von Stolterfoth's poem describes in profuse detail the fierce winter storms endured by Blücher and his forces as they passed the tiny multiturreted castle of the Pfalz in the mid-Rhine.[61] The poet then makes a contemporary reference to the international machinations soon to erupt into the London Treaty crisis of July 1840: " 'Forward!' calls the voice of battle, 'our Rhine is still not free.' "

Lützow The poet Theodor Körner, who himself experienced a heroic death at age twenty-two in Lützow's volunteer corps, based three Rheinlieder poems of 1813 on the Rhine exploits of the Prussian Freikorps leader Adolf Freiherr von Lützow (1782–1834). The latter established the *Schwarze Schar* (Black troop) that year. These poems are titled "Jägerlied" (Hunter's song), "Lied der schwarzen Jäger" (Song of the black huntsman), and "Lützows wilde Jagd" (Lützow's wild hunt). "Piercing horns," according to Körner, announce the raiding forces of "Lützow's wild hunt" as the Germans pursue the French across the Rhine. This victory eliminated the tyrannical Gallic intrusions into the land of the Germans, united by the "holy" bonds of a common language, God, fatherland, and blood. Again one sees the symbolic justification of nationhood as sacred and familial.

Gutenberg Several Rheinlieder poems center on the figure of Johann Gutenberg (1394–1468), the inventor of printing with movable type (see figure 5.1 and the discussion of the Gutenberg music festivals in chapter 5). They include the anonymous "Deutsches Lied zur vierten Säcular-Feier des Gutenberg-Festes" (German song for the fourth secular celebration of the Gutenberg Festival) and "Festgesang zur Errichtung des Gutenberg'schen

Denkmals in Mainz" (Festival song for the erection of the Gutenberg Monument in Mainz). The Gutenberg group also includes Georg Herwegh's (1817–75) "Der beste Berg" (The best mountain) and Ludwig Giesebrecht's (1814–89) "Gutenbergsbild" (Gutenberg's picture). Herwegh's poem, written in 1841, exhausts an elementary but untranslatable pun as a device to celebrate the renowned fifteenth-century printer of Mainz. Gutenberg (literally, "good mountain") is "der beste von allen Bergen" (the best of all mountains). Yet he "heget keine Veste" (contains no fortress; that is, he is not a *Burg*, or castle fortress, but a *Berg*). And he "pfleget keinen Wein" (cultivates no wine, what a *Berg* does). The poet, attempting to portray the printer as the permanent defender of Germans from "Mainz on the Rhine to the sea," then proceeds to offer a strained comparison between Gutenberg and the hallowed Emperor Friedrich Barbarossa I: "For too long was the Kyffhäuser the Redbeard's death night; there the good *Berg* [Gutenberg, or the Kyffhäuser mountain] was awakened for his emperor. . . . The best *Berg* on earth, that is the Gutenberg."[52]

Giesebrecht's poem does not resort to such fatiguing wordplay. The poet ceremoniously salutes Gutenberg's revolutionary invention, which forever enriched the entire world, especially that of art.

KRIEGSLIEDER

A modest number of patriotic Rhine poems admit no solution to the French Rhine threat other than unconditional warfare. In "Wer ist frei?" (Who is free?) from 1841, Herwegh proclaims that the liberation of the Germans' Rhine would ensue only from battle, for the French would forever remain untrustworthy. Ferdinand Freiligrath's "Hurrah Germania!" espouses open aggression more defensively than Herwegh's verses. Freiligrath, a genuine foe of tyranny and an equally renowned political lyricist of the 1840s, portrays the figure of Germania poised "boldly, with body bent forward over the Rhine, a proud, beautiful woman" protecting the German hearth (see figure 2.4). At the summons to battle, the poem continues, Germania had merely chosen to continue garnering the harvest in innocent pacifist intent. On the arrival of the "malicious" French, however, she obviously stood ready to call all Germans to defend the Rhine as their own. Any threat to German law, customs, and treasured artifacts would justify war without reservation.

The anonymously authored "Des Kriegers Abschied" (The soldier's farewell) indulges in a more subjective tone recollecting that of certain Rhine poems from *Wunderhorn*. In the mode of the traditional farewell song, a soldier stoically forsakes his bride for the cause of his "holy duty" to liberate the Germans from the "arrogant French." Joining his comrades in the pursuit of the enemy across the "old German Rhine," he entreats his beloved to endure his death "there on the beautiful Rhine" because that sacrifice for the sake of German freedom symbolizes the ultimate act of heroism.

THE LORELEY AND NIBELUNG

More than any of the symbols thus far examined, the Rhine figures of the Loreley and Nibelung, though having quite different literary and historical origins, sharply illuminate some of the most significant German Romantic notions. This pair of Rhine symbols, animistic in their personification of nature, combines all of the attributes contained in the Rheinlieder texts just examined. The river itself signifies the cosmos in its state of perpetual movement and change. Works of art concerned with the Rhine testify to humanity's feeling of oneness, of organic unity, with this powerful object of nature. The formulation of the Loreley and Nibelung images in German Romantic lieder realized that coming-to-consciousness underlying many characteristic German Romantic themes: *Sehnsucht, Wanderlust, Werden,* and *Weltschmerz,* all of which line the trail of the oedipal odyssey. The Loreley and Nibelung also attest to the nineteenth-century fascination with the real and imagined past. And, as personifications of nature itself, they bring to light even more the German Romantic preoccupation with the ideals of the *Volk* and *Volkstümlichkeit.*

These figures above all stand for the beauty and mystery of the Rhine as a supreme emblem of nature. Their very "act" of doing so in the Rheinlieder poems is a cosmic expression of beauty as allegory. The Rheinlieder treating the Loreley and Nibelung subjects thus gave the nineteenth-century Germans profound cause for joining in a common dream of nationhood. These two images belonged to all the Germans, to all the *Volk.*

ANIMISM IN THE RHEINLIEDER: THE HUMANIZATION OF NATURE

In the far reaches of the semimythic past, King Nibelung I reigned over a distant realm. The obscure dwarf Alberich served as lord treasurer. According to the thirteenth-century *Nibelungenlied,* the Nibelung name eventually passed to the Burgundians on the Rhine, over which loomed a legend-laden cliff, the Loreley. From this outcrop, early records attest, the haunting echoes of sailors' cries reminded Rhine travelers of ancient fatal seductions by a fair-haired maiden on high (see figure 3.4). Etymological and geographical studies of ancient Loreley legends, in fact, linked her singing with the Nibelungen hoard.

Neither the ancient Nibelung nor Loreley figures assumed a supernaturally human identity until the German Romantics transformed them into animistic personifications of nature, in this case, the Rhine. German Romantic landscape art, literature, and music exemplified the metamorphosis of relatively unpoetic subjects, the Loreley cliff and the Nibelung folk, into works of art, ranging from the pedestrian to the sublime. These were viewed as personifying nature's feelings and motivations. Like the Danube, Seine, Amazon, and Nile, the Rhine has flowed majestically through history, its watersheds scenes of ancient significance. The coincidence of time and place in the nineteenth century transformed the Rhine into an evocative example of nature-become-symbol, relating to humankind's physical survival, political identity, and sense of beauty. This convergence of humanity and the river occurred during turbulent social, economic, and political struggles

Fig. 3.4. The Loreley Cliff *(at left). Steel engraving by C. Frommel, ca. 1840 (in possession of the author).*

coinciding with the appearance of myriad works of art. These works expressed a new awareness of the recondite splendor and awesome workings of the world and the human psyche.

The German Romantics' rediscovery of ancient and medieval myth, epic, and folklore, moreover, led them to reincarnate archaic imagery in a new mythology. Poets and dramatists (many of their works were set to music), as well as painters, were moved equally by their love of nature and an awareness of their national past to fashion mermaids and wicked old dwarfs in a corporate reenactment of the organic ascent to consciousness.

Wagner, for example, fashioned the Nibelungs—Alberich, Mime, and their subterranean cronies—into creatures with humanoid physiques and emotions, possessing the magical ability to forge the Rhine's gold into wondrous objects. Bernard Shaw caricatured Alberich as "a poor devil of a dwarf stealing along the slippery rocks of the river bed, a creature with energy enough to make him strong of body and fierce of passion, but with a brutish narrowness of intelligence and selfishness of imagination."[53]

Similarly, Heinrich Heine envisioned the Loreley as a seductive sorceress in his lyric "Die Lorelei," of 1824, set by Liszt, Silcher, and seventeen other composers (see the Index of Rheinlieder nos. 258–76).

> I know not what it should mean
> That I am so sad;
> A fairy tale from olden times,
> I cannot comprehend it.
> The air is cool and it darkens,
> And the Rhine flows peacefully by;
> The peak of the mountain glitters
> In the evening sunshine.
> The gloriously beautiful maiden sits
> Up there wondrously,
> Her golden jewelry gleams,
> She combs her golden hair
> And, doing so, sings a song;
> It has a wondrous,
> Compelling melody.
> It grips the sailor in his little boat
> With savage grief.
> He looks not at the craggy reef,
> He looks only upward to the heights.

> I believe, at the end
> The waves swallow up
> Both sailor and boat;
> And that is what
> The Loreley did with her singing.[54]

Wagner, too, created his own version of Loreleys, his mermaid Rhine Maidens, whom Shaw lampooned "as simply trolling any nonsense that comes into their heads in time to the dancing of the water and the rhythm of their swimming."[55]

As we have seen, central themes in the Rheinlieder typified the German Romantics' notion of nature's kinetic development in an evolving organic process, like the eternal movement of the river they exalted. The Loreley and Nibelung images embodied allegorically that very striving toward conscious expression that was the ultimate goal of this process. With these animistic symbols, art became an expression of nature's inner being, rather than simply mimesis, or the literal imitation of the natural world. This view of nature's process, whereby unconscious reason generates conscious forms, thus implied the humanization of nature. The inanimate became animate, manifested in such creatures as wood nymphs and water sprites. Animate and inanimate nature, mute in the presence of others, became articulate. Spirits and elves became self-evident in that ascent to consciousness that Gotthilf Heinrich von Schubert called nature's "night side."[56]

THE LORELEY

The Loreley image emerged from the body of legendary lore compiled by the Heidelberg Romantics. This literature was represented chiefly by Clemens Brentano's collection of folksong poems, *Des Knaben Wunderhorn*, assembled in collaboration with Arnim between 1805 and 1808, and by the Grimms' compilations of Germanic fairy tales and legends, completed between 1812 and 1822.

The appearance of the Romantic Loreley image in the work of Brentano and the Heidelberg Romantics illustrated the process whereby a culture's need to rediscover its mythic past resulted in the formulation of a new mythology based on an object of nature's beauty, the Rhine and its surrogate symbols.

Signifying the encroachment of nationalism upon literature, this apotheosis of the Teutonic past also gave rise to an expanding corpus of lyric poems, attaining its most calculating ironic effects in the works of Heinrich Heine.[57] His Rhine poems—some, like "Die Lorelei," set to music—glorified the German past while endowing nature with human feeling. Heine's personified imagery, moreover, was heightened by the pungent thrusts of his irony. Friedrich de la Motte Fouqué's (1777–1843) fairy-tale novella *Undine* (1811), concerning a Loreley-like water sprite, prompted operas by E. T. A. Hofmann and Lortzing (see figure 3.5). Brentano's magical "Lore Lay," in its transmutation from external nature to humanization, manifested Rhine animism at its zenith.

FROM THE PAST

The ancient mermaid image—variously identified as nymphs, sirens, nereids, nixies, kelpies, tritons, or silkies—had evolved through the ages from the mythology and folklore of many civilizations. The generic nixie was pictured as soullessly flaunting her half-fish body and golden hair in inevitably fatal open-water seductions of guileless sailors. Through the ages, the mythological image of water has been intimately associated with the traumatic theme of birth or rebirth, through a return to the womb or with a life-threatening potential. Thus such female divinities as sirens and mer-

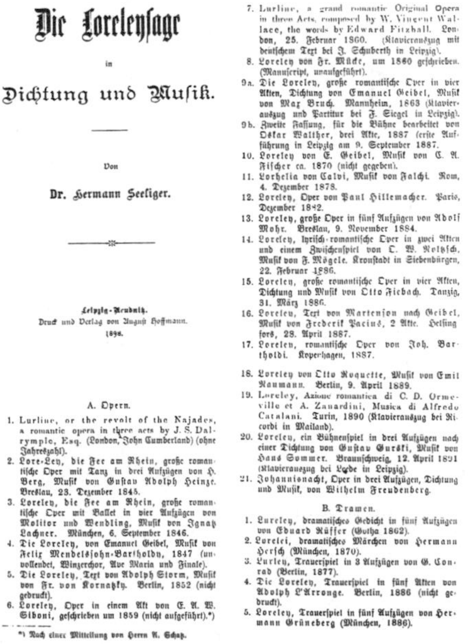
Die Loreleysage

in

Dichtung und Musik.

Von

Dr. Hermann Seeliger.

Leipzig-Reudnitz.
Druck und Verlag von August Hoffmann.
1898.

A. Opern.

1. Lurline, or the revolt of the Najades, a romantic opera in three acts by J. S. Dalrymple, Esq. (London, John Cumberland) (ohne Jahreszahl).
2. Lore-Ley, die Fee am Rhein, große romantische Oper mit Tanz in drei Aufzügen von H. Berg, Musik von Gustav Adolph Heinze. Breslau, 23. Dezember 1845.
3. Loreley, die Fee am Rhein, große romantische Oper mit Ballet in vier Aufzügen von Molitor und Wendling, Musik von Ignatz Lachner. München, 6. September 1846.
4. Die Loreley, von Emanuel Geibel, Musik von Felix Mendelssohn-Bartholdy, 1847 (unvollendet, Winzerchor, Ave Maria und Finale).
5. Die Loreley, Text von Adolph Storm, Musik von Fr. von Kornatzky. Berlin, 1852 (nicht gedruckt).
6. Loreley, Oper in einem Akt von E. A. W. Siboni, geschrieben um 1859 (nicht aufgeführt).*)

*) Nach einer Mitteilung von Herrn A. Schatz.

7. Lurline, a grand romantic Original Opera in three Acts, composed by W. Vincent Wallace, the words by Edward Fitzball. London, 25. Februar 1860. (Klavierauszug mit deutschem Text bei J. Schuberth in Leipzig).
8. Loreley von Fr. Mücke, um 1860 geschrieben. (Manuscript, unaufgeführt).
9a. Die Loreley, große romantische Oper in vier Akten, Dichtung von Emanuel Geibel, Musik von Max Bruch. Mannheim, 1863 (Klavierauszug und Partitur bei F. Siegel in Leipzig).
9b. Zweite Fassung, für die Bühne bearbeitet von Oskar Walther, drei Akte, 1887 (erste Aufführung in Leipzig am 9. September 1887.
10. Loreley von E. Geibel, Musik von C. A. Fischer ca. 1870 (nicht gegeben).
11. Lorhelia von Calvi, Musik von Falchi. Rom, 4. Dezember 1878.
12. Loreley, Oper von Paul Hillemacher. Paris, Dezember 1882.
13. Loreley, große Oper in fünf Aufzügen von Adolf Mohr. Breslau, 9. November 1884.
14. Loreley, lyrisch-romantische Oper in zwei Akten und einem Zwischenspiel von C. W. Noltzsch, Musik von F. Mögele. Kronstadt in Siebenbürgen, 22. Februar 1886.
15. Loreley, große romantische Oper in vier Akten, Dichtung und Musik von Otto Fiebach. Danzig, 31. März 1886.
16. Loreley, Text von Martenson nach Geibel, Musik von Frederik Pacius, 2 Akte. Helsingfors, 28. April 1887.
17. Loreley, romantische Oper von Joh. Bartholdi. Kopenhagen, 1887.
18. Loreley von Otto Roquette, Musik von Emil Naumann. Berlin, 9. April 1889.
19. Loreley, Azione romantica di C. D. Ormeville et A. Zanardini, Musica di Alfredo Catalani. Turin, 1890 (Klavierauszug bei Ricordi in Mailand).
20. Loreley, ein Bühnenspiel in drei Aufzügen nach einer Dichtung von Gustav Gurski, Musik von Hans Sommer. Braunschweig, 12. April 1891 (Klavierauszug bei Leede in Leipzig).
21. Johannisnacht, Oper in drei Aufzügen, Dichtung und Musik, von Wilhelm Freudenberg.

B. Dramen.

1. Lureley, dramatisches Gedicht in fünf Aufzügen von Eduard Rüffer (Gotha 1862).
2. Lorelei, dramatisches Märchen von Hermann Hersch (München, 1870).
3. Lurley, Trauerspiel in 3 Aufzügen von G. Conrad (Berlin, 1877).
4. Die Loreley, Trauerspiel in fünf Akten von Adolph L'Arronge. Berlin, 1886 (nicht gedruckt).
5. Loreley, Trauerspiel in fünf Aufzügen von Hermann Grüneberg (München, 1886).

Fig. 3.5. Hermann Seesiger, "Die Loreleysage in Dichtung und Musik" (Leipzig-Reudnitz: August Hoffmann, 1898).

maids frequently have appeared as guardians, or manifestations, of rivers, streams, wells, and oceans.[58]

Ancient Greek myths, epics, and vase paintings endowed the sirens with magical, fatal song encountered by such mythical heroes as Orpheus and Odysseus. Pliny the Elder, in his *Natural History*, dating from the first century C.E., reported observing "true" mermaids. Christian iconography perpetuated the notion of legendary sirens, preserving this ancient symbolism until the age of Columbus. At that time, voyagers of discovery revived the mermaid image to satisfy their compatriots' growing fascination with exotic creatures they imagined populating the newly explored lands. In Shakespeare's *A Midsummer Night's Dream*, Oberon

> heard a mermaid on a dolphin's back
> Uttering such dulcet and harmonious breath
> That the rude sea grew civil at her song.[59]

Romantic fish-women proliferated as the temptresses in the paintings of Herbert Draper and John William Waterhouse, in the familial water sprites of Arnold Böcklin's (1827–1901) works, in Alfred, Lord Tennyson's (1809–92) poeticized mer-persons, and in the mermaid wallpaper of the Pre-Raphaelites Edward Burne-Jones and William Morris. The illustrator Arthur Rackham (1867–1939), among others, fashioned sea nymphs to accompany passages from William Shakespeare and Richard Wagner, while Edvard Munch and Gustav Klimt produced paintings of modern-day neurotic sirens (see figure 3.6).[60]

As with these ancient and legendary mermaid figures, the Loreley image personified, for the German Romantics, a profound ambivalence toward nature in the Rhine's visible, irresistible beauty in conflict with its hidden, fatal potential. The late thirteenth-century *Kolmarer Liederhandschrift* and etymological and geographical studies refer to an old tradition identifying the voice of a seductress with echoes produced by the concave Loreley overhang that looms high above the Middle Rhine. In his *Distichon* of 1502, the German humanist poet Konrad Pickel, called "Celtes," mentioned a folk saga linking spirits with the Loreley cliff and its echo. The *Origines palatinae* of the sixteenth-century German scholar Marquard Freher located a thirteenth-century reference to the Nibelungen treasure's being preserved beneath the Loreley rock.[61]

In his novel *Godwi* of 1802, Clemens Brentano populated the omnipresent

Fig. 3.6. Arthur Rackham, Alberich and the Rhine Maidens. *Drawing, 1910. William Heinemann Ltd. Courtesy of Reed Consumer Books Ltd.*

Rhine with multifarious fairy-tale spirits in a subjective, animistic experi-
encing of nature, the river itself acting and feeling as beauty intermingled
with magic: "I looked . . . where the Rhine kissed the foot of the green
mountains, whose heads seemed to turn, drunken from his rushing embrace;
and it seemed to me as if the soul of the powerful river would flow upward
through the arteries of the mountain like warm, living blood, and as if the
ground lived under me, and as if everything were a single life, the pulse of
which was beating in my heart."[62]

Brentano's "Lore Lay," a *Ballade* interpolated into the second part of
Godwi, introduced this magical Rhine seductress as an incarnation of the
landscape where her fatal song and body guarded the Nibelung treasure for
Father Rhine.[63]

THE LORELEY RHEINLIEDER

I have identified at least thirty Loreley Rheinlieder published in the 1840s
(see the Index of Rheinlieder). The poets of these works include Heinrich
Heine, Karl Simrock, Joseph Freiherr von Eichendorff, and Emanuel Geibel
(1815–84); as well as the little-known Wilhelmine Lorenz, Bornemann, von
Loeben, Vogt, Adolph Böttger, and Seidler. Over twenty operas on the
Loreley theme, moreover, were composed between ca. 1840 and 1890, indi-
cating the compelling force of this image in the German Romantic mind.[64]
Felix Mendelssohn (1809–47), for example, set a fragment of Emanuel
Geibel's Loreley text to music shortly before his death in 1847.

The ravishing Loreley in Eichendorff's "Waldgespräch" (Forest dialogue) of 1815 haunts the chilly nocturnal woods. The guileless lone rider
recognizes the seductive nymph, who personifies the wild forest with the
Rhine distantly implied. His discovery spells his inevitable doom, thereby
reenacting the Romantic wanderer's ascent to ultimate consciousness.[65]
Schumann's setting of Eichendorff's "Waldesgespräch," op. 39, no. 3, from
the composer's *Liederkreis* cycle of 1840, maintains what Jack Stein calls the
poem's "fairy tale frame" and "stereotyped folklike ring."[66]

Heine's famous "Die Lorelei," from his cycle *Die Heimkehr* (1824), is a
melancholic fairy-tale narrative that envisions a landscape pervaded by a
sense of preordained destruction. (See example A.1 for Clara Schumann's
setting of Heine's "Die Lorelei.") The songstress's delusively luminous allure is visually conveyed through her golden jewels, hair, and comb, which
reflect the sunset above, against the Rhine's cool, dark tranquillity below.

The poet sets heaven against hell, life against death, perhaps bearing some comparison with such strata in Wagner's later *Ring*.[67] Otto Heinrich von Loeben's "Der Lurleyfels" of 1821 comfortably fits what became the standard Loreley formula: the blue-eyed, golden-haired enchantress upon the cliff, who seduces a sailor below with her magical song of the Rhine's supposedly innocent beauty.

In Karl Simrock's "Warnung vor dem Rhein" (Rhine warning), published in 1839, an earnest father moralistically cautions his ingenuous Siegfried-like son against the deceptively picturesque Rhine vista of castles and cathedrals, haunted by a deadly nixie.

Wilhelmine Lorenz's poem "Lorelei" of 1832 exhausts the by-now-familiar clichés. In a diluted aura of magic and mystery, Rhine waves whisper over the Loreley's quiet abode as she intones "Remember me!" beneath the stillness of the full moon in a foreboding picture of the archaic river's ominous depths.

THE NIBELUNGEN

The Nibelungs likewise symbolize nature on several levels. Their intensely human lust and avarice reflect human passions. Their violence equals that of the physical world. In contrast to the Loreley's relatively recent, circumscribed, and utterly feminine Rhine animism, the conspicuously masculine Nibelungs emerged from a vast complex of ancient themes and associations. From the fourth to the twelfth century, the intricately involved legacy of Nibelungen themes was preserved in a continuous evolution of oral heroic poetry spread among most of the Germanic populations of Europe.

Thus the thirteenth-century *Nibelungenlied* itself evolved cumulatively over centuries from the merger of historical or near-historical events, myths, legends, and literary reformulations. The sources and parallels mention various mythic Rhine occurrences: for example, a Nibelung dynasty ridiculed as *nebulones Franci* ("Frankish windbags"), along with Rhine Burgundians called "Niflungs," rich in gold and mermaids.[68]

As the surviving manuscripts reveal, interest in the *Nibelungenlied* fluctuated widely over the centuries. By the third decade of the fourteenth century, the transmission of *Nibelungenlied* manuscripts had ceased in favor of other heroic epics. Edward R. Haymes attributes the waning vogue of the *Nibelungenlied* to its aura of overwhelming tragedy. The latter conflicted with the earlier courtly preference for happy endings, which reinforced the Germans' ideal of their supposed golden age, their chivalric past.[69]

The German Romantics' nearly obsessive fascination with the *Nibelungen-lied* signified a renewed appreciation of their cultural and national past. Among the Romantics contributing to the rapid acceleration of *Nibelunglied* scholarship, Ludwig Tieck and Friedrich von Schlegel sought to collaborate on an edition of the epic. Both the latter and his brother, August Wilhelm von Schlegel, presented lectures on the work in Berlin from 1801 to 1803 and in Cologne in 1807. The medievalist Friedrich Heinrich von der Hagen (1780–1856), whose studies of the *Nibelungenlied* provided Richard Wagner with poetic material for his *Ring* cycle, published several of the first scholarly editions of the medieval work between 1807 and 1820.

Further editions appearing throughout the century included those of Joseph Maria Christoph Freiherr von Lassberg (1770–1855); Karl Lachmann (1793–1851), whose work Wagner also incorporated in the *Ring*; Victor von Scheffel; and Karl August Barack. In 1815 August Zeune, the founder of the German Language Society, produced the first school edition of the *Nibelungenlied*. Von Lassberg's two editions appeared, respectively, in 1821 and 1846, Lachmann's five between 1826 and 1878, von Scheffel's in 1859, and Barack's in 1865.[70]

The epic meanwhile inspired numerous dramatic re-creations, from 1781 on, including Friedrich (Maler) Mueller's (1749–1825) *Nibelungenlied* play; Friedrich de la Motte Fouqué's trilogy *Der Held des Nordens* of 1810; Ernst Raupach's five-act drama with prologue *Der Nibelungen-Hort*, staged in 1828 and published in 1834; Emanuel Geibel's drama *Brunhild* of 1857; Christian Friedrich Hebbel's dramatic trilogy *Die Nibelungen*, completed in 1860 and published two years later; and Wilhelm Jordan's two epics, collectively entitled *Die Nibelunge*, written between 1864 and 1874. Heinrich Dorn's (1804–92) opera *Die Nibelungen* was premiered in Berlin in 1854.[71]

Among the massive complexities of the Nibelung subject matter in its Rhine context is the legend of Genoveva, a saint of royal lineage and wife of a Rhenish Siegfried. German dramas based on this figure include Maler Mueller's *Golo und Genoveva* (1780), Tieck's *Leben und Tod der Heiligen Genoveva* (1800), and Hebbel's *Genoveva* (1843). The saintly subject led Robert Schumann to compose a four-act opera, *Genoveva*, op. 81, composed for the most part in 1848. The ultimate form of the libretto was mainly the work of Schumann himself, though it was based largely on Robert Reinick's text, the latter largely derived from Tieck's and Hebbel's versions. Felix Mendelssohn, Niels Gade, and reportedly Schumann expressed interest in composing a Nibelungen opera.[72]

In part 1 of the medieval *Nibelungenlied* itself, the "original" Nibelungs form a royal dynasty, mere background earthlings devoid of any supernatural attributes. They consist of Nibelung I, lord of Nibelungland; his sons, Schilbung and Nibelung II; and the seemingly inconsequential dwarf Alberich, lord treasurer of the Nibelung dynasty and thereby protector of the treasure and of the cloak of invisibility. Finding the cloak's secret, Alberich proclaimed, would make its discoverer lord of all mankind, but its theft, he added, would also assure an ensuing tragedy.

The second stratum of Nibelungs arises when Siegfried, though never a principal hero, slays Nibelung II. With this act he wins the hoard and becomes a second-generation Nibelung, reigning over Nibelungland, the Netherlands, and Norway (all merged mythically with his capital, Xanten, on the Rhine).

After Siegfried's murder at Worms by Hagen, the Rhine Burgundians in part 2 proceed to Hungary, or Hunland, assuming the name "Nibelung" as an alternative designation. These Burgundian Nibelungs include Gunther, the "senior king"; his brothers, the vice-kings Gernot and Giselher; their sister, Kriemhild; queen Brunhild; and a heroic Hagen, Burgundian kinsman and vassal.[73] The latter, together with Kriemhild, as avenger of her husband Siegfried's death, is the primary protagonist.

The genesis of the *Nibelungenlied* indicates a tangled conglomeration of history, myth, folklore, and literary reformulation, from which a concept of the Nibelungs emerges rather unobtrusively as one of several ancient folk among others. The medieval poet only casually hints at the symbolic imagery and associations found so abundantly and pronounced in the Rheinlieder and Wagner's *Ring*. In the *Nibelungenlied*, the poet alludes merely vaguely to the supernatural in reference to the treasure, cloak of invisibility, and Sieglind, one of two doom-prophesying water fairies of the Danube.[74]

Moreover, as the natural world also does not figure aesthetically in the medieval epic, so human nature rarely approaches the personal or individualistic. Psychological motivation—the lust for power, fame, revenge, and honor—and emotions such as passion, hatred, grief, and pessimism tend chiefly toward corporate expression or codified ritual, as, for example, in Kriemhild's weeping. Thus the expression of emotions is described by the *Nibelungenlied* poet in the collective terms of a chivalric age, rather than in the subjective, individualistic manner of Romanticism.[75]

Similarly, symbolic tokens are treated rather incidentally in the medieval epic, tending to provoke only impersonal reactions. This approach differs fundamentally from that of the nineteenth century. Even the golden Nibelung treasure won by Siegfried and stolen by the Burgundians has only secondary importance as part of the medieval dowry concept, and Hagen's act of sinking it in the Rhine never incites truly aggressive reactions. With its endless battles, tournaments, and feasts, the panorama of the entire epic, in fact, extends over a landscape colorfully populated with casts of thousands. The anonymity of such a scene diverges sharply from the subjective. nature landscapes of German Romantic art.

THE NAZARENES AND THE
NIBELUNGENLIED

One of the most literal re-creations of the *Nibelungenlied* was the landscape art of the German Romantic Nazarene painters. In their depictions, the neo-Classical idealization of the ancient Greco-Roman heritage merged with medieval religious motives and a nostalgic glorification of the Teutonic past. Originally inspired in their nostalgic spirituality by the writings of Wilhelm Heinrich Wackenroder (1773–98), Ludwig Tieck, and Friedrich Schlegel, the Nazarenes christened themselves the *Lukasbund* (League of St. Luke) in Vienna ca. 1808–9, and then had abandoned this French-occupied city in 1810 for Rome.[76]

Other German Romantics, too, such as the lyric poet Friedrich Hölderlin, sought to reconcile an idealized Classical Greek beauty with Romantic longing. Hölderlin's influential poem "Der Rhein" is an example. Hegel likewise equated ancient Classical mythology with its northern counterparts: "Without doubt, priests and poets have never known, under an abstract and general form, the thoughts that constitute the basis of mythological representations, and it is not by design that they have been enveloped in a symbolical veil. But it does not follow that their representations cannot be symbols and ought not to be considered as such."[77] Hegel, moreover, connected the artistic creation of "forms of the imagination" with the German Romantic theme of the ascent to consciousness from an unconscious truth.

Combining the introspective examination of inner human passions and motivations with a precise, more personal rendering of the Rhine and other landscapes, Nazarene art openly expressed a sense of German identity. This was reinforced by memories of the Germans' earlier anti-Napoleonic sympathies and by darker themes from their even more distant history. Nazarene art was a form of cultural and patriotic propaganda.

NIBELUNGENLIED ART

In 1817 the Nazarene Peter Joseph von Cornelius produced landscape engravings based on the *Nibelungenlied*, as did Alfred Rethel in the 1840s.[78] In 1825 Ludwig I of Bavaria commissioned Julius Schnorr von Carolsfeld (1794–1872), father of the Wagnerian tenor Ludwig Schnorr von Carolsfeld, to decorate the new wing of his royal Residenz in Munich with seven frescoes from the *Nibelungenlied*, a forty-year project. In 1825 Schnorr also painted an oil triptych on a dramatic and pivotal confrontation in the epic, *Hagen Exhorts Brunhilde to Avenge Herself*, based on the famous "quarrel of the queens" episode (see figure 3.7). During the dispute of the queens, Brunhilde had just discovered that Siegfried, rather than her husband, Gunther, had seduced her while keeping himself invisible with the *Tarnkappe* (cape of darkness). In the central panel of this landscape, Hagen, one of Gunther's vassals, convinces Brunhilde to permit him to avenge the deed and later murders Siegfried during a hunt. In his woodcut *Der Nibelungen Noth* (*The Plight of the Nibelungen*) of 1843, Schnorr reinforced the deep nature symbolism of the Rhine theme through detailed emphasis on the wild darkness of the setting (see figure 3.8).[79] Schnorr also illustrated two editions of the

Fig. 3.7. Julius Schnorr von Carolsfeld, Hagen Exhorts Brunhilde to Avenge Herself. *Oil on canvas. Courtesy of the Sammlung Georg Schäfer Schweinfurt.*

Fig. 3.8. Julius Schnorr von Carolsfeld, The Plight of the Nibelungen. *Woodcut, Tübingen,*
1843. Courtesy of the Kunstbibliothek, Staatliche Museen zu Berlin Preussischer Kulturbesitz,
Berlin.

Nibelungenlied in 1843 and 1867 and painted frescoes on *Nibelungenlied*-related episodes from historical accounts of Charlemagne and Friedrich Barbarossa.

Other German Romantic artists, among them sculptors and architects, likewise based works on *Nibelungenlied* themes; they included Bengt Erland Folgelberg's sculpture *Wotan* of 1830 and Michael Echter's gilded letters in Munich's Residenz Palace illustrating passages from Wagner's *Ring*. Ludwig I of Bavaria, grandfather of Wagner's patron Ludwig II, even commissioned the building of the Walhalla, a Greek Doric temple typifying the German Romantic identification of the Teutonic past with the glories of ancient classicism.[80] Moritz von Schwind (1804–71) painted *Daughters of the Rhine*, a watercolor of 1869 illustrating a scene from Wagner's *Das Rheingold*, premiered that year as the prelude to *Der Ring des Nibelungen*.[81]

RHEINLIEDER BASED ON THE
NIBELUNGENLIED

Predating Wagner's magical, semi-humanized Nibelungs and Rhine Maidens were the Nibelung references saturating the texts of the Rheinlieder published in the 1840s. These poems represented a wide-reaching constellation of landscape images associated with the Rhine as symbol. The poems of these settings, reinforced through musical means, "humanized" the Rhine variously as God, father, a fruitful masculine Erda, king, or immortal hero. This humanization of the river and its symbolic surrogates—the Nibelungs, Siegfried, giants, dragons—brought to consciousness a profound sense of the German cultural and national past. This process also revealed that with this humanization, or animistic representation, came a powerful concern with elemental human emotions that an array of nascent nineteenth-century sciences were also scrutinizing. As with contemporary fields dealing with the human mind, the *Nibelungenlied*-oriented Rheinlieder and their linking of pride, love, hate, and fear in cause-and-effect relationships with "mysterious" events revealed the depths of German Romantic thought.

In "Das Lied vom Rhein," the poet Max von Schenkendorf (1783–1817) describes Siegfried and other Nibelungs as ancient, wondrous beings from "the distant period of giants." In this, von Schenkendorf anticipated Wagner's intermingling of subterranean creatures with earthlings and divinities. The poet obliterated Hagen's Nibelung kinship, replacing his medieval heroism with villainy. The Nibelung treasure gains Grail-like significance as the symbolic goal of German national consciousness, though the hoard also symbolizes the Nibelungs' avarice and the Rhine's ominous power. "The Nibelungen hoard," the poet relates, "arises and gleams anew! It is the old German honors that again make their appearance: the discipline and courage and fame of the fathers, the Holy German Empire! We swear allegiance to our master, we drink his wine. Freedom be the star! The watchword be the Rhine!"

In Karl Simrock's poem "Der Nibelungen Hort," Lohengrin appears as the Rhine's proud "swan knight." This anthropomorphic representation of nature, combined with Nibelung accoutrements (the hero's sword and horn of magical Rhine gold) moralistically portrays the Nibelungs' treasure as nature's sinister force in its provocation of greed and hatred. The hoard must return to the Rhine with its wine of joyous golden beauty.

The poem "Siegfrieds Schwert" by Ludwig Uhland describes the young hero abandoning his father's castle to venture out into the world. The wanderer apprentices himself to a smith in order to forge his own sword and thus equip himself, "like other knights," to slay "giants and dragons in forest and field." Similarly, in Karl Immermann's "Auf dem Rhein," the Nibelungs' secret treasure symbolizes nature's oppressive forces. The poet's love, like the gold, is doomed to sink into the Rhine. Schumann set this poem in 1846 and in 1854 threw his gold wedding ring into the Rhine in an attempted suicide.

Arthur Lütze's ballad "Der Drachenfels," with its pronounced Nibelung associations, opposes a golden-haired maiden against a fearsome dragon, to be slain ultimately by Siegfried. The creature inhabits a massive Rhine cliff, the site of a ruined early twelfth-century castle surrounded by vineyards producing the wine Drachenblut (dragon's blood).

In a different vein, an anonymous Rheinlied glorifies the Nibelungs and their treasure as the Rhine's supernatural essence, luminously promising national unity despite the river's murky threat of oppression.

It is clear that the Rheinlieder of the 1840s, though not fully personalizing the Nibelungs, abundantly endowed these Rhine symbols with elemental human emotions.

WAGNER'S NIBELUNGS

As we know, Wagner's voluminous manuscripts resulting in his ultimate *Ring* poem attest to years of absorption and audacious speculation in Germanic history, myth, and folklore. His cycle contains a diverse assortment of personages and motives that at times intermixes the most disparate Teutonic and Norse elements. Wagner sifted this vast lode of material through his peculiar instinctual and visionary processes and reduced it to his own complex of individually conceived ideas and characters.[82]

As the composer proceeded through the various drafts of the *Ring* text, his thinking often underwent radical changes, especially in the psychological and ethical sphere. In the ultimate version of the *Ring*, the Nibelungs display an assortment of emotions and motivations so intense as to result in quasi-caricatures of human subjectivity. The violence of their passions, in fact, reflects feelings aroused by nature and transposed to nature. Even supernatural qualities are organically fused with the Nibelungs' superhuman attributes, for incarnate in these dwarfish gnomes rage the ominous powers of sorcery.

Within the Rhine-dominated setting of the *Ring*, Wagner made much of the blood ties, absent in ancient lore, uniting the earthling mortals, the Gibichungs, and a god on high. In accord with the same idealization of familial connectedness that prevails in the Rheinlieder, as generally in the German Romantic concept of nationalism, these ties, moreover, "genealogically" reinforce the three-level intermingling of character "realms" in the *Ring* itself. Loge, the roguish demigod of fire, shares his cunning with his sub-Rhine cousins Mime and Alberich, father of the equally treacherous Hagen. The latter, in turn, is a half-brother to the Rhine-dwelling Gibichungs Gunther and Gutruna. In addition, Wagner's *Ring* characters, while representing different dramatic strata, also freely intermix: subterranean elves interact with water-bound fish-women, earthly beings, and cosmic divinities.

And, like Wagner's Nibelungs, his Rhine Maidens represent personalized compressions of human emotions and forces in nature that found equally pantheistic expression in German Romantic lyric poetry and landscape art. In sum, the *Ring*, with its Nibelungs and Rhine Maiden Loreleys, romanticizes a supreme emblem of nature, the evocatively beautiful Rhine, as the collective human psyche.

Wagner's figures thus reflect the conscious artistic visualization of the unconscious reaches of nature, a realization of the organic process in dramatic-musical guise. From the Nibelungs' loss of the Ring to its return to the Rhine's primally innocent Loreleys, a gigantic cyclic process is at work. And this process demonstrates on a massive scale the organic concept central to German Romantic literature, art, philosophy, natural science, and psychology, to name but a few fields of thought.

From all these examples, it is clear that the nineteenth-century Germans transformed a semimythic Nibelung folk and legend-laden Loreley cliff into Romantic images of enchantment. In doing so they revealed the feelings, dreams, and desires bequeathed to an ancient river. The confluence of old and new marked the Germans' rite of passage from their heroic Nordic past. This process, with its convergence of historical and ideological forces, made the Rhine a focus for the evocation of nature, personified by the Loreley and Nibelung.

The American psychoanalyst Jacob Arlow once defined myths as needful means for extending individual to communal experience. Artistic imagery, he noted, resolves personal guilt into "mutual exculpation."[83] This metaphoric restatement of unconscious wishes girds the masses with particular force in national emergencies.

The Rheinlieder appeared as the consequence of just such a national emergency. The Romantic "animizing" of the Rhine through the ancient Loreley and Nibelung figures created a new mythology that heartened the Germans in their crisis of national identity and survival during the 1840s, as subsequently throughout the century. This new mythology, established by the German Romantics in the Rheinlieder and other works of literature and art, hastened the dawn of that era soon to resound with Wagner's Nibelungs and Loreley Rhine Maidens.

The brothers Jacob and Wilhelm Grimm distinguished the fairy tale as "more poetic" than legends, the latter retaining more historical, local elements. The Romantic Loreley and Nibelung, intermingling both genres, offer a poetic reformulation of old material, a new stratum of metaphoric mystique summoned to rescue and preserve the collective German psyche. As the Grimms noted in 1816:

"One must quietly lift the leaves and carefully bend back the bough so as not to disturb the folk, if one wishes to steal a furtive glance into the strange world of nature. . . . Around everything that appears extraordinary to the human senses—existing either as part of Nature's possessions in a given landscape, or as something that history calls to man's attention—there gathers the scent of song and legend. From the coexistence with rocky crags, lakes, castle ruins, and with trees there emerges a bond creating that homesick feeling universally human. Without this poetry that is their companion whole peoples would have languished and faded into oblivion. . . . Thus, we can understand the essence and the virtue of the German folk legend that proffers fear and warnings of evil together with a joyous appreciation of the good. . . . History and legend flow together, intermingling with one another as in rivers.[84]

VOLKSTÜMLICHKEIT
AND THE MUSIC OF THE
RHEINLIEDER

*F*or the Germans of the *Vormärz*, engaged as they were with such aspects of humanity as the individual psyche and the collective unconscious, the idealization of *das Volk* and its past pervaded many areas of thought. And, as we have seen, the notion of *Volkstümlichkeit*, the nineteenth-century version of which primarily implied "availability" to the people as a whole, was a dominant theme of the times. In music, *Volkstümlichkeit* took various forms. Four-hand piano arrangements of symphonies, for example, gave general access to music in the homes of the middle classes as a substitute for concert hall performances of large-scale orchestral music. Versions for two players could reach relatively wide "domestic" audiences.

Chapter 1, furthermore, has shown how *volkstümlich*, or folklike, in nature were the myriad *Liedertafeln*. These song societies afforded the growing middle strata of society the opportunity for singing music for which their modest amateur skills were adequate. Similarly, chapter 5 sorts out some of the sociomusical complexities of an age in which the *Volkstümlichkeit* ideal of the expanding blue- and white-collar bourgeoisie confronted the tastes and standards of a professional elite becoming increasingly powerful in its own right. In chapter 5 we shall see the effects of this conflict between practiced amateurs and professional musicians in the Rhineland itself, a critical player in German protonationalism.

These and other sociomusical considerations helped define the context of a *Volkstümlichkeit* ideal that pervaded the Rheinlieder as a whole, from the largest group—that of the easily singable examples—to the much smaller number of more "sophisticated" art songs.

A *VOLKSTÜMLICH* MUSICAL STYLE

The musical style characterizing the majority of the Rheinlieder published in the 1840s derived from the realm of the essentially *volkstümlich*, or folk-song-like. That is, they are works created with a consciously artless intention.

In the Rheinlieder adhering to *volkstümlich* principles, the voice, if accompanied instrumentally, was supported, or even doubled, in an unassuming piano part or not infrequently by the guitar. These were the two instruments, of course, that at the time most typified amateur domestic music making. The accompaniment generally adhered, that is, to the rhythm of the poem with only a modicum of expressive musical devices and compass.

In the much smaller group of art songs, the composer has shaped the vocal and keyboard parts to express, in greater or lesser extent, the emotional tone peculiar to the given poem. The metrical and rhythmic scheme, for example, may be designed to reinforce the meaning of the words. At times even more intensely, the voice part is correspondingly fashioned to convey the psychological depths of the poem in the musical process of "tone painting." The piano part characteristically assumes a semi-independent role of its own, enriching and setting off the vocal line with fine gradations in harmony, rhythm, and texture. Schumann's and Liszt's settings of "Im Rhein" are good examples of this type of art song. In addition, *volkstümlich* tendencies often permeate the art songs in varying amounts, as in Schumann's "Sonntags am Rhein" and Kreutzer's Becker setting. In the final analysis, therefore, no precise line enables us to distinguish absolutely between the art songs and *volkstümlich* examples of the Rheinlieder.

Among all these songs, moreover, almost one-half are settings for solo voice. The rest are designed for chorus, typically male chorus, or both solo voice and chorus. Over half of the total number of songs appear in the sources with accompaniment. One-fourth of the Rheinlieder are exclusively part-songs, that is, choral settings, and are predominately unaccompanied. About one-eighth of the Rheinlieder are written for solo voice combined with chorus. Some of these songs appear with a modest guitar accompaniment that occasionally serves as an alternative to the piano.

In a dozen or so solo songs and a few part-songs (those given, for example, in Franz Samans's *365 fröhliche Guitarrlieder*), letter tablature indicates guitar harmonization.[1]

The Hofmeister catalogues list fifty-one Rheinlieder as both part-songs and solo lieder. Several of these appear without any music at all, for example, as in a collection containing some music, but at times offering only the poem with the indication "to be sung to the melody of . . ." Singers apparently used such compilations to recall the tunes from memory. The following table breaks down the Rheinlieder in the Hofmeister catalogues according to performance medium.

TYPES OF RHEINLIEDER SETTINGS

Solo voice	
with accompaniment	143
without accompaniment	46
Part-songs	
with accompaniment	16
without accompaniment	78
Both solo voice (with	
accompaniment) and	
part-song	51
Settings unknown	48
Total	382

THE *VOLKSTÜMLICH* STYLE

Among the *volkstümlich* Rheinlieder, both the solo settings and the part-songs share the same modesty of musical means. One is, in fact, almost tempted to agree with G. W. Fink, critic of the *Allgemeine musikalische Zeitung*, that measure-by-measure musical analyses of these simple songs would produce "vain and boring" results—though, as this chapter reveals, exceptions do occur.[2] With few deviations, these lieder are in a major key, melodically and harmonically unpretentious or even elementary, rhythmically uniform and plain, and in simple strophic form, that is, with the same music repeated for each verse of the poem.[3] Perhaps offering the examples of a single lied in both part-song and solo-with-piano versions most directly demonstrates the style of the *volkstümliche* Rheinlieder (see examples 4.1a and 4.1b).

Since many of these songs have openly patriotic texts, they are often provided with melodies marked by martial dotted rhythms and melodies. Many other Rheinlieder, however, although lacking patriotic texts, have

Ex. 4.1a. F. Silcher, "Die Lorelei" (Heine), for unaccompanied four-part men's chorus. In Volksliederbuch für Männerchor 1, ed. Friedlaender (Leipzig: C. F. Peters, 1907), no. 172, p. 392, meas. 1–2.

Ex. 4.1b. F. Silcher, "Die Lorelei" (Heine), for solo voice and piano. Trans. C. Everest (Philadelphia: Lee and Walker, 1859), meas. 5–12.

equally "four-square" melodic designs. Not surprisingly, considering their intended function, their vocal ranges are generally rather limited, hence, of course, singable by *das Volk.* Within the strophe, most of the Rheinlieder consist of a restricted number of basic melodic phrases arranged in a balanced, repetitive scheme.[4] In only a smattering of instances does the composer attempt any tone painting of the text. If he resorts to this practice at all, it is in order to emphasize such crucial words as "They shall not have it" (the famous opening line of Becker's Rhine poem), "free," "German," or "Rhine." Otherwise the musical setting remains brief, direct, and sometimes unmistakably trite. Even the occasional embroidering of the melody usually proves rather mundane and cursory.

Of the Rheinlieder poems composed as part-songs, half have four-voice settings. The remainder are written for two or three parts or employ a chorus in unison. Most represent part-writing throughout, though several also contain one or more sections for solo voice in addition to the chorus. Hofmeister lists most of these part-songs as intended for male chorus. In the songbooks, however, the music is usually printed in the treble clef and on a single staff (see example 4.2).

PERFORMANCE

The latter procedure suggests several interesting implications for performance practice and intended use. Crowding as many as four parts on one minuscule staff (which additionally allows a single line of text to serve for all the voices) enabled the inclusion of an extensive selection of songs within a single diminutive volume. More such collections could be printed at a lower cost than otherwise possible to accommodate the ever-expanding multitude of choral societies. As a rule, however, these part-songs lack an indication as to the number of voices intended for each part.

The fact that the limited size and hence reduced cost of these lieder books easily promoted wide dissemination provided clear testimony to the flourishing of a golden age of the lied, so central to the music of German Romanticism. Lieder collections sufficiently small for easy transportability, furthermore, suited the convenience of singers engaged in the typically German Romantic custom of *Wanderschaft* (wayfaring), domestic music making, and *Liedertafel* sessions. Yet it should be noted that, while this type of songbook format endowed the nineteenth-century German bourgeoisie with an unending supply of *volkstümlich* songs, they also fulfilled a need that, for

Ex. 4.2. C. M. von Weber, "Lützows wilde Jagd" (Körner), for unaccompanied four-part men's chorus. In Auswahl deutscher Lieder, ed. Steiner (Leipzig: Serig'sche Buchhandlung, 1844), no. 43, p. 73, meas. 1–2.

better or for worse, evidenced the overtones of commercialism, so resonant in the musical environment of that era.

The cramped, closed score (in the treble clef) of many part-song publications, moreover, closely resembles the writing style of a chordal right-hand piano part; counterpoint remains minimal.[5] With no demands placed on the performers for truly independent part-singing or for keyboard virtuosity, ease of execution proved the rule of the day. (In the case of the contemporary art song, of course, the piano and its compositional idiom had assumed a rather independent role, which typically required considerable skill from the accompanist.) Thus, with the *volkstümlich* part-song, we again witness that aesthetic leveling-off, to be recounted later in this study, that so frustrated the Düsseldorf music directors from Mendelssohn to Schumann, as well as much of the professional world—connected, for instance, with the Lower Rhine Music Festivals.

In further consideration, for a moment, of the inclination to resort to the treble clef for choral, even male choral, writing, one might note a complaint issued by the *Allgemeine musikalische Zeitung* in January 1844. In part-songs for *Männerchor*, it objected, composers were increasingly extending the higher vocal ranges, seriously threatening the continued availability of competent tenors. The author further lamented:

> At *Männergesang* festivals one seldom hears fresh, powerful voices; or even though one is present, it is so covered by a multitude of hoarse and croaking voices that it cannot make itself heard. Outcries on several sides have already been raised against "too much"; for such zeal, once awakened, rules out needed restraint. Most of the time the singers participating in *Liedertafeln* banquets are, in fact, disabled, [and these events] usually degenerate into drinking bouts with shouting and tobacco smoke.[6]

Hence the manner of printing the music in these songbooks discloses much information concerning the singing societies, especially the male choruses of the 1840s. In short, these Rheinlieder exhibit *Volkstümlichkeit* in every sense. Balanced in form, immediately singable and available, they represent the nineteenth-century heirs of Schulz's collection *Lieder im Volkstum*.

SETTINGS OF BECKER'S "RHEINLIED"

Twelve settings of Becker's Rhine poem offer a fair sampling of Rheinlieder adhering closely to the ideal of *Volkstümlichkeit*. Among the examples examined here, four are for solo voice with piano accompaniment, by Conradin Kreutzer, Carl Krebs, Gustav Kunze, and Gustav Reichardt. Eight are part-songs: two for four-part unaccompanied male chorus, by Felix Gröben-schütz and Hermann Pistorius; two for four-part male chorus with piano or guitar, by R. E. Bochmann and Sigismund Neukomm; one for unison unaccompanied male chorus, by Carl Reinecke; one for soprano with chorus and piano, by Ferdinand Walter; one for solo quartet with a four-part chorus, by Loewe; and one for four-part unaccompanied male chorus (alternating with a solo voice) and piano, by Schumann.

Kreutzer's Becker setting (see example 4.3) won the immediate favor of the Colognese at its premiere on 15 October 1840. Every aspect of his lied confirmed the *volkstümlich* ideal: strophic form; an unassuming melody and plain harmony; balanced phrases, extended by the "echo" repeats ending the initial two lines; and a simple texture, with the highest line of the piano part almost always doubling the voice. The idiomatic keyboard writing and lively, though minimal, prelude and postlude, however, elevate this setting above the totally folklike or commonplace.

The Krebs version, for solo voice and piano, offers an extensive discourse on the German claim to the Rhine (see example 4.4). The patriotic tone is conveyed through overt statements of militant dotted rhythms; a continual stream of aggressive double octaves and saber-rattling tremolos in the piano part; and ever-inflected shadings in tempo and dynamics (with particular emphasis on *fortissimo*, *crescendo*, and *marcatissimo*) in accordance with the slight-est textual innuendo. The conspicuous patriotic tone is further heightened by bellicose repetitions of "Sie sollen ihn nicht haben" (They shall not have it [the Rhine]) and other crucial phrases; a resolute vocal line; and an impul-sive shift from C major to a distant E-flat major at the mention of the peacefully coursing Rhine. This touch of harmonic tranquillity is further emphasized by a turn to mellifluous chordal writing in the piano part. Cer-tain features lift this lied above simply "academic" *Volkstümlichkeit*: dramatic flourishes of chords and Waldhorn calls, expressive harmonic sorties at "bis seine Fluth begraben" (until its flood inters), and other dramatic, dynamic touches. All these devices sharpen the emotional excitement of the whole.

The Becker setting by Gustav Kunze, which won one of the prize competi-tions, follows the *volkstümlich* model, although the composer indulges in mild chromatic variations of the harmony (see example 4.5).

Reichardt maintains a soft-spoken musical patriotism. His setting for solo voice and piano (example 4.6) displays the expected *volkstümlich* and martial

Ex. 4.3. C. Kreutzer, "Der deutsche Rhein" (N. Becker), for solo voice and piano or guitar (Cologne: Eck, 1840), meas. 1–14.

Ex. 4.4. C. Krebs, "Der deutsche Rhein" (N. Becker), for solo voice and piano (Hamburg and Leipzig: Schuberth, 1840), meas. 1–10.

Ex. 4.5. G. Kunze, "Der deutsche Rhein" (N. Becker), for solo voice and piano (Leipzig and Berlin: C. F. Peters, 1870), meas. 1–5.

Ex. 4.6. G. Reichardt, "Der deutsche Rhein" (N. Becker), for solo voice and piano (Berlin: Bote and G. Bock, 1840), meas. 1–8.

features: symmetrical phrase structure, unvarying strophic form, an uncomplicated texture and harmony, a facile melodic style, pungent rhythms, and an
unembellished piano part. If it were not for the awkward text repetitions,
these features, along with a bold piano introduction, would completely fulfill
the composer's intention: *Frisch, kräftig, aber gemessen, in der Bewegung des Parade-
Marsches* (Fresh, powerful, but solid, in the movement of a parade march).

With the exception of Walter's setting for soloist and women's voices and
Reinecke's for unison and unaccompanied chorus, all the choral Rheinlieder
were written for four-part male chorus. This *Klangideal* of texture and sonority
directly implied the mood of imminent battle, what one might call militaristic *Volkstümlichkeit*. This group of Rheinlieder, too, never deviate from the
prescribed patriotic formula—an artless musical style and bracing dotted
rhythms. The musical amplification of emotional turns in the poetry occurs
rarely and only with stereotyped expressive devices: accents emphasizing significant words (as in the renowned first line), transient touches of harmonic
color, or naïve manipulations of *forte* and *piano* (see examples 4.7 and 4.8).

R. E. Bochmann's setting for four-part male chorus and piano (example
4.9) proceeds in a lilting triple meter with a hymnlike simplicity of texture
and the vocal line doubled in the piano.

The setting for four-part male chorus (only the two-part section appears
in example 4.10) and piano or guitar by Sigismund Neukomm displays
modest counterpoint in the accompaniment.

Carl Reinecke designed his setting for unison a cappella male chorus
(see example 4.11).

*Ex. 4.7. F. Gröbenschütz, "Der deutsche Rhein" (N. Becker), for unaccompanied four-part men's
chorus (Berlin: F. S. Lischke, 1840), meas. 1–4.*

Ex. 4.8. H. Pistorius, "Der deutsche Rhein" (N. Becker), for unaccompanied four-part men's chorus (Berlin: C. A. Challier, 1840), meas. 1–4.

Ex. 4.9. R. E. Bochmann, "Der deutsche Rhein" (N. Becker), for four-part men's chorus and piano. Published by the composer, n.d., meas. 1–14.

Ferdinand Walter's arrangement (example 4.12) was dedicated to "the Ladies' Society in Nikolaus Becker's native town" (Haushauven-Geilenkirchen, on the Rhine near Cologne). In this setting, a unison chorus joins the soloist on the final line of each verse. Carl Loewe's version alternates a solo quartet with a four-part chorus (see example 4.13).

After completing a setting of Becker's poem for solo voice, chorus, and piano, Schumann composed one for four-part unaccompanied male chorus,

Ex. 4.10. S. Neukomm, "Der deutsche Rhein" (N. Becker), for four part men's chorus with or without piano (Mainz, Antwerp, and Brussels: B. Schott, 1840), meas. 6–13.

Ex. 4.11. C. Reinecke, "Der deutsche Rhein" (N. Becker), for solo voice unaccompanied (Leipzig: Breitkopf & Härtel, 1843, 1883), meas. 1–7.

the setting to be discussed here (example 4.14). Although of more interest than the general run of Becker settings, Schumann's music remains, like the others, essentially *volkstümlich* in its uncomplicated choral writing, harmony, and form. The composer modifies the structure somewhat by using Becker's famous opening line as a refrain; here the full chorus in four-part harmony dramatically alternates with a half-chorus in unison. Schumann's setting of Becker's poem won no prize in the composition contests.

BIEDERMEIER *VOLKSTÜMLICHKEIT*

The difficulties inherent in attempting an absolute distinction between the simple, ingenuous *volkstümlich* setting and the "art song" easily become ap-

Ex. 4.12. F. Walter, "Der deutsche Rhein" (N. Becker), for solo voice and piano (Bonn: Adolph Marcus, 1840), meas. 1–5.

Ex. 4.13. C. Loewe, "Der deutsche Rhein" (N. Becker), for unaccompanied four-part men's chorus (Hildburghausen: F. W. Gadow, 1840), meas. 1–4.

parent when one encounters examples that bridge both styles. Like many lieder displaying *volkstümlich* features only partially, two examples by Schumann seem to have captured that "artless" Biedermeier ambience of idealized simplicity, that vision of the nineteenth-century German everyday. As with his settings of Rhine poems by Heine and Eichendorff, Schumann's setting of Robert Reinick's "Sonntags am Rhein," the first of the *Sechs Gedichte*, op. 36, dates from 1840. The very artlessness of the poetry permits no more than unostentatious music in order that the image of a perfectly *volkstümlich* idyll be preserved: the blissful contemplation of a Rhine stroll on a serene Sunday morning. Amid naïvely described landscape details reverberating with organ-accompanied hymn singing in the village church, a castle towering over the Rhine symbolically recalls a wondrous medieval German past. Reinick, for example, acclaims "the splendid Rhine," its banks wreathed in grapevines. The river, he intones, glorifies "the pious,

Ex. 4.14. R. Schumann, *"Der deutsche Rhein"* (*N. Becker*), *for unaccompanied four-part men's chorus. In* Volksliederbuch für Männerchor *1, ed. Friedlaender (Leipzig: C. F. Peters, 1907), no. 133, p. 296, meas. 1–6.*

faithful fatherland in its full splendor, contemplated by the dear God with joy and songs of all kinds."

Schumann's setting is equally ingenuous (see example 4.15). The simple, strophically inclined form and the organization of various themes directly paralleling the verse structure create an easy symmetry. This *volkstümlich* approach is further maintained by the unprepossessing vocal line and basically chordal piano part. At times the role of the latter is extended, however, through dissonant harmony, gentle echoes of the vocal line, and a considerable postlude. Only at the reference to the German fatherland suffused in "joy and songs" does one observe a slight emotional dramatizing: the vocal line broadens into more expansive intervals while the piano proceeds into chords of increased density further thickened by a weighty bass sonority.

Karl Leberecht Immermann's "Auf dem Rhein" is another Rhenish sabbath ode set by Schumann in 1840 as his op. 51, no. 4 (see example 4.16). Although the text centers on a potentially profound analogy between the golden Nibelungen hoard, deposited in the far depths of the Rhine, and a treasure forever submerged in the luckless lover's heart, the poet offers only the most mundane imagery. Fittingly, however, Schumann provides totally unpretentious music; the piano doubles the voice and supports it in an unobtrusively chordal, hymnlike manner.

Schumann's "Lorelei," op. 53, no. 2, a setting of yet another inconsequential poem on the subject of the Rhine siren, this time by Wilhelmine

Ex. 4.15. R. Schumann, "Sonntags am Rhein" (R. Reinick), op. 36, no. 1, for solo voice and piano. In 109 Lieder für eine Singstimme und Pianoforte von Robert Schumann *(Leipzig: Steingräber, [18??]), p. 182, meas. 1–9.*

Lorenz, likewise dates from 1840, the composer's "song-writing year."[7] As the central idea of the text, the Loreley figure hauntingly beckons, "Remember me!" to the sounds of whispering Rhine waves that engulf her erstwhile tranquil dwelling. The musical writing generally and the melodic invention particularly never transcend a paucity of expression, as in the limited number of melodic motives reiterated ad absurdum. Again no more than a cliché, continual piano arpeggios offer the all too ordinary reference to waves, as they feebly ramble along in the lilting rhythm of barcarole style (see example 4.17).[8]

Two Rheinlieder settings of Felix Mendelssohn were published in the 1840s: those of Karl Simrock's "Warnung vor dem Rhein" (*Nachlass*) and Georg Herwegh's popular "Rheinweinlied," op. 76, no. 2 (also set by Franz Liszt, H. Marschner, and fourteen other composers). Simrock's Rhine poem is an artful example of graceful Biedermeier *Volkstümlichkeit*. Despite the protective father's angst at thoughts of the fatal Rhine siren, as the poem goes, Mendelssohn resorts to the usual unadorned piano part, symmetrical phrase structure, and a simple strophic framework (see example 4.18). Even the composer's extension of the text through his modestly com-

Ex. 4.16. R. Schumann, "Auf dem Rhein" (K. Immermann), op. 51, no. 4, for solo voice and piano. In Lieder und Gesäng für eine Singstimme mit Begleitung des Pianoforte von Robert Schumann *(Leipzig: F. Whistling, [1850]), vol. 2, p. 12, meas. 1–9.*

Ex. 4.17. R. Schumann, "Lorelei" (W. Lorenz), op. 53, no. 2, for solo voice and piano. In Sämtliche Lieder, *rev. Dörffel (Leipzig: C. F. Peters, [188?]), vol. 2, p. 143, meas. 1–8.*

pelling refrain "An den Rhein" (to the Rhine) imparts only a hint of the apprehension dominating the poem.

The Herwegh setting, completed in 1844, adheres, for the most part, to the typical *volkstümlich* prescription for a four-part unaccompanied male chorus (see example 4.19).[9] "Conservative" in all aspects of its musical style, this brief German drinking song exudes sheer patriotism with its martial

Ex. 4.18. F. Mendelssohn, "Warnung vor dem Rhein" (K. Simrock), for solo voice and piano. In Nachlass: Sämtliche Lieder für eine Singstimme und Pianoforte von F. Mendelssohn Bartholdy, rev. Riemann (Leipzig: Steingräber, n.d.), p. 180.

Ex. 4.19. F. Mendelssohn, "Rheinweinlied" (Herwegh), op. 76, no. 2, for unaccompanied four-part men's chorus. In Felix Mendelssohn Bartholdy's Werke, ed. Rietz (Leipzig: Breitkopf & Härtel, n.d.), vol. 17, meas. 1–3.

melody and dotted rhythms, particularly effective at "Stosst an" (touch glasses). Fleeting touches of Mendelssohn's more sophisticated style nevertheless pervade the setting. The composer, for instance, sharply contrasts the tenor and bass voices, indulges in colorful changes of key, and introduces abrupt harmonic shifts from minor to major to emphasize the insistent refrain, "Der Rhein soll deutsch verbleiben" (The Rhine shall remain German).

Like Schumann, Liszt, and Wilhelm Stade, Robert Franz set Heine's "Im Rhein, im heiligen Strome" (On the Rhine, on the holy river), as his op. 18, no. 2 (see example 4.20). Despite Heine's caustic irony in disdainfully comparing the Virgin with the poet's beloved, Franz renders the scene with utter Biedermeier grace and tranquillity. In spite of his instruction "Im Legendton," in fact, the unpretentious writing gives no suggestion of a distant, mysterious past. Melodic, harmonic, and rhythmic artlessness is absorbed in the hypnotic rhythmic swells of barcarole style. Other Biedermeier factors include doubling of the vocal part in the pianist's right hand, and a modified strophic form (aabcaa) grouping the lines of the poem into symmetrical pairs. At the reference to the Virgin's image in the cathedral (curiously altered to "auf goldenem Grunde" [on a golden base] from "auf goldenem Leder" [leather]), Franz moves directly and prosaically from G major to F major, while adding a smidgen of harmonic shadings at "in meines Lebens Wildnis" (in my life's savage wilderness).

THE RHEINLIEDER AS ART SONGS:
THE SHADOW OF *VOLKSTÜMLICHKEIT*

Although a relatively small proportion of Rheinlieder published in the 1840s fully merit the designation "art song," a significant number of distinguished composers nevertheless made contributions to this intimate category of German Romantic musical literature that, for the most part, reflect the highest aesthetic values. At least three of these composers—Schumann, Mendelssohn, and Liszt—actually lived in the Rhineland and participated directly in its musical life. Elements of *Volkstümlichkeit*, varying in the extent of both folklike and nationalistic shadings, moreover, pervade their Rheinlieder, further demonstrating that reciprocity of cultural values and musical expression that lay deep in the heart of German Romanticism.

Schumann   Robert Schumann composed by far the most imposing constellation of Rheinlieder, nine altogether, including the four already exam-

Ex. 4.20. R. Franz, "Im Rhein" (Heine), op. 18, no. 2, for solo voice and piano. In Franz-Album (Leipzig: C. F. W. Siegel's Musikalienhandlung, 1897), vol. 1, pp. 38–39, meas. 1–16.

ined. A pair of Heine settings from the *Dichterliebe* cycle of 1840, op. 48, merge both vocal line and piano part in a musical "personification" of the Rhine that reaches the apogee of German Romantic nature animism.

In Schumann's "Im Rhein, im heiligen Strome," op. 48, no. 6, the motivic structure of the piano part transmits the poetic aura of hallowed, ancient times and sense of perpetuity (see example 4.21). It does this independently of, yet in conjunction with, the imagery conveyed in the voice part. The dotted rhythms and descending, recurring introductory chordal figure, cou-

Ex. 4.21. R. Schumann, "Im Rhein" (Heine), op. 48, no. 6, for solo voice and piano. In Sämtliche Lieder für eine Singstimme mit Klavierbegleitung von Robert Schumann, *rev. Dörffel (Leipzig: C. F. Peters, [188?]), vol. 1, p. 114, meas. 1–25.*

pled with the indication *ziemlich langsam* (rather slow) and its solemn
E-minor tonality, create a vision of the river's antediluvian majesty and of
the magnificent cathedral reflected in it. This emotional tone continues,
consistently, yet transfigured, beyond the poem's conclusion into the piano
epilogue.[10]

Further devices heighten the sense of the Rhine's timeless presence. As
the lied opens, the bass line starkly doubles the most salient notes in the
voice, later parallels it in rich thirds and sixths, and again duplicates it with
the right hand in an inner voice. The entire procedure results in a certain
austerity of texture reinforcing the innuendos of archaic times.

Other musical events intensify the ironic imagery of the sacred river: the
lowered second degree (an archaic Phrygian touch) in the voice at *heilige*; the
precipitous shift to G major at *ein Bildniss, auf goldenem Leder*); and the enrichment of the texture by doubling the chief motive in thirds, as emotion rises
at mention of the Virgin. In addition, the Schumannesque conclusion of
the voice part on the dominant chord, not resolved to the tonic until the
piano postlude, sharpens Heine's bitter comparison of the beloved with
this holy figure. One could, in fact, liken Schumann's musical setting to
Gustav Mahler's ironic references in his orchestral writing to a folkish
past.[11]

Schumann's final lied in the *Dichterliebe* cycle, "Die alten, bösen Lieder"
(The old, wicked songs), op. 48, no. 16, alludes, rather than directly referring, to the symbolic river by enumerating the Heidelberger Fass (a famous
wine vat), the Mainz bridge, and the Cologne Cathedral (see example 4.22).
Again, assuming the literary position, one could argue that Schumann's
setting falls short of the artful and witty self-mockery of the poem. The
latter, as Stein observes, simultaneously parodies "its own macabre content
(the burying of his verses); a poem about poems; and a poem with a surprise
ending—the coffin for his verse being giant size because his love and pain
are also to be buried in it."[12]

As a musical work of art, however, Schumann's setting does convey the
aura of Rhine-suffused antiquity and morbidity in both the voice and piano
parts equally, which contend contrapuntally against one another. The opening piano octaves, for example, anticipate the starkly descending vocal motive of a perfect fourth and fifth. These austere open intervals, along with
the minor tonality, immediately transmit the archaic atmosphere of "die
alten, bösen Lieder," Heine's central image. This brazen motive, inverted

Ex. 4.22. R. Schumann, "Die alten, bösen Lieder" (Heine), op. 48, no. 16, for solo voice and piano. In Sämtliche Lieder, *vol. 1, pp. 138–39, meas. 1–19, 25–43.*

and modified in accordance with specific emotional innuendos in the poem, generates the remaining melodic writing.

Counterpoised against this audacious vocal line, the piano part surges forth with a relentless dancelike figure. More forceful rhythmically than melodically, the fury of this motive leaves the poet's angry despair in little doubt. Schumann's piano writing, one could conclude, openly supports Heine's caustic comparisons at the obvious level rather than subtly intimating the poem's bitter bite.[13] Whether or not the mellifluous piano epilogue evades or strengthens the irony of the poem, it does create a sense of distance from the passionate agony expressed in the preceding measures. At any rate, through various stylistic means, Schumann has conveyed the poet's feelings of loss. In a way, these parallel the Rhine's ancient aura of the irretrievability of the past, with all its ancient landmarks.

Schumann's setting of a third Heine poem, "Berg' und Burgen" (Mountains and castles), op. 24, no. 7, transmutes quite a different river atmosphere into a gentle barcarole, reproducing the illusory serenity of the folksong-like poem (see example 4.23). As in the two examples previously discussed, Schumann apparently missed the full ironic thrust of Heine's text. This occurs most conspicuously in the nearly precise musical repetition at the final strophe, where, to the contrary, Heine brutally changes the tone, as he scathingly equates the delusive allure of the Rhine with that of his beloved. Yet Schumann does not dissipate all of the poet's anger. The frequent dissonances, the slight rhythmic alteration at the emotionally charged words *Strom* (river) and *freundlich* (friendly), the chromaticism at *auch*, and other procedures do underline Heine's acrid comparison. The internal counterpoint, along with the jarring turn to the supertonic key, highlights Heine's ironic contrasts.

Two of Schumann's settings of Eichendorff poems from the composer's *Liederkreis* cycle, op. 39, also composed in 1840, evidence a consciously conceived *Volkstümlichkeit* musically supporting the intentional folkish, fairy-tale ambience of the poetry.[14] In his Loreleyesque ballad "Waldesgespräch," Schumann's utter simplicity, modification of strophic form, and barcarole style undergird what Stein calls the legendary atmosphere of the poem (see example 4.24).[15] Musical devices, however, such as the dotted rhythms characterizing the lone rider and hunting-horn figures, betray the horror of the scene.

Additional features of the musical setting heighten specific emotional elements of the poem: shifts in the texture of the piano part; the quickening

Ex. 4.23. R. Schumann, "Berg' und Burgen" (Heine), op. 24, no. 7, for solo voice and piano. In Sämtliche Lieder, vol. 1, pp. 18–19, meas. 1–12, 25–36.

of the pace through repeated chords; harplike figuration coloring the Loreley's magical witchery; abrupt chords and the emphasis on *bist* (are); unexpected harmonic turns and other musical references at the sudden recognition of the Loreley's identity. Schumann has musically characterized the agony of human love as idealized in the figure of this siren of the Rhine, whom Eichendorff, as Eric Sams observes, "transfers to his own ground; and here she is less Circe than Diana the huntress, nature herself."[16]

In contrast, "Auf einer Burg" ("Upon a castle"), no. 7 of Schumann's *Liederkreis*, musically portrays a timeless Rhine vista, idealized as a quiescent Biedermeier landscape (see example 4.25). Through the reference to the twelfth-century emperor Friedrich Barbarossa, Eichendorff summons the past, embodied in medieval knighthood, while also intimating undertones of decline and death. The prominent descending open fifth, tossed between voice and piano, particularly underscores the aura of antiquity.[17] In startling opposition, the poet then discloses a music- and sun-filled wedding scene below on the Rhine. As part of the flavor of unadorned *Volkstümlichkeit*,

Ex. 4.24. R. Schumann, "Waldesgespräch" (Eichendorff), op. 39, no. 3, for solo voice and piano. In Sämtliche Lieder, *vol. 1, pp. 62–64, meas. 1–18, 41–47.*

Ex. 4.25. R. Schumann, "Auf einer Burg" (Eichendorff), op. 39, no. 7, for solo voice and piano. In Sämtliche Lieder, *vol. 1, pp. 72–73, meas. 1–8, 27–39.*

Schumann provides a deceptively artless vocal line, unassuming chordal framework, and strophic structure (disturbed only by a syncopated figure at the jolting mention of a wedding). All of these portray a calm but mournful setting above the Rhine. The composer even deepens the illusion of simplicity through the prevalent static rhythmic motion of the whole.

Liszt   During the early 1840s Franz Liszt composed several Rheinlieder for solo voice and piano: settings of Heine's "Im Rhein" (entitled "Am Rhein" by the composer) and "Die Loreley," as well as Prince Felix Lichnowsky's (1814–48) "Die Zelle in Nonnenwerth" (The cell in Nonnenwerth).[18] Liszt also set Arndt's well-known "Das deutsche Vaterland" and Herwegh's "Rheinweinlied," both of which were also arranged for four-part male chorus.

The first version of Liszt's "Am Rhein," composed ca. 1840 and published three years later, sustains and extends Heine's form and imagery (see example 4.26).[19] Although Stein censured Schumann for misinterpreting the irony of this poem, one might equally reprove Liszt for "erring" at the opposite extreme. Liszt tends to drive the imagery of the ironically sacrilegious comparison to its death by sheer musical overstatement. That is, the barcarole-style vocal line, undulating piano arpeggios, and lengthy postlude rather literally enforce the Rhine's overbearing presence.[20]

Liszt's harmonic turns of color, such as sudden key changes, openly spell out Heine's bitter inflections of sentiment. At the first mention of the "great cathedral," for example, the tonality immediately shifts from E major to the distant key of F major as the voice dramatically ascends over an octave. At a corresponding point in the next strophe, at the despairing exclamation "Ach, in meines Lebens Wildnis" (Alas, in the savage wilderness of my life), Liszt turns to F minor as the vocal part twists in convulsive chromatic inflections. When Heine sardonically compares his beloved to the Virgin, brief touches of G and C major momentarily sharpen the emotional tone. One could argue, however, that all this coloristic harmony serves more the cause of the composer's own characteristic means of expression than the poet's peculiarly acid imagery.

In "Die Loreley," composed in 1841 and published in 1843, Liszt ignores Heine's strophic structure in favor of a free-flowing setting of the poetic narrative. Internal musical repetition, however, delicately accords with the poem's rhyme scheme (see example 4.27).[21] The opening vocal recitative, more spoken than sung, is extended into a tranquil barcarole section alluding to the peaceful coursing of the Rhine. When the poet introduces the Loreley figure, however, with her golden attributes and strangely compelling song, Liszt retains the barcarole style in the vocal line but temporarily transforms the piano part into expectant repeated chords, after which lacy, ethereal arpeggios underscore the element of mystery and magic. At the climactic moment when the boatman yields to the temptress's allure and succumbs to the Rhine's depths, the vocal part withdraws into a rather elemental speechlike *parlando*. The piano tremolos (*allegro agitato molto*), incessantly repeated figures, and thrusts of added harmonic color reinforce the terror of the occasion. Yet at Heine's last thought, that the Loreley had brought about the calamity through her singing, Liszt returns to his initial recitative and gentle barcarole as a closure.

In 1841 Liszt composed two Rheinlieder for four-part male chorus with piano accompaniment. The first version of the Arndt setting, "Das deutsche Vaterland," is lengthy, overtly patriotic, and grandiose—in the use of the extremes of the vocal range, for instance. The first performance of the work, dedicated to Friedrich Wilhelm IV of Prussia, took place in Leipzig in December 1841. Publication followed in 1843. Liszt's setting of Herwegh's "Rheinweinlied" numbers among a quartet of four-part choruses composed for the benefit of the Mozart Foundation. Provided with piano accompaniment and also published in 1843, it was introduced at Jena on 30 November 1841.[22]

Loewe   Six songs by Carl Loewe (1796–1869) form an impressive part of the Rheinlieder literature. In "Die Glocken zu Speier" (The bells at Speyer), op. 67, no. 2, dating from 1837, Loewe set a ballad by Max von Oër. The simple and elegant writing re-creates the poem's aura of death, magic, and music (see example 4.28). Loewe's folklike style supports the mood of reflection on the past and on the demise of great kings: the modest vocal line inclines toward spoken narrative within a strophic structure; the harmony remains unassuming throughout; the piano writing consists solely of simple chordal accompaniment, with the right hand doubling the chief notes of the voice; and obvious tone painting occurs only at a bass pedal point depicting the tolling of funeral bells.

Volkstümlichkeit likewise pervades Loewe's "Graf Eberstein," op. 9, no. 5, a setting of a ballad by Ludwig Uhland. The narrative recounts tumultuous ongoings occurring in a Rhenish castle at Speyer (see example 4.29). The piano part transmits the spirited essence of a round dance, with its whirling internal repetitions, effervescent doublings at the sixth and octave, incessant sixteenth-note motion, and elemental triple meter. The folkish bearing of the whole is further secured by the unostentatious vocal line (again, doubled by the right hand of the piano) and the strophic form.[23] The piano prelude, interludes, and postlude artfully extend the *Volkstümlichkeit* of the text, except for the abrupt dominant ending, the unfinished effect of which sharpens the drama of the tale.

Two further Rheinlieder of Loewe represent the ballad genre for solo voice with piano: settings of Friedrich von Schiller's "Der Graf von Habsburg" (The count of Habsburg), op. 98, and of Arthur Lütze's "Der Drachenfels" (The Dragon's Rock), op. 121, no. 2. Certain features of these songs betray pure *volkstümlich* artlessness: the rhythmic stolidity of their vocal melodies, emphasizing the narrative ballad style; "unaffected" diatonic harmony; and modified strophic structure, particularly in "Der Drachenfels."

Ex. 4.26. F. Liszt, "Am Rhein" (Heine), Raabe 567a, for solo voice and piano (first version). In Franz Liszts Musikalische Werke 7/1, Buch der Lieder 1/2 (Leipzig: Breitkopf & Härtel, [1918]), pp. 2(20)–8(26), meas. 1–16, 29–36, 49–56.

In opposition to his folklike treatment of the voice, Loewe treats the keyboard part of each one in a genuinely pianistic manner. Sonority, range, and figuration accordingly correspond to specific ideas or objects in the poems, and to emotional fluctuations in the narratives. Both songs, particularly "Der Graf von Habsburg," evidence the extreme length characteristic of narrative ballads based on legendary or historical subject matter.

In "Der Graf von Habsburg," Loewe preserves the strophic form of Schiller's poem by altering the musical style to accord with the evolving drama and fluctuating emotional tone coursing through the five major sections of the narrative (see example 4.30). And he carries out his sensitive depiction mainly through his detailed treatment of the piano. In this inter-

Ex. 4.27. F. Liszt, "Die Loreley" (Heine), Raabe 591b, for solo voice and piano (second version). In Franz Liszts Musikalische Werke 7/2 (Leipzig: Breitkopf & Härtel, [1921]), pp. 2(16)–6(20), meas. 1–18, 30–44, 53–63, 84–90.

Ex. 4.28. C. Loewe, "Die Glocken zu Speier" (v. Oër), op. 67, no. 2, for solo voice and piano. In Carl Loewe: Balladen und Lieder, *ed. Moser (Leipzig: C. F. Peters, n.d.), vol. 1, pp. 62–64, meas. 1–4, 16–24, 59–68.*

minable tale about the path to earthly and heavenly redemption in Aachen, Loewe also adheres to the strophic structure of this folktale text by aligning musical phrases with pairs of verse lines within each section. Various musical inflections imitate "natural" sounds and movement, revealing the more earthy connotations of *Volkstümlichkeit.* At *der Sturmwind saust* (the storm wind howls), for example, Loewe suddenly abandons the tonic key, a procedure that he accompanies with a restless flurry of broken chords. Horn motives appearing in both the voice and keyboard suggest the hunt. Similarly, dotted rhythms establish the sense of movement described in the poem; a motive high in the keyboard echoes *ein Glöcklein* (a little bell); and a rippling effect in the piano occurs with *ein Bächlein* (a brooklet).

Loewe again merges folklike elements within an art song context in "Der

Ex. 4.29. C. Loewe, "Graf Eberstein" (Uhland), op. 9, vol. 6, no. 5, for solo voice and piano. In Carl Loewe: Balladen und Lieder, *ed. Moser (Leipzig: C. F. Peters, n.d.), vol 2, p. 30, meas. 1–18.*

Drachenfels," op. 121, no. 2 (see example 4.31). A. Lütze's poem concerns a mythical dragon inhabiting a massive cliff overhanging the Rhine at the site of a mysterious castle ruin. The melodramatic ballad tone is deepened through the use of the minor mode, picturesque chromatic harmony, wrenching shifts of key, and descriptive pianistic figuration matching the Rhine's atmosphere of magic and horror. The poem's folksong-like ambience is reinforced through varied strophic form, each verse being introduced by identical music, which then changes with the particular dramatic action being depicted.

Two additional Rheinlieder of Loewe verge only slightly toward the realm of the art song. *Volkstümlich* simplicity dominates. The composer set Ludwig Giesebrecht's poem "Gutenbergsbild," published in 1837, for the Rhenish commemoration that year of the newly erected monument to the famous early printer of Mainz (see chapter 5). Loewe also contributed to the corpus of musical settings based on Becker's poem "Der deutsche Rhein." Both of these lieder, for four-part unaccompanied male chorus, display the unadorned setting, virtually standardized by this time, for the patriotic song: major keys, strophic form, symmetrical phrase structure, uncomplicated texture and harmony, and a nationalistic tone assured by unison writing or a hymnlike style.

Cornelius and Franz   In his Rheinlied "Botschaft" (Message), op. 5, no. 1,

Ex. 4.30. C. Loewe, "Der Graf von Habsburg" (Schiller), op. 98, for solo voice and piano (Leipzig: Gustav Heinze, [184?]), pp. 3–13, meas. 1–11, 72–80, 108–10, 134–41.

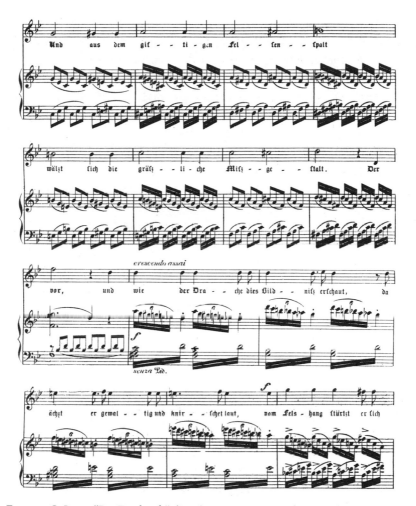

Ex. 4.31. C. Loewe, *"Der Drachenfels"* (Lütze), op. 121, no. 2, for solo voice and piano. In Zwei Balladen von Dr. C. Loewe *(Dresden: F. W. Arnold, n.d.), pp. 3–9, meas. 6–11, 47–54, 59–66, 82–87.*

Peter Cornelius carefully balances elements of musical *Volkstümlichkeit* with those of the art song (see example 4.32). The poem, his own, is a balmy reflection of love's longing at the Rhine's bank, a mood that the composer casts in the soothing idiom of the barcarole. A basic folksong manner is achieved with strophic form and a modest vocal line. Aspects of art song style include the chromaticism, gently illuminating the mellow inflections of the text, and the piano's independent prelude, interlude, and postlude.

Franz's "Am Rheinfall," op. 44, no. 6, a setting of a text by Ida Gräfin Hahn-Hahn, is an impassioned rendering of a remarkably ordinary poem (see example 4.33). At the closing reference to the "raging" and "storming" Rhine falls, the poet continues, "thy glance so closely, softly, mildly protects my soul." At this, the voice rises to the peak of its range against a dramatically lowered bass line sinking to the lowest note on the keyboard. At "meine Seele" (my soul), moreover, the tempo slackens momentarily to *più lento* (slower). This occurs simultaneously with an equally abrupt *diminuendo*. Otherwise, the *volkstümlich* manner prevails.

Methfessel   The Rheinlieder of the Wars of Liberation composer Albert Methfessel, while retaining the serious mien of the art song, nevertheless adhere substantially to the *volkstümlich* model of utter simplicity in expres-

Ex. 4.32. P. Cornelius, "Botschaft" (Cornelius), op. 5, no. 1, for solo voice and piano. In Lieder für eine Singstimme mit Pianofortebegleitung von Peter Cornelius, *ed. Friedlaender (Leipzig: C. F. Peters, [19??]), p. 36, meas. 1–14.*

Ex. 4.33. R. Franz, "Am Rheinfall" (Hahn-Hahn), op. 44, no. 6, for solo voice and piano (Leipzig: F. Kistner, n.d.), meas. 30–39.

sion. These songs, republished in the 1840s, include settings of Arndt's "Scharnhorst" for unaccompanied chorus; Werner's "Kriegslied" (War song); and the anonymously authored "Des Kriegers Abschied" (The warrior's farewell; see example 4.34). The latter two belong to the composer's *Sechs deutsche Kriegslieder*, op. 35 (1814), for solo voice and piano. Methfessel also set Becker's "Der deutsche Rhein" for four-part male chorus; Arndt's "Der Freiheit Schlachtruf" (The battle cry of freedom) for solo voice, with

Ex. 4.34. A. Methfessel, "Des Kriegers Abschied" (Anonymous), op. 35, for solo voice and "forte-piano." In Sechs deutsche Kriegslieder, 2d ed. (Rudolstadt: Hof- Buch- und Kunst-Handlung, 1814), p. 10, meas. 1–5.

or without accompaniment; Arndt's "Vaterlandslied" for solo voice and piano; K. Göttling's "Rheinweinlied" for unaccompanied three-part chorus; "Unser Berather" (Our councilor) for unaccompanied solo voice; and O. L. B. Wolff's "Wo möcht' ich sein?" (Where may I be?) for solo voice with guitar.[24] The settings employ the most elemental chordal keyboard support. Of the examples for solo voice, one includes a chorus on the refrain.

All these Rheinlieder share basic strophic form, remain in major keys and 4/4 meter throughout, and evidence purely diatonic vocal lines. (Sentimental chromaticism occurs in a single case.) These songs, which contain various types of internal repetition to achieve coherence within strophes, voice an innocent patriotic intent, shown in their melodies consisting of perfect fourths, fifths, and triads, and in the repeated display of crisp martial dotted rhythms.

Weber   Two Rheinlieder by another, more famous Wars of Liberation composer, Carl Maria von Weber, remain faithful to the *volkstümlich* prescription set forth by Schulz and the Berlin lieder school (see example 4.2). Both settings—an anonymous "Wanderlied" (Song of the wayfarer) and Theodor Körner's "Lützows wilde Jagd" (Lützow's wild hunt)—conform to the expected folklike simplicity in their strophic pattern, symmetrical phrase structure, and four-part texture for unaccompanied male chorus. ("Wanderlied" contains one section combining "four or eight solo voices" with a unison chorus on the refrain.) References to the folk and nature are made with bold triadic melodies and the mimicking of woodland bird calls and hunting horns. In "Lützows wilde Jagd," poetic intimations of horror, magic, and mystery are portrayed by touches of chromaticism.

"THE WATCH ON THE RHINE": RHEINLIEDER AND GERMAN NATIONAL ANTHEMS

Because Becker's "Der deutsche Rhein" expressly answered the Germans' immediate yearning to affirm their sense of cultural and national identity at a time of extreme urgency, countless patriots devoted massive efforts in attempting to elevate the poem to the status of a national anthem. The prodigious number of impassioned settings and heated composition contests attests to the powerful collective public yearning for a representative German song. No one could arrive at a common consensus, however, in the determination of the definitive setting of Becker's verses. Meanwhile a competitor arose to challenge the momentary preeminence of "Sie sollen ihn nicht haben."

Late in 1840 the Württemberg merchant Max von Schneckenburger brought forth another Rhine poem, his pious but militant "Die Wacht am Rhein" (The watch on the Rhine; see figure 2.4). In 1842 a Bern organist, Johann Mendel (fl. 1830–60), set these verses to music. It was not until 1854, however, that Krefeld's (a Rhine town) choral conductor Carl Wilhelm composed his setting, conforming perfectly to the conventional *volkstümlich* mode. Wilhelm's version, originally intended for male chorus, was first introduced to the public at Krefeld on 11 June 1854.[25] Although continually sung during the Franco-Prussian War of 1870–71, Wilhelm's "Die Wacht am Rhein" did not attain in the nineteenth century the truly wide national popularity that it ultimately gained in the twentieth.

The French National Anthem and the Rhine   The history of German national anthems intersects somewhat with the appearance of the French "Marseillaise," which the French Rhine army immediately assumed as its battle cry in 1792. The song soon captivated all the French. The poem and music were written by Claude-Joseph Rouget de l'Isle (1760–1836) in April 1792. It was first played in Strassburg by the band of the Garde Nationale as a marching song for the French army of the Rhine.[26] From 1795 until Napoleon's fall from power, the French considered it their official national anthem. It lost favor for a while until its permanent return to national recognition in 1870.

Challenged by the effectiveness of the "Marseillaise" in bolstering French patriotic sentiments, the occasional poet Lorenz Leopold Haschka produced "Gott, erhalte Franz den Kaiser" ("God, preserve the Emperor Franz") in 1797. Joseph Haydn set this text to music, and on 12 February of that year (the Austrian emperor's birthday), the Haydn-Haschka anthem was premiered at the Wiener Burgtheater. During the ensuing years, the poem underwent several revisions. In 1853 the version of Johann G. Seidl, glorifying Habsburg Austria as well as the emperor, was officially recognized as the Austrian national anthem.

The Germans   From the final demise of the Holy Roman Empire of the German Nation early in the century, however, Germans had longed for an anthem of their own. A year after the Rhine crisis provoked by the London Treaty, the poet Hoffmann von Fallersleben, following the example of Nikolaus Becker and Carl Wilhelm, composed verses entitled "Deutschland,

Deutschland über alles."[27] Completed on 26 August 1841 and first published with Haydn's melody to "Gott, erhalte Franz den Kaiser" on 1 September of that year in Hamburg, this patriotic anthem—which mentions rivers, but curiously not the Rhine—soon gained wide popularity throughout Germany that persisted well past the Franco-Prussian War. The first two of the three verses are a paean to German Romantic feelings of cultural nationalism and common origins:

> Germany, Germany, above all,
> Above everything in the world,
> When it always, in defense and offense,
> Remains fraternally together,
> From the Maas up to the Memel,
> From the Etsch up to the Belt—
> Germany, Germany above all,
> Above everything in the world!
>
> German women, German loyalty,
> German wine, and German song
> Shall maintain in the world
> Their old, beautiful sound,
> To inspire us to noble deeds
> Our whole life long—
> German women, German loyalty,
> German wine, and German song![28]

During the Franco-Prussian War another hybrid nationalistic song, "Heil dir im Siegerkranz" ("Hail to thee with victor's crown") also found favor among the Germans. The text of this "Kaiserlied" was the work of Heinrich Harries, whose poem was set to the melody of the English national hymn, "God Save the Queen." Ultimately, on 11 August 1922, Reichspräsident Friedrich Ebert declared "Deutschland, Deutschland über alles" the official German national anthem.[29] When Germany was divided after its defeat in World War II, the fledgling East Germany adopted an entirely new anthem, while the West chose the third verse of Hoffmann von Fallersleben's text as its official song in 1950.[30]

IN THE FINAL ANALYSIS

The unsettling political crisis of 1840, while attributable to complex international machinations, gave rise among the Germans to a significant body of political music, most notably the Rheinlieder and future German national anthems. The *volkstümlich* musical style of the Rheinlieder, to whatever degree, fulfilled certain sociopolitical, as well as artistic, needs of the times. At informal gatherings or regularly scheduled meetings, the local *Liedertafeln* vented in song their feelings of a common cultural identity.

With the art songs, the *volkstümlich* symbol of the Rhine even took an individualistic and sophisticated turn, although certain musical idioms recur among the settings. The relentless grandeur prevailing in Schumann's "Im Rhein," for example, pictures the awesome majesty of the river and Cologne Cathedral, which is relatively untapped by Liszt or Franz. The Rheinlieder, *volkstümlich* in whatever respect, epitomized the style of the German Romantic lied in its various manifestations: the barcarole, the round dance, the ballad, hunting-horn figures, the conscious restriction to folksong-like melodic simplicity, repetitive strophic form, and deliberate archaisms, such as open perfect intervals. All these endowed the Rhine as symbol with a *volkstümlich* hue shaded with either down-to-earth folkishness or spirited patriotic pride or both.

Volkstümlichkeit in the Rheinlieder was dramatically self-propagating, for it also served the extramusical purposes of German society in that era. In our own day, rock music has continued to flourish not only because of its aesthetic values in its particular cultural milieu but also because the development of its characteristic idioms coincided with and accommodated the contemporaneous need to protest. More comprehensively, it provided a critique on sociopolitical issues of the times to an extent possible through no other type of music. Likewise, the *Volkstümlichkeit* characterizing the Rheinlieder of the 1840s clearly illustrated the reciprocity of cultural values and musical expression. It also demonstrated the dual role of the Rhine as both a cultural and national image and musical symbol of the times.

One might attribute this particular musical manifestation of popular culture to the circumstance that the majority of the composers in question could claim merely amateur rank. If—with the exception of Schumann, Liszt, Franz, Loewe, and a few others—we could dismiss the Rheinlieder composers simply as zealous but dilettantish dabblers in the art of music, then their genial *Volkstümlichkeit*, in both style and patriotic emotional fervor, would need no further explanation. Such is not the case, however. Virtually all the Rheinlieder composers received serious, thorough musical educations from respected professional teachers, and themselves served in one or more strictly professional musical capacities: as city kapellmeister, for instance, or sometimes even as *Hofkapellmeister;* as the conductor of any of various vocal or instrumental institutions; as *Stadtkantor* (city cantor); as conductor of a court opera establishment; as director or conductor of a music festival; as a teacher of composition, theory, voice, or instruments; as a composer, usually of lieder and often of other genres; as a performer; as an author of books on musical theory, composition, aesthetics, or even occasionally of novels steeped in musical Romanticism; and as a contributor of serious essays to musical journals. Many Rheinlieder composers actively assumed more than one of these roles. The "average" professional musician was thus drawn to express popular patriotic sentiment through the medium of a thoroughly middle-class art, the *volkstümlich* lied. At the same time, some of the most eminent composers of the day elevated *Volkstümlichkeit,* variously transformed by their own individualistic aesthetics, into the realm of the art song.

The Rheinlieder composers, furthermore, represented every area of Germany, confirming the cause of the Rhine as indeed national and not merely regional. The proliferation of these composers, as well as of their lieder, further indicates the vast extent to which the German Romantics were preoccupied with song and to which music had come to function as a means of cultural and national propaganda. By no means, then, did a feeling of cultural identity in nineteenth-century music restrict itself to opera or the mazurka. *Lieder im Volkston* continued to survive and flourish far into the nineteenth century, now borne, however, on the wings of a newly intensified patriotic élan.

THE RHINE, *VOLKSTÜMLICHKEIT*, AND MUSIC IN PRACTICE

RHINE MUSIC FESTIVALS

*O*ur examination of the Rheinlieder and their historical context has shown that the image of the Rhine
offered the German Romantics an extraordinary
cultural and national symbol to sustain their dreams
of nationhood. The Rheinlieder themselves, in fact, epitomized the expression of those dreams. To understand that expression more deeply, however,
we must also examine a related historical phenomenon of the times: the
practice of music in the Rhineland itself, one of the most crucial and
vulnerable crossroads in Europe. An overview of Rhineland *Liedertafeln* festivals, of the musical life of Düsseldorf—the capital of the Prussian Rhine
Province—and of the Lower Rhine Music Festivals (which also involved
the province's cities of Elberfeld, Cologne, and Aachen) will serve to reinforce some of the major themes of the German *Vormärz* brought to light by
the Rheinlieder and their historical context.

Several extramusical factors made the four Rhine Province cities participating in the Lower Rhine Music Festivals important cultural centers.
Aachen and Cologne were ancient cathedral towns with long-established
musical traditions of their own. Elberfeld, a thriving commercial center,
had firmly established musical institutions. Düsseldorf, a chief vortex of the
coming industrial age, was also a principal contender in the Germans' drive
toward national unity. The importance of this city lay not only in its close
political, economic, and cultural connections with Berlin but also in its role
as the seat of a highly influential European school of art. All four cities,

joined by the Rhine and its tributaries, formed the very heartland of the rising middle classes. In this growing urban industrial complex, these same bourgeoisie were assuming control of commerce and hence of culture.

As we have seen with the Rheinlieder, the ideals of a very German Rhine and of *Volkstümlichkeit* formed an intricate matrix of interrelated forces. These forces gain in richness of perspective when we see, for example, that *Liedertafeln* festivals were openly dedicated to German cultural nationalism. Their repertory consisted of *volkstümlich* lieder, including Rhine-texted works. A German repertoire, moreover, made up principally of oratorios and symphonies and, later on, lieder and opera arias, dominated the programs of the Lower Rhine Music Festivals. In 1826 the German music theorist Adolf Bernhard Marx (1795–1866) summoned the Germans to become more aware of the symphonies of Haydn, Mozart, and Beethoven as part of their cultural and national heritage: "We must be aware of [symphonies] if we want to recognize our age and ourselves."[1]

The performers, organizers, and publics of all these events, moreover, represented the very core of the emerging middle classes. In their growing affluence, the latter guided the public performance-in-practice of *Volkstümlichkeit*, meaning most comprehensively a German *Volkstümlichkeit*. The German population, moreover, had tripled in size between 1750 and 1850.[2]

The various Rhine festivals signified a new stage in the development of the German amateur choral tradition: a community of singers united fraternally for the ongoing cause of Germanness in music and music making. The Rhine festivals as a whole, in fact, were but cultural and national manifestations of the already politically aware Rhinelanders, who could not forget the previous French occupation. As seen in earlier chapters, the wide coverage afforded the Rhine festivals in professional musical journals attested to the importance that Germans as a whole attached to these Rhine celebrations.

In the purely social gatherings accompanying these festivals, the performers and members of the audience "acted out" some of the Rheinlieder themes. After rehearsals and concerts, participants and guests alike undertook lively river excursions, heightened by singing and Rhine wine. Not less important, the natural beauty of the Rhine landscape answered that characteristically German urge, *Wanderlust*.

Thus these social events, too, illustrated in an informal way how the new mobility and leisure ethic of the *Volk* enabled them to establish and develop these festivals. In so doing, these celebrations in their own way reinforced that measure of communal feeling basic to cultural and national visions.

THE EMERGENCE OF NEW PATRONS

Some of the proliferating rural emigrants to such industrial centers of opportunity as the Rhineland swelled the ranks of the nouveau riche. This emerging upper stratum of the middle classes consisted chiefly of legal and medical professionals, industrialists, and ranking municipal bureaucrats, who together formed a "homogenized" coalition of society.[3]

Thus a novel amalgam of music patrons gradually evolved, advanced through the aristocracy's mutual wealth and education or hard won by the bourgeois elite. By the 1830s and 1840s, as the Düsseldorf coterie around its music directors demonstrated, this coalition had developed into a highly effective, status-oriented entity in city after city, furnishing concert patrons and arbiters of public taste alike. This new leadership in public concert life accorded with the expanding control being assumed by city administrations and a rising new economy throughout Europe.

From these facts we can conclude that the Rhine festivals—in fact, the public musical life of the Rhine cities as a whole—embodied many of the forces at work during the *Vormärz*, the identical forces that the Rheinlieder themselves represented.

CULTURAL NATIONALISM AND
GERMAN *LIEDERTAFELN* FESTIVALS

Inspired by the Swiss music festivals that had taken place regularly since 1808, similar celebrations emerged in Germany, spurred on by an intensifying patriotism. The first of these, which occurred in Frankenhausen in 1810, was directed by the well-known violinist and composer Ludwig Spohr (1784–1859). A music festival held there in October 1815 commemorated the defeat of Napoleon at the Battle of Leipzig two years previously, an event that restored to the Germans all their previously occupied territory east of the Rhine.

Through the first half of the nineteenth century, German music festivals concentrated chiefly on oratorios and symphonies by such "Teutonic" composers as Spohr, Gottfried Weber, Handel, Haydn, Mozart, and Beethoven. This nascent sense of German identity also evidenced itself in the inclusion of openly patriotic lieder and an emphasis on German performers. In 1845, the date of the first pan-German *Sängerfest*, seventeen hundred singers representing all German territories converged on Würzburg. From 1815 on, that is, through the post-Napoleonic era, similar festivals were held in Hildesheim, Hannover, Hamburg, and other German cities. The Rhineland, too, provided an active theater for such events.

By the 1820s and 1830s, the more specialized public *Sängerfest*, an alliance of numerous individual *Liedertafeln*, had appeared. Its primary aim was to champion the *volkstümlich Männerchor* repertoire with its associated intimations of regional and pan-German loyalties. Festival programs and accounts indicate, in fact, that Rheinlieder frequently formed part of the concert repertoire.

The number of patriotic *Sängerfeste* in the Rhineland steadily increased from the end of the 1830s into the early 1840s and the succeeding period. Even the tiniest market crossroads could boast of its own *Männergesangverein* (men's song society). And the union of such organizations in festivals commonly produced gigantic choruses. At the unveiling of the Gutenberg Monument in Mainz in 1837, a twelve-hundred-voice male chorus presented a Loewe oratorio (see figure 5.1).[4] In 1838 a group of seven hundred singers from smaller towns along the Rhine and its tributaries—the Main, Neckar, and Lahn—as well as from other Rhineland areas, assembled at Frankfurt am Main for a great festival. As Julius Bautz observed: "National enthusiasm found here, as at earlier . . . festivals, the most glowing expression. The lofty mission of the German lied stood out during such days more than many governments would have liked. They saw with mistrust that the German *Männergesang* was capable of exercising a powerful effect and of elevating patriotic hopes."[5]

In the Rhine crisis year of 1840, two thousand singers of both sexes, representing Rhenish *Liedertafeln*, gathered around the Gutenberg monument in Mainz to commemorate the invention of printing from movable type.[6] In that same year Cologne's *Männergesangverein* added its support to the project of completing and restoring the city cathedral by organizing special performances with equally colossal forces.

According to the *Allgemeine musikalische Zeitung* of Leipzig, the *Neue Zeitschrift für Musik, Caecilia: Eine Zeitschrift für die musikalische Welt*, and *Iris im Gebiete der Tonkunst*, the following special events occurred in the Rhineland from September 1837 through June 1846: the annual Alsatian Music Festival in Strassburg; the Lower Rhine Music Festivals (examined later in this chap-

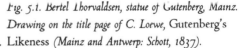

Fig. 5.1. Bertel Thorvaldsen, statue of Gutenberg, Mainz. Drawing on the title page of C. Loewe, Gutenberg's Likeness (Mainz and Antwerp: Schott, 1837).

ter); the vocal festivals commemorating the printer Gutenberg, given in Mainz in 1837 and 1840; the great *Männergesangfest* sponsored by the Mainz *Liederkranz* in Frankfurt am Main in 1838; the music festival at Neustadt, in the Bavarian Palatinate, in 1842; the two *Dombaufeste* (festivals celebrating the completion and reconstruction of the cathedral) held in Cologne in 1842; the music festival organized in Mainz by the city *Liedertafel* in 1842 and consisting of eleven hundred *Gesangvereine* drawn from nearby regions; the annual music festival at Heidelberg; the musical celebration commemorating the unveiling of the Beethoven monument in Bonn during 1845; the 1845 *Sängerfest* in Würzburg; the Heidelberg festival of 1845; a *Wettgesang* (singing competition) involving a sizable number of *Gesangvereine* in Mainz during June 1846; and a patriotic *Sängerfest* in Cologne during the same year (see figure 5.2).[7] The Rhine-texted cantata "Das Heidelberger Fass," composed by the city's music director, Louis Hetsch, was performed at the Heidelberg Music Festival in 1845.

Musical periodicals of this period cited numerous examples of Rheinlieder and other songs being performed at these events. They additionally reported on a considerable degree of more "routine" musical activity in the

Fig. 5.2. Seventh Sängerfest, Düsseldorf, 1852. View of the prize distribution, showing the Geisler Hall from inside and the expansion that was constructed expressly for this musical event. From Paul Kast, ed., Schumanns rheinische Jahre *(Düsseldorf: Droste, 1981), no. 122, p. 10. Courtesy of the Stadtmuseum Düsseldorf.*

Rhine area. The repertoire included concertos, symphonies, four-part songs for male voices (with many Rheinlieder among them), oratorios, operas, masses, and other religious works.

THE REIGN OF THE RHENISH *DILETTANTI:* DÜSSELDORF FROM MENDELSSOHN TO SCHUMANN

Robert Schumann composed both his Third Symphony (the "Rhenish"), op. 97, and his Festival Overture with Chorus on the "Rheinweinlied," op. 123, in Düsseldorf. This handsome city on the right bank of the Lower Rhine, about forty kilometers north of Cologne, represented a way station for nineteenth-century musicians eyeing more prominent German cities as eventual settings for their professional futures.[8] Felix Mendelssohn accepted the music directorship there only after his failure to obtain the corresponding post at the Berlin Singakademie; barely two years later he abandoned the city to assume the conductorship of the Leipzig Gewandhaus Orchestra. Schumann's unsuccessful application for this position and the second conductorship at the Dresden court theater apparently compelled him to accept the Düsseldorf conductorship by default. Two less prominent but worthy musicians successively followed in Mendelssohn's footsteps as Düsseldorf's music director. Julius Rietz (1812–77), a cellist, composer, and conductor, moved there in 1834 as Mendelssohn's assistant at the City Theater opera productions; in 1847, the year of Mendelssohn's death, Rietz accepted positions as theater kapellmeister and conductor of the Singakademie at Leipzig. The Düsseldorf music directorship also served as a transition stage for the distinguished pianist, composer, and writer Ferdinand Hiller (1811–85). This directorship was preceded by conducting positions at Leipzig and Dresden and followed by his appointment as music director at Cologne. Schumann succeeded Hiller at Düsseldorf in 1850.

In the spring of 1842, during Rietz's tenure there, Düsseldorf also provided Richard Wagner with a brief interlude as he undertook a private Rhine journey after leaving Paris for a position in Dresden.[9] Indeed, this intermission marked the earlier portion of a critical "Rhine" decade that would conclude with his gestation of the poem for *Der Ring des Nibelungen*, his massive tetralogy begotten from the image of that very river.

Despite the city's seemingly only "temporary" usefulness, music in Düsseldorf, as elsewhere in Europe, was nevertheless undergoing profound transitions reflecting fundamental historical processes at work in the century of Romanticism: the shift from dilettante to professional and even virtuoso standards; the removal of music from a court establishment to its incorporation as an urban institution; and the broadening of its role as chiefly an elitist pursuit to that of an instrument of *Volkstümlichkeit*—that is, music as an essentially folklike element of middle-class life and as an expression of Germanness. A perusal of the roles of Mendelssohn, Rietz, Hiller, and Schumann in this busy Rhine capital and of its musical institutions adds another dimension to the array of cultural and national forces already demonstrated by the Rheinlieder and their historical milieu. In doing so, this examination will also enrich our understanding of certain sociocultural aspects of music in nineteenth-century Germany as a whole.

The extensive processes of transition occurring in the musical life of Düsseldorf and other industrial cities of the Rhine formed part of the massive, inextricably interrelated upheavals and their repercussions that were already transforming the socioeconomic structure of most European cities from 1800 on. This was happening amid the cataclysmic new forces of industrialization, commercialization, and urbanization—the more visible aspects of the Romantic epoch.[10]

COURTING THE CROWDS:
MUSIC AS A COMMODITY

As will be seen from the often labored contract negotiations regarding salaries and official responsibilities between the Düsseldorf bureaucracy and its music directors from Mendelssohn on, the drastic changes overtaking the first half of the nineteenth century in the Rhineland and other urban industrial centers of Germany deeply affected the growth of the arts. This development eventually thrust musicians into the role of independent agents in an open market. Composers and performers necessarily became entrepreneurs compelled to "function" before the expanding concert public, the new consumers. As in the Düsseldorf situation, some of them managed this transformation more easily than others, becoming in the process the nineteenth-century superstars of the international music world. The flourishing publication of music and music journals at this time further expressed the spirit of commercial opportunism, which included a "Rhine phase," as already discussed. The intensifying commercialization of society, emphasizing profit making and the selling of labor and goods for money, had thus forced even the arts into the value system of a market economy.[11]

With the civic replacing the courtly establishment, music had traded its primarily functional role for its new status as property. The increasingly affluent upper middle classes, now providing public patronage, were nurturing an expanding group of professional musicians, while likewise contributing to the notion of art works as cheapened "commodities."[12] The motives driving the upper-middle-class cultivation of music began to reflect the spirit of commercial opportunism, a transformation already experienced in literature and painting. As sponsors of virtuosic exhibition, business magnates pompously displayed their wealth, while educated professionals and bureaucrats exploited their intellectual connoisseurship by supporting less ostentatious "classical" music. In both ways, the bourgeois elite sought to gratify its status-oriented ambitions through the merchandizing of music and other cultural "products." This attitude was clearly evident in Düsseldorf's struggles to finance its new municipally structured musical life.[13]

The growing esteem of industrial "progress" indirectly produced a curious contradiction in the performance levels of music, apparent in Düsseldorf as in other Rhine cities. Dilettantism in the performance of "serious" music gradually was yielding, on the one hand, to an exclusive professionalism that reached its extreme in the cult of the virtuoso. This idealization

of musical productivity and success also undermined the earlier, democrati-
cally directed musical institutions in Düsseldorf. Amateurism, on the other
hand, was undergoing a dramatic renewal in industrial cities. It was most
concentrated in the Rhine factory centers. An element of devotion to the
industrial spirit thus also contributed to a new sense of blue-collar camaraderie. Artisans and factory employees, proud of their manufacturing
achievements, organized themselves into urban *Liedertafeln*. Vaguely in the
tradition of the mastersinger, these workers consecrated their singing to the
ideal of *Volkstümlichkeit*, that peculiarly German conglomeration of homey
cultural-national feeling joined with a popular, folksong-like musical style
and an informal mode of performance (see chapter 1).

This transformation sweeping over Europe surfaced in Düsseldorf in
many ways, as the eventual Rhine Province capital within the Prussian orbit
moved from one type of provincialism into another.

FROM COURT TO PROVINCIAL
CAPITAL: A RHINE CITY
IN TRANSITION

Until the early eighteenth century, life in Düsseldorf centered around the
court. Strategically located on the Lower Rhine, the city was the residence
of the dukes of Berg from the early sixteenth century. The court enjoyed
the services of such artists as Hans Holbein the Younger (1497?–1543). From
1609 Düsseldorf was the seat of the Palatine electors of the Wittelsbach
lines of Pfalz-Neuburg and Pfalz-Sulzbach, during whose reign Italian and
Netherlandish artists and musicians crowded into the city. At the splendid
Versailles-like court of the Elector Johann Wilhelm (1692–1716), one encounters such names as Steffani, Corelli, Ariosti, Draghi, Bernabei, Pistoc-
chi, Veracini, and Handel. The elector also established a magnificent
painting collection.[14]

Johann Wilhelm, however, removed the court from Düsseldorf to Heidelberg in 1702.[15] By November 1720 his successor and younger brother,
Duke Carl Philipp, had transferred the residence from Heidelberg to
Mannheim. In 1767 the Palatine elector, Duke Carl Theodor (1724–99), a
noted patron of music and the arts, transformed the Mannheim court into
one of the most splendid cultural centers of Europe. He also established
the Düsseldorf Academy of Art, which flourished until the advent of Napoleon. Thus by the early eighteenth century, although Düsseldorf was no

longer a court residence, painting and sculpture thrived. Music making, however, entered a lull, resting solely with its citizenry, who could enjoy only occasional traveling opera troupes.

Between the late eighteenth and early nineteenth centuries, the city twice changed hands between the French and Germans. After the Revolution of 1789 the French invaded the Rhinelands, and in July 1806 Napoleon Bonaparte established the sixteen-state Rhenish Confederation, as described earlier. This newly organized state included the Grand Duchy of Berg (governed by his brother-in-law, Joachim Murat), of which Düsseldorf became the capital. In October 1813, however, the crucial Battle of Leipzig freed Germany east of the Rhine from French domination. On 3 May 1815 the Congress of Vienna allocated a large section of the Rhinelands to Prussia, creating the Prussian Rhine Province as part of the Germanic Confederation, with Düsseldorf as its capital.[16]

This reordering of German states and consequent "coalition" of Prussia and Düsseldorf created a political, socioeconomic, and cultural interdependency between Berlin and the little Rhine city that revitalized music making in the provincial capital. The Prussian hegemony on the Rhine created important musical and artistic ties between Berlin and Düsseldorf, as in, for example, the situations of Felix Mendelssohn and the eminent artist Friedrich Wilhelm von Schadow (1788–1862). The new political stability and economic security afforded Düsseldorf through Prussian rule speeded the process of industrialization by opening the city to major trade routes and strengthening its money and credit. With the spread of steamboat and railway travel, the Düsseldorf metropolitan area, which boasted one of the largest inland harbors on the continent, became an important center in the European coal and iron industry.[17] Middle-class Düsseldorfers consequently began to assume an increasing affluence capable of supporting more intensive social and cultural organizations.

The Revolution of 1789, followed by the French occupation of the Rhineland, furthermore, had aroused the political consciousness of its inhabitants. As chapter 2 has revealed, their experience with the *Code Napoléon* (Civil Code of 1804) had substantially advanced the administrative expertise of the middle class.[18]

In addition, the Rhineland's acquired allegiance to Prussia, the vanguard of an approaching German Empire, had begun to nourish nascent Rhenish and pan-German nationalistic feelings, coupled with volatile liberal sensibilities. Nationhood appealed especially to an industrial middle class such as that of Düsseldorf, for it promised a further expansion of local economic interests while also offering a compensating new focus of power to replace vanished aristocratic dynasties and political ideals. To Berlin's advantage, Düsseldorf and the Ruhr area supplied Prussia with vast coal stores and related industrial forces, both material and human, that any nineteenth-century government in the pursuit of power would covet.[19] Control of the Rhine also provided Prussia with a critical European corridor for an ever-accelerating international commerce. Like Germanic generations back to ancient times, moreover, Prussia viewed its strategic Rhine Province as the paramount political frontier defense against an ever-dissatisfied France.

For these reasons, the interests of Düsseldorf and Berlin had coalesced into a mutually advantageous symbiosis, and the time was now ripe for reciprocal cultural interchange. The Prussian capital itself, of course, was a thriving center of literature, art, music, and other "intellectual" pursuits. Berlin thus incorporated the Rhine city into its already rich cultural milieu. (The role of the Mendelssohn family illustrates in beautiful microcosm the rich complexity of Berlin's myriad cultural institutions.)

Düsseldorf's succession of music directors consequently inherited the potential support and patronage of Berlin's musicians, artists, literati, professional classes, and even its military representatives. The alliance of Düsseldorf with Prussia, as the following examination of the Mendelssohn-to-Schumann era shows, had thus established tangible reasons for the Germans' symbolic focus on the Rhine. This image infused both Berlin and Düsseldorf Prussians with a common ardor and purpose that was to promulgate not only war but also art, literature, and music.

RENEWAL: NEW MONEY AND THE REVIVAL OF ART

After its splendid blossoming within the eighteenth-century court establishment, art in Düsseldorf suffered a severe setback when, in 1805, during the Napoleonic occupation, the city's celebrated art collection was removed to Munich. Art enjoyed a renaissance in 1821, however, when the distinguished painter Peter Joseph von Cornelius was appointed director of the Art Academy, now endowed by Prussia.[20] The revival continued when Johann Gottfried Schadow, a professor at the Berlin Art Academy, arrived in Düsseldorf in 1826 to succeed Cornelius (see figure 5.3). Most of Schadow's students accompanied him from Berlin, opening an even more brilliant epoch in the

Fig. 5.3. Theodor Hildebrandt, Old Academy of Art *(formerly Electoral Gallery and Library), Düsseldorf. Watercolor, nineteenth century. Stadtmuseum Düsseldorf. From* Düsseldorf: Wandlungen einer Westdeutschen Residenz *(Düsseldorf: August Bagel, 1938), p. 108. Courtesy of the Stadtmuseum Düsseldorf.*

history of the Düsseldorf Academy. Schadow and his circle were to have influential connections with the city music directors from Mendelssohn to Schumann.[21]

Under Schadow's leadership, extending from 1826 to 1859, the Art Academy developed into a major center of historical and landscape painting, with the Rhine providing a favored subject. This institution further intensified municipal life through its establishment of the *Kunstverein für die Rheinlande und Westfalen* (Artists' Society for the Rhinelands and Westphalia), founded in 1829. This organization exhibited many works in a campaign to combat public taste for the trivial.[22] By the nineteenth century, then, Düsseldorf, now politically stable, prospering in its economy, and supporting a rich cultural existence, had readied itself to support an organized public musical life as well.

MUSIC IN DÜSSELDORF PRIOR
TO PRUSSIAN RULE

During the pre-Prussian years, Düsseldorf enjoyed the modest concert life of a typical medium-sized German city bereft of court patronage. Music making took place among local dilettante enthusiasts, who established a Musik-Academie in 1800. According to its revised constitution of 1807, "The Academie gathers [weekly] in an association, where, from 6 to 8 o'clock, a small concert is given, card tables are set up, and, around 8:30 until early morning, a ball is offered in the salon. . . . Throughout the year, 12 great concerts will be given, . . . to which the society members will always have free access."[23]

In 1805 Düsseldorfers organized an amateur *Musik-Liebhabers-Gesellschaft* (music-lovers' society) to present vocal and instrumental concerts by local dilettantes. The enticement of a post-performance ball to attract a paying audience guaranteed financial success for these concerts. For, during these earlier Napoleonic years, the municipality itself, though "emotionally" supportive of these musical events, could not yet provide them with a concrete financial base. That dilettante tradition of intermingling both social and musically edifying motives, however, continued in Düsseldorf far past the midcentury.[24]

To the municipal backing of organized music was added financial support on 21 September 1812, when the Düsseldorf city council named Johann Friedrich August Burgmüller (1766–1824) as the first city music director, a position he held until his death. Though the French still occupied the Rhine Province, albeit barely, city council members were allowed to negotiate Burgmüller's salary and contract, which specified the conducting of all church music. The agreement also included other requirements, such as the directing of "concerts for the poor and the instruction of all the children of the city *Musikanten* and other citizens desiring to participate in public concerts, for otherwise all public music would soon disappear from the city because here we have no means to be able to pay professional singers at concerts."[25]

With Burgmüller's appointment, an eventually troublesome tradition had already emerged: choosing a music director sheerly for his prestigious name. This process evinced a deeply middle-class value system that, as John Kenneth Galbraith defines it, survives into the twentieth century.[26] As the city council itself acknowledged shortly after Burgmüller's death: "An annual salary of 600 francs was allotted to [him], from 21 September 1812 on, not because [the city] sought a director for the church music and a singing teacher for school youth, but because it . . . wanted to entice to this position a musical artist with the outstanding service and reputation of Herr Burgmüller."[27]

AFTER 1815: PRUSSIAN SOVEREIGNTY

From 1800 to 1818 Düsseldorf had doubled its population from about ten thousand to twenty thousand residents. In the spring of the latter year, the leading local *dilettanti* founded the municipally funded *Städtischer Musikverein* (City Music Society), to be conducted by Burgmüller, as the central organizing force for the Lower Rhine Music Festivals. The society aspired to enhance its members' musical edification through the encouragement of worthwhile religious and secular music. The performers were practiced amateurs and students, the latter drawn predominantly from the Art Academy.

MENDELSSOHN

From the death of Burgmüller, a chief founder of the Lower Rhine Music Festivals, in 1824 until Mendelssohn arrived in 1833, financial problems forced the Music Society's executive committee and the city council to leave open the position of city music director.[28] In late January 1833, however, the seventeen-member governing board of the Lower Rhine Music Festival (consisting of such middle-class Düsseldorf leaders as the provincial government president, von Woringen, and the mayor, von Fuchsius) asked the twenty-four-year-old Felix Mendelssohn to conduct the festival to be held in the city on 26, 27, and 28 May of that year. Mendelssohn's glorious success and public recognition as conductor of this event prompted the Music Society to present him with a three-year contract as city music director.[29] In mid-September Mendelssohn assumed a comprehensive assignment: to conduct the winter subscription concerts of the Music Society, the performances of the 120-member Choral Society, Catholic and Protestant church music, and the operas at the newly founded City Theater. Mendelssohn acknowledged a personal motive in accepting the position: "in reality for the purpose of securing quiet and leisure for composition."[30] In February 1834 he remarked, "When I do not feel inclined to compose, there is conducting and rehearsing, and it is quite a pleasure to see how well and brightly things go."[31] Mendelssohn's salary of six hundred thalers was paid by the *Verein zur Beförderung der Tonkunst* (Society for the Advancement of Music), a new amalgam including the Music Society.

Mendelssohn raised performance standards in Düsseldorf considerably in both the chorus and orchestra, enforcing discipline and demanding regular rehearsals while mercilessly removing the bad and engaging the best performers. Despite his achievements, the dilettante base of Düsseldorf's music making nevertheless gradually undermined Mendelssohn's morale. On 14 March 1835 he wrote:

> There is simply nothing to be done here in the way of music, and I long for a better orchestra. . . . There is plenty of taste and feeling for music; only the means are so limited . . . and all one's trouble goes for nothing. I assure you that at the beat, they all come in separately, . . . and in the *pianos* the flute is always too sharp, and not a single Düsseldorfer can play a triplet clearly, . . . and every *Allegro* leaves off twice as fast as it began, and the oboe plays E natural in C minor, and they carry their fiddles under their coats when it rains, and when it is fine they don't cover them at all—and if you once heard me conduct this orchestra, not even four horses could bring you there a second time. . . . All the *dilettanti* fight to the death, and nobody will sing the solos, or rather everybody wants to, and they hate putting themselves forward, though they are always doing it; but you know what music is in a small German town—Heaven help us![32]

Even as church music director, Mendelssohn confronted dilettante standards: "Then came the procession with my solemn march in E-flat, where the bass [repeated] the first part while the treble [went] straight on; but that does no harm in the open air."[33] Soon afterward, he noted:

> No really appropriate epithet exists for the [church] music. . . . The chaplain came and complained to me of his dilemma: the mayor had said . . . that the music should be of a better class. A very peevish old musician, in a threadbare coat, was summoned. Hitherto it had been his office to beat time. . . . He declared that he neither could nor would have better music; that if we wanted to have it, we should look for somebody else; that he knew perfectly well what vast pretensions some people had nowadays; everything was expected to sound so beautiful; this had not been the case in his day, and he played just as well now as formerly.[34]

Mendelssohn's relationship with the celebrated Düsseldorf Academy of Art nevertheless proceeded harmoniously. He lived in Schadow's house. Here he became acquainted with academy artists such as Eduard Bendemann and Johann Wilhelm Schirmer, a distinguished professor of landscape painting with whom the composer studied watercolors. Mendelssohn had already developed friendships with some of these painters during 1830 in Rome, where Schadow had been a protégé of Mendelssohn's maternal uncle, the art-loving Prussian General Consul J. S. Bartholdy (see chapter 3). The Düsseldorf artists, perhaps the most socially influential group in the city, warmly supported the composer in his musical endeavors.[35] These artist friends also participated in choral concerts in the churches; designed scenery, decorations, and costuming for the theater; and provided the great hall of the Art Academy for oratorio performances.[36]

According to the nineteenth-century music historian August Reissmann, however, Mendelssohn experienced problems in his Düsseldorf position. Reissmann offered this explanation: "The city was . . . not large enough—even with the most active interest—to assume and bear undertakings of such far-reaching significance. In any case, however, . . . our master raised the public musical life of Düsseldorf to a height corresponding to the great artistic importance that the city had won through the Art Academy."[37]

Mendelssohn left Düsseldorf permanently after conducting the Lower Rhine Music Festival in Cologne in early June 1835. Two months later he assumed his new Leipzig post at the Gewandhaus.

RIETZ

The cellist, composer, and editor August Wilhelm Julius Rietz accepted Mendelssohn's invitation in 1834 to come to Düsseldorf as second conductor at Immermann's City Theater (see figure 5.4). He assumed this position

Fig. 5.4. Julius Rietz in Düsseldorf, *drawing. From Richard Fellner,* Geschichte einer Deutschen Musterbühne: Karl Immermanns Leitung des Stadttheaters zu Düsseldorf *(Stuttgart: Hoffmann, 1888).*

on 1 October of that year. The city council named Rietz to succeed Mendelssohn as Düsseldorf's music director on 24 July 1835. Rietz assumed the by now traditional responsibilities: conducting the public subscription concerts of the city orchestra and chorus, directing the music of the two principal churches, and serving as musical intendant of the city theater. Yet he had to supplement his small salary as the Rhine capital's music director by giving private lessons in singing, piano, and cello. Rietz also officiated as chief conductor of the Lower Rhine Music Festivals held in Düsseldorf in 1845, 1856, and 1869. He also conducted these events in Aachen in 1864, 1867, and 1873.[38]

Although he encountered recurring discipline problems in the orchestra, Rietz's determination eventually raised performance standards to a new high. Through his diligence he also reorganized several rival associations, including the powerful *Verein zur Beförderung der Tonkunst* (Society for the Advancement of Music) into the *Allgemeiner Musikverein* (General Music Society), thereby efficiently concentrating the city's musical forces.[39]

Like Mendelssohn, Rietz experienced difficulties with Immermann, who opposed Rietz's preference for German over Italian operas. For the commercial survival of the theater, however, Immermann favored modish Italian operas, insisting that "we cannot pay great virtuosos, but, rather, everything must proceed from . . . average powers." Eventually the theater council, backed by Immermann, thus managed to dismiss Rietz in the summer of 1835, though the latter returned as musical intendant at the beginning of 1842, two years after Immermann's death.[40]

With the cooperation of influential citizens, Rietz had also sought to increase Düsseldorf's share in financing the Lower Rhine Music Festivals. These events incurred mounting deficits because of the greatly expanded concerts, number of performers, and increased honoraria for professionals and virtuosos. The financing of the Rhine capital's civic musical activities, in fact, had grown quite complex. In early 1833 the struggling Society for the Advancement of Music, responsible for the public subscription concerts, nevertheless had temporarily paid over half of Mendelssohn's salary, but could not maintain this practice. The Choral Society was then compelled to fund the remaining amount.[41]

As with Mendelssohn, Rietz enjoyed the company of the local nobility, the highest-ranking civil servants, and industrialists, all united by education and wealth in a newly powerful upper layer of the middle classes. Again as with Mendelssohn, this group also included the city's "Berlin colony," headed by Prince Friedrich of Prussia and many Prussian military officers and government bureaucrats, as well as Mendelssohn's artist friends Hilde-brandt, Plüddemann, Lessing, and Schirmer. Rietz described Düsseldorf as "Florence on the Rhine."[42]

During Rietz's twelve years as the city's music director, his reputation as a conductor continually rose. Like Mendelssohn earlier and Schumann later, Rietz, too, composed major works in this provincial capital. He also performed occasionally on the cello with such distinguished musicians as his friend Ferdinand Hiller, then kapellmeister in Dresden, who directly succeeded him in his city post. While Rietz directed Düsseldorf's music, moreover, an important new dilettante musical organization emerged, the *Männergesangverein* (Men's Song Society), established in 1842.[43] Rietz left Düs-seldorf in June 1847 to replace Ferdinand Stegmayr (1803–63) as director of the Leipzig Singakademie and Niels Gade (1817–90) as the theater kapell-meister there beginning on 1 October 1847. On 27 November 1848 Rietz explained his departure from Düsseldorf in a letter to Breitkopf and Härtel: "I have been . . . compelled to give up my position here because of the truly disagreeable relationships and the vulgarity, transcending all description, of the musicians, whom I have had to endure for 12 years."[44]

HILLER

The city music directorship therefore fell vacant until November, when Hiller assumed the position. He already had acquired a distinguished repu-tation as a conductor, teacher, composer, essayist, and pianist while main-taining close friendships with Chopin, Liszt, Berlioz, Spohr, Mendelssohn, the Schumanns, David, Joachim, and many other important nineteenth-century musicians. He would also establish good relations with some of the Düsseldorf artists so supportive of Mendelssohn (see figure 5.5).

The negotiations between Hiller and the General Music Society execu-tive committee illustrate how the citizens of a moderately sized nineteenth-century German city chose to realize their high musical ideals and objec-tives. The physician Wolfgang Müller von Königswinter (1816–73), one of Düsseldorf's enlightened musical connoisseurs and an important member of the General Music Society, guided the contract bargaining. On 12 June 1847 Müller set forth Hiller's duties and salary. Hiller would annually con-duct ten General Music Society winter subscription concerts, three to four masses, the evening performances in the two principal city churches during

Fig. 5.5. Chr.P——s (?), Ferdinand Hiller in Musicians' Circle: Recollections of the music festival in Düsseldorf. Lithograph, 1853. Hiller is surrounded by the musicians David, Pixis, von Königslöw, von Wasielewski, Grützmacher, and others. Hiller's left index finger points to an image, possibly of the famous music critic Hanslick. From Kast, Schumanns rheinische *Jahre, no. 134, p. 122. Courtesy of the Stadtmuseum Düsseldorf.*

Holy Week, and the weekly rehearsals of the Choral Society. He would also give private music lessons and conduct opera at the City Theater.[45]

Müller extolled Düsseldorf's enlightened support of serious music, urging Hiller "not to believe what Mendelssohn [had] said against Düsseldorf." But he apologized for the city's lack of truly "superior musicians."[46] In reply, Hiller emphasized his achievements in Dresden, where he had founded subscription concerts, conducted a Choral Society, and prepared a new opera, soon to be performed. Yet, apparently unaware of Düsseldorf's value in Prussian eyes, Hiller complained that the Rhine capital, unlike Dresden, lay "a bit far from the centers of German music." He also objected that the salary offered, "although quite respectable," was "hardly sufficient" to cover his relocation.[47] Like his predecessors, he additionally requested a vacation long enough for composition.

As negotiations dragged on their bureaucratic way, Müller blamed the committee's delay in its decision on the critical pre-1848 economic and political situation. On 28 September 1847 Müller declared that the executive committee had unanimously voted to approve Hiller's appointment. Earlier Müller had disclosed that two committee members had especially favored Hiller: the influential Düsseldorf notary Joseph Euler (1804–86), later to be Schumann's steadfast supporter, and the city attorney, Bloem.[48] Müller also divulged that Hiller's excellent professional reputation had substantially influenced the final decision, as with Burgmüller and Mendelssohn earlier and Schumann later. Hiller assumed the city music directorship in November 1847.

During the following February, Hiller, as Euler had predicted, praised Düsseldorf's "friendly, cultivated people." He lauded their "dependable hospitality typical of Rhinelanders" and their positive response to his musical ambitions: "All lies in my hands—the concerts, the excellent Choral Society, etc. . . . The advantages of my position here are that it does not give me too much and [gives] only musically significant things to do. . . . I have thereby the greatest external and inner peace for my new works because everything is tightly regulated."[49]

Because of the pressures from organizing concerts, participation in local politics, and connections with the Düsseldorf art establishment, Hiller nevertheless composed relatively little in the Rhine city. In 1850 he became music director of Cologne, another major urban center in the Prussian Rhine Province. There he established the city conservatory, became its first director, and otherwise continued to exercise an important influence on music in the Rhineland. For example, he conducted the Lower Rhine Music Festivals held in Düsseldorf in 1853, 1855, and 1860 and those in Cologne in 1858, 1862, 1865, and 1883.[50]

SCHUMANN'S STORMY TENURE

On 2 September 1850 a train drew into Düsseldorf bringing Robert Schumann and his family from Dresden to their new home, where the composer had been named city music director.[51] Hiller and the General Music Society executive committee greeted the Schumanns at the railway station. That evening the local *Liedertafel*, under its conductor, Julius Tausch (1827–95), serenaded the new arrivals. Within a week the city orchestra had performed in the Schumanns' honor and the committee had sponsored a concert by local dilettante singers consisting exclusively of Schumann's compositions. A banquet and formal ball followed with dignified speeches offered by such city government officials as Deputy Mayor Wortmann.[52]

This extraordinary attention paid to Schumann attested to the executive committee's and city council's unqualified confidence that the prestige of the composer and his wife, Clara, "the outstanding piano virtuoso," would benefit Düsseldorf. Only a year after the city's initial glorious welcome, however, relationships between Schumann and the city's dilettante musical establishment had deteriorated alarmingly. The situation degenerated steadily and irreversibly until the composer attempted suicide in the Rhine in February 1854.

At first, Schumann's relationship with Düsseldorf offered much promise. The composer's contract had been determined by the General Music Society's executive committee and the city council. It specified that Schumann, more or less like his predecessors, would annually conduct nine or ten General Music Society subscription concerts, the weekly rehearsals of the Choral Society, and regular performances in the two city churches on Catholic feast days.[53] Schumann began with a well-drilled orchestra, his legacy from Mendelssohn, Rietz, and Hiller. His correspondence between January 1850 and June 1851 revealed his high opinion of Düsseldorf's musical organizations and its public, although Schumann had recollected Mendelssohn's and Rietz's warnings about the powerful dilettante segment of the city orchestra.[54]

Clara Schumann's diary, too, indicated the favorable beginning of the relationship between Schumann and the Düsseldorf musical establishment. In September 1850 she wrote, "Robert was very pleased with the [Choral Society]; it is very large, and the sopranos especially sound quite beautifully fresh. . . . For the little city," she added a few days later, "the orchestra is quite excellent, which makes Robert very satisfied."[55]

Clara additionally emphasized Robert's warm relations and personal music making with the dilettante connoisseurs such as the aging Schadow and his circle of artists: Theodor Hildebrandt (1804–61), Christian Köhler (1809–61), Carl Friedrich Lessing (1808–80), and Carl Ferdinand Sohn (1805–67). The Schumanns' group of supporters further included the amateur composer, poet, and conductor Dr. Richard Hasenclever (1813–76), a member of the city board of health and one of the family's personal physician-friends. The cénacle further consisted of the city notary Euler and Hiller's earlier negotiator, Wolfgang Müller von Königswinter, another Schumann physician-friend.[56]

In the fall of 1851 Schumann established two new dilettante musical organizations that he would direct: a Sängerkränzchen and Quartettkränzchen, each meeting every two weeks in private homes. The repertoire of the first consisted of lieder, Bach motets, and Renaissance choral music. The other group performed instrumental chamber music, including recently composed works.[57] Although both organizations failed within a few months, the *Düsseldorfer Journal* nevertheless boasted about city musical life during Schumann's first season there: "The public musical life of Düsseldorf . . . has already assumed an honored place, for a number of years, among comparable artistic efforts of the greatest cities of Germany."[58]

Schumann's Rhenish Symphony and Overture to Hermann und Dorothea: *Products of Düsseldorf*   The Düsseldorf premiere of Schumann's Third Symphony in E-flat Major, op. 97, took place on 6 February 1851. The composer's concertmaster, Wasielewski, christened it the "Rhenish." (Schumann's Rhine-connected opera *Genoveva* had been first performed in Leipzig on 25 June 1850.) The last of his four symphonies in order of composition, the "Rhenish" was composed between 2 November and 9 December 1850. Schumann himself conducted the premiere as part of eight City Orchestra subscription concerts presented under his direction during the 1850–51 season.

The composition of the Third Symphony had followed upon a visit by the Schumanns to Cologne on 29 September 1850. There they had been profoundly moved by the majestic beauty of the cathedral, the site on the following day of Cardinal Archbishop Geissel's enthronement.

To describe it in the most general terms, Schumann's final symphony consists of a suite of five movements, each a musical landscape idyll in which the symphonic ideal is often propelled by the forces of *Volkstümlichkeit* (see example 5.1). After the ebullient opening movement (*Lebhaft*), where traditional sonata form mingles with cyclic procedures connecting the first and second themes, Schumann presents a rustic scherzo displaying the *volkstümlich* earthiness of a *Ländler*, the elemental dance character of which is reinforced by powerful unison writing.

After a delicate intermezzo (*Nicht schnell*), the fourth movement (*Feierlich*), traditionally called the "Cathedral Scene," evokes a solemn image of the lofty Cologne landmark. The force of the movement's driving polyphony—a musical allusion to the medieval past of the cathedral and of the ancient Rhine over which it stands—is made all the more compelling by the density of its orchestration. The archaic character also derives from the commanding pronouncements of the horns and trombones. In the finale (again *Lebhaft*), the thrust of the brass, emboldened by lusty passages of

Ex. 5.1. R. Schumann, Third Symphony in E-flat Major ("Rhenish"), op. 97, fourth movement. In Robert Schumann's Werke, *ed. C. Schumann (Leipzig: Breitkopf & Härtel, 1887), 1/4, p. 279(37), meas. 1–6.*

syncopation, is largely accountable for the relentless fury of the movement. The latter is introduced by a theme that, in its underlying interval of a fourth, suggests cyclic kinship with the initial subjects of the first, second, and fourth movements. Though in the major mode, a later reminiscence of the fourth movement's pressing theme and other scattered thematic remembrances contribute to the unity of the symphony as a whole.

In this work, which Schumann had originally envisioned as a depiction of life on the Rhine, the composer's musical imagination ranges over a broad spectrum of styles and procedures. Above all, he captures two facets of nature also encapsulated in the Rheinlieder of the 1840–50 decade, immediately prior to the composition of the symphony: touches of homespun *Volkstümlichkeit*, as in the scherzo, re-creating that German Romantic ideal of humankind's affinity to nature at its most fundamental; and the evocation in the fourth movement, which taps the core of that man-made beauty, of the Cologne Cathedral, so closely associated with the ancient Rhine itself. Expressed in many different nineteenth-century art forms, the Germans' awe of the grandeur of the structure, in fact, exemplifies once more that peculiarly Romantic attachment to the Gothic, which Caspar David Friedrich and Johann Wolfgang von Goethe identified with the enfolding branches of trees. This was nature at its most sublime. Indeed, the entire symphony could be described as a series of musical panoramas emblematic of the Rhine itself. At the same time, Schumann's Third Symphony realized an ideal presented earlier in this study, a notion central to nineteenth-century thinking: art not as an imitation of nature, but as the deepest expression of feelings attributed to nature, the inner nature of the world and of humankind. Schumann found his version of this expression in the art of symphonic composition.

The year 1851 also marked the appearance of another Rhine-related work, Schumann's Overture to *Hermann und Dorothea*, op. 136. It was written to accompany Goethe's *Volks-Epos* dating from the spring of 1797. The action of the epic poem takes place in the Rhine area near Strassburg, where hordes of refugees streamed across the river in a crisis of 1732. Goethe, a native Rhinelander, transposed the tale of two heroic and royal lovers to the milieu of the common *Volk*, although the poem was intended as a response to the politically uneasy times following the French Revolution.[59]

Troubling Times   Despite his early successes in Düsseldorf, however, friction erupted between Schumann and the city's musical establishment even during that initial year. In March 1851 a local newspaper reported criticism of Schumann's conducting by an anonymous member of the General Music Society's executive committee. The Choral Society, consisting mostly of inexperienced dilettantes, complained that it had been accustomed to rehearsing with the conductor himself at the piano. Schumann, the organization complained, directed the performers from a desk with Clara accompanying at the keyboard. In addition, the chorus faulted the composer's conducting style as unintelligible, reserved, even taciturn, and many society members balked at Schumann's scheduling of extra rehearsals. Clara herself once remarked that, when conducting, her husband would lose himself in the music, forgetting performers awaiting his cues, then would become irritated by imprecise entrances and unexpected dissonances. This turmoil, in turn, eroded discipline and regular attendance.[60]

By September 1851 both Schumann's mental condition and his relationship with the dilettante musical establishment had further eroded. On 6 September, after a planning conference for the coming season held by the Choral Society's executive committee, Clara noted in her diary, "storm with [Deputy Mayor] Wortmann." Distraught by a rehearsal of Bach's *St. Matthew Passion* in March 1852, she lamented over the mostly dilettante chorus: "The people here have respect neither for art nor for the conductor! . . . The ladies hardly open their mouths, and they behave (naturally with the exception of several trained singers) so impolitely, sit down when singing, throw their feet and hands around like quite undisciplined youngsters."[61]

In the spring of 1852 the General Music Society's executive committee, many performers, and a sizable segment of the public increasingly criticized Schumann's conducting, complaining about his distracted personal manner and clumsiness. Choral and orchestral discipline steadily deteriorated, however, and by the summer Schumann's debilitating ill health forced him temporarily to relinquish conducting to Julius Tausch, his deputy.[62] After the composer's return in December, the General Music Society executive committee directed Tausch to conduct all rehearsals, leaving Schumann only performances to conduct. Two days later, Ruppert Becker (1830–87), who had succeeded Schumann's later biographer Josef Wilhelm von Wasielewski as the orchestra's concertmaster, noted, "This evening brought news that enraged everybody: the concert directors of the Choral Society had written Schumann an uncivil letter in which they sought to rid themselves of his conducting."[63] On 29 December Becker continued: "The orchestra could accomplish salutary things only through the greatest strictness and through subordination to the conductor. Both are lacking. . . . The dilettantes . . . as everywhere, ruin the situation. How unpleasant it is to make music with them!"[64]

Deputy Mayor Wortmann remarked that the orchestra, which contained both amateur and professional players, "misses, under Herr Schumann, the solid, sure indication of tempos, even beats, clear, definite, and comprehensible directions."[65] During the 1852–53 season, moreover, Schumann's worsening illness even caused tempos to appear too fast to him.[66] His letters of this period, however, reveal some interesting aspects of the power wielded by the Düsseldorf middle-class *dilettanti*. The General Music Society executive committee, he noted, shared with him the selection of music for the winter subscription concert series as well as the program and virtuoso soloists for the Lower Rhine Music Festival held at Düsseldorf in 1853, at which Schumann conducted.[67]

Schumann's Festival Overture on the "Rheinweinlied"   Schumann's *Fest-Ouverture mit Gesang über das "Rheinweinlied" für Orchester und Chor*, op. 123, was premiered at this festival during the performance of 17 May.[68] Completed in April 1853, it was the composer's setting (with a text version by Wilhelm Müller) of Johann André's "Rheinweinlied," in turn a setting of Matthias Claudius's poem "Bekränzt mit Laub" (see example 5.2). The latter was listed in the Hofmeister catalogue as published in the 1840–50 decade (see the Index of Rheinlieder). This joyous paean to the Rhine and its wine preserves the *volkstümlich* original melody while extending it with a lengthy, densely scored orchestral introduction. In its martial simplicity and solemnity, the introduction resembles the more openly "patriotic" type of Rheinlied. The first part, a dignified, celebratory fantasy on André's melody, juxtaposes two contrasting styles in alternation: a section in which the full orchestra spews forth exuberant fanfares offered by a brass and woodwind section of eight members each, and lighter episodes that revel in Schumann's characteristic mood of caprice. Here, as in the heroic stance of the tenor's reflective, recitative-like solo and in the following choral proclamation of the lied (reduced to soloists at one point), one might sense the grandiose spirit of the finale of Beethoven's Ninth Symphony or of a choral scene in Wagner's *Tannhäuser*. Yet Schumann preserves the *Volkstümlichkeit* of a modest *Volkslied* in tones of cultural and national pride, as, for example, when the chorus confidently concludes, "If anyone be sad, give him [Rhine] wine."

Further Strife   But from the beginning of Düsseldorf's 1853–54 season, complaints about Schumann's conducting continued and even intensified. Wortmann complained that Schumann had "changed the programs, or-

Ex. 5.2. R. Schumann, Fest-Ouverture mit Gesang über das Rheinweinlied "Bekränzt mit Laub" für Orchester und Chor, *op. 123, Choral Entrance. In* Robert Schumann's Werke, *2/5, p. 24.*

dered music, engaged out-of-town artists, and generally behaved as if no [General Music Society] executive committee existed." He even altered the orchestra rehearsal schedule.[69] A disastrous Choral Society performance of a mass by Moritz Hauptmann (1792–1860) conducted by Schumann at the Maximilian Church on 16 October 1853 angered the city's musical leaders, ultimately triggering the calamitous conclusion of the composer's music directorship. At the rehearsal, a bewildered Schumann had continued to conduct even after the miserable music making had ended. The Choral Society informed Schumann that it would no longer sing under him. The General Music Society executive committee ultimately and unanimously directed Schumann to relinquish to Tausch the conducting of all but his own compositions.[70]

During the following weeks, public opinion, voiced through official channels, continued to disparage the composer's conducting. An anonymous essayist for Cologne's *Niederrheinische Musikzeitung* on 12 November 1853 reflected that Schumann "lacks all stimulating liveliness, certainty, and agility, which are the most indispensable for a musical conductor precisely . . . where, as with us, the orchestra partly, the chorus completely consists of dilettantes."[71]

Through this tragic affair, one can nevertheless observe the plethora of conflicting personal and political relationships within Düsseldorf's musical and municipal power structure, about which Schumann himself once remarked sardonically, in regard to this situation, that there was "no special harmony, about as much as exists in the first chord of the finale in [Beethoven's] Ninth Symphony."[72] On 6 December 1853 Mayor Hammers wrote to Schumann, offering to arbitrate or at least investigate the situation through a subcommittee of the city council. The municipality itself compassionately continued to pay Schumann's salary until mid-1855.[73] Because of Schumann's irreversibly deteriorating condition, however, the city council chose Tausch to succeed him, halting the battles at last. On 27 February 1854 the composer attempted suicide in the Rhine in an extreme gesture of pathological Rhine symbolism. On 4 March 1854 he was committed to a private mental hospital at Endenich near Bonn, where he died over two years later. The *Niederrheinische Musikzeitung* of 28 February 1855 sadly observed, "With a position in which men like Mendelssohn, Rietz, Hiller, and Schumann have worked, . . . even here one is convinced that a famous name and great compositional talent—in spite of the splendor that they indeed lent it—do not suffice to bring a city's musical life to full bloom."[74]

DÜSSELDORF AT THE HEART OF
CHANGE: ART IMITATING LIFE

The twenty-year period encompassing the music directorships of Mendelssohn through Schumann in Düsseldorf coincided with a socioeconomic and political upheaval that transformed the European continent, and with particular intensity in such expanding urban centers as those in the Rhine area. Düsseldorf, strategically located on this vital ancient waterway coursing through the heart of a continent, lay in the epicenter of the nascent Industrial Revolution, making it highly vulnerable to forces that metamorphosed the organization and performance of music.

The shift from aristocratic to public patronage signified other changes as well. With the court system, one tends to perceive the patron as a single entity, while in the "liberated" nineteenth century "the patron" was more diversified, more diffuse in outlook, and more numerous. In this latter situation, the composer faced a relatively greater range of choices and responsibilities in the creation and disposition of his compositions and, with the conductor and performer, may have become more dependent on instantaneous, mass public response. This altered set of circumstances, on the one hand, explains Arnold Hauser's view that Romantic works of art in all fields, in fact, exposed their creators to an inexorable "state of tension and opposition towards the public, as the century evolved."[75] This conflict plagued the Düsseldorf music directors and the municipal arts establishment into the 1850s. On the other hand, with the nineteenth-century transition from courtly to corporate patrons, perhaps one set of intrigues was merely replaced with another. One need only reflect on the factions aligned in the various musical controversies in Düsseldorf at this time to see clear evidence of this state of affairs.

Contradictions also arose in the course of professionalization. Despite his struggles with Düsseldorf's dilettante organizations, for example, Schumann and his virtuoso wife routinely included amateur-connoisseurs in their domestic music making. The composer himself, moreover, established two amateur choral groups, thus obfuscating distinctions between dilettante and professional even further. In addition, several musical amateur-connoisseurs, though troubled by Schumann's deteriorating musical performance, later contributed emotional and financial support to the ailing composer during the painful controversies of his final tragic months.

As the ideals of Rhineland organizations and the texts of the Rheinlieder have shown, the burgeoning of *Liedertafeln* produced a new sense of "Germanic" camaraderie among the Germans in the post-Napoleonic decades.[76] This phenomenon, consummately represented by nineteenth-century Düsseldorf, raises some interesting questions about the social uses of music. Did the rising number of *Liedertafeln*, with their democratic orientation, absorb the very dilettantes now being excluded from the more organized and regulated orchestral and choral institutions by the increasing proportion of professional musicians? Did professionalism thus indirectly lend support to the cultural nationalism nurtured in these organizations by forcing the displaced dilettantes to assemble under the convenient guise of "Germanness"?

"Provincial" though it was, Düsseldorf lay directly in the midst of a pan-European upheaval that gradually permitted the upper middle classes to assume the roles of musical patron and public. Their sovereignty has endured into the twentieth century. For seemingly diverse causes, "the reign of the *dilettanti*" had shifted permanently and inexorably from the arena of performance to that of the administration of an urban musical culture. The Rhine capital's distinguished music directors had thus met headlong those overwhelming forces of change against which they could not remain immune. As Leon Mayhew observes: "Artists themselves are not free from the web of affiliation; indeed they are dependent upon it for sustenance, and hence are caught up (even tossed about) in the trends and transformations we call social change."[77]

As viewed in Düsseldorf during the Rhine crisis decade and a few years before and after that period, these socioeconomic transformations showed "in practice" many of the themes voiced in the Rheinlieder of that era, particularly the dreams of a single German nation.

THE NEW PUBLIC AND THE REORDERING OF THE MUSICAL ESTABLISHMENT: THE LOWER RHINE MUSIC FESTIVALS, 1818–1867

The first half-century of the Lower Rhine Music Festivals extended from 1818 to 1867.[78] The "Rheinlieder Decade" of 1840–50 marked the midway point in this span of years. As with Düsseldorf itself, these events further exemplified the process by which an expanding, increasingly affluent, enlightened, and urban bourgeoisie, especially powerful in the Rhineland, acquired control over the musical establishment and provided the substance of a new mass public. The festivals, inaugurated by knowledgeable musical amateurs in Düsseldorf, nearby Elberfeld, Cologne, and Aachen, evolved into an imposing organization of professional musicians administered by city governments.

Like Düsseldorf in particular, the Rhineland as a whole was an important center of German Romantic music, as the Lower Rhine Music Festivals demonstrated. A look at some of the salient aspects of these events brings to light issues fundamental to an understanding of the musical phenomena characterizing German nineteenth-century history: stability and changes in the repertoire; the dramatic rise in professionalism, accompanied nevertheless by an enduring dilettantism; changing proportions of vocal and instrumental musicians; the role of various municipalities in the organization of these events; the social aspects of the festivals; and expansion in geographical area, in the number of performers, and in the size of the audience, necessitating continually improved concert facilities. Moreover, the festivals were indirect expressions of *Volkstümlichkeit* in the massive extent of their performing forces and in the equally gigantic size of their audiences. In addition, lieder gradually became accepted into the repertoire, if only in a somewhat random way at first.

The examination of the Rheinlieder and their impact in chapter 2 demonstrated that, in the realm of music alone, the spread of periodicals, the expansion of publication, and the growth of criticism attested to a new commercial spirit, attuned to the requirements of public demand. This demand, moreover, was coupled with the rise of a vast complex of bourgeois musical organizations.

Furthermore, with the French menace temporarily removed and the consequent restoration of civil stability following the Wars of Liberation, German Romantics could freely indulge in the ideal of *Volkstümlichkeit* that these festivals embodied. The mass musical gatherings were occasions for spirited communal relationships in the name of art and for the expression of mounting pride in the German musical legacy, so evident in the Rheinlieder texts. The view that the Lower Rhine Music Festivals directly voiced cultural and national impulses was expressed by the *Kölner Zeitung* less than a year after the Rhine crisis. The comment concerned the twenty-third festival, held in Cologne: "That is a true national festival, to become conscious of the noblest treasures of the nation in inspired association, for that is a spiritual possession no one can steal."[79]

This development, characteristic throughout urban areas of the Rhine-land and elsewhere in Germany from early in the century, was clearly encouraged by certain external forces. These included the late eighteenth-century English choral movement and the Pestalozzian ideal of the Swiss Hans Georg Nägeli: that choral singing unites the folk in the common pursuit of good music. Carl Friedrich Zelter's founding of the Berlin *Lieder-tafel*, as described earlier, inaugurated another significant phase in the development of male choral singing.[80] And for the rest of the Prussian Rhine Province, the choral movement offered a channel for the expression of common feelings of fellowship, as well as sentiments of regional and pan-German patriotism unleashed by the years of French presence.

An analogous proliferation of similarly motivated singing groups and choral festivals elsewhere in nineteenth-century Europe paralleled developments in Germany. A profusion of lay choral societies, the *Orphéons*, spread extensively through France from about the 1830s. Large numbers of dilettante singing societies had for decades formed an important element of English musical life. Mammoth choral performances long remained the vogue among the Swiss, Dutch, and Flemish. *Volkstümlichkeit* was also mirrored in the camaraderie of these events. But, in the case of Rhine music festivals, *volkstümlich* sociability was aided by a fascination with nature that was easily encouraged by the Rhineland's literally "down-to-earth" scenic beauties.

Both the more general music festivals and more specialized ones held by choral societies represented the musical manifestation of German nationalistic meetings in various fields organized from the early 1820s. Periodic national conferences of *Germanisten* (teachers of German and Germanic philology), fellow German academicians, scientists, farmers, attorneys, and other special interest groups had already been well established by the 1840s.[81]

In 1843 the Rhenish political scientist Peter Kaufmann (1804–72) conceived the idea of establishing more generalized "national festivals of the German people." These were to take place every three years, for the purpose of intensifying the idealization of German nationalistic sentiments. Kaufmann proposed that these festivals be combined with the more specialized ones already instituted. Those selected as the finest representatives of the German fatherland would win "national prizes."[82]

Julius Alf listed several indications that the *Volkstümlichkeit* ideal, implying for the German Romantics both popular appeal and patriotism, was at work in the Lower Rhine festivals at a fairly early date. The *Allgemeine musikalische Zeitung* reported that at the festival of 1828, "concertos and [solo] songs are excluded" at the Lower Rhine Music Festivals, for the latter are "serious matters and employ" the broadest means.[83] The festival statutes of 1830 continued to state that solo performances were to be prohibited. In referring to the festival of 1835, Otto Jahn remarked that "such a large, mixed public demands a completely precise category of works, . . . those that have their effect through the masses and on the masses."[84]

But the official festival programs do not tell the whole story. In describing the 1842 festival at Düsseldorf, Alf commented that "the newspapers took special pains to extol the '*Volkstümlichkeit*' of the institution [i.e., festival] and spent many words on justifying the festival as a 'Rhenish national celebration.' "[85]

All of these cultural factors provided formative influences in shaping the Lower Rhine Music Festivals. In part through these festivals, their host cities became important arbiters of culture engrossed in developing and subsidizing their local musical institutions. The urban citizenry supported the festival concerts, not only through their willingness to press for municipal subsidy and their enthusiastic musical entrepreneurship, but also through the purchase of tickets for participation in, and attendance at, the concerts. In the 1820s and 1830s, for example, the sale of concert tickets combined with municipal subsidies generally covered expenses, which had risen during this time from three thousand to four thousand thalers. The cost of several of these earlier festivals nevertheless could be completely defrayed only through additional city funds. By the 1840s municipal subsidies and admission prices were considerably increased, rehearsals were opened to a constantly expanding public, and further city subsidies were granted. By the 1860s festival expenses had risen to annual sums between six thousand and seven thousand thalers, particularly as a result of honoraria paid to professional performers, though substantial surpluses were gained at Düsseldorf and Aachen.[86]

Despite the declarations of Schumann's *Davidsbündler*, however, that the Romantic musical public tended to favor mediocrity and commercial gain over deeper aesthetic values, the history of the Lower Rhine Music Festivals discloses that more than just occasionally even the "ordinary" middle classes sought the highest standards in music and music making. In reviewing the first Lower Rhine Music Festival held in Aachen in 1825, the Leipzig *Allgemeine musikalische Zeitung* reported: "The musical alliance on the Lower Rhine

. . . has made its task the annual preparation of a Whitsuntide festival to the muse of music through the performance of the most significant works of older and more recent times."[87]

Similarly, the chronicler Hauchecorne, reminiscing over the first half-century of these Lower Rhine events, concluded: "The friends of music, who join annually for the performance of greater classical works of music of older and more recent times and who make arrangements thereto, have enjoyed the most salutary effects of their unselfish endeavors for the development and the propagation of good music on the Lower Rhine and in the adjoining regions."[88]

MUSICAL LIFE IN THE FESTIVAL CITIES

Düsseldorf, Elberfeld, Cologne, and Aachen belonged to the Prussian Rhine Province, created in 1815. All four had enjoyed long musical traditions. At the founding of the Lower Rhine Music Festivals in 1818, Düsseldorf, the capital of the province, was also its musical center. We have already explored several decades in its musical life.

Elberfeld   Elberfeld, twenty-five kilometers east of Düsseldorf in the Ruhr valley, had attained a prominent commercial and industrial position by 1850, thereby affording stable support for musical ventures.[89] The civil stability gained by the Wars of Liberation and the excitement stimulated by the Lower Rhine Music Festivals considerably encouraged the town's spirit of musical enterprise. The *Singschule* was enlarged in 1815 into the Elberfeld *Gesangverein*, a pivotal group in the founding of these festivals. Toward midcentury other municipal musical organizations gradually emerged, the most important of which were the town's first permanent orchestra, founded in 1845; the *Instrumentalverein* (instrumental society), organized in 1856 and expanded into the municipal orchestra in 1864; and the *Konzertgesellschaft* (concert society), started in 1862, which regularly attracted distinguished solo artists.[90]

Aachen   Aachen marked the western frontier of the Prussian Rhine Province. Charlemagne's northern capital, site of a great cathedral and a popular spa, it had been a cultural crossroads between Germans and Lowlanders for centuries. Through the eighteenth century, musical activity in Aachen centered around the requirements of the cathedral and the tastes of a sophisticated spa public that favored professional orchestral concerts with famous traveling virtuosi. But the Napoleonic occupation from 1794 to 1814 significantly altered the structure of musical life in Aachen. Thus, by the time the Prussians had arrived, the ties between music and a secular or religious elite had yielded in Aachen, as elsewhere in the Rhineland, to a broader civic orientation of culture based on the musical interests of merchants, professionals, and civil servants.

The position of city music director, with a salary paid by the city council, was established in 1804, absorbing the office of cathedral kapellmeister until 1852. At this date the administration of cathedral music again became an independent matter. In 1828 the Aachen city council additionally assigned to the music director the duties of theater kapellmeister. The first music director, Karl Mathias Engels (1764–1823), was succeeded in 1835 by Beethoven's amanuensis Anton Schindler (1795–1864). The Hungarian pianist Karl von Turanyi (1805–73), who held the position from 1841 to 1858, was succeeded by Franz Wüllner (1832–1902), Schindler's one-time student. Wüllner presided until 1865. A number of musical organizations also emerged under municipal control: the Aachen *Bläserkorps*, established in 1804; a twenty-seven-member orchestra, organized in 1827, chiefly to serve the city opera; a thirty-two-member professional municipal orchestra, the first city orchestra in the Rhineland, formed in 1852 from Aachen's *Harmoniekorps*; and the *Städtischer Gesangverein*, municipalized in 1854.[91] The latter, especially, manifested the surge of amateur choral singing—most commonly in exclusively male organizations—that developed in Aachen from around 1820.

Cologne   The nineteenth-century bourgeoisie of Cologne inherited substantial musical traditions from the previous century and continued to experience the lingering musical influence of the city's ancient religious establishments. Before 1800 the *Ratskapelle* and musicians' guilds contributed substantially to Cologne's musical life. The *Musikalische Akademie*, founded in 1743, sponsored programs typically consisting of symphonies and a concluding oratorio or passion; and *Kaufmannskonzerte* (merchants' concerts) were instituted through an alliance of several musical organizations.[92] The French, who occupied Cologne in 1794, however, noticeably impaired the city's economy and cultural life. Numerous religious establishments with long musical traditions, for example, were dissolved or destroyed.

The advent of Prussian rule in 1815 and the rapid development of steamboat and railway systems restored civil and political stability and gave Cologne a share of control over Rhineland trade and German commerce.[93] Soon new performing societies and other important urban musical institutions made their appearance. A group of musical amateurs organized the *Musikalische Gesellschaft* in 1812 and the *Singverein* in 1820. Its members included representatives of the city's most distinguished families, such as that of the lord mayor, Steinberger.[94] In 1827 these two societies merged to form the municipal *Konzertgesellschaft*, the orchestra of which consisted of amateurs, military musicians, members of the reorganized cathedral chapel, and theater musicians.[95]

During the 1830s and 1840s many other musical institutions appeared in Cologne: the *Singakademie* and the *Liedertafel* in 1836; the Cologne Quartet in 1839; the *Städtischer Gesangverein* (consisting of members of the *Singakademie*, the *Liedertafel*, and the *Musikalische Gesellschaft*) in 1840; the *Kölner-Männer-Gesang-Verein* in 1842; and the *Philharmonische Gesellschaft* in 1846.[96]

The socioeconomic equilibrium and prosperity enjoyed by the Colognese in the post-Napoleonic era had also sustained long-standing operatic traditions. The city opened its first standing theater in 1822 and its second in 1829. In addition, Cologne welcomed, though not so intensively as Aachen, a plethora of traveling virtuosi en route to Paris and London.[97]

As in other cities, the role of the urban populace in Cologne's musical establishment was further secured with the creation of a city music directorship in the Rhine crisis year of 1840.[98] The major responsibilities of the director, an employee of the city council, included the *Singverein*, the *Konzertgesellschaft*, the Lower Rhine Music Festivals, and the opera. The first musician to hold this post was Conradin Kreutzer (1840–42), whose setting of Becker's Rhine poem was hailed as the "Colognaise" (see example 4.3). Kreutzer was succeeded by Heinrich Dorn (1842–49) and Ferdinand Hiller (1850–85), the latter having just left Düsseldorf. In 1845 Dorn, as music director, founded the *Rheinische Musikschule*, yet another municipal institution controlled and subsidized by the city council. It was the predecessor of Cologne's *Konservatorium*, established in 1850 by Hiller.[99]

THE LOWER RHINE MUSIC FESTIVALS

On the evening of 3 November 1817, in Düsseldorf's Hotel Brass, a zealous band of informed musical amateurs met with Johannes Schornstein (d. 1853), music director in Elberfeld and organist of the Reformed Church there. Together they began plans to organize a two-day music festival to be held during Whitsuntide the following spring.[100] Through the establishment of these festivals, the group aspired to advance the performance of good music on the Lower Rhine by combining vocal and instrumental resources not available in any single city.[101]

The first half-century of the Lower Rhine Music Festivals provides a rich sampling of the municipalization of music during Germany's Romantic era. These festivals, at first lasting two days with a concert on each, rapidly increased in popularity. Eventually the festival organizers added a third day's concert as well as open rehearsals. Fireworks, steamboat and railway excursions, dancing, and Rhine wine further enlivened the holiday atmosphere.

Responsibility for the organization of these festivals during their first fifty years fell to a core of energetic, knowledgeable musical dilettantes, the majority of whom formed the governmental and mercantile backbone of the Rhenish municipalities concerned. These civic leaders—judges, mayors, notaries, physicians, attorneys, building inspectors, merchants, industrialists, and military officers—joined with a few professional musicians to form the board of festival directors for the host city of the year.[102]

For nearly a year before each event, the board, consulting with civic and musical leaders in the other festival towns, worked with the conductors and music director of the host city to determine the programs. The board also bore the responsibility for reserving concert halls, obtaining necessary scores and parts, choosing the soloists, and arranging living accommodations for festival participants and guests from other cities, as well as the juggling of finances.

During their first half-century, the Lower Rhine celebrations passed through four stages. From 1818 to 1824, the first stage, the festivals alternated between Düsseldorf, Elberfeld, and after 1821, Cologne. An oratorio, performed on the first day's concert, became the traditional centerpiece of each festival through the decades. Except for 1824, a Beethoven symphony always followed as the major work of the second day. Occasionally a concerto, along with an aria, overture, and cantata or other shorter choral work, made up the remainder of the program on the second day. All the composers represented were German.[103]

The number of performers more than doubled from 209 in 1818 to 475 by 1824, as detailed in table 5.1.

Although initially the chorus and orchestra had remained of equal dimensions, with about a hundred performers in each group, by 1824 the chorus was half again the size of the orchestra.[104] The festival audience,

TABLE 5.1. FESTIVAL PERSONNEL

	ALL PERFORMERS*	CHORUS	ORCHESTRA
Stage 1			
1818	209	100	95
1819	208	100	100
1820	208	100	100
1821	394	222	158
1822	321	190	123
1823	312	180	120
1824	475	286	178
1818–24 (Average)	304	168 (55%)	125 (41%)
Stage 2			
1825	423	266	147
1826	341	200	130
1827	340	200	130
1828	486	281	193
1829	367	223	135
1830	448	274	163
1832	565	349	205
1833	420	267	142
1834	482	338	133
1825–34 (Average)	430	266 (62%)	153 (36%)
Stage 3			
1835	619	427	179
1836	538	356	172
1837	489	340	141
1838	641	390	169
1839	576	411	155
1840	549	402	134
1841	697	505	182
1842	582	403	170
1843	599	458	132
1844	591	417	167
1845	375*	246*	120*
1846	631	487	131
1847	789	616	164
1835–47 (Average)	590	420 (71%)	155 (26%)

TABLE 5.1 (*continued*)

	ALL PERFORMERS*	CHORUS	ORCHESTRA
Stage 4			
1851	538	392	136
1853	664	490	160
1854	540	392	135
1855	822	649	165
1856	898	723	164
1857	568	417	137
1858	683	519	153
1860	798	630	160
1861	570	425	135
1862	716	569	139
1863	938	781	146
1864	591	451	131
1865	768	621	139
1866	888	734	141
1867	538	407	124
1851–67 (Average)	701	547 (78%)	144 (21%)

(*"All performers" includes chorus, orchestra, vocal and instrumental soloists, and conductors. Next to the figures for 1845, Hauchecorne gives alternative numbers for participants cited as *angemeldet* [registered]: chorus, 464; orchestra, 174; total, 647.)

moreover, increased from around six hundred to approximately one thousand.[105] All the vocal soloists appearing during these years were dilettantes. Their exclusive reign was perhaps the single most prominent characteristic marking the early years of the Lower Rhine Music Festivals.

The second phase of the celebrations extended from 1825, when Aachen joined the host cities, until 1834, a period of further expansion and developing fame. After 1827, indeed, Elberfeld had to withdraw as a festival site, for the town's concert facilities no longer sufficed to accommodate the greatly enlarged festivals.[106]

The number of performers during this period fluctuated somewhat erratically from year to year (see table 5.1, stage 2). In 1832 the figure, though, had reached 565; and by 1834 the chorus size, with 338 members, was over twice that of the orchestra. During this period, the audience increased to 1,410, and several illustrious conductors participated, including Mendelssohn, Ferdinand Ries, Spohr, and Bernard Klein.[107]

Among the seventy-two solo singers of this era, only seven were professionals (see table 5.2). Moreover, only one truly celebrated instrumental soloist participated: the pianist Felix Mendelssohn, who in 1833 first conducted a Lower Rhine Music Festival. This high regard for dilettantes was expressed unambiguously in 1829. A board of directors asked Ferdinand Ries, the conductor of the forthcoming festival, whether he would not prefer a professional soprano soloist from Aachen for his oratorio *Der Sieg des Glaubens*, op. 157, composed specifically for the Lower Rhine Music Festival that year. Ries retorted: "The beautiful voice of the lovely Madame F. would be very pleasant to me; only it is dangerous, and I cannot advise it. You must try to fill the soloist positions with amateurs; it enlivens the participants more and has its own charm. Also it could be objectionable to some participants to have someone from the theater."[108]

For the 1825 festival, the Leipzig *Allgemeine musikalische Zeitung* had similarly commented regarding the vocal soloists, one professional and the remainder dilettantes: "All the solo parts [in Handel's *Alexander's Feast*, Beethoven's *Christus am Ölberge*, and Mozart's *Davidde penitente*] were executed very well and in part with excellent virtuosity. In addition to the most gloriously noted bass Mr. Pillwitz, it was surely dilettantes whose good offices deserve suitable recognition."[109]

The 1825–34 phase was also marked by an expansion of the programming. Now another oratorio or a partial one frequently was presented on the second day.[110] New oratorios, in fact, were written specifically for the festivals, such as Klein's *Jephta* for 1828 and Ries's *Der Sieg des Glaubens* for 1829. The composition of new oratorios went hand in hand with the "restoration" of Handel's at these celebrations. From the 1830s through the end of this half-century, a complete Handel oratorio was given at almost every festival. At this time, too, one observes the first appearance at these events of movements from masses, as well as the frequent enlargement of the

TABLE 5.2. VOCAL SOLOISTS

	DILETTANTE	PROFESSIONAL	TOTAL
1818–24	59	0	59
1825–34	65	7	72
1835–47	47	45	92
1851–67	19	72	91

The sources of the figures constituting this table are Jahn, *Aufsätze*; Hauchecorne, *Blätter*; and the Leipzig *Allgemeine musikalische Zeitung*.

first day's program to include a symphony, overture, or cantata besides an oratorio.[111]

The third stage of the festivals, from 1835 to 1847, the eve of the revolutionary year, was distinguished by continuing growth and strikingly increased professionalism. The number of participants rose from 619 to 789 by the end of these years, while the chorus expanded from a size over twice that of the orchestra in 1835 to four times its number, or 616 singers, in 1847 (see table 5.1, stage 3). Many distinguished conductors presided: Mendelssohn, Heinrich Dorn, Ries, Spohr, Konradin Kreutzer, Spontini, and George Onslow.[112] There were other signs of continually rising professionalism during this period. Five festivals between 1839 and 1846 extended into a third day of music largely devoted to virtuoso performance. On these occasions eminent soloists appeared, among them the singers Clara Novello, Sophie Schloss, and Jenny Lind, along with Mendelssohn and the Cologne Quartet.[113] Of the ninety-two solo singers performing during this phase of the festivals, half were professionals, a marked increase over the proportion of professionals in the preceding stage.[114]

The oratorio, above all, and the symphony, second in prominence, continued to dominate the programs of these years, as they had in the earlier phases of the festivals.[115] Four of the programs were lengthened by a third day's concert consisting of one major instrumental work—a concerto or a string quartet, for instance—along with other musical genres essentially new to the festival repertoire: arias, lieder, and shorter virtuoso instrumental pieces. No lieder, in fact, had ever been presented before the 1835–47 phase. The potpourri type of program typical of the third day additionally contained the usual mixture of overtures and choruses on religious or edifying themes.[116] Two other musical events occurred during the third stage of the festivals: the presentation of Weber's *Euryanthe* at the 1844 celebration and of the overture and second act of Spontini's *Olympia* at the 1847 festival. These were the only occasions when any significant amount of operatic music was heard in the first half-century of the festivals.

The last phase of these celebrations spanned the years from 1851 to 1867, when professionalism took over.[117] Schumann, while music director at Düsseldorf, and Liszt, court kapellmeister at Weimar, headed the array of eminent conductors at the festivals of 1853 and 1857, respectively. Other prominent conductors included Peter Lindpaintner (1791–1856), court kapellmeister in Stuttgart; Karl von Turanyi; Ferdinand Hiller, music director at Cologne; Julius Tausch, Schumann's successor as Düsseldorf's music director; Julius Rietz, Mendelssohn's successor at Düsseldorf and subsequently conductor of the Gewandhaus Concerts at Leipzig; Franz Lachner (1803–90), the intimate friend of Schubert and general music director at Munich; Franz Wüllner, Turanyi's successor as music director at Aachen; Otto Goldschmidt (1829–1907), Jenny Lind's pianist-husband; and Ferdinand Breunung (1830–83), Wüllner's successor as music director at Aachen.

Every festival during this phase concluded with a third day's program of vocal and instrumental performance by such celebrities as the pianists Clara Schumann and Hans von Bülow; the violinists Joseph Joachim, Henri Vieuxtemps, Theodor Pixis, Ferdinand David, and Leopold Auer; and the singers Jenny Lind, Julius Stockhausen, Sophie Schloss, and Clara Novello. Professional solo singers meanwhile now outnumbered dilettantes by more than three to one (see table 5.2). The change in outlook was reflected, for instance, in Otto Jahn's assessment of the amateur bass who sang in Beethoven's Ninth Symphony at the 1856 festival: "He has, like so many dilettantes, preferred to cultivate the imperfections and mistakes of insufficient schooling as presumed merits."[118]

Compared with the programs of the earlier years, those of this phase were expanded in various ways. Besides the established offering of oratorios, symphonies, overtures, masses, cantatas, shorter choral religious works, and instrumental display pieces, the number of arias and lieder performed increased substantially (although their titles were often omitted), as did concertos. A symphonic poem and an orchestral suite, moreover, were first presented during the period 1851–67.[119] The concerts included more works of J. S. Bach, a certain amount of early Baroque and Renaissance music, and the traditional homage to Beethoven, Haydn, and Mozart. The length of the concerts was greater than ever before; a third day was to be expected and its concert consisted of twelve to fifteen works, as compared with an average of ten compositions in the period 1835–47.

By this phase of their first half-century, the Lower Rhine Music Festivals had enlarged substantially in several ways. The number of participants between 1851 and 1867 reached its peak for the entire fifty years: a staggering 938 in 1863 (see table 5.1, stage 4).[120] In 1851 the size of the chorus was nearly three times that of the orchestra; in the climactic year of 1863, with 781 singers, it had risen to five times.

The relative size of the orchestra diminished equally steadily as compared with the total number of performers. In the first three years of the festivals, it represented 45 to 48 percent of the performing body; from 1821 through the 1840s, 21 to 40 percent; by the 1850s and 1860s, only between 16 and 25 percent. The actual size of the orchestra varied considerably; at its smallest, around 100 members, between 1818 and 1820, it continually vacillated between 130 and 180 members from the mid-1820s on.

The steady growth in festival participation thus occurred primarily in the chorus. At a time when musical professionalism was becoming the norm and virtuosity was clearly mounting, solid dilettantism continued to flourish in the mammoth chorus. This was the equivalent of the *Männerchor*, so prevalent in the Rheinlieder settings and *Liedertafeln* festivals discussed earlier. As for the mounting size of the audience, Jahn reported that by 1855 all two thousand seats in Düsseldorf's Geissler Garden Hall were filled and that, besides, "several hundred" additional people had to be accommodated on a specially constructed platform and through standing room.[121]

Although the years wrought changes in the programs, certain kinds of works continued to dominate, especially the oratorio and the symphony. In a special encomium praising the high musical standards of the Rhineland, Ludwig Bischoff (1794–1867), founder and editor of two Cologne music journals, commented on the 1862 Lower Rhine Music Festival: "As generally at our music festivals, so too at those celebrated in Cologne, newer things have found an honorable place; but it is significant that the performance of classical masterworks . . . attracts by far the largest group of listeners. And the participation of the public, which has increased continually since the resumption of the festival in 1851 after a three-year interruption, is gratifying proof of the success of artistic life on the Rhine in its noble course toward the highest genres of music: the oratorio and the symphony."[122]

Of the composers represented at the festivals, Beethoven reigned supreme, while Handel and Mozart consistently predominated, though not always in the same order, among the four composers ranking next in popularity (see table 5.3).

From 1818 through 1827 Weber and Friedrich Schneider (1786–1853) also counted among the leading five. In the second decade Ferdinand Ries and Cherubini replaced these two; in the next, the Rhine crisis decade, Mendelssohn usurped Ries's position; in the fourth and fifth decades, Schumann succeeded Cherubini.

For all five decades the most popular composers, as ranked according to the total number of works performed during the first half-century of the festivals, were Beethoven, then Handel, Mozart, Mendelssohn, and

TABLE 5.3. THE LEADING FIVE
COMPOSERS FOR FIVE DECADES
OF FESTIVALS

DECADE	COMPOSER	TOTAL NUMBER OF WORKS
1818–27	Beethoven	13
	Handel	6
	Mozart	6
	Weber	6
	Schneider	4
1828–37	Beethoven	16
	Ries	7
	Handel	6
	Cherubini	5
	Mozart	4
1838–47	Beethoven	15
	Handel	13
	Mozart	13
	Mendelssohn	9
	Cherubini	7
1851–57	Beethoven	18
	Handel	11
	Mendelssohn	10
	Mozart	9
	Schumann	7
1858–67	Beethoven	22
	Handel	21
	Schumann	19
	Mozart	16
	Mendelssohn	15

Schumann—surely a prestigious quintet. Some Rhine-texted works were presented, but no Rheinlieder, unlike the repertoire of the *Liedertafeln* festivals already discussed.

The constant shift in proportions between chorus and orchestra over these years in favor of the singers could not have failed, either, to have affected the combined choral-instrumental sound. It is intriguing and perhaps a little frightening to contemplate this balance further in the light of contemporaneous reports that, at the 1856 festival, a third of the chorus of 730 consisted of basses, 237 of them, along with a 164-member orchestra.[123] Tone color changed within the festival orchestra itself. At the end of the

TABLE 5.4. IMPORTANT COMPOSERS AT THE FESTIVALS, 1818–1867

	NUMBER OF FESTIVALS	SPAN
Beethoven	41	1819–67
Handel	37	1819–67
Mozart	30	1819–67
Weber	20	1822–67
Mendelssohn	18	1839–67
Cherubini	16	1829–67
Haydn	14	1818–65
Gluck	11	1839–67
Schumann	11	1853–67
Ries	10	1824–38
J. S. Bach	9	1838–67
Spohr	9	1820–66
Schubert	7	1840–67

first phase, 1818–24, the weight of orchestral sonority lay in the strings; in 1824, for example, twelve to fifteen double basses, for an orchestra of 178 players, had to be collected and transported from various cities, since no single town contained that many.[124] For the 1862 celebration, however, with an orchestra of 139 players, Bischoff reported: "Besides the woodwinds, which are now employed more extensively and in greater mass than previously, the recent symphony orchestra has strengthened the third tone color, the brass, into a burgeoning force by doubling the horns, by frequently using valve trumpets, and by supplementing the trombone quartet with a tuba. This sound suppresses the heart of orchestral music, the principal tone color provided by the soaring strings, in that the powerful and artistic bowing stroke is overwhelmed by brass mouthpieces and lung power."[125]

The prosperous course of these festivals also brought the constant renovation of concert facilities and the construction of new ones to accommodate the burgeoning audiences. In Düsseldorf, the first festival (1818) had taken place in the Jansen Hall, replaced in 1822 by the larger, former Knight's Hall of the old castle; in 1826 by the city theater; in 1853 by the Geissler Garden Hall; and in 1866 by the sizable new Kaiser Hall, noted for its superb acoustics. The 1819 festival was held in Elberfeld in the local musical society hall, that of 1823 in the enlarged Casino there, and that of 1827 in the converted riding school. Aachen's newly built theater was the site of its first festival in 1825. In 1836 that building was expanded, and in 1864 the festival moved to the Kursaal, the magnificent new spa concert hall.[126] Cologne accommodated its first Lower Rhine Music Festival in 1821, in the old Gürzenich Hall, which for the 1824 celebration had gained a new roof. By 1828 this hall had been enlarged, in 1832 redecorated, and by 1858 rebuilt.

This examination of the Lower Rhine Music Festivals has traced the emerging importance of the influential urban bourgeoisie in German musical life during the earlier nineteenth century. Various aspects of these festivals, with their almost exclusively German repertoire, help account for the state of music at a time when the affluent, informed middle classes were asserting their leadership in society as the basis both of the musical establishment and of a new mass public. W. Jackson Bate's observation on the place of Samuel Johnson in the world of eighteenth-century English letters indicates that this situation ranged further than music alone: Johnson "was caught between two worlds. Traditional patronage from individuals or the government, which had supported literature before, was waning rapidly. It had not yet been replaced by the immense expansion of the reading public, throughout the growing middle class, which was to appear in the later 1700s and to transform the entire sociological character of literature in the nineteenth century."[127]

These changing conditions in the realm of English literature parallel a number of forces active in the music of German Romanticism, as the Lower Rhine Music Festivals demonstrate.

EPILOGUE: LIEDER, RHEINLIEDER, AND THE LOWER RHINE MUSIC FESTIVALS

In 1839, the year before the Rhine crisis, lieder (Mendelssohn's new *Sechs schottische National-Lieder*) were first performed at the Lower Rhine Music Festivals. In 1840, 1842, 1846, and 1851 lieder by Schubert, Mendelssohn (some of his listed only as "Lieder"), and Lindpaintner were presented. Also at the 1839 festival, the Britisher Clara Novello sang "God Save the Queen," after which the audience demanded she perform this melody with the patriotic German text "Heil dir im Siegerkranz." Toward the end, the entire hall, including the chorus and orchestra, rose and joined in with Novello.[128] Through the 1850s and 1860s various lieder by Beethoven, Mendelssohn, Schubert, Silcher, Schumann, Brahms, and others were sung at the festivals.

In 1853 Robert Schumann's Festival Overture with Chorus on the "Rheinweinlied" was premiered. The festival of 1860 included two Rheinlieder, Schumann's "Waldesgespräch" (and again in 1863) and Ferdinand Hiller's "Das Wirthshaus am Rhein" (The Inn on the Rhine). In 1862 the overture to Schumann's Rhine-oriented opera *Genoveva* appeared on the festival program, as did Mendelssohn's "Rheinisches Volkslied" in 1864 and Schumann's "Sonntags am Rhein" in 1867.

One must also take into account, however, that lieder were performed on the sidelines of the festivals as early as 1829. On the eve of the June 1829 festival in Aachen, the city's *Liedertafel* serenaded the conductor, Ferdinand Ries, with four-part *Männergesänge* in front of his home. On the first morning of the 1835 festival in Cologne, *Liedertafeln* from Elberfeld and Aachen joined with other groups to perform their repertoire.[129]

Camaraderie coupled with patriotism pervaded the *Liedertafeln* of the 1830s and 1840s.[130] For the Rhenish *Liedertafeln* of the 1840s, this was especially the case. These groups, moreover, directly participated in the "Morning Entertainments" of the Lower Rhine Music Festivals. These were impromptu concerts given to honor the conductors and soloists of these events. When the festival was canceled in the revolutionary year of 1848, in fact, a nationalistic *Männergesangfest* in Düsseldorf replaced it, setting a precedent for such occasions.[131]

We can draw several conclusions from viewing the first half-century of the Lower Rhine Music Festivals in light of the Rheinlieder publication in the 1840s, the decade forming the exact midpoint in the first half-century of the latter events. Both the Rheinlieder and these celebrations, as well as the Rhenish *Liedertafeln* festivals, involved a mass public and mass participation in the cause of German music. With the Rheinlieder, we have an immense body of German poets, composers, and music, all directed toward a vast, heterogeneous, and essentially German public. In the case of all these festivals, we again note vast hordes in the number of performers and size of the audience, as well as large numbers of citizens coordinating festivals that joined a number of Rhineland cities and villages. Both the grand scale of these events and their repertoire were aimed at the German *Volk* at large. This was patently *Volkstümlichkeit* in the very practice of music. And it was a

Volkstümlichkeit accompanied by a full panoply of nineteenth-century German cultural and national implications.

There are further parallels. Both the festivals and the Rheinlieder phenomenon in all its aspects were marked by tensions resulting from dilettantes confronting professional musicians. And all four of the Düsseldorf music directors examined here wrote Rheinlieder, as did the many kapellmeisters of the smallest hamlets.

Together the Rheinlieder, the Lower Rhine Music Festivals, and the musical life of such Rhine cities as Düsseldorf demonstrated the high value placed on this region by musical figures in such artistic and intellectual centers as Berlin and Leipzig. The Germans, divided though they yet were into countless states and tiny monarchies, found in a body of musical and poetic literature and in its performance milieu a voice and focus for their national aspirations. That *volkstümlich* body of literature and its context can best be explained through the cultural and national metaphor of the Rhine River.

CONCLUSION: THE
RHINE AS MUSICAL
METAPHOR

*J*n his path-breaking biography of Johann Sebastian
Bach, completed in 1880, Julius August Philipp Spitta
offered an impassioned statement of German cultural
identity. Perhaps the greatest significance of this Bach
scholar's remarks vis-à-vis *The Rhine As Musical Metaphor* lies in his confident
proclamation of faith in a notion that, only a few decades earlier, was just
beginning to crystallize. Spitta, for example, considered Sebastian Bach's
paternal great-uncle Heinrich Bach "a foster-father of [German] culture."
This older family member was town musician and organist of the Lieb-
frauenkirche in Arnstadt from 1641. And Spitta praised the mammoth musical legacy of the Bach family, "who cherished and hid the precious essence
of German national feeling" despite the devastations of such events as the
Thirty Years' War.

Bach's biographer, in fact, even equated the Bachs with "the German
nation." Spitta's views issued from his conviction that the greatness of the
Bachs' musical contributions to human history had derived from strong
genetic relationships. "Truly," he argued, "did Sebastian Bach spring from
the very core and marrow of the German people." More than once, Spitta
referred to the Bachs as "the German nation." He maintained, moreover,
that the sublimity of the Bachs' music was due to the very circumstance
that they had joined together in musicians' guilds, in which many of the
members were already related by kinship or ultimately by marriage.

We have seen that earlier in the nineteenth century the Rhine provided
a focus for the Germans' sense of a common culture based largely on their
faith in the bonds of kinship. Likewise, Spitta was convinced, the Bachs

and their music represented a powerful symbol of the Germans' mutual familial heritage.

Vater Rhein, too, had long reigned paternally as a supreme "foster-father of culture" in the eyes of Germans striving toward a national unity that, by Spitta's day, had become a reality.

Thus one can see that the German Romantics over many decades adhered to a familial ideal of nationalism, a concept, furthermore, glorifying music itself as the font of Germanness. In addition, two of the primary symbols of Germanness, especially in music, belonged to the Romantics' glorified realm of nature, for a mighty river and an extraordinary family served as quintessential emblems of German cultural identity. This identity was based on pride in a glorious ancestral homeland and deep familial roots. And the latter defined a *Volk* at the heart, mind, and soul of which was music.

The metaphorical force of the Rhine image has also brought to light the unique importance of the lied in German Romanticism. Its predominately serious tone, particularly when impelled by the cause of cultural nationalism, cannot be compared with the "mindset" of the French chanson, Italian aria, or English air. The lied of German Romanticism—peculiarly German, like the Lutheran chorale—was, in addition, a singularly middle-class genre. Although varying extensively in sheer artistic worth, the lied genre captured the attention of a prodigious number of major and "secondary" German composers, publishers, and critics. It also called into being that characteristic German Romantic institution, the *Liedertafel*, the chief milieu of the Rheinlieder. There are, in fact, few more precise illustrations of nineteenth-century *Volkstümlichkeit* in musical style and performance practice than the *Liedertafel* and its repertoire.

The present study has necessarily been confined principally to the lied. But to some extent, of course, other realms of German Romantic music were touched by elements of the Rhine theme. We must not overlook, for example, the fact that the Rheinlieder event of the 1840s was in full flower at the same time that Wagner was producing the gripping male-chorus finale of *Tannhäuser*, act 2. This opera, moreover, was set in Thuringia, the ancient land of the Bachs. Wagner's choice for the center of the action, in fact, was the eleventh-century Wartburg—a fortress towering over Johann Sebastian Bach's native city of Eisenach—site of the medieval minnesinger contests, and Martin Luther's home when he translated the New Testament. It goes without saying that all these associations lend ample support to

Spitta's concept of German nationhood, and most importantly, a concept based on a sense of cultural identity.

As the four hundred Rheinlieder published in the 1840–50 decade have demonstrated, as have related historical phenomena in "extramusical" spheres, Germany's majestic river came to symbolize a wide spectrum of nineteenth-century Teutonic themes: the humanization of nature and of its mysterious beauty; the depth of human emotion and its connections with the ideals of longing, becoming, and wayfaring; hero worship in a messianic age; the concept of love-death; the amateur choral movement and growing tensions between dilettantes and professional musicians; the ancient political antagonisms rending the Middle East from Western Europe and Germany from France; the socioeconomic upheavals of a nascent Age of Industrialization; *Volkstümlichkeit*, with its cultural and national ramifications in music and other arts; the rise of urban musical institutions and entrepreneurship; the increasing influence of musical criticism; and the blossoming of the lied, central in its role as an art form of the middle classes, who continued to expand in size and influence throughout the nineteenth century and over Europe as a whole.

Vater Rhein, for millennia a prime artery of international commerce and communication, became a focal point for mid-nineteenth-century German culture in general, and for music in particular. In examining this little-known body of musical literature, we become more closely acquainted with the broad base of German Romantic music without resort to its icons alone. We also gain a better understanding of cultural nationalism, as it developed in the past and in its positive dimension as a force representing the beauties of one's homeland and origins. Finally, we acquire an enriched appreciation of the present that can enable us to address such issues of the current post–Cold War era as ethnicity with far-sightedness, patience, and hope.

INDEX OF RHEINLIEDER
PUBLISHED IN THE
1840S

In the following index, I have sought to record all the Rheinlieder of which I have knowledge that were published or selected for republication during the decade 1840–50. The total number of songs from this period that treat the subject of the Rhine or its associations, however, will probably never be known. The reader may locate a song either by referring to the poet, whose name appears in alphabetical order; to the title of the poem or first line (in parentheses)—disregarding the article *der, die, das*—when the poet is not named in the sources; or to the composer, given in the alphabetical Index of Composers following the Index of Rheinlieder. The contents of each listing vary in extent according to the amount of information obtainable. Each listing also includes the following publication information: the particular Hofmeister catalogue citation (a single asterisk * indicating the volume covering 1839–44 and two asterisks ** representing the volume including 1844–51) or other citation, and the publishing firm and its location; the songbook (if used for the analytical portions of the study) in which the lied is additionally or exclusively found; and the type or types of setting known to have been made. When a Rheinlied poem has been set by more than one composer, the composers are listed separately and alphabetically, along with the publication data and type of setting—all this being noted immediately after the first mention of a poem.

For the purposes of saving space, the following abbreviations have been used:

AdL: *Auswahl deutscher Lieder*. Ed. Irwin H. Steiner. Leipzig: Serig'sche Buchhandlung, 1844.

365fG: *365 fröhliche Guitarrlieder,* vol. 3. Ed. Franz Samans. Wesel: J. Bagel, 1848.

ALfdaK: *Ausgewählte Lieder für die ausziehenden Krieger,* 4th ed. Ed. Arno Krehan. Weimar: R. Borkmann, 1917.

CB: *Commers-Buch für die deutschen Studenten,* 3d ed. Ed. Max Friedlaender. Magdeburg and Leipzig: Gebrüder Baensch, 1858.

DdF: *Die deutschen Freiheitskriege in Liedern und Gedichten.* Ed. Ludwig Erk. Leipzig: Rudolf Winklers Verlag, 1913.

DLSl: *Erk's deutscher Liederschatz,* vol. 1. Ed. Ludwig Erk and rev. Max Friedlaender. Leipzig: Peters, 1890.

LS: *Lieder-Schatz: Eine Auswahl der beliebtesten Volks-, Vaterlands-, Soldaten-, Jäger-, Studenten- und Liebes-Lieder für eine Singstimme mit Pianoforte-Begleitung.* Leipzig and Berlin: Peters, 1870.

VfMI: *Volksliederbuch für Männerchor,* vol. 1. Ed. Max Friedlaender. Leipzig: Peters, 1907.

VfMII: *Volksliederbuch für Männerchor,* vol. 2. Ed. Max Friedlaender. Leipzig: Peters, 1907.

Hase: *Liederbuch des deutschen Volkes,* 2d ed. Ed. Carl Hase, Felix Dahn, and Carl Reinecke. Leipzig: Breitkopf & Härtel, 1883. (Note: basically consists of lieder from the original edition of 1843.)

Hofm. 1844: *C. F. Whistling's Handbuch der musikalischen Literatur,* 3d ed. Ed. Adolph Hofmeister. Leipzig: Friedrich Hofmeister, 1845.

Hofm. 1851: *C. F. Whistling's Handbuch der musikalischen Literatur,* 3d ed., 1st supplement. Ed. Adolph Hofmeister. Leipzig: Friedrich Hofmeister, 1852.

NZfM: *Neue Zeitschrift für Musik.*

Settings have been abbreviated as follows: "P" is part-song; "SV" is solo voice; "U" indicates unaccompanied; "p" after "SV" or "P" indicates piano accompaniment, while "g" in the same circumstance refers to guitar accompaniment. Thus "UP" indicates an unaccompanied part-song, "USV" signifies unaccompanied solo voice or unaccompanied unison chorus, and "SV-p" denotes a solo voice with piano accompaniment. If no musical setting is indicated, the reader is to assume that the Rheinlied in question appears in the source(s) with its text alone.

HOW MANY RHEINLIEDER?

The extent to which the image of the Rhine captivated the German musical mind of the *Vormärz* is dramatically indicated by the profusion of Rheinlieder appearing in Germany during that period. Although their total number can never be precisely determined, I believe a useful estimate of its extent and significance has been established by following several assumptions:

a. A Rheinlied is simply a German song on the subject of the Rhine, the Rhinelands, or their associated symbols, regardless of the identity of poet or composer.

b. The decade 1840–50—or, more exactly, the period 1839–51 documented by Hofmeister (see below)—virtually inaugurated by the appearance of Becker's Rheinlied, captured an essence of Rheinlied production with respect to both quantity and subject matter.

c. The publication of a Rheinlied during that decade, apart from its date of origin, reliably indicates its importance as an expression of "Rhine fever"; conversely, manuscripts of Rheinlieder are of negligible value for this purpose. In other words, publication most accurately expressed public sentiment.

d. The third edition of the monumental, comprehensive Hofmeister *Handbuch der musikalischen Literatur*, the most important part of which attempts to list all musical publications in Germany and neighboring lands between 1839 and 1851, provides a dependable yardstick for measuring the extent of Rheinlied production ("production" meaning printing, regardless of date of composition) in that decade, especially when it is used as a natural point of departure in the perusal of unlisted single songs (inside and outside of anthologies) and isolated mentions.

e. Such a perusal, however, has as its main objective not the statistical supplementation of the Hofmeister *Handbuch* in matters of quantity, but the study of poetry and music. The dozens of anthologies examined in this process are included in the bibliography; of these, nine proved most useful in their avoidance of duplication and their presentation of sufficient quantities of Rheinlieder in convenient form. These nine comprise the primary basis of this index of Rheinlieder published in the 1840s. The total number of actual songs, published in the 1840s and used to study poetry and music, is around two hundred, although the examination of many more Rheinlieder appearing later contributed much to my understanding of the texts and settings from the 1840–50 decade.

THE HOFMEISTER *HANDBUCH*

During its entire history the *Handbuch* covered all the music, books on music, and iconographic representations printed by all the German music publishing firms of the time. The *Handbuch* virtually made the reputation of Friedrich Hofmeister (1782–1864) among German music bibliographers, although he did not begin it. The first edition of these catalogues was produced by Carl Friedrich Whistling (1788–after 1849), a German music publisher established at Leipzig. It was printed in 1817 by Anton Meysel as the *Handbuch der musikalischen Literatur, oder Allgemeines systematisch geordnetes Verzeichniss gedruckter Musikalien, auch musikalischen Schriften und Abbildungen mit Anzeige des Verlegers und Preise.* It attempted to present a complete listing of music published in Germany, along with additional listings from neighboring countries, between 1780 and 1817. Friedrich, the elder Hofmeister, bought the *Handbuch* in 1819 and resold it to Whistling in 1825.

After the publication of the 1817 volume, ten yearly supplements to this first edition carried it to 1827. A second edition appeared in 1828. The work of Whistling, it contained three parts along with a supplement. In 1829 the Hofmeisters bought Whistling's entire firm, publishing two further supplements to carry the work up to 1838. Adolph Hofmeister had meanwhile entered into these efforts in 1834 as editor of the second supplement. Adolph published the first volume of the third edition in 1845, covering music printed between 1839 and January 1844. The second volume appeared in 1852, updating the collection to the end of 1851.

The Rheinlieder published in the 1840s have been located either by the simple noting of a title or first line as it appears in Hofmeister, or by the roundabout procedure of (a) finding a lied (singly or in a collection) with Rhine-associated texts but without mention of the Rhine in its title or first line, and (b) having ascertained that it is a Rheinlied, locating it in Hofmeister to confirm that it falls within the 1839–51 period.

POET	TITLE/FIRST LINE	COMPOSER	PUB. INFO.	SETTING
1. Anonymous	"Abschied"	F. Möhring	***Bonn: Simrock	SV-p
2. Anonymous	"Abschied von Köln" ("Köln am Rhein, du schönes Städtchen")	Volksweise	VfMI	UP
3. Anonymous	"Alter Schlachtgesang aus Cöln"	J. Rietz	***Arnold: Elberfeld	UP
4. Anonymous	"Bierlied" ("Auf, singet, und trinket")	Unknown	365fG	USV
5. Anonymous	"Coblenz"	F. Möhring	***Bonn: Simrock	SV-p
6. Anonymous	"Cöln"	F. Möhring	***Bonn: Simrock	SV-p
7. Anonymous	"Den Deputirten des 8ten rheinischen Landtags"	F. Möhring	***Bonn: Simrock	SV-p
8. Anonymous	"Deutsches Lied zur vierten Säcular-Feier des Gutenberg-Festes"	C. G. Reissiger	*Leipzig: Teubner	SV-p; UP
9. Anonymous	"Drei Sterne am Rhein"	F. Hünten	Cited by Kossmaly	SV-p
10. Anonymous	"Der Engländer am Lurleyfelsen"	F. Möhring	***Bonn: Simrock	SV-p
11. Anonymous	"Festgesang zur Errichtung des Gutenberg'schen Denkmals in Mainz"	G. Meyerbeer	*Mainz: Schott	P-p
12. Anonymous	"Festlied Friedrich's von den Bergen" ("Süss ist unter Brüdern deutsches Fröhlichsein")	F. Samans	365fG	USV
13. Anonymous	"Der Fischer am Rhein"	C. Keller	*Cologne: Dunst	P-p
14. Anonymous	"Fischlein im Rhein"	Angelina	***Vienna: Mechetti	SV-p
15. Anonymous	"Handwerksburschen-Abschied" ("Es, es, es und es, es ist ein harter Schluss")	Volkslied	LS	SV-p, g
16. Anonymous	"Im alten Fass zu Heidelberg" or "Das Lied vom Heidelberger Fass" or "Das Heidelberger Fass"	L. Hetsch	***Heidelberg: Meder	SV-p
17. Ibid.	Ibid.	H. Marschner	Kötzschke	?
18. Ibid.	Ibid.	C. G. Reissiger	***Berlin: Schlesinger	UP

POET	TITLE/FIRST LINE	COMPOSER	PUB. INFO.	SETTING
19. Anonymous	"Klage eines hohensteinischen Mädchens"	C. Klage	***Leipzig: Hofmeister	SV-p
20. Anonymous	"Klänge vom Rhein"	H. B. Wiss	**Stuttgart: Hollberger	UP
21. Anonymous	"Des Kriegers Abschied" ("Leb' wohl, mein Bräutschen schön!")	A. Methfessel	Op. 35, *Sechs deutsche Kriegslieder, 10*	USV; SV-p
22. Anonymous	"Lied der Lorle"	G. Reichardt	***Augsburg: Böhm	SV-p
23. Anonymous	"Das Lied vom Rhein"	Rettich	***Bonn: Simrock	UP
24. Ibid.	Ibid.	A. Schick	***Zürich: Nägeli	UP
25. Anonymous	"Lurlei"	O. Trehsen	***Vienna: Mechetti	SV-p
26. Anonymous	"Die Lurley"	C. G. Reissiger	***Dresden: Paul	SV-p
27. Anonymous	"Mainz"	F. Möhring	***Bonn: Simrock	SV-p
28. Anonymous	"Mainzer Casino-Lied"	A. Leroux	***Mainz: Schott	SV-p
29. Anonymous	"Mainzer Siegeslied"	J. F. Kelz	*Berlin: Paez	UP
30. Ibid.	Ibid.	F. Knuth	*Berlin: Challier	UP
31. Anonymous	"Nach dem Rheine"	J. C. Schärtlich	***Berlin: Bote und Bock	UP
32. Anonymous	"O Jugend" ("Rheinisches Volkslied")	F. Mendelssohn	***Leipzig: Breitkopf & Härtel	SV-p
33. Anonymous	"Der Philister" ("Wisst Ihr, was ein Philister heisst?")	A. H. Neithardt	AdL	UP
34. Anonymous	"Rheines Trinklied"	F. Derckum	***Bonn: Simrock	UP
35. Anonymous	"Der Rheingraf hielt ein festlich Mahl"	F. F. G. Kirchhof	***Aachen: E. ter Meer	SV-p
36. Anonymous	"Der rheinische Wein" ("Seht doch, wie der Rheinwein tanzt in dem schönen Glase")	A. Krieger	VfMII	SV-cont
37. Anonymous	"Rheinischer Bundesring"	A. G. Ritter	***Magdeburg: Heinrichshofen	UP

38. Anonymous	"Rheinischer Schifferreigen"	C. Banck	*	UP
39. Anonymous	"Rheinländisches Wiegenlied"	F. Kücken	*Berlin: Schlesinger	UP
40. Anonymous	"Rheinlied" ("Hebt an den Chor, ihr meine deutschen Brüder!")	H. Winkelmeier	***Speyer: Lang; 365fG, No. 217, 257	USV
41. Anonymous	"Rheinpreussens Loblied zum 15. Oktober" ("Völker der Erde, so gross und so klein!")	Unknown	365fG, No. 84, 102	USV
42. Anonymous	"Der Rheinstrom"	F. Möhring	***Bonn: Simrock	SV-p
43. Ibid.	Ibid.	A. Schick	***Zürich: Nägeli	UP
44. Anonymous	"Rheinweine"	F. Hiller	***Mainz: Schott	UP
45. Anonymous	"Romanze vom Wolfsbrunnen"	K. F. L. Hetsch	*** *Die historische Cantate "Das Heidelberger Schloss,"* Heidelberg: Meder	SV-p
46. Anonymous	"Rückkehr zum Rhein"	F. Möhring	***Bonn: Simrock	SV-p
47. Anonymous	"Rüdesheim"	F. Möhring	***Leipzig: Siegel	UP
48. Anonymous	"Saarbrücken"	F. Möhring	***Bonn: Simrock	SV-p
49. Anonymous	"Sehnsucht nach dem Rheine" or "Rheinsehnsucht" ("Dort, wo der Rhein")	C. F. Ehrlich	*Vier Gesänge für 1 Singstimme,* op. 15, no. 2, Magdeburg: Heinrichshofen	SV-p, g
50. Ibid.	Ibid.	F. Möhring	***Berlin: Trautwein	SV-p
51. Ibid.	Ibid.	H. Proch	***Vienna: Diabelli	SV-p
52. Ibid.	Ibid.	G. Schmitt	***Mainz: Schott	SV-p
53. Ibid.	Ibid.	L. Schröter	***Magdeburg: Heinrichshofen	UP
54. Anonymous	"Siegesgesang aus der Hermannsschlacht" or "Siegesgesang der Deutschen nach der Hermannsschlacht"	F. Abt	Kötzschke	P with inst

POET	TITLE/FIRST LINE	COMPOSER	PUB. INFO.	SETTING
55. Ibid.	Ibid.	F. Lachner	Kötzschke	?
56. Anonymous	"Trinklied am Rhein"	N. Gade	**Leipzig: Breitkopf & Härtel	UP
57. Anonymous	Volkslied: "Der unerbittliche Hauptmann" or "Die Fremdenlegion" ("O Strassburg, O Strassburg, du wunderschöne Stadt!")	F. Commer	ALfdak	USV
58. Ibid.	Ibid.	Volksweise	VfMI; Leipzig: F. Pfeiffer	USV
59. Anonymous	"Vor dem Königsschusse" ("Ihr Schützen, lasst die Fahnen weh'n")	v. Pressler	365fG	UP
60. Anonymous	"Wasser und Wein; Wer seinen Wein"	H. Esser & V. Lachner	*Mainz: Schott	UP
61. Anonymous	"Der weisse Adler am Rhein"	C. Kossmaly	Mainz: Schott	?
62. Anonymous	"Wie schön ist's am Rhein"	C. Saling	**Magdeburg: Heinrichshofen	SV-p
63. Anonymous	"Das Wirthshaus am Rhein"	H. Esser	**Mainz: Schott	SV-p, g
64. Ibid.	Ibid.	F. Hiller	**Cologne: Schloss	SV-p
65. Anonymous	"Wum, wum, nur fröhliche Leute"	E. Berner	AdL	UP
66. Anonymous	"Zu Cöln am Rhein"	Unknown	**Oldenburg: Schulze	SV-p
67. Anonymous	"Zu Miltenberg am Maine" ("Zu Miltenberg am Maine, zu Würzburg an dem Steine")	E. Widmann	VfMII	UP
68. Anonymous	"Zur goldnen Bremm"	F. Möhring	**Bonn: Simrock	SV-p
69. Arndt, E. M.	"Blücher" or "Das Lied vom Feldmarschall" ("Was blasen die Trompeten? Husaren heraus!")	Volksweise	Hase; AdL; Erk, DdF; VfMI; Erk, DLSI	USV; SV-p, UP
70. Ibid.	Ibid.	Unknown	LS	SV-p

#	Author	Title	Composer	Source	Code
71.	Arndt, E. M.	"Das deutsche Vaterland" ("Was ist des deutschen Vaterland?")	J. Cotta	Erk, DdF, No. 60, 62; Hase, No. 777, 478; AlfdaK, No. I, 13	UP
72.	Ibid.	Ibid.	C. Krebs	**Hamburg; Schuberth	UP; SV-p
73.	Ibid.	Ibid.	F. Liszt	Berlin: Schlesinger	UP
74.	Ibid.	Ibid.	G. Reichardt	**VfMI; LS; Erk, DLSI; 365fG; Leipzig: Hofmeister; Berlin: Schlesinger	SV-p
75.	Ibid.	Ibid.	Unknown	AdL	UP
76.	Ibid.	Ibid.	C. F. Zelter	VfMI	UP
77.	Arndt, E. M.	"Der Freiheit Schlachtruf" or "Vaterlandslied" ("Der Gott, der Eisen wachsen liess")	A. Methfessel	AdL, No. 24, 39; LS, No. 21, 132; Erk, DLSI, No. 132, 140	USV; UP; SV-p
78.	Ibid.	Ibid.	Unknown	Erk, DdF	UP
79.	Arndt, E. M.	"Scharnhorst" ("Wer ist würdig unsrer grossen Todten?")	A. Methfessel	Erk, DdF, No. 28, 31	UP
80.	Arndt, E. M.	"Victoria" ("Auf Victoria: auf Victorial welch ein Klang aus Niederland!")	Unknown	Hase	UP
81.	Arndt, E. M.	"Wem deutsches Blut in seinen Pulsen brennet"	Unknown	AdL	UP
82.	Arndt, E. M.	"Zur Feier des 18. Oktobers" ("Es ist in diesen Tagen")	Unknown	Erk, DdF	UP
83.	Arnim & Brentano	"Der Baum im Odenwald" ("Es steht ein Baum in Odenwald"), Wunderhorn	J. F. Reichardt	CB; Hase; Erk, DLSI; AdL	USV; SV-p
84.	Arnim & Brentano	"Der Bettelvogt" ("Ich war noch so jung"), Wunderhorn	F. H. Himmel	AdL	UP
85.	Arnim & Brentano	"Liebesdienst" ("Es war ein Markgraf überm Rhein"), Wunderhorn	C. Loewe	Hase	SV-p
86.	Ibid.	Ibid.	Volksweise	VfMII	USV; UP
87.	Arnim & Brentano	"Das Ringlein" ("Bald gras' ich am Neckar, bald gras' ich am Rhein"), Wunderhorn	F. Kücken	**Leipzig: Kistner	UP

POET	TITLE/FIRST LINE	COMPOSER	PUB. INFO.	SETTING
88. Ibid.		Unknown	LS	SV-p, g
89. Ibid.		Volksweise	AdL; Erk, DLSI; CB; Hase	USV; SV-p, g
90. Arnim & Bren-tano	"Der Schweizer" ("Zu Strassburg auf der Schanz"), *Wunderhorn*	R. Franz	**Offenbach: André	SV-p
91. Ibid.		F. Silcher	Erk, DLSI; LS; VfMI	SV-p, g; UP
92. Ibid.		Volksweise	Cited in Walzel	?
93. Assmann, Frei-herr von Ab-schatz	"An die Deutschen" ("Nun ist es Zeit zu wachen")	Unknown	Hase, No. 759, 466	SV-p
94. Bechstein	"Am Rhein"	F. C. Fuchs	**Vienna: Witzendorf	SV-p
95. Becker, Nikolaus	"Der deutsche Rhein" or "Rheinlied" or "Der teutsche Rhein" ("Sie sollen ihn nicht haben")	J. Abenheim	*Stuttgart: Schilz	SV-p
96. Ibid.		F. Aller	*Mainz: Schott	UP
97. Ibid.		A. F. Anacker	*Dresden: Arnold	SV-p
98. Ibid.		C. Banck	*Dresden: Arnold	SV-p; P-p
99. Ibid.		Bandmann	*Breslau: Weinhold	SV-p
100. Ibid.		C. Becker	*Berlin: Challier	SV-p
101. Ibid.		J. Becker	*Leipzig: Schuberth	SV-p; P-p
102. Ibid.		J. W. Betzhold	*Elberfeld: Betzhold	SV-p; UP
103. Ibid.		E. Blumenroder	*Nürnberg: Riegel et W.	P with wind

No.			Composer	Publisher	
104.	Ibid.	Ibid.	R. E. Bochmann	Score pub. by composer	SV-p; P-p
105.	Ibid.	Ibid.	G. Börner	*Breslau: Weinhold	UP
106.	Ibid.	Ibid.	J. H. K. Bornhardt	*Hannover: Bachmann	SV-p
107.	Ibid.	Ibid.	F. Brandenburg	*Barmen: Langewiesche	SV-p; UP
108.	Ibid.	Ibid.	C. Bräuer	*Altenburg: Helbig	UP
109.	Ibid.	Ibid.	H. K. Breidenstein	NZfM; Bonn: Simrock	?
110.	Ibid.	Ibid.	C. B. Breuer	Cologne: pub. by composer	?
111.	Ibid.	Ibid.	F. X. Chivatal	*Magdeburg; Heinrichshofen	SV-p
112.	Ibid.	Ibid.	Christern	*Hamburg: Niemeyer	SV-p
113.	Ibid.	Ibid.	F. Derckum	*Cologne: Du Mont-Schauberg	SV-p
114.	Ibid.	Ibid.	H. A. Dresel	*Lemgo: Meyer'sche Hofbuchhandlung	SV-p; UP
115.	Ibid.	Ibid.	F. v. Drieberg	*Berlin: Trautwein	UP
116.	Ibid.	Ibid.	C. A. v. Eckenbrecher	*Berlin: Bethge	SV-p; UP
117.	Ibid.	Ibid.	J. J. Eickhoff	*Wesel: Prinz	UP
118.	Ibid.	Ibid.	H. Engels	*Elberfeld: Arnold	SV-p
119.	Ibid.	Ibid.	M. Ernemann	*Breslau: Grosser	SV-p
120.	Ibid.	Ibid.	J. Eschborn	*Mannheim: Heckel	SV-p
121.	Ibid.	Ibid.	C. Freudenberg	*Breslau: Leuckart	SV-p
122.	Ibid.	Ibid.	Friedrich Wilhelm III of Prussia	*Hamburg: Schuberth	UP

POET	TITLE/FIRST LINE	COMPOSER	PUB. INFO.	SETTING
123. Ibid.		K. Geissler	*Chemnitz: Häcker	SV-p
124. Ibid.		C. F. J. Girschner	*Cologne: Kohnen	SV-p
125. Ibid.		F. Gnüge	*Dresden: Heydt	SV-p; UP
126. Ibid.		C. Gollmick	Kossmaly in NZfM	?
127. Ibid.		F. Gröbenschütz	*Berlin: Paez; F. S. Lischke	UP
128. Ibid.		G. A. Gross	*Hamburg: Niemeyer	UP; SV-g
129. Ibid.		F. W. Grund	*Hamburg: Böhme	SV-g; P-p
130. Ibid.		A. Gyrowetz	*Vienna: Diabelli	SV-g
131. Ibid.		A. Hackel	*Vienna: Haslinger	P-p
132. Ibid.		M. C. Heerdmenger	*Leipzig: Brauns; Wöller	SV-p; UP
133. Ibid.		L. Huth	*Berlin: Schlesinger	UP; SV-p, g
134. Ibid.		E. Kirsch	*Schweidnitz: Franke	UP
135. Ibid.		C. Klage	*Berlin: Krigar	SV-g, p
136. Ibid.		J. Klein	Cologne: Eck	?
137. Ibid.		F. W. Klingenberg	*Görlitz: Koblitz	SV-p, g
138. Ibid.		F. Knuth	*Berlin: Challier	UP
139. Ibid.		J. H. C. Koopmann	*Carlsruhe: Holtzmann	UP; P-p; SV-p
140. Ibid.		C. A. Krebs	*&***Hamburg: Schuberth	SV-p; UP

141. Ibid.	C. Kreutzer	*Mainz: Schott; Cologne: Eck	UP; SV-p, g; P
142. Ibid.	G. W. Kündiger	*Nürnberg: Ebner	SV-p
143. Ibid.	F. J. Kunkel	*Stuttgart: Zumsteeg	SV-p
144. Ibid.	G. Kunze	*Leipzig: Schuberth; LS; Erk, DLSI	UP (men, children); SV-p; SV-p, g
145. Ibid.	J. G. Lägel	*Gera: Blachmann	SV-p
146. Ibid.	J. Lang	*Berlin: Challier	SV-p
147. Ibid.	C. Langrock	*Leipzig: Whistling	UP; SV-p
148. Ibid.	C. Leibl	Cologne: Eck	?
149. Ibid.	J. Lenz	*Breslau: Leuckart	SV-orch; P-orch
150. Ibid.	C. Loewe	*Leipzig: Hofmeister	UP
151. Ibid.	C. Lührss	*Berlin & Leipzig: Whistling	SV-p
152. Ibid.	F. v. Maczewski	*Mitau: Reyher	UP
153. Ibid.	J. J. Maier	*Erlangen: Bläsing	UP
154. Ibid.	C. L. A. Mangold	*Mainz: Schott	SV-p; P-p
155. Ibid.	Marcellin	*Berlin: Challier	SV-p, g
156. Ibid.	H. Marschner	*Leipzig: Hofmeister	UP
157. Ibid.	E. Marxsen	*Hamburg: Cranz	SV-p; UP
158. Ibid.	J. Matthieux	*Bonn & Leipzig: Kistner	SV-p
159. Ibid.	A. Methfessel	*Braunschweig: Leibrock	UP

POET	TITLE/FIRST LINE	COMPOSER	PUB. INFO.	SETTING
160. Ibid.		A. Metzler	*Breslau: Grosser	SV-p
161. Ibid.		A. Michel	*Gotha: Müller	SV-p, g
162. Ibid.		A. Müller	*Vienna: Haslinger	SV-p, with chorus
163. Ibid.		P. Müller	*Mainz: Faber	UP
164. Ibid.		A. H. Neithardt	*Berlin: Trautwein	SV-p; UP
165. Ibid.		S. Neukomm	*Mainz: Schott	SV-p; P-p; UP; P w. orch
166. Ibid.		E. J. Otto	*Dresden: Meser	SV-p
167. Ibid.		H. A. Pistorius	*Berlin: Challier	SV-p; UP
168. Ibid.		A. Pollmann	*Elberfeld: Arnold	SV-p
169. Ibid.		F. W. Preusse	*Breslau: Weinhold	SV-p
170. Ibid.		G. Preyer	*Vienna: Diabelli	SV-p; P-p, g
171. Ibid.		G. Rain	*Leipzig: Hartung	UP; SV-p
172. Ibid.		G. Reichardt	*Berlin: Bote & Bock	UP; SV-p
173. Ibid.		C. H. C. Reinecke	*Hamburg: Cranz; Hase	SV-p; USV
174. Ibid.		C. G. Reissiger	*Dresden: Meser	SV-p
175. Ibid.		E. Richter	*Breslau: Grosser	SV-p
176. Ibid.		E. Salleneuve	*Berlin: Esslinger	SV-p; P; UP

No.	Source	Composer	Publisher	Rights
177.	Ibid.	G. Schäfer	Hamburg: Berendssohn	?
178.	Ibid.	A. Schäffer	*Berlin: Schlesinger	SV-p; UP
179.	Ibid.	H. Schäffer	*Hamburg: Böhme	SV-p; P-p or inst
180.	Ibid.	J. C. Schärtlich	*Berlin & Potsdam: Crantz	SV-p; UP
181.	Ibid.	H. Schmidt	*Berlin: Bote & Bock	UP; SV-p
182.	Ibid.	J. P. S. Schmidt	*Berlin: Schlesinger	SV-p
183.	Ibid.	J. C. F. Schneider	*Dessau: Ackermann	UP
184.	Ibid.	M. Schön	*Breslau: Leuckart	SV-p
185.	Ibid.	R. Schumann	*Leipzig: Friese; Breitkopf & Härtel	UP; SV-p
186.	Ibid.	C. T. Seiffert	*Breslau: Leuckart	UP
187.	Ibid.	C. F. Seyffert	*Brandenburg: Müller	SV-p; UP
188.	Ibid.	C. L. Spohn	*Carlsruhe: Holtzmann	SV-p; UP
189.	Ibid.	A. Stahlknecht	*Chemnitz: Häcker	SV-p
190.	Ibid.	E. W. Staudt	*Schaffhausen: Brodtmann'sche Buchhandlung	SV-p; UP
191.	Ibid.	S. T. Steinbrunn	*Bromberg: Mittler	UP
192.	Ibid.	J. Stern	*Berlin: Simion	SV-p
193.	Ibid.	X. Stolzenberg	*Cologne: Dunst	SV-p, g; UP
194.	Ibid.	J. H. Stuntz	*Frankfurt: Dunst	UP; SV-p, g

POET	TITLE/FIRST LINE	COMPOSER	PUB. INFO.	SETTING
195. Ibid.		Unknown	Kossmaly in NZfM	?
196. Ibid.		J. J. H. Verhulst	*Leipzig: Whistling	SV-p, g; P-p
197. Ibid.		W. V. Volckmar	*Düsseldorf: Forberg	SV-p
198. Ibid.		H. Wächter	*Hannover: Bachmann	SV-p
199. Ibid.		H. Waldow	*Stolp: Fritsch	SV-p
200. Ibid.		F. Walter	*Bonn: Marcus	SV-p
201. Ibid.		A. Weinbrenner	*Elberfeld: Hassel	SV-p
202. Ibid.		C. F. Weisheit	Schmalkalden: F. Pistor	SV-p
203. Ibid.		L. Weiss	*Vienna: Diabelli	SV-p
204. Ibid.		F. Weller	*Berlin: Schlesinger	SV-p, g
205. Ibid.		A. Zeiss	*Rinteln: Bösendahl	UP
206. Bornemann	"Lurley-Lied"	H. Stümer	**Berlin: Schlesinger	UP
207. Böttger, A.	"Lorelei, die Fee"	J. Becker	*Leipzig: Klemm	SV-p
208. Boyen, Hermann v.	"Preussens Losung" ("Der Preussen Losung ist die Drei'")	Unknown	*DdF, No. 57, 58	UP
209. Brentano, Clemens	"Am Rheine"	J. Heuchemer	**Aachen: E. ter Meer	SV-p
210. Ibid.		H. Marschner	**Hamburg: Schuberth	SV-p, g
211. Bürger, G. A.	"Bacchus" ("Herr Bacchus ist ein braver Mann")	J. A. P. Schulz	Hase, No. 256, 167	USV
212. Claudius, Matthias	"Rheinweinlied" ("Bekränzt mit Laub den lieben, vollen Becher")	J. André	***Offenbach: André; LS, No. 3, 179	SV-p; SV-p, g; P-p, g; USV

213. Ibid.	Ibid.	J. A. P. Schulz	AdL, LS	USV; SV-p, g
214. Cornelius, P.	"Botschaft" ("Liebendes Wort, cich send' ich fort!")	P. Cornelius	Leipzig: Peters (see example 4.32)	SV-p, g
215. Cramer	"Kriegslied" ("Feinde ringsum!")	Unknown	AdL	UP
216. Drimborn, E. G.	"Kaiser Wenzel" ("Was schiert mich Reich und Kaiserprunk")	C. Böhmer	CB, No. 161, 164	USV
217. Eichendorff, J. F. v.	"Auf einer Burg" ("Eingeschlafen auf der Lauer")	R. Schumann	Op. 39, no. 7	SV-p
218. Eichendorff, J. F. v.	"Die Rheinfahrt"	H. C. Dammas	*Magdeburg; Heinrichshofen	P-p
219. Ibid.	Ibid.	C. E. Pax	*Berlin: Paez	P-p
220. Ibid.	Ibid.	G. Wöhler	***Leipzig: Breitkopf & Härtel	SV-p
221. Eichendorff, J. F. v.	"Waldes[ge]spräch" ("Es ist schon spät, es ist schon kalt'")	R. Schumann	Op. 39, no. 3	SV-p
222. Ernst, B.	"Wo ist des Rheines Hort"	J. V. Hamm	***Mainz: Schott	SV-p
223. Ibid.	Ibid.	F. Möhring	***Bonn: Simrock	SV-p
224. Ibid.	Ibid.	H. Schnaubelt	***Vienna: Glöggl	SV-p
225. Fink, G. W.	"Die Pfälzer Eisenbahnen"	G. Hammer	*Speyer: Lang	UP
226. Fischback, P.	"Das Fürstenwort in Brühl"	R. J. Dürrner	***Elberfeld: Arnold	SV-p
227. Follen, A. L.	"Der Bursch und Philister" ("Ein Wille, fest und scharf wie Stahl")	Unknown	AdL	USV
228. Follen, A. L.	"Vaterlands Söhne" ("Vaterlands Söhne, traute Genossen!")	Unknown	Hase; AdL	UP
229. Follen, K.	"Bundeslied" or "Lied der Deutschen" ("Brause, du Freiheitssang, brause wie Wogendrang")	Unknown	Hase; 365fG; AdL	USV; UP

POET	TITLE/FIRST LINE	COMPOSER	PUB. INFO.	SETTING
230. Freiligrath, F.	"Hurrah Germania!" ("Hurrah, du stolzes schönes Weib, Hurrah Germania!")	T. Mohr	Hase, No. 795, 493	SV-p
231. Friedrichsen	"Deutschland und Welschland" ("Mag alles Wunder von dem Lande singen")	A. L. Follen	AdL	?
232. Geibel, E.	"Die Rheinsage" or "Rheinsage vom Kaiser Karl"	C. Decker	***Leipzig: Hofmeister	SV
233. Ibid.		C. A. F. Eckert	**B. Bogler	UP
234. Ibid.		J. Matthieux	**Berlin: Trautwein	SV-p
235. Ibid.		G. Rebling	***Magdeburg: Heinrichshofen	UP
236. Ibid.		C. H. C. Reinecke	***Leipzig: Breitkopf & Härtel	SV-p
237. Ibid.		R. F. Siebenkees	***Leipzig: Whistling	SV-p, g
238. Geibel, E.	"Der Ritter vom Rhein" ("Ich weiss einen Helden von seltener Art")	Unknown	Hase	USV
239. Geibel, E.	"Unter der Loreley"	H. Marschner	***Offenbach: André	SV-p, g
240. Giesebrecht, L.	"Gutenbergsbild" ("In dem Lichtmeer ohne Schranke")	C. Czerny	*Mainz: Schott	P-p
241. Ibid.		C. Loewe	*Mainz: Schott	UP
242. Göttling, K.	"Rheinweinlied" ("Rheinwein nur aus Römerbechern trink'")	A. Methfessel	AdL, No. 22, 208	UP
243. Göttling, K.	"Unser Berather" ("Nie kommen auf die Ruhgedanken")	A. Methfessel	AdL, No. 23, 209	USV
244. Gräter	"Ein Hoch dem Schütz Armin und Berthold Schwarz" ("Es leben alle Schützen hoch im deutschen Vaterland!")	Unknown	365fG, No. 168, 264	?

Author	Title	Composer	Publisher / Opus	Format
245. Hahn-Hahn, Countess I.	"[Am] Rheinfall" ("In den Abgrund lass mich schauen")	R. Franz	Op. 44, no. 6; Leipzig: Fr. Kistner (see example 4.33)	SV-p, g
246. Ibid.		F. S. Hölzel	***Vienna: Mechetti	SV-p
247. Hammerschmidt, M.	"Das rheinische Mädchen"	H. Lucan	***Bonn: Simrock	SV-p
248. Ibid.		Unknown	VfMI; Erk, DLSI	SV-p, g
249. Haupt, L.	"Weh dir, mein Vaterland"	Unknown	AdL, No. 113, 161	?
250. Haupt, T. v.	"Der Herbst am Rhein"	J. Panny	*Op. 32, no. 4; Mainz: Schott	P with orch
251. Haupt, T. v.	"Der Rhein"	J. Panny	*Op. 25, no. I; Mainz: Schott	P-p; P with inst; UP; SV-p, g
252. Heine, H.	"Die alten, bösen Lieder" ("Die alten, bösen Lieder")	R. Schumann	Op. 48, no. 16	SV-p
253. Heine, H.	"Berg' und Burgen" ("Berg' und Burgen schau'n herunter")	R. Schumann	Op. 24, no. 7	SV-p
254. Heine, H.	"Im Rhein" or "Am Rhein" ("Im [Am] Rhein, im heiligen [schönen] Strome")	R. Franz	***Op. 18, no. 2; Leipzig: Peters	SV-p, g
255. Ibid.		F. Liszt	*Berlin: Schlesinger (1st version)	SV-p
256. Ibid.		R. Schumann	Op. 48, no. 6; ***Leipzig: Peters	SV-p
257. Ibid.		W. Stade	***Leipzig: Whistling	SV-p
258. Heine, H.	"Die Lorelei" or "Lorelei;" "Die Lorelzy," "Loreley," "Die Lore-Ley" ("Ich weiss nicht, was soll es bedeuten")	J. Becker	*Leipzig: Klemm	SV-p
259. Ibid.		J. Bürde	***Magdeburg: Heinrichshofen	SV-p

POET	TITLE/FIRST LINE	COMPOSER	PUB. INFO.	SETTING
260. Ibid.		L. Ehlert	**Leipzig: Peters	SV-p; SV-p, g
261. Ibid.		C. W. Ellisen	***Hannover: Hornemann	SV-p
262. Ibid.		Fr. Gretscher	***Coblenz: Falckenberg	SV-p
263. Ibid.		J. Grill	*Mainz: Schott	SV with cello & p
264. Ibid.		G. A. Heinze	***Amsterdam: Roothaan	SV-p
265. Ibid.		J. Hoven	***Vienna: Haslinger	SV-p
266. Ibid.		E. Klietzsch	Leipzig: Breitkopf & Härtel	SV-p, g
267. Ibid.		F. Kücken	*Op. 3; Leipzig: Hof-meister	SV-p
268. Ibid.		F. Liszt	**Berlin: Schlesinger (1st version)	SV-p
269. Ibid.		J. Matthieux	***Berlin: Trautwein	SV-p
270. Ibid.		J. Netzer	*Leipzig: Hofmeister	P-p, g or misc
271. Ibid.		C. Oberthür	***Mainz: Schott	SV-p
272. Ibid.		L. Schlotman	***Berlin: Guttentag	SV-p
273. Ibid.		F. Silcher	***Stuttgart: Zumsteeg	SV-p, g; UP; USV
274. Ibid.		E. Steinkühler	***Mainz: Schott	SV-p
275. Ibid.		F. H. Truhn	***Berlin: Schlesinger	UP

#	Author	Title	Composer	Publisher	
276.	Ibid.		Unknown	***Hannover: Nagel	SV-p
277.	Heine, H.	"Die Wallfahrt nach Kevlaar" ("Am Fenster stand die Mutter")	Unknown	Hase	?
278.	Heisterbergk	"[Turners] Wanderlied" ("Auf, schmücket die Hüte mit grünen-den Maien")	Unknown	365fG	?
279.	Ibid.		C. M. v. Weber	AdL	UP
280.	Herwegh, G.	"Der beste Berg" ("Es ist ein Berg auf Erden")	Unknown	Hase, No. 840, 526	?
281.	Herwegh, G.	"Rheinweinlied" ("Wo solch ein Feuer noch gedeiht")	W. Bauck	***Berlin: Schlesinger; AdL, No. 21, 204	SV-p
282.	Ibid.		W. Dettmer	***Offenbach: André	SV-p
283.	Ibid.		C. Diehl	***Mainz: Schott	SV-p
284.	Ibid.		R. J. Dürrner	VfMI	?
285.	Ibid.		D. Elster	AdL	UP
286.	Ibid.		R. Franz	VfMI	UP
287.	Ibid.		G. Hammer	***Mainz: Schott	SV-p
288.	Ibid.		F. Liszt	*Mainz: Schott	P-p, g
289.	Ibid.		H. Marschner	*Leipzig: Hofmeister	UP
290.	Ibid.		F. Mendelssohn	**Op. 76, no. 2; Leipzig: Kistner	UP
291.	Ibid.		H. T. Petschke	***Leipzig: Breitkopf & Härtel	UP
292.	Ibid.		G. Reichardt	*Berlin: Bote & Bock	UP
293.	Ibid.		E. Richter	***Berlin: Bote & Bock	P-p, g; UP
294.	Ibid.		Unknown	365fG	USV
295.	Ibid.		Unknown	***Augsburg: Kreuzer	UP

POET	TITLE/FIRST LINE	COMPOSER	PUB. INFO.	SETTING
296. Ibid.	Ibid.	Unknown	Hase	USV
297. Ibid.	Ibid.	Volksweise	Hase	?
298. Ibid.	Ibid.	S. A. Zimmermann	**Mainz: Schott	UP
299. Herwegh, G.	"Wer ist frei?" ("Der ist allein ein freier Mann")	W. Baumgartner	Hase	USV
300. Hoffmann, H. H.	"Hermann" or "Loblied auf Hermann" ("Preis dir, Hermann, Volkserretter")	Unknown	Hase	USV
301. Ibid.	Ibid.	Unknown	365fG	USV
302. Hoffmann, H. H.	"Lob und Dank dem Vater Rhein!"	F. J. Messer	*Mainz: Schott	P-p
303. Hoffmann von Fallersleben, A. H.	"Rheinlied und Rheinlied" ("In jedem Haus ein Klimperkasten")	Volksweise	AdL	USV
304. Hoffmann von Fallersleben, A. H.	"Wer in Deutschland"	Unknown	Kossmaly in NZfM	?
305. Immermann, K. L.	"Auf dem Rhein" ("Auf deinem Grunde haben sie an verborg'-nem Ort")	R. Schumann	**Op. 51, no. 4	SV-p
306. Katsch, A.	"Hundert Semester" ("Als ich schlummernd lag heut' Nacht")	A. Schlieben	CB	?
307. Keil, R.	"Die lustigen Brüder"	R. Keil	CB	?
308. Kerner, J.	"Der reichste Fürst" ("Preisen mit viel schönen Reden")	Volksweise	AdL	USV
309. Kopisch, A.	"Blücher am Rhein" ("Die Heere bleiben am Rheine stehn")	C. G. Reissiger	Berlin: Schlesinger	SV-p and chorus
310. Körner, T.	"Jägerlied" ("Frisch auf, ihr Jäger, frei und flink")	C. F. D. Schubart	Hase	USW

311. Körner, T.	"Lied der schwarzen Jäger"	"Melody of another lied"	Hase	USV
312. Körner, T.	"Lützows wilde Jagd" ("Was glänzt dort vom Walde")	C. M. v. Weber	VfMI, No. 254, 613; AdL, No. 43, 72; LS, No. 20, 170	UP; SV-p; USV
313. Körner, T.	"Trinklied" ("Gläser klingen, Nektar glüht in dem vollen Becher")	Unknown	AdL	USV
314. Ibid.	Ibid.	C. F. Zöllner	Leipzig: Fr. Kistner	UP
315. Lichnowsky, Prince F.	"Die Zelle in Nonnenwerth"	F. Liszt	*Cologne: Eck (1st version)	SV-p
316. Lorenz, W.	"Loreley" or "Lorelei" ("Es flüstern und rauschen die Wogen")	R. Schumann	**Op. 53, no. 2; Leipzig: Whistling	SV-p
317. Löwenstein, R.	"Was frägt der Trinker nach Censur?"	Unknown	AdL	USV
318. Lütze, A.	"Der Drachenfels" ("Sag an, was hinauf zur Drachenkluft")	C. Loewe	Op. 121, no. 2; Dresden: F. W. Arnold (see example 4.31)	SV-p
319. Mahlmann, A.	"Weinlied" ("Mein Lebenslauf ist Lieb' und Lust und lauter Liederklang")	Unknown	VfMII, No. 347, 116; CB, No. 118, 122	UP
320. Matthisson, F. v.	"Jünglingswonne" ("So lang im deutschen Eichentale")	F. Schubert	VfMI	UP
321. Miller, J. M.	"Auf, ihr meine deutschen Brüder"	Unknown	AdL, No. 19, 202	USV
322. Müchler, K.	"Ich trinke!" ("Im kühlen Keller sitz' ich hier auf einem Fass vol Reben")	K. L. Fische=	Erk	USV
323. Müller, C. Wilhelm	"Die nächtliche Erscheinung zu Speier"	C. Koch	**Berlin: Abelsdorff	SV-p
324. Müller, C. W.	"Die Arche Noah" ("Das Essen nicht das Trinken")	J. C. F. Schneider	Hase, No. 276, 185; AdL, No. 14, 192	USV; UP

POET	TITLE/FIRST LINE	COMPOSER	PUB. INFO.	SETTING
325. Müller, C. W.	"Doppeltes Vaterland" ("An der Elbe Strand ist mein Vaterland")	F. E. Fesca	AdL, No. 31, 219	USV
326. Müller, C. W.	"Der Frühling am Rhein"	H. Dorn	***Cologne: Eck	SV-p
327. Nolden, P.	"Der Rhein ist 'ne Perl"	A. Pütz	***Mainz: Schott	SV-p
328. Nonne, J. H. C.	"Beim Siegesfeuer am 18. Oktober" ("Flamme, empor!")	C. L. T. Gläser	Erk, DdF	UP
329. Oër, Max v.	"Die Glocken zu Speier" ("Zu Lüttich, im letzten Häuselein")	C. Loewe	Op. 67, no. 2	SV-p
330. Pfeffel, G. C.	"Die Tabakspfeife" or "Der Edelmann und der Invalide" or "Die Türkenpfeife" ("Der Edelmann: 'Gott grüss' euch, Alter!'")	C. P. E. Pilz	Erk, DSLI; 365fG	USV
331. Pfeiffer	"Kehre wieder, alte Treue!" ("Deutsche Eichen seh' ich streben")	Unknown	AdL	?
332. Reiff, J. J.	"Kriegslied" ("Rhein-Preussiches Kriegerlied")	H. Neumann	*Elberfeld: Arnold	P with inst
333. Ibid.	Ibid.	F. Weber	*Bonn: Simrock	P-p or orch
334. Reinick, R.	"Sonntags am Rhein" ("Des Sonntags in der Morgenstund")	R. Schumann	Op. 36, no. I	SV-p
335. Ibid.	Ibid.	G. Vierling	***Berlin: Guttentag	P-p, g
336. Rinne, C.	"Vaterlandslied" or "Ein Deutschland" ("Und hörst du das mächtige Klingen?")	A. E. Marschner	VfMl; ALfdaK	UP
337. Rückert, F.	"Marschall Vorwärts" ("Marschall Vorwärts! tapfrer Preusse, deinen Blücher")	Unknown	Erk, DdF	?
338. Rustige, H. v.	"Auf, mein Deutschland" ("Auf, mein Deutschland, schirm, dein Haus!")	F. Kücken	ALfdaK	USV
339. Salchow, G. A.	"Morgenlied der Schwarzen Freischaar, 1813" ("Heraus, heraus die Klingen")	Unknown	AdL, No. 170, 400	USV
340. Scheffel, J. V. v.	"Alt Heidelberg" or "Lied des Trompeters von Säckingen" ("Alt Heidelberg, du feine, du Stadt an Ehren reich")	C. Kuntze	Hase	USV

341. Ibid.	Ibid.	S. A. Zimmermann	CB	?
342. Scheffel, J. V. v.	"Die Fahndung" ("Und wieder sprach der Rodenstein; 'Pelzkappenschwerenot!'")	Unknown	CB	?
343. Scheffel, J. V. v.	"Perkêo" ("Das war der Zwerg 'Perkêo'")	S. Gruwe	CB, No. 33, 37	USV
344. Scheffel, J. V. v.	"Rodenstein im Waldhorn" ("Und wieder sass beim Weine im Waldhorn ob der Brück")	J. J. A. Barth	Hase	USV
345. Scheffel, J. V. v.	"Rodensteins Auszug" ("Es regt sich was im Odenwald")	C. Hering	CB, No. 67, 83	USV
346. Scheffel, J. V. v.	"Die Teutoburger Schlacht" ("Als die Römer frech geworden")	A. Anger	Hase	USV
347. Scheffel, J. V. v.	"Der Überfall" ("Und wieder sprach der Rodenstein")	Unknown	CB	?
348. Scheffel, J. V. v.	"Das wilde Heer" ("Das war der Herr von Rodenstein")	C. Schmezer	Erk, DLSl, No. 20, 23l	SV-p, g
349. Scheffel, J. V. v.	"Der Willekumm" ("Und als der Herr von Rodenstein zum Frankenstein sich wandte")	W. Tappert	Hase	?
350. Schenkendorf, M. v. & L. F. Jahn	"Die deutschen Ströme" ("Lasst uns die deutschen Ströme singen im deutschen, festlichen Verein")	Unknown	AdL	USV
351. Schenkendorf, M. v.	"Frühlingsgruss (an das Vaterland, 1814)" ("Wie mir deine Freuden winken")	B. Klein	Erk, DdF; Hase	UP
352. Schenkendorf, M. v.	"Das Lied vom Rhein" ("Es klingt ein heller Klang")	H. G. Nägeli	VfMl, No. 120, 268; CB, No. 62, 66; Erk, DLSl, No. 29, 242; Hase, No. 781, 828	UP; USV; P; SV-p, g
353. Ibid.	Ibid.	Unknown	AdL	UP
354. Schiller, F.	"Der Graf von Habsburg" ("Zu Aachen, in seiner Kaiserpracht")	C. Loewe	Op. 98	SV-p
355. Schmidt v. Lübeck, G. P.	"An die Deutschen" ("Vom alten deutschen Meer umflossen")	R. Müller	Hase	USV

POET	TITLE/FIRST LINE	COMPOSER	PUB. INFO.	SETTING
356. Schmidt v. Lübeck, G. P.	"Deutscher Ehrenpreis" ("Von allen Ländern in der Welt das deutsche mir am besten gefällt")	E. Kuhl	Hase	USV
357. Schneckenburger, M.	"Die Wacht am Rhein" ("Es braust ein Ruf wie Donnerhall")	J. Mendel	Essen: Baedeker	SV-p
358. Ibid.	Ibid.	C. Wilhelm	Leipzig: Peters	SV-p
359. Schreiber, A.	"Der Königstuhl bei Rhense" ("Am Rhein da stand vor Alters ein Stuhl aus grauem Stein")	Unknown	Hase, No. 770, 473	USV
360. Schröer, W.	"Von der Katzbach zog ein Held" ("Von der Katzbach zog ein Held")	Volksweise	Erk, DdF	USV; p
361. Seidler	"Die Loreley"	E. Steinkühler	**Mainz: Schott	SV-p or inst
362. Simrock, K.	"Der Nibelungen Hort" ("Es war einmal ein König, ein König war's am Rhein")	Unknown	Hase, No. 648, 395; Erk, No. 64, 76	USV; UP
363. Simrock, K.	"Warnung vor dem Rhein" ("An den Rhein, an den Rhein, zieh' nicht an den Rhein")	F. Mendelssohn	**Bonn: Simrock	SV-p
364. Stolterforth, A. v.	"Blüchers Rheinübergang" ("Gott mit uns! und nun zu Schiffe'")	Unknown	Erk, DdF, No. 38, 40	?
365. Strakerian	"Setzt euch, Brüder, in die Runde"	J. C. F. Schneider	AdL	UP
366. Tenner, C.	"Mutterseelen Allein" ("Es blickt so still der Mond mich an")	A. Bräuer	Erk, DLSI	SV-p, g
367. Tenner, C.	"Rheinisches Trinklied"	F. Kücken	Berlin: Schlesinger	P
368. Thümmel, v.	"Zitherbubens Morgenlied" ("Fröhlich und wohlgemuth")	J. H. K. Bornhardt	LS	SV-p, g
369. Uhland, L.	"Graf Eberstein" ("Zu Speier im Saale")	C. Loewe	Op. 9	SV-p
370. Uhland, L.	"Rheinsehnsucht" ("Mein Herz ist am Rheine")	H. Marschner	**Dresden: Paul	SV-p

371. Ibid.	Ibid.	W. Speyer	**Stuttgart: Göpel; Offenbach: André; Frankfurt: Hedler	SV-p
372. Ibid.	Ibid.	F. Weber	**Cologne: Eck; Leipzig: Hofmeister	SV-p
373. Uhland, L.	"Siegfrieds Schwert"	Unknown	Hase, No. 831, 521	SV-p
374. Uhland, L.	"Die sterbenden Helden" ("Germanenschwerter drängen Feindes Heer wild vor sich her")	Unknown	AdL	UP
375. Uhland, L.	"Vorwärts" ("Vorwärts! Fort und immer fort!")	Unknown	Hase	?
376. Uhland, L.	"Der Wirtin Töchterlein" ("Es zogen drei Bursche wohl über den Rhein")	C. Loewe	**Berlin: Schlesinger	SV-p
377. Voss, J. H.	"Rheinweinlied" ("Mit Eichenlaub den Hut bekränzt!")	Unknown	Hase, No. 764, 469	USV
378. Weissmann, A. H.	"Festlied"	J. H. Stuntz	Mainz: Schott	P-p
379. Werner	"Kriegslied" ("Gott mit uns! Wir ziehn in den heiligen Krieg!")	A. Methfessel	Op. 35	P-p
380. Wihl, L.	"Das neue Lied vom Rhein"	F. W. Markull	**Leipzig: Siegel	UP
381. Wolff, O. L. B.	"Wo möcht' ich sein?" ("Wo möcht' ich sein?")	A. Methfessel	365fG	USV
382. Zuccarini	"Arthurs Tafelrunde" ("Es schlingt sich die Runde, es kreist der Pokal")	Unknown	AdL	USV

INDEX OF COMPOSERS
LISTED IN THE
RHEINLIEDER INDEX

(Alphabetical list of composers and item numbers corresponding to their names in the preceding Index of Rheinlieder Published in the 1840s)

Note: Clara Schumann's setting of Heine's "Die Lorelei," completed on 8 June 1843, was not published in her lifetime (see example A.1).

Ex. A.1. C. Schumann, "Die Lorelei" (Heine). In the Archives of the Robert-Schumann-Haus, Zwickau, file no. 5987-A, meas. 1–20. Courtesy of the Staatsbibliothek zu Berlin, Preussischer Kulturbesitz, Musikabteilung mit Mendelssohn-Archiv.

NOTES

INTRODUCTION

1. Schumann's ninth Rheinlied, a setting of K. L. Immermann's "Auf dem Rhein" ("Auf deinem Grunde haben sie an verborgnem Ort"), was written in 1846.

2. C. F. Whistling's *Handbuch der musikalischen Literatur, oder allgemeines systematisch geordnetes Verzeichniss der in Deutschland und in den angrenzenden Ländern gedruckten Musikalien, auch musikalischen Schriften und Abbildungen, mit Anzeige des Verleger und Preise*, 3d ed., 3 vols. and supplementary vol. (1839 to the beginning of 1844 and January 1844 to the end of 1851), ed. Adolph Hofmeister (Leipzig: Friedrich Hofmeister, 1845, 1852).

3. Richard Wagner, *Prose Works*, trans. William Ashton Ellis (London: Kegan Paul, 1892–99) 1:19.

4. See Joseph Kerman, *Contemplating Music: Challenges to Musicology* (Cambridge, Mass.: Harvard University Press, 1985), 12.

5. Regarding these two themes and the vast but particular socioeconomic upheavals in nineteenth-century Germany, I agree with Edward F. Kravitt that the entirety of a culture's socioeconomic, political, and ideological context limits the concept of musical Romanticism to a specific time and place, rather than assigning it to a universal position ever in flux in alternation with an equally amorphous Classicism. See Kravitt, "Romanticism Today," *Musical Quarterly* 76/1 (spring 1992): 104–5.

6. See Barbara Tuchman, *Practicing History: Selected Essays* (New York: Knopf, 1981), 23, and Gertrude Himmelfarb, *The New History and the Old* (Cambridge, Mass.: Harvard University Press, 1987), 69.

7. Dale H. Porter, *The Emergence of the Past: A Theory of Historical Explanation* (Chicago: University of Chicago Press, 1981), 178.

CHAPTER ONE

1. Hanslick cited in Julius Bautz, *Geschichte des deutschen Männergesangs in übersichtlicher Darstellung* (Frankfurt am Main: Steyl & Thomas, 1890), 61.

2. Gottschalk Wedel, "Deutsches Volkslied," *Neue Zeitschrift für Musik* (hereafter, *NZfM*) (13 May 1842): 153.

3. Ibid., (17 May 1842): 158.

4. Johann Gottfried Herder, *Fragmente über die neuere deutsche Literatur* and *Ideen zur Philosophie der Geschichte der Menschheit* (Riga and Leipzig, 1791), cited in H. G. Schenk, *The Mind of the European Romantics* (Garden City, N.Y.: Doubleday, 1969), 16.

5. Jahn cited in Hans Kohn, *The Mind of Germany: The Education of a Nation* (New York: Harper & Row, 1960), 89.

6. Georg Wilhelm Friedrich Hegel, *Philosophy of Right*, trans. S. W. Dyde (London: Blackwood, 1896), 257–73; also Hegel, *Philosophy of History*, cited in Boyd C. Shafer, *Nationalism: Myth and Reality* (New York: Harcourt, Brace and World, 1955), 25–26.

7. Shafer, *Nationalism*, 104.

8. In his *Encyclopédie* of 1780 Denis Diderot defined a citizen as a member of a free society of several families. The *patrie* was symbolized by a father and his children, i.e., the family unit. See Shafer, *Nationalism*, 104.

9. Kohn, *The Mind of Germany*, 90.

10. Jakob Venedey, *La France, l'Allemagne et les Provinces Rhénanes* (Paris, 1840), 68–69.

11. Hector Berlioz described the war songs, including one of his own, heard in Paris during the heated postrevolution days. See *Memoirs of Hector Berlioz from 1803 to 1865, Comprising his Travels in Germany, Italy, Russia, and England*, trans. Ernest Newman, rev. ed. (New York: Dover, 1966), 107.

12. See Irene Collins, "Liberalism in Nineteenth-Century Europe," in *European Political History, 1815–1870: Aspects of Liberalism*, vol. 5, ed. Eugene C. Black (New York: Harper & Row, 1967), 103–27.

13. The Rhenish Catholic middle classes, for example, active politically and strong economically, hoped to retain the civil equalities granted under French rule. Therefore they strongly opposed annexation by Prussia.

14. Karl-Georg Faber, *Die Rheinlande zwischen Restauration und Revolution: Probleme der rheinischen Geschichte von 1814 bis 1848 im Spiegel der zeitgenössichen Publizistik* (Wiesbaden: Franz Steiner, 1966), 369–71. In addition, a considerable number of émigrés from the French Revolution of 1789 had settled in the Rhinelands, reinforcing pro-French sympathies there.

15. Jacques Droz, *Europe between Revolutions, 1815–1848*, ed. J. H. Plumb, trans. Robert Baldick (New York: Harper & Row, 1968), 153–54.

16. Or the *kleindeutsch* view, as opposed to the *grossdeutsch* outlook.

17. Krause, in *Von der musikalischen Poesie* of 1752, advocated composing song melodies that only modestly enhanced the poetry. The Krause aesthetic long endured. Close adherence to this style of easy accessibility, however, led to the mass production of lieder that in the later eighteenth century threatened to dissolve into mere

triviality. See Max Friedlaender, ed., *Das deutsche Lied im 18. Jahrhundert*, 3 vols. (Stuttgart and Berlin: J. G. Cotta, 1902; reprint, Hildesheim: Georg Olms, 1962).

18. Walter Wiora, *Das deutsche Lied: zur Geschichte und Ästhetik einer musikalischen Gattung* (Wolfenbüttel: Möseler, 1971), 132–33.

19. E.g., Ludwig Erk, *Die deutschen Volkslieder mit ihren Singweisen*, 3 vols. (Berlin, 1838); Wilhelm von Zuccalmaglio and A. Kretzschmer, *Deutsche Volkslieder mit ihren Original-Weisen*, 2 vols. (Berlin: Vereins-Buchhandlung, 1840); and August Heinrich Hoffmann von Fallersleben, ed., *Deutsches Volksgesangbuch* (Leipzig: Wilhelm Engelmann, 1848).

20. Walter Wiora, "Die Romantisierung alter Mollmelodik im Liede von Schubert bis Wolf," in *Deutsches Jahrbuch der Musikwissenschaft für 1966* II, ed. Rudolf Eller (Leipzig: Peters, 1967), 61–71. In some instances, Wiora notes, the *volkstümlich* idiom derived from an intermediary source, itself an art song. He notes, however, that earlier nineteenth-century German folksong collectors frequently sought out ancient melodies atypically in minor. The very scarcity of the latter reinforced the Romantics' notion that such melodies, by association with certain old church modes, were sacred relics of a distant German past.

21. Wiora, *Das deutsche Lied*, 129. *Volkstümliche* lieder, Wiora adds, demonstrate melodic characteristics corresponding to these "spheres" of the poetic life, as in the case of a piano accompaniment suggesting the playing style of folk instruments.

22. See Friedrich Blume, *Classic and Romantic Music*, trans. M. D. Herter Norton (New York: Norton, 1970), 111–12.

23. August Reissmann, *Das deutsche Lied in seiner historischen Entwicklung* (Cassel: Oswald Bertram, 1861), 89.

24. Schulz considered "the appearance of the familiar" as the essence of *Volkston*.

25. Reissmann, *Geschichte des deutschen Liedes* (Berlin: J. Guttentag [D. Collin], 1874), 153. His list of *volkstümlich* song composers included these writers of Rheinlieder: F. H. Himmel, H. G. Nägeli, C. Kreutzer, F. Schneider, G. Reichardt, F. Silcher, A. Methfessel, A. Neithardt, and C. M. von Weber.

26. Ibid., 158–63, 167–68, et passim. Reissmann's *volkstümlich* examples included Schubert's "Das Wandern ist des Müllers Lust" and "Sah ein Knab' ein Röslein stehn"; Mendelssohn's "Auf Flügeln des Gesanges"; and Handel's *Messiah*. He considered Mozart's last seven operas even more *volkstümlich* than Handel's oratorios, for the former represented actual, not abstract, life as it continually changes. Yet he judged Mozart's operas also as the highest form of art music, unlike the *volkstümliche* lieder of Hiller and others.

27. Michel le Bris, *Romantics and Romanticism*, trans. Barbara Bray and Bernard C. Swift (New York: Rizzoli, 1981), 178. See also Fritz Novotny, *Painting and Sculpture in Europe, 1780–1880*, 2d ed. (Baltimore: Penguin Books, 1971), 227–33.

28. Hans Joachim Moser, *Das deutsche Lied seit Mozart* (Berlin: Atlantis, 1937), 1:141–42.

29. Ibid., 150–51. See also Gunter Pulvermacher, "Biedermeier," *The New Grove Dictionary of Music and Musicians*, ed. Stanley Sadie (London: Macmillan, 1980), 2:695–97.

30. Ernst Bücken, *Das deutsche Lied: Probleme und Gestalten* (Hamburg: Hanseatische Verlangsanstalt, 1939), 114–22. Hans Hermann Rosenwald classifies the Biedermeier lied as a *gesellig* (social) type of *volkstümlich* music as opposed to the Romantic *Stimmungslieder* (mood songs) of Schubert and Schumann. See Rosenwald, *Geschichte des deutschen Liedes zwischen Schubert und Schumann* (Berlin: Benno Balan, 1930), 4. All the Biedermeier song composers that he lists (Weber, Marschner, Kreutzer, Silcher, and Reissiger) wrote Rheinlieder.

31. Wilhelm Heinrich Riehl, "Geleitsbrief," *Hausmusik* (1855), cited in Bücken, *Lied*, 122–23.

32. Richard Kötzschke, *Geschichte des deutschen Männergesanges* (Dresden: Wilhelm Limpert, 1927), 78. This statement echoes general opinion in the mid-nineteenth century, as in Gottschalk Wedel, "Deutsches Volkslied," *NZfM* (17 May 1842): 162–63. Wedel disparages "battle" folk songs inspired by the Wars of Liberation as merely "one-sided," unlike nonmilitary folk songs embracing a full range of both positive and negative human feelings. See also C. A. Föppl, "Über den gegenwärtigen Zustand der teutschen Tonkunst, wie er ist und sein sollte," *Caecilia* 90 (1844): 85. Föppl, lauding the *Männergesang* as a unique and "truly German art," lists an array of composers contributing to the genre: J. M. Haydn, H. G. Nägeli, A. Methfessel, C. M. von Weber, F. Kuhlau, L. Spohr, K. Kreutzer, F. Schubert, K. F. Zelter, et al. See also Benedikt Widmann, *Die kunsthistorische Entwickelung des Männerchors in drei Vorlesungen dargestellt* (Leipzig: C. Merseburger, 1884); and Otto Elben, *Der volkstümliche deutsche Männergesang* (Tübingen: Verlag der H. Laupp'schen Buchhandlung, 1887), 402–3 et passim.

33. See Kötzschke, *Geschichte*, 70.

34. Albert Methfessel, "Vorwort," in *Sechs deutsche Kriegslieder für eine und mehrere Stimmen, mit Chören und willkührlicher Begleitung des Fortepiano, in Musik gesetzt und allen braven deutschen Kriegern gewidmet*, Op. 35 (1813), 2d. ed. (Rudolstadt: Hof- Buch- und Kunst-Handlung, 1814). Methfessel's group consisted entirely of Wars of Liberation veterans, who especially favored a repertoire of *Vaterlandslieder* that included two Rheinlieder for male voices: a setting of Claudius's "Stimmt an mit hellem hohen Klang" and of Arndt's "Der Gott der Eisen wachsen liess."

35. See Rosenwald, *Geschichte*, 49–50. One of this study's chief sources of Rheinlieder is also a major repository of German student songs: Irwin H. Steiner, ed., *Auswahl deutscher Lieder*, 6th ed. (Leipzig: Serig'sche Buchhandlung, 1844).

36. Cf. "Zur Geschichte des Männergesanges," *Allgemeine musikalische Zeitung* (hereafter, *AmZ*) (24 January 1844): 49.

37. Franz Samans, ed., "Vorwort," *365 fröhliche Guitarrlieder* 3 (Wesel: J. Bagel, 1848). Indeed, the Thüringer Sängerbund, established in Erfurt, held open-air

meetings annually through the 1840s. Beautiful landscapes determined the site of each event. According to a contemporary participant at one of these convocations, "There it seems as if the harmonies would be carried away to the distant mountains—the forest night, the forest darkness stand before us as if alive." See the anonymously authored "Zur Geschichte des Männergesanges," *AmZ* (31 January 1844): 65.

38. Carl Hase, "Vorrede" (reprinted from the 1843 ed.), *Liederbuch des deutschen Volkes*, 2d ed., ed. Felix Dahn, Carl Hase, and Carl Reinecke (Leipzig: Breitkopf & Härtel, 1883), 3–5. All Hase's comments regarding these lieder, he notes, apply equally to the 1883 edition.

39. The Siebengebirge are the storied Seven Mountains rising over the Rhine in the vicinity of Cologne and Bonn.

40. Wedel, "Vierstimmiger Gesang," *NZfM* (15 April 1842): 122.

41. The text and music of the a cappella songs performed by the first Berlin *Liedertafel* were contributed almost totally by club members, to whom Goethe offered several poems for musical settings. See Bautz, *Geschichte*, 87.

42. A *Jüngere Berliner Liedertafel* was established by Ludwig Berger and Bernhard Klein in 1819. The group consisted of both amateur and professional musicians, the latter including the critic Ludwig Rellstab and Rheinlied composer Gustav Reichardt, whose popular setting of "Was ist des deutschen Vaterland?" was composed specifically for this club. See Kötzschke, *Geschichte*, 74.

43. In 1805 Nägeli organized a Singinstitut for children and in 1812 the Züricher Stadtsängerverein. The latter was open to singers from all social levels and dedicated to furthering the *Männergesang*. In his *Gesangbildungslehre für den Männerchor* (Zürich, 1817), he expressed a preference for male voices for reasons of enunciation of texts and penetrating tone quality. See Bautz, *Geschichte*, 8–9.

44. The Frankfurt am Main *Liederkranz* undertook the foundation of "brother song clubs" along the Rhine and its tributary, the Main. In January 1844 the *AmZ* claimed that in Swabia and Franconia "almost every city and even every larger village has its own *Liederkranz*"; see "Zur Geschichte des Männergesanges," *AmZ* (24 January 1844): 52. Kötzschke, *Geschichte*, 74ff., lists important *Liedertafeln* of the time and songs most performed by them. Rheinlieder are conspicuous: the Stuttgart *Liederkranz* (Weber's setting of Körner's "Lützows wilde Jagd"); the Leipzig *Liedertafel* (H. Marschner's setting of "Im alten Fass zu Heidelberg," Mendelssohn's setting of Herwegh's "Rheinweinlied," and K. F. Zöllner's setting of "Wo möcht' ich sein?"; the Dresden *Liedertafel*, conducted by R. Schumann from 1847 to 1848 (his setting of Becker's Rheinlied, C. G. Reissiger's setting of "Blücher am Rhein," and R. J. Dürrner's setting of "Zwischen Frankreich und dem Böhmerwald"); the Munich *Liedertafel* (Franz Lachner's setting of the "Siegesgesang aus der Hermannsschlacht"); the Tübingen *Liedertafel* (Silcher's setting of Heine's "Die Lorelei" and

of "Zu Strassburg auf der Schanz"); the Brunswick *Liedertafel* (Franz Abt's setting of "Siegesgesang der Deutschen nach der Hermannsschlacht"); the Krefeld *Liedertafel* (K. Wilhelm's setting of Schneckenburger's "Die Wacht am Rhein"); and the Männergesangverein of Jena University (Weber's setting of Körner's "Lützows wilde Jagd," along with an unidentified setting of "Was ist des deutschen Vaterland?").

The majority of the *Männergesang* composers listed above, as well as others, either belonged to or conducted *Liedertafeln*. A comprehensive survey of *Liedertafeln* and their repertoires would no doubt turn up many more Rheinlieder than those noted above.

45. Heinz Blommen, *Anfänge und Entwicklung des Männerchorwesens am Niederrhein: Beiträge zur rheinischen Musikgeschichte 42* (Cologne: Arno Volk-Verlag, 1960), 250.

46. The enduring vigor of this amateur "movement" testified to the sharply rising income and living standard even of the German lower middle classes at this time. Their concerts had originated in social music making enjoyed in taverns, cafés, parks, churches, and dance halls as those of the upper bourgeois and nobility had developed from salons. Artisans and factory workers constituted the largest working force of urban society in Germany and elsewhere by the mid-nineteenth century. By the 1860s artisans formed 50 percent of Prussia's manufacturing force, though factory employees soon outnumbered them. In such new Rhineland manufacturing cities as Essen, only seventy-seven kilometers north of Düsseldorf, factory workers represented the majority of the population by ca. 1850. See William Weber, *Music and the Middle Class* (New York: Holmes & Meier, 1975), 85; and Peter N. Stearns, *European Society in Upheaval: Social History since 1750*, 2d ed. (New York: Macmillan, 1975), 144 et passim.

47. The following chronological list provides a sampling of Rhenish *Sängerfeste* (song festivals) that included Rheinlieder: Mainz, 1835, a great *Sängerfest* of four hundred singers (Meyerbeer's "Ein Festgesang zu Ehren Gutenbergs"); Krefeld, 10 May 1837, *Liedertafel* festival (G. Reichardt, "Was ist des deutschen Vaterland?"); Mainz, 1837, *Sängerfest* honoring its native Gutenberg (Loewe's "festival oratorio" *Gutenberg*, including the Rheinlied "Gutenbergs Bild"); Frankfurt am Main, 1838, *Sängerfest* (Weber's "Lützows wilde Jagd"); Düsseldorf, May 1839, Rhenish music festival (an unidentified setting of Arndt's "Was ist des deutschen Vaterland?"); Heidelberg, 17 May 1843, music festival (Louis Hetsch's cantata *Das Heidelberger Schloss* with the Rheinlied "Romanze von Wolfsbrunnen"); Kleve, 1845, Lower Rhine–Netherlands *Sängerfest* (C. G. Reissiger's Rheinlied "Blücher am Rhein"); Cologne, June 1836, the first German-Flemish *Sängerfest* (Franz Weber's Rheinlied "Rheinprussisches Kriegerlied," C. Müller's setting of Geibel's poem "Der Ritter vom Rhein," and Reichardt's "Was ist des deutschen Vaterland?"); Cologne, 14–15 June 1846, national German *Gesangfest* (anonymous Rheinlied "Rhein- und Schelde-

klänge" and Reichardt's "Was ist des deutschen Vaterland?"); see Bautz, *Geschichte*, 41–42; Blommen, *Anfänge*, 262, 275–77. Also see the *AmZ* 51 (20 December 1837): 835; 24 (12 June 1839): 463–64; 19 (10 May 1843): 350; and F. M. Gredy, "Wettgesang in Mainz und Sängerfest in Cöln im Juni 1846," *Caecilia* 100 (1846): 254–55.

48. Weber, *Music*, 100–101, observes that in the nineteenth century the sense of pride and unity so characteristic of choral organizations was nurtured through the development of musical discipline, the moral edification gained from singing sacred music, and the philanthropic beneficence derived from giving concerts devoted to charitable or civic causes. Such occasions, for example, were often the basis of mid-nineteenth-century *Liedertafeln* and their festivals.

49. Cf. "Zur Geschichte des Männergesanges," *AmZ* (24 January 1844).

50. Ibid. (31 January 1844).

51. *NZfM* 21, cited in F. M. Gredy "Über Liedertafeln im Allgemeinen und die von Mainz ins besondere," *Caecilia* 95 (1845): 159.

52. Ibid.

53. Ibid., 160.

54. Ibid., 407.

55. Ibid., 161.

56. Ibid., 162–63. An unnamed writer for the *AmZ*, reviewing lieder recently composed for the Mainz *Liedertafel* and the city's *Damen-gesangverein*, remarked that the setting of a Heine text by Franz Messer, then conductor of both groups, demonstrated "that the Mainz *Liedertafel* belonged among those [song clubs] that, out of love for music and for their director, are also agreeable to accomplishing even more difficult tasks"; see *AmZ* (16 January 1839): 42.

57. See *Hugo Riemanns Musiklexikon*, 11th ed., rev. Alfred Einstein (Berlin: Max Hesses Verlag, 1929), 1039–40; and Kötzschke, *Geschichte*, 78–93.

58. See René Wellek, "Romanticism Re-examined," in *Concepts of Criticism* (New Haven, Conn.: Yale University Press, 1963), 220.

59. See Tacitus, *The "Agricola" and the "Germania,"* trans. and ed. H. Mattingly and S. A. Handford (New York: Penguin Books, 1983).

60. The poet was the smithy and mastersinger Barthel Regenbogen. For the rich history of politics and the arts on the Rhine corridor, see Georg Hölscher, *Das Buch vom Rhein*, 7th ed. (Cologne: Hoursch & Bechstedt, 1927), 60 et passim.

61. Ibid., 61; see also Heinz Stephan, *Die Entstehung der Rheinromantik*, Rheinische Sammlung 2 and 3, ed. C. Enders and P. Bourfeind (Cologne: Rheinland-Verlag, 1922), 39–40.

62. Ibid., 13–16.

63. The Hain included the famous poets Friedrich Leopold, Graf zu Stolberg, Johann Heinrich Voss, Ludwig Heinrich Christoph Hölty, and Matthias Claudius. Klopstock himself wrote a Rhine poem concerning German liberty: "An die

Natur." See Friedrich Bruns, ed., *Die Lese der deutschen Lyrik von Klopstock bis Rilke* (New York: Appleton-Century-Crofts, n.d.), 9–11.

64. Stephan, *Entstehung,* 5–6.

65. Resulting from Goethe's Rhine journey of 1774, his poem "Burg Lahneck" reveals a sense of awe in confronting the river. See *Goethe und das Rheinland: Rheinische Landschaft, Rheinische Sitten, Rheinische Kunstdenkmäler,* Ed. Rheinischer Verein für Denkmalpflege und Heimatschutz 27 (Düsseldorf, 1932).

66. Stephan, *Entstehung,* 19–20, 46; also Karl J. Simrock, *Das malerische und romantische Rheinland,* 4th ed. (Bonn: Cohen, 1865). For Schumann's use of this subject as the text of his opera *Genoveva,* see p. 114.

67. René Wellek, "German and English Romanticism: A Confrontation," *Studies in Romanticism* 4/1 (Boston University Graduate School, autumn 1964): 42.

68. At Heidelberg, the Grimm brothers, Jacob (1785–1863) and Wilhelm (1786–1859), collected folk tales drawn from oral tradition that preserved and offered to the Germans what they believed were profound truths concerning the beginnings of civilization. This literature of the Heidelberg *Jüngere Romantik* directly influenced the central Romantic quest for a group identity rooted in a common German ancestral past. See Stephan, *Entstehung,* 37.

69. See Bruns, *Lese,* 20–22, 166–72.

70. Stephan, *Entstehung,* 35, 49. Schlegel's poem "Am Rheine," published in *Europa* (1803), idealized the German age of chivalry with overtones of a latent nationalism.

71. The literary and intellectual ties between the Rhine Romantics and such influential Berlin figures as Schlegel are examined at length in chapter 5.

CHAPTER 2

1. Golo Mann, *The History of Germany since 1789,* trans. Marian Jackson (New York: Praeger, 1968), 72.

2. Following the Wars of Liberation, the Concert included France. The Belgians' acquisition of independence in 1830, with all its international repercussions, had first tested the soundness of the Concert ideal, but the question of the East most endangered European peace in the 1830s. See Jacques Droz, *Europe between Revolutions, 1815–1848,* ed. J. H. Plumb, trans. Robert Baldick (New York: Harper & Row, 1968), 238, and M. Sabry, *L'Empire égyptien sous Mohamed-Ali et la question d'Orient (1811–1849): Égypte, Arabie, Soudan, Morée, Crète, Syrie, Palestine: Histoire diplomatique d'après des sources privées et des documents inédits recueillis aux archives du Caire, de Paris, de Londres et de Vienne* (Paris: Librairie Orientaliste Paul Geuthner, 1930), 493ff.

3. In establishing the Institut d'Égypte and a new science of Egyptology, Napoleon had reinforced an already considerable French fascination with Egyptian civilization while nurturing Egyptian national pride as well. See Saint-Marc Girardin, "Méhémet-Ali," review of Clot-Bey's *Aperçu général sur l'Égypte, Revue des deux mondes*

4/23 (14 September 1840): 905–20; "Chronique de la quinzaine," *Revue des deux mondes* 4/23 (14 August 1840): 649; René Albrecht-Carrié, *A Diplomatic History of Europe since the Congress of Vienna* (New York: Harper & Row, 1958), 50; John Marlowe, *Anglo-Egyptian Relations, 1800–1953* (London: Cresset Press, 1954), 50; Adolphe Thiers, letter to Baron Jean-Frédéric Cotta, Paris, 18 August 1828, in Robert Marquant, *Thiers et le Baron Cotta*, Travaux et mémoires des Instituts François en Allemagne 7 (Paris: Presses Universitaires de France, 1959), 463–65; and Charles C. Gillispie, "The Scientific Importance of Napoleon's Egyptian Campaign," *Scientific American* 27/3 (September 1994): 78–85.

4. Thiers deluged the entire French foreign service from Europe to the Mediterranean with war-mongering dispatches intending to force a revocation of the London agreement. See Sabry, *L'Empire*, 493–524. The *British and Continental Examiner* of Leipzig warned on 15 August 1840, 21, that "Thiers has turned his countrymen into 'dogs of war.' . . . Of the frightfully rabid state of these creatures we have but too indisputable proof in the foam and froath [sic] that has been issuing from their mouths for the last several days." See also "Chronique de la quinzaine," *Revue des deux mondes* 4/23 (31 July 1840): 487; and Adolphe Thiers, letter of 7 September 1840, in François Charles-Roux, *Thiers et Méhmet-Ali* (Paris: Librairie Plon, 1951), 178. In early August 1840 the *Revue des deux mondes* had indicated the sense of rage and betrayal that the treaty had evoked generally throughout the French press. In the name of French national honor, the *Revue* suggested that Britain should align with France behind Muhammad's cause to control jointly the critical passage from Europe to the Orient and dispel the growing specter of Russia in the East.

5. "Chronique de la quinzaine," *Revue des deux mondes* 4/23 (14 August 1840): 651 and (14 September 1840): 50, 943.

6. See John M. S. Allison, *Thiers and the French Monarchy* (London: Archon, 1968), 264–65. Thiers demanded, for example, the return of Napoleon's ashes to Les Invalides in May 1840. See also L. de Carné, "De la popularité de Napoléon," *Revue des deux mondes* 4/22 (1 April 1840): 857–69; and Charles-Roux, *Thiers*, 189, 262–63.

7. Prim Berland, *Le Rhin allemand de Nicolas Becker* (Paris: Jean Flory, 1942), 114.

8. Pierre Renouvin, ed., *Le XIXe siècle, part I (de 1815 à 1871): L'Europe des nationalités et l'éveil des nouveaux mondes*, Histoire de relations internationales 5 (Paris: Librairie Hachette, 1954), 121. On 28 October 1840 the French Chamber of Deputies ordered military preparations and fortifications, which were under way by November.

9. Renouvin, *Le XIXe siècle*, 123. The Bavarian monarch had even demanded the French return Strassburg.

10. Major Rhenish newspapers reprinted Matzerath's article. This pro-Prussian but Rhenish Catholic patriot belonged to the Bonn circle of Romantic literati around the Rheinlied poet Karl Simrock. See also Karl-Georg Faber, *Die Rheinlande zwischen Restauration und Revolution: Probleme der rheinischen Geschichte von 1814 bis 1848 im Spiegel der zeitgenössischen Publizistik* (Wiesbaden: Franz Steiner, 1966), 374, 383–84.

11. *British and Continental Examiner* (Leipzig, 24 October 1840): 32.

12. The Confederation also included the ten small annexed counts or princes under Karl Theodor von Dalberg (d. 1817), a German diplomat admired by Napoleon who obtained control of Frankfurt and adjacent territories. The Confederation generally extended over all Germany east of the Rhine, excluding Münster, Bremen, and Hamburg, which belonged to the French Empire. Prussia and Austria remained independent of the Confederation. See George Rudé, *Revolutionary Europe, 1783–1815* (New York: Harper, 1964), 193–97. Napoleon assigned the German grand duchy of Berg (with Düsseldorf as its capital), on the lower Rhine's right bank, to his brother-in-law, Joachim Murat. He also sought family ties with German dynasties in Bavaria, Baden, and Württemberg through arranged marriages.

13. See Hajo Holborn, *A History of Modern Germany* (New York: Knopf, 1964–71), 371–426. To counteract French influence, Prussia established reform policies directed toward eliminating the French presence in Germany. Prussia's motto, "With God for King and Fatherland," revealed, Holborn notes, "that monarchism, isolationism, and an obscure amalgam of Prussian and German national feelings merged into a quasi-religious obligation."

14. For Rheinlieder texts commemorating Blücher and this event, see chapter 3.

15. The Confederation included East Prussia and Austria (excluding Hungary) on the east, Trieste and the Tyrol on the south. In the southwest it stretched to the borders of Switzerland, Alsace, and Lorraine. Encompassing Luxembourg and extending west to the Netherlands border, it also encompassed Holstein on the north, with the Baltic Sea as its uppermost boundary. Religious and other internal conflicts further impeded the encouragement of pan-German patriotism at this time. See Lewis B. Namier, "Nationality and Liberty," in *European Political History, 1815–1870: Aspects of Liberalism*, vol. 6, ed. Eugene C. Black (New York: Harper & Row, 1967), 144. Even after the Wars of Liberation, the force of German particularism, benefiting from tensions between Austria and Prussia, restricted the forging of German unity to the establishment of a German federation, rather than the creation of a federal republic. John McManners, *European History, 1789–1914: Men, Machines, and Freedom* (New York: Harper & Row, 1969), 147, describes the newly established Confederation as "a caricature of coherence," particularly hindered by its cumbersome bureaucratic structure.

16. Eventually the Prussians' obligation to defend the Rhine became an unquestioned sine qua non of "German" destiny. On the Upper Rhine, the year 1815 also marked the cession of Landau to the Bavarian Palatinate. Britain played a vital role at the Vienna Congress in supporting Prussia's lead in uniting Germany, especially on the Rhine frontier, by then an even more strategic bulwark against France. See McManners, *European History*, 115.

17. Kohn, *The Mind of Germany*, 75.

18. Ibid., 24.

19. Ibid.

20. See McManners, *European History*, 149. See p. 96 regarding Arndt's poem "Was ist des Deutschen Vaterland?"

21. According to the Leipzig *Zeitung für die elegante Welt* 214 (31 October 1840): 31.

22. For the original German, see Ernst Volkmann, ed., *Um Einheit und Freiheit, 1815–1848: Vom Wiener Kongress bis zur Märzrevolution*, Deutsche Literatur: Politische Dichtung 3 (Leipzig: Philipp Reclam jun., 1936), 141–42. Nikolaus Becker, son of a Bonn merchant, practiced law in Haushauven-Geilenkirchen, near Cologne. See also Victor Rosenwald, "Nicolas Becker," *Nouvelle biographie générale depuis les temps les plus reculés jusqu'à nos jours, avec les renseignments bibliographiques et l'indication des sources à consulter*, ed. Hoefer (Paris, 1855), 5:99–100.

23. *Rheinisches Jahrbuch für Kunst und Poesie* (Cologne, 1841), 2:365–66. The series was published first in the *Augsburger allgemeine Zeitung*. Matzerath, a Cologne court assessor, had written a poem in 1836 extolling the Rhineland visit of the Prussian crown prince. Though a Rhenish Catholic, Matzerath actively supported Prussian state control of the Rhine Province as a step toward German national unity.

24. See Berland, *Le Rhin*, 46, and Faber, *Die Rheinlande*, 385.

25. *NZfM* (21 November 1840): 168.

26. Friedrich Wilhelm's father, Friedrich Wilhelm III, had died on 7 June 1840. Prussia anticipated great advantages from the developing industrialization of its Rhineland. See Geoffrey Bruun, *Europe and the French Imperium, 1799–1814* (New York: Harper & Row, 1938), 56–57.

27. Max von Boehn, *Biedermeier: Deutschland von 1815 bis 1847* (Berlin: Bruno Cassirer, 1918), 102, 112.

28. Most mid-nineteenth-century music journals were allied with various music publishers, though *Iris im Gebiete der Tonkunst* and the *NZfM* numbered among the relatively objective ones. See Leon B. Plantinga, *Schumann As Critic* (New Haven, Conn.: Yale University Press, 1967), 31.

29. See *AmZ* (9 December 1840): 1030–31; the *NZfM* (12 December 1840): 192; "Intelligenzblatt" 1 (in which the Leipzig music publisher Julius Ferdinand Georg Schuberth confessed that he had favored Julius Becker's setting although he had published Kunze's winning composition), *NZfM* (January and February 1841); *AmZ* (27 January 1841); G. W. Fink, *AmZ* (3 March 1841) and (5 May 1841): 366; and Eduard Krüger, *AmZ* (2 June 1841).

30. "Intelligenzblatt" 2, *NZfM* (February 1841). Schumann's setting won no prize and was not publicly advertised. See Paula and Walter Rehberg, *Robert Schumann: Sein Leben und sein Werk* (Zürich: Artemis, 1954), 591. The critic Eduard Krüger (1807–85) reported that two concerts had been given in Breslau's Krollscher Wintergarten on unspecified days during the musical season 1840–41 to the end of April. At one event the sizable audience had declared Lenz's Becker setting the winner over en-

tries submitted by four other well-regarded local composers: Bialeki, Moritz Ernemann, Johann Freudenberg, and Ernst Friedrich Richter.

31. "Intelligenzblatt" 7, *NZfM* (November 1840) and 1 (January 1841). This publication also listed seven new settings of Becker's poem.

32. *AmZ* (3 March 1841): 191.

33. Heinrich Eduard Jacob, *Felix Mendelssohn und seine Zeit* (Frankfurt am Main: V. S. Fischer, 1959), 281–82.

34. Ibid.

35. Ibid.

36. *AmZ* (December 1840).

37. Notice in the *NZfM* (12 December 1840): 192; "Intelligenzblatt" 1, ibid. (January 1841); and *AmZ* (27 January 1841): 80–81.

38. *AmZ* (5 May 1841): 366.

39. See Volkmann, *Um Einheit*, 142–43, for the German text.

40. For the last two lines, see note 42. For the musical setting, see Irwin H. Steiner, ed., *Auswahl deutscher Lieder*, 6th ed. (Leipzig: Serig'sche Buchhandlung, 1844), no. 108, 156–57.

41. Staatsarchiv, Koblenz, Abt. 403, no. 6578, cited in Faber, *Rheinlande*, 403–4. Another anonymous poem (fol. 8–10), "Rheinlands Gesinnung" ("Rhineland Sentiment"), opens, "On the Rhine, on the Rhine, there they freely press the vines [one of many allusions to Claudius's famous "Rheinweinlied"] / that give us the wine, yet they will not give us a free press / On the free German Rhine." The last line refers to Becker's poem. By 1845 another disillusioned Rhenish pamphleteer, Karl Heinzen, nastily appealed to the "natural hate" guarding every Rhinelander's "heart against the false, hypocritical, thoroughly Russian *Berlinertum.*"

42. Heinrich Heine, "Caput V," "Deutschland, ein Wintermärchen," in *Sämtliche Schriften*, vol. 4, ed. Klaus Briegleb (Munich: Carl Hanser, 1971), 587–89. Biberich, a town across the Rhine from Mainz, refers to the fierce political-economic competition of Heine's day; in 1841 a Hessian minister sank over one hundred stone-filled boats at Biberich to divert commercial traffic from Nassau.

43. Prutz's poem first appeared in the pamphlet "Der Rhein" (Leipzig, 1840). See Volkmann, *Einheit*, 145–47.

44. Arnold Ruge, "Besprechung des Rheinliedes von Becker an Lamartine und des Rheinliedes von Prutz," *Hallische Jahrbücher* 311 (Leipzig: 28 December 1840), 62–82.

45. Nikolaus Müller, ed., *Deutschland und Frankreich am Neujahr 1841: Worte zur Zeit, mit deutschen Vaterlandsgesängen* (Mainz: Seifert'sche Buchdruckerei, 1841), 7–18, 26.

46. Volkmann, *Einheit*, 152.

47. "Die politische Bedeutung des Rheinliedes von Nicolas Becker; ein Resumé von einem Norddeutschen," *Deutsche Jahrbücher für Wissenschaft und Kunst* 214, ed. Arnold Ruge (Dresden, 19 February 1841): 294–300.

48. Faber, *Rheinlande*, 388.

49. See W. Deetjen, *Sie sollen ihn nicht haben! Tatsachen und Stimmen aus dem Jahre 1840* (Weimar: n.p., 1920), 35.

50. For Arminius, see chapter 3. See Alphonse de Lamartine, *Oeuvres poétiques complètes*, ed. Marius-François Guyard (Paris: Gallimard, 1963), 1173–77. Like Musset, Lamartine composed one other Rhine poem, "La Chute du Rhin à Läuffen (Paysage)" [The Rhine Falls at Läuffen (Landscape)]. See Berland, *Le Rhin*, 38, who notes that Lamartine first read Becker's Rheinlied on 16 May 1841.

51. The French version, from "Poésies nouvelles," appears in Alfred de Musset's *Poésies complètes*, vol. 1 of *Oeuvres*, ed. Maurice Allem (Paris: Librairie Gallimard, 1957), 403–4.

52. Alphonse de Lamartine, *Cours familier de littérature: Un entretien par mois* (Paris: Chez l'auteur, 1856–62), 19:16.

53. Ibid. Berland, *Le Rhin*, 46, adds that Musset's poem later was set to the music of an unnamed composer and sung before a French audience at the outbreak of the Franco-German conflict of 1870.

54. See Johannes Scherr, *Menschliche Tragikomödie: Gesammelte Studien, Skizzen und Bilder*, 3d ed., vol. 12 (Leipzig: Otto Wigand, 1884), 90–114.

55. *Athenäum: Zeitschrift für das gebildete Deutschland* (Berlin, 10 July 1843): 10–12, (19 July 1841): 375.

56. Ibid. (26 June 1841): 397–98.

57. An earlier version of this section of chapter 2, "The *Rheinlieder* Critics: A Case of Musical Nationalism," appeared in *Musical Quarterly* 63/1 (January 1977): 74–98.

58. During the 1840s the editors of the *AmZ*, published in Leipzig by Breitkopf & Härtel, were Gottfried Wilhelm Fink (1828–42), Carl Ferdinand Becker (1842–43), Moritz Hauptmann (1843–44), the publishers in a general editorship (1844–46), and Johann Christian Lobe (1846–48). During the same period the *NZfM*, published in Leipzig by Robert Friese, was edited by Robert Schumann (1834–44), Oswald Lorenz (1844–45), and Franz Brendel (1845–68). *Iris im Gebiete der Tonkunst (Iris)*, published in Berlin by T. Trautwein, was edited by Ludwig Rellstab (1830–41). Rheinlieder reviews of the 1840s represent a climax of comment and the most useful contemporary assessment of these songs, but some earlier Rhine songs had been discussed during the 1830s in the *AmZ*.

59. This tendency can be traced to the eighteenth-century music journals of Johann Mattheson (1681–1764), Lorenz Christoph Mizler (1711–78), Johann Adolf Scheibe (1708–76), and Friedrich Wilhelm Marpurg (1718–95). Johann Nikolaus Forkel (1749–1818) and Johann Friedrich Reichardt (1752–1814) led the movement late in the century to educate public taste.

60. Imogen Fellinger, "Zeitschriften," *Die Musik in Geschichte und Gegenwart* 14: 1179.

61. "An die Leser," *AmZ* (28 December 1848): 859. The journal's first editor was Friedrich Rochlitz (1798–1818), followed in 1818 by the respected Leipzig publisher Gottfried Härtel (1763–1827) and until 1841 by G. W. Fink. Resurrected in 1863, the *AmZ* again assumed a decisive role in the musical activity of its day, but it never attained the importance that it had enjoyed under Rochlitz. Until 1868 the newly revitalized journal emphasized contemporary music making, but Friedrich Chrysander (1826–1901) redirected it toward research in music theory.

62. Martha Bigenwald, "Die Anfänge der *Leipziger allgemeinen musikalischen Zeitung*," (dissertation, Freiburg, 1938), 60, cited in Plantinga, *Schumann*, 45.

63. The *Allgemeine musikalische Zeitung* introduced the line of large, comprehensive, internationally respected musical journals, which included a number of nineteenth-century journals published outside Germany such as the Austrian *Allgemeine musikalische Zeitung mit besonderer Rücksicht auf den österreichischen Kaiserstaat, 1817–1824*, and the French *Revue et gazette musicale de Paris*, a continuation of the *Revue musicale* begun by Fétis in 1827 and extending from 1834 to 1880. See Fellinger, "Zeitschriften," 1182–83. During its earlier years, the music reviews in the *AmZ* continued the policies inaugurated by such *Kenner und Liebhaber* (connoisseurs and amateurs) journals as Johann Adam Hiller's *Wöchentliche Nachrichten und Anmerkungen die Musik betreffend* (Leipzig, 1766–70), with regularly featured, lengthy, and mildly critical music reviews. See Plantinga, *Schumann*, 43. The amount of space allotted to each critique revealed how highly the *AmZ* valued the quality of the published music that it discussed. Music rated as poor was simply disregarded—a procedure discontinued with Fink's arrival as editor (1827–41).

64. The first issue of another musical journal, *Cäcilia: Eine Zeitschrift für die musikalische Welt* (ed. Gottfried Weber [1824–42] and Siegfried Wilhelm Dehn [1842–48]; published in Mainz, Brussels, and Antwerp by B. Schott's Sons), appeared in 1824, offering important discussions of music history and music theory, as well as musical ethnological, pedagogic, and instrumental topics.

65. Schumann, "Einleitung," *Gesammelte Schriften über Musik und Musiker*, 5th ed. (Leipzig: Wigand, 1854; reprint, Leipzig: M. Kreisig, 1914), and "Zur Eröffnung des Jahrgangs, 1835," cited in Fellinger, "Zeitschriften," 1181. Franz Brendel (1811–68) edited the *NZfM* from 1845 until his death.

66. The growing importance of professional musical journals directed toward special-interest groups thus reflected the rapid expansion of public musical life and institutions toward the mid-nineteenth century. The increasing proliferation of *Gesangvereine* and *Liedertafeln*, for example, created a new readership for journals devoted exclusively to the *Männergesang* and *Chorgesang*: in Germany, *Teutonia* (published 1846–1849) and *Die Sängerhalle* (1861–1908; from 1909 on titled the *Deutsche Sängerbun-*

deszeitung); in Austria, the *Liedergenossen* (1861–65); and in France, *L'Orphéon* (1855–1939).

67. The *Kenner und Liebhaber* musical journals of the later eighteenth century first offered reviews of published music. Plantinga, *Schumann*, 55, notes that Schumann, unlike most music journal editors of his day, exercised great discrimination in selecting for review the compositions sent to him by composers and publishers, even consulting Hofmeister's monthly reports.

68. According to Plantinga, *Schumann*, 47, among musical journals of its time, the *NZfM* was "unique; partisan, but progressive, seeking to enlighten rather than to entertain, it had, in a certain sense, more in common with contemporary literary journals than with the musical ones."

69. Note that the *NZfM* neglected Rheinlieder for male chorus, in contrast to the far greater attention paid to this subgenre in the other two publications.

70. Carl Kossmaly, "Musikalische Charakteristiken von C. Kossmaly (Über das 'Lied' im Allgemeinen,—Das 'Volkslied,'—N. Becker's Gedicht—Über die Compositionen desselben)," *NZfM* (19 February 1841): 59–60; (22 February 1841): 63–64; (26 February 1841): 49–50; and (17 August 1841): 53–54. Carl Kossmaly studied music in Berlin (1828–30) with Berger, Zelter, and Klein. He had a long career as a theater kapellmeister in Wiesbaden, Mainz, Amsterdam, Bremen, Detmold, and Stettin. Also one of the philosophizing members of the Davidsbund, Kossmaly was invited by Schumann to write for his *NZfM* in 1837. He was also a lieder composer and compiled a lexicon of Silesian composers. See Wolfgang Boetticher, "Karl Kossmaly," *Die Musik in Geschichte und Gegenwart* 7:1643–44.

71. See Plantinga, *Schumann*, 47, and Imogen Fellinger, *Verzeichnis der Musikzeitschriften des 19. Jahrhunderts*, Studien zur Musikgeschichte des 19. Jahrhunderts 10 (Regensburg: Gustav Bosse, 1968).

72. Kossmaly, "Musikalische," *NZfM* (19 February 1841): 59.

73. Ibid., 67, 69. For the references to Arminius (Hermann) and German oaks, see chapter 3. Schumann first set the poem for solo voice and chorus with piano; he then arranged the lied for four-part male chorus, a cappella, the version described here.

74. Kossmaly, "Musikalische," *NZfM* (13 August 1841): 50.

75. Rellstab, *Iris* 7 (12 February 1841): 27–28: a review of "Ei Franzmann, was fällt Dir ein," an anonymous Rhine poem set by Mangold, op. 19. Rellstab, who edited and contributed to a number of German musical periodicals, was a composer, an artillery officer, a teacher of mathematics and history, and an author. *Iris* was published from 1830 to 1841. Rellstab, editing it practically always singlehandedly, intended that his journal impart to its readers "a review of the entire state of music . . . as much in regard to events as to phenomena"; see Rellstab, *Iris* 2 (1831): 1. Rellstab's reviews of settings of the Becker poem appeared in *Iris* 3 (15 January

1841): 11–12; 4 (22 January 1841): 15; 12 (19 March 1841): 47–48; 15 (9 April 1841): 59–60; and 31 (30 July 1841): 123–24.

76. Critique of Hünten's lied "Drei Sterne am Rhein" in *Iris* 8 (19 February 1841), 30.

77. Rellstab, review in *Iris* 12 (19 March 1841): 47.

78. Rellstab, *Iris* 15 (9 April 1841): 59–60. The composer Lenz was the prizewinner also maligned by Kossmaly.

79. Rellstab, *Iris* 4 (22 January 1841): 15.

80. *AmZ* (4 October 1843): 711–13.

81. Fink's article listing the settings of Becker's poem was published in three installments of the *AmZ*: (3 March 1841): 191–94; (31 March 1841): 275; and (23 June 1841): 495. Fink, born in Thuringia, spent his early years in the ministry at Leipzig. Beginning in 1808 he wrote for the *AmZ*, and he edited it from 1827 to 1841. He also served as music director of the University of Leipzig, lectured there, composed vocal and instrumental works, and was the compiler of several lieder collections and the author of numerous books on music.

82. Kossmaly, "Musikalische," *NZfM* (19 February 1841): 64. Here Kossmaly distinguished this type of lied as the highest of three genres of song, the criterion for judgment being poetic-musical relationships. In the first and simplest category ("Salon and Conversation Music") he placed songs in which the music conformed so literally and superficially to the words as to be applicable to any other poem with the same meter. The middle genre consisted of lieder having not merely an external but also a spiritual (*geistig*), inward, intimate correspondence of melody and text, both welded so closely together as to appear written simultaneously.

83. Kossmaly, "Musikalische," *NZfM* (1 March 1841): 71–72; (13 August 1841): 49; (17 August 1841): 53; and (26 February 1841): 69. Constantin Julius Becker (1811–59) was Kossmaly's fellow critic on the *NZfM*. Becker, not related to the poet Nikolaus Becker as far as is known, was a music teacher in Dresden, composed operas as well as choral and instrumental works, and wrote books on musical theory and Romantic novels.

84. Julius Becker, review in *NZfM* (2 November 1841): 143.

85. Kossmaly, "Musikalische," *NZfM* (19 February 1841): 63; (1 March 1841): 71–72.

86. Ibid. (26 February 1841): 68.

87. Ibid., 68–69.

88. Julius Becker, "Liederschau," *NZfM* (26 October 1841): 135.

89. Kossmaly, "Musikalische," *NZfM* (19 February 1841): 63.

90. Plantinga, *Schumann*, 31, emphasizes the official connections between most music journals and the music publishers toward the mid-nineteenth century, but he argues that criticism in *Iris* and the *NZfM* was unaffected by the commercial

urge. See *AmZ* (9 December 1840): 1030–31; notice in *NZfM* (12 December 1840): 192; "Intelligenzblatt" 1, *NZfM* (January 1841); *AmZ* (27 January 1841): 80–81; "Intelligenzblatt" 2, *NZfM* (February 1841); G. W. Fink, *AmZ* (3 March 1841): 191; *AmZ* (5 May 1841): 366; and Eduard Krüger, *AmZ* (2 June 1841): 442–44.

CHAPTER 3

1. Hegel, "Of the Symbolic Form of Art," in *Lectures on Aesthetics*, vol. 1 of *Philosophy of Hegel*, ed. Carl J. Friedrich (New York: Modern Library, 1954), 339.

2. Heine, "Über Polen," in *Vermischte Schriften*, vol. 5/1 of *Sämmtliche Werke* (Philadelphia, 1856), 400.

3. Another section (46 through 61) of *Childe Harold* idealized the Rhine as the height of divine nature. See George Gordon, Lord Byron, *Childe Harold's Pilgrimage and Other Romantic Poems*, ed. Samuel C. Chew (New York: Odyssey Press, 1936), 100–106. The American poet Henry Wadsworth Longfellow also sang the Rhine's praises in "The Golden Legend" (1851), part 2 of his verse trilogy *Christus: A Mystery*.

4. The French lexicographer Maximilien Littre gave 1802 as the date marking the first use of the term *biology*; see Crane Brinton, *Ideas and Men: The Story of Western Thought* (New York: Prentice-Hall, 1950), 411.

5. Hennell's artificial production of ethyl alcohol in 1826 and, two years later, Friederich Woehler's manufacture of urea from cyanic acid and ammonia demonstrated that substances until then observed only in organic matter could be manufactured in the laboratory. See W. C. Dampier, *A History of Science and its Relations with Philosophy and Religion*, 4th ed. (Cambridge: Cambridge University Press, 1961), 253–61.

6. Herbert Butterfield, *The Origins of Modern Science* (New York: Macmillan, 1956), 172–77. Leibnitz's monads, or elements of reality, were viewed as self-contained energy centers, each having its own source of striving as a self-motivated entity, foreshadowing Freud's dynamic notion. Leibnitz also anticipated concepts of the unconscious; a century later Herbart expanded these ideas into a mathematics depicting the conflict of ideas in their striving toward consciousness. See also Melvin H. Marx and W. A. Cronan-Hillix, *Systems and Theories in Psychology*, 4th ed. (New York: McGraw-Hill, 1987), 248–50. This was indeed the age of utopian dreams, played out in America by such groups as the Quakers and Shakers.

7. Bonnet's achievements likewise influenced Lamarck's contemporary, the French naturalist Georges Léopold Cuvier (1769–1832), who, again through fossil remains, hypothesized parallel lines of development in the various separate animal groups rather than a single cause of evolution. See Butterfield, *Origins*, 178–80.

8. The imagery of fire and water as agents of creation, death, and rebirth pervades ancient mythology and other folk literature genres; Wagner's *Ring* continues

this concept of symbolism in the omnipresence of "reminders" of Valhalla's flames and the Rhine's watery depths.

9. See Charles Darwin, *Narrative of the Surveying Voyages of Her Majesty's Ships "Adventure" and "Beagle,"* vol. 3 (London, 1839–40) in *The Darwin Reader,* ed. Marston Bates and Philip S. Humphrey (New York: Scribner's, 1956), 35. In his *Essay on Population* of 1798, Malthus had maintained that only famine, disease, and war could limit population size to counter mankind's characteristic striving to exceed its means of subsistence. The evidence Darwin collected on the *Beagle* voyages of 1831, moreover, further substantiated his doctrines of the interdependence of all living things, the transmutation of species, and the survival of the fittest. See Dampier, *History of Science,* 275.

10. Butterfield, *Origins,* 172.

11. Ibid., 169–70.

12. See H. G. Schenk, *The Mind of the European Romantics* (Garden City, N.Y.: Doubleday, 1969), 43–44.

13. Even earlier, such Enlightenment thinkers as Jean-Jacques Rousseau (1712–78) had conceived of the nation as essentially a "natural" association. See Schenk, *European Romantics,* 44.

14. See ibid., 3–18.

15. "For us, to exist is to feel; and our sensibility is incontestably prior to our reason." See ibid., 4 and 252, n. 6.

16. Herder's treatise of 1778, *Vom Erkennen und Empfinden der menschlichen Seele* (Concerning human perception and consciousness), had contributed toward transmitting the Neoplatonic idea of nature's quintessential integrity to natural philosophy, with its pantheistic premise of infinity encompassing everything finite. This organic view of all nature and mankind as a single unified entity striving for self-consciousness implied the humanization of nature as a corollary. The psyche as an object of analysis occupied Plato, St. Augustine, the humanists, and Spinoza. In 1803 the German physician Johann Christian Reil published the first systematic treatise on psychotherapy, in which he emphasized the interaction between psychological and physiological phenomena in the organism. "Feelings and ideas, briefly, psychic influences, are the proper means," he insisted, "by which disturbances of the brain can be corrected and its vitality can be restored." See Franz G. Alexander and Sheldon T. Selesnick, *The History of Psychiatry: An Evaluation of Psychiatric Thought and Practice from Prehistoric Times to the Present* (New York: Harper & Row, 1966), 133–36.

17. Alexander and Selesnick, *History of Psychiatry,* 137. Esquirol, however, advanced so far as to advocate that an individual's capacity to think rationally about abstract concerns might be diminished by his preoccupation with his personal thoughts and feelings.

18. Ibid., 139–43.

19. Peter L. Rudnytsky, *Freud and Oedipus* (New York: Columbia University Press, 1987), 119.

20. Schiller, *Naive and Sentimental Poetry and On the Sublime* (1795–1801), trans. Julius Elias (New York: Unger, 1966), 100–111.

21. See Rudnytsky, *Freud and Oedipus*, 130, 150.

22. Ibid.

23. Hugh Honour, *Romanticism* (New York: Harper & Row, 1979), 316; see also Lancelot Lew Whyte, *The Unconscious before Freud* (New York: Doubleday, 1962), 124.

24. See Alfred Einstein, *Music in the Romantic Era* (New York: Norton, 1947), 338–40.

25. Oskar Walzel, *German Romanticism*, trans. Alma Elise Lussky (New York: Putnam, 1932; reprint, New York: Capricorn Books, 1966), 20–30 et passim.

26. August Wilhelm von Schlegel, *A Course of Lectures on Dramatic Art and Literature*, trans. J. Black (London: Wyeth, 1846), 23–27.

27. Theodore Gish, "*Wanderlust* and *Wanderleid:* The Motif of the Wandering Hero in German Romanticism," *Studies in Romanticism* 3/4 (Boston University Graduate School, summer 1964): 225–39.

28. Enzo Carli, *The Landscape in Art*, ed. Mia Cinotti (New York: Morrow, 1980), 124.

29. Fritz Novotny, *Painting and Sculpture in Europe, 1780–1880*, 2d ed., trans. R. H. Boothroyd (Baltimore: Pelican, 1971), 85, 422. See also Helmut Häuser, *Ansichten vom Rhein: Stahlstichbücher des 19. Jahrhunderts* (Cologne: Greven, 1963), 31 et passim.

30. See Benedetto Croce, *Aesthetic* (New York: Farrar, Straus and Giroux, 1922); also Bernard Bosanquet, *A History of Aesthetic* (Cleveland: World, 1932), 280ff.

31. Michel Le Bris, *Romantics and Romanticism* (New York: Rizzoli, 1981), 80. Friedrich felt the impact of the Romantic religious revival as represented, e.g., by the German Protestant theologian Ernst Daniel Schleiermacher (1768–1834). The latter advocated the preservation of the spiritual basis of religion through denying its conventional external trappings. Friedrich's disciple the painter-philosopher Carl Gustav Carus (1789–1869) espoused a similar pantheism emphasizing the organic process and structure of life. Likewise, the poet Novalis believed that "the individual soul must achieve harmony with the soul of the world." See Robert Rosenblum, *Modern Painting and the Northern Romantic Tradition* (New York: Harper & Row, 1975), 19–21.

32. See Novotny, *Painting*, 117. Runge saturated his visionary landscapes with supernatural flower genii allegorizing nature's magical phenomena. In great contrast, Friedrich's landscapes expressed nature's vast infinity, so immense that it dwarfed human figures. See also Marco Valsecchi, *Landscape Painting of the 19th Century*, trans. Arthur A. Coppotelli (Greenwich, Conn.: New York Graphic Society, 1971); and Paul Ferdinand Schmidt, *Deutsche Landschaftsmalerei von 1750 bis 1830*, vol. 1, *Deutsche Malerei um 1800* (Munich: R. Piper, 1922).

33. The Königsstuhl project, launched in 1843, represented one of many such nationalistic endeavors in the historic preservation of German Rhine landmarks during the Rhine crisis decade. Two of the other festivities centered around the restoration and completion of the Cologne Cathedral and the Gutenberg monument in Mainz. Rheinlieder texts were generated by these occasions. There are also Rheinlieder poems recounting an early fifteenth-century incident in which the Rhenish electors slighted the Bohemian King Wenzel by selecting the Palatinate Count Rupert III as emperor. The Wars of Liberation poet Ferdinand Freiligrath, for example, composed a poem in his *Glaubensbekenntnis* (Mainz, 1844) for the Königsstuhl project that opened thus: "Newly built at old Rhens / Stands once more the election throne, / But ducks, alas! and geese / Graze quacking and cackling around it. . . . When into the black-red-gold banner / Fresh and free the Rhine wind blew; / When they shoved a drunkard / From the throne, according to his deserts. / Wicked Wenzel! Never do we yearn today to return to thee!" See Hölscher, *Buch*, 291–92.

34. When I visited the site in the 1970s, it was devoid of other pilgrims and littered with refuse.

35. This probably refers intentionally to Matthias Claudius's (1740–1815) celebrated "Rheinweinlied." This is one of several such allusions to this poem, and especially to this line that occurs among the Rheinlieder texts.

36. Heinrich Heine, "Anno 1839," in *Sämtliche Schriften*, vol. 4, ed. Klaus Briegleb (Munich: Carl Hanser, 1971), 379–80.

37. Heine, letter from Göttingen to Rudolf Christiani, 7 March 1824, in *Briefe*, vol. 1, ed. Friedrich Hirth (Mainz: Kupferberg, 1950), 150.

38. Heine, "Vorwort," "Deutschland; ein Wintermärchen," in *Sämtliche Schriften*, vol. 4, ed. Klaus Briegleb (Munich: Carl Hanser, 1971), 574.

39. This rocky cliff supports an early twelfth-century castle erected by the archbishop of Cologne but devastated during the Thirty Years' War. A cavern halfway up the Drachenfels once supposedly "housed the dragon slain by Siegfried, . . . who, having bathed himself in its blood, became invulnerable." Cf. Karl Baedeker, *The Rhine from Rotterdam to Constance: Handbook for Travellers*, 16th rev. English ed. (Leipzig: Karl Baedeker, 1906), 94. The wine grown in this region is appropriately called *Drachenblut*, or dragon's blood.

40. *Die wilde Jagd* (the wild hunt) is one of countless Germanic folk legends surviving to the present with regional variations.

41. Müller was also the poet of Schubert's *Müllerlieder*, *Winterreise*, and other works.

42. Walzel, *German Romanticism*, 148.

43. This is the familiar line quoted or paraphrased in many other Rheinlieder poems.

44. Thomas Carlyle, "The Hero As Divinity," lecture 1 (5 May 1840), "On

Heroes, Hero-Worship, and the Heroic in History," in *The Complete Works of Thomas Carlyle*, vol. 1 (New York: Kelmscott Society, n.d.), 245.

45. Daniel Casper von Lohenstein, *Grossmüthiger Feldherr Arminius, oder Hermann als ein tapfferer Beschirmer der deutschen Freyheit, nebst seiner durchlauchtigen Thusnelda in einer sinnreichen Staats- Liebes- und Helden-Geschichte, dem Vaterlande zu Liebe dem deutschen Adel aber zu Ehren und rühmlichen Kupffern gezieret*, 2 vols. (Leipzig, 1689).

46. J. E. Schlegel's *Hermann, ein Trauerspiel* dates from 1743. Möser's *Hermann* appeared in 1749. Klopstock's three-drama cycle on Hermann comprises *Hermanns Schlacht* (1769), *Hermann und die Fürsten* (1784), and *Hermanns Tod* (1787).

47. Walzel, *German Romanticism*, 179. Fragments of a tragedy entitled *Hermann* were published by Ernst Moritz Arndt in 1809. Jahn's "Rede des Arminius vor der Teutoburger Schlacht" dates from 1813. During the Wars of Liberation era, countless mostly second-rate literary idealizations of Hermann abounded in German nationalist publications.

48. The deity Tuisco is often linked with Hermann in these Rheinlieder poems. In myth and legend the Germans descended from Mannus, Tuisco's son, in turn the progeny of Earth.

49. Large drinking glasses.

50. Martin Luther and the Reformation became identified with the cause of nationalism in German minds. Patriotic German students and other intellectuals, for example, celebrated the defeat of Napoleon on the Reformation tercentenary in 1817 at the Wartburg castle overlooking Eisenach, J. S. Bach's birthplace. It was at the Wartburg that the medieval minnesingers held their storied contests and Luther finished translating the New Testament into German. Several Rheinlieder poems exalting Hermann identify him with such other heroic figures as Wilhelm Tell and Elijah.

51. The Pfalz is a fourteenth-century structure built for the lords of the Palatinate and perched on a rock ledge in the Rhine at Kaub.

52. The legendary Barbarossa had been bewitched and slept deep within the Kyffhäusser mountain in Thuringia. Yet he remained a protector of German destiny and "on call" as the national savior, whom mythical encircling ravens (also mentioned in the poem) would awaken to rescue the Germans from the hopelessness of the repressed to a new age of gold.

53. George Bernard Shaw, *The Perfect Wagnerite: A Commentary on the Nibelung's Ring* (London, 1898; reprint, New York: Time, 1972), 2–3.

54. Heinrich Heine, "Die Lorelei," in *Buch der Lieder*; see Friedrich Bruns, ed., *Die Lese der deutschen Lyrik von Klopstock bis Rilke* (New York: Appleton-Century-Crofts, n.d.), 228.

55. Shaw, *Perfect Wagnerite*, 3.

56. "At the very origin of art," Hegel observed, "there existed the tendency of the imagination to struggle upward out of Nature into spirituality. Whatever can

find room in the human heart, as feeling, idea, and purpose; whatever it is capable of shaping into art—all this diversity of material is capable of entering into the varied content of painting." See Whyte, *The Unconscious before Freud*, 163.

The paintings of the highly regarded Viennese landscapist Moritz von Schwind depicted local forests populated with hosts of Biedermeier nymphs, giants, and other fairy-tale figures. These illustrated the Grimm brothers' German folktale collections and Arnim and Brentano's Rhine-related compilation *Des Knaben Wunderhorn*. Schwind also painted characters from Wagner's *Ring*. See Gert Schiff, "An Epoch of Longing: An Introduction to German Painting of the Nineteenth Century," in *German Masters of the Nineteenth Century* (New York: Metropolitan Museum of Art, 1981), 21.

57. See Wolfgang Kayser, *The Grotesque: Its Configuration in Painting and Literature*, Eng. trans. (Bloomington: Indiana University Press, 1963).

58. See Joseph Campbell, *The Masks of God: Primitive Mythology* (New York: Viking Press, 1959), 61–62.

59. William Shakespeare, *A Midsummer Night's Dream* 2/1, 11, 150–53, in *The Complete Plays and Poems of William Shakespeare*, ed. William Allan Neilson and Charles Jarvis Hill (Boston: Houghton Mifflin, 1942), 96.

60. Böcklin studied with the landscapist Johann Wilhelm Schirmer, also Mendelssohn's teacher earlier at the Düsseldorf Academy. See also Carrol B. Fleming, "Maidens of the Sea," *Smithsonian* 14/3 (June 1983): 86–92. Offenbach's famous ghostly barcarole in *Les Contes d'Hoffmann*, the rhythmic motive of which suggests water imagery in much Romantic music, was taken from his opera-ballet *Die Rheinnixen* (Vienna, February 1864).

61. The *Lurlenberg*, or *Lurelei*, was mentioned by the thirteenth-century poet Konrad Marner. The term *Lorelei* probably derived from the Middle High German term *luren*, meaning "to stare"; a later usage implied "duping." *Lei* refers to "slate cliff." See Hölscher, *Buch*, 272.

62. Stephan, *Entstehung*, 46–47. The novel specifically refers to such Rhine sites as the Loreley.

63. Brentano, *Godwi*, part 2, chap. 36. The nixie seduces unsuspecting knights into a Rhine doom, her captivating love thereby implying death and delusion. In his poem "Ahnen des Müller's Radlauf," from 1816, Brentano's alluring animistic Rhine maiden is the songstress nymph daughter of Father Rhine. She guards the Nibelungen treasure. See Hölscher, *Buch*, 273; also Stephan, *Entstehung*, 58, and K. Hessel, "Die Echtheit der Loreleisage," *Zeitschrift für den deutschen Unterricht* 19 (1905), 481ff.

64. See Hölscher, *Buch*, 281, for additional Loreley poems of Eichendorff ("Der stille Grund" and "Verloren"); Geibel ("Der Verliebte Steuermann"); and Julius Wolff ("Lurley"). Mendelssohn's *Loreley* fragment, op. 98 (finale of act 1 and Vint-

ners' Chorus), to a three-act opera text by Emanuel Geibel, was completed in 1847 and premiered in 1852.

65. Schumann changed Eichendorff's title to "Waldesgespräch," which appears in Eichendorff's novel *Ahnung und Gegenwart*. Eichendorff was associated with Arnim and his circle and had contributed to *Wunderhorn*. See also Theodor Ibing, "Das Verhältnis des Dichters Freiherr Josef von Eichendorff zu Volksbrauch, Aberglaube, Sage und Märchen" (diss., University of Marburg, 1912), 98; also Joseph von Eichendorff, *Werke*, vol. 1, ed. Ansgar Hillach (Munich: Winkler, 1970), 986.

66. Jack M. Stein, *Poem and Music in the German Lied from Gluck to Hugo Wolf* (Cambridge, Mass.: Harvard University Press, 1971), 112–13.

67. Heine once recalled, "When I sat now on the ruins of the old [Rhine] castle and declaimed this song [a poem by Uhland], I heard . . . the nixies in the Rhine that flows by mimic my words." See Heine, "Die romantische Schule," in *Sämmtliche Werke* 5/1:231–32. The familiar setting of Heine's Loreley poem is sung even today on Rhine boats as they pass the Loreley. The melody is commonly ascribed to Friedrich Silcher (1789–1860) but actually dates from a lied of 1746, "Die unzufriedene Sylvia" by Adolf Carl Kuntzen (1720–81).

68. See *The Nibelungenlied*, trans. A. T. Hatto (Harmondsworth, Middlesem Pen guin Books, 1965); *Das Nibelungenlied*, ed. Helmut de Boor (Wiesbaden: Brockhaus, 1979); and *Das Nibelungenlied: Paralleldruck der Handschriften A, B, und C nebst Lesarten der übrigen Handschriften*, ed. Michael S. Batts (Tübingen: Niemeyer, 1971). Numerous scholars have concluded that between 1191 and 1204 a single anonymous poet creatively organized his material into a final version subsequently lost. Clear relationships among the three manuscript versions (A, B, and C) unearthed between the mid-eighteenth century and early nineteenth have thus far not been ascertained. The first *Nibelungenlied* manuscript was discovered in 1750; the first complete edition appeared in 1782. All together, the *Nibelungenlied* was transmitted in some thirty manuscripts and fragments dating from the thirteenth to the sixteenth centuries. See also Edward R. Haymes, *The Nibelungenlied: History and Interpretation* (Urbana: University of Illinois Press, 1986), 129. The Rhine marked a crucial segment of the ancient route connecting France with Constantinople. The Nibelungs emerged from an intermixture of historical or near-historical personages and associated events and from existing mythical and legendary material. The entire Nibelung narrative can be traced to the historically attested destruction of the Burgundian kingdom at Worms on the Rhine by Attila's and subsequent Huns in the mid-fifth century C.E. Worms, established as the Roman fortress Borbetomagus, was destroyed in 407 C.E. by the Alemanni, Vandals, and Alans; but it then fell to the incoming Burgundians, who established themselves there in 413. Latin laws and chronicles from the sixth century on allude to mythic elements in these Rhine events; the tenth-century Latin epic *Waltharius* derides a Nibelung dynasty as *nebulones Franci* ("Frankish rascals" or "windbags"); twelfth-century lays on the death

of Sigurd (Siegfried) and the fall of the Niflungs (Nibelungs) preserved in the thirteenth-century *Poetic Edda* and in Snorri Sturluson's (1178–1241) *Prose Edda*, associate the "Niflungs" with the Burgundians on the Rhine. The latter were said to protect variously their "god-given" gold, two Rhine mermaids, a gold ring, or a treasure. The twelfth-century Latin *Gesta danorum* by the Danish historian Saxo Grammaticus refers to an oral version of the Nibelung story, as does the eighth-century *Beowulf*, in which Siegmund slays the dragon, thereby winning the treasure. See Haymes, *Nibelungenlied*, 27.

69. Ibid.

70. See Hölscher, *Buch*, 92. See also Heinz Engels, ed., *Die Handschrift C des Nibelungenliedes und der Klage: Handschrift C der F. F. Hofbibliothek Donaueschingen* (Stuttgart, 1968). Stephan, *Entstehung*, 79, mentions Görres's essay "Der gehörnte Siegfried und die Nibelungen" and Jakob Grimm's monograph "Über das Nibelungen-Liet."

71. Fouqué subsequently added *Sigurds Rache* and *Aslanga* to the "Heldenspiel" *Sigurd der Schlangentödter* in 1808, thus completing the trilogy; the latter, together with Raupach's *Der Nibelungen-Hort*, exercised some influence on the Nibelung dramas of Hebbel and Wagner.

72. In a letter of 14 November 1840 (i.e., written at the height of the Rhine crisis), Mendelssohn responded favorably to his sister Fanny for her suggesting he consider material from the *Nibelungenlied* as an opera text. See Felix Mendelssohn, *Letters*, ed. G. Selden-Goth, trans. Marion Soerchinger (New York: Pantheon Books, 1945; reprint, New York: Vienna House, 1973), 296–97; also Ernest Newman, *The Life of Richard Wagner* (New York: Knopf, 1969), 3:27–28, n. 9.

73. Hagen's stature as hero, despite his role as villain, has been much scrutinized by literary scholars; Haymes, for example, classifies Hagen as the Germanic archetypal "dark hero," in contrast to such "bright" counterparts as Beowulf and Siegfried. See Haymes, *Nibelungenlied*, 87.

74. In the *Nibelungenlied*, "wild nixies" of the Danube announced to Hagen his coming doom. These ur-Rhinemaidens are further described as "water-fairies endowed with second sight." The *Thidrekssaga*, several decades later in origin than the *Nibelungenlied*, calls these same water sprites "two mermaids from the Rhine."

75. See Haymes, *Nibelungenlied*, 110, 116; Gottfried Weber, *Das Nibelungenlied: Problem und Idee* (Stuttgart: Metzler, 1964), 7; and Walter Haug, "Höfische Idealität und heroische Tradition im Nibelungenlied," in *Atti dei convegni lincei* (Rome: Accademia Nazionale dei Lincei, 1974), 35–50.

76. St. Luke was the patron saint of the medieval painters' guilds. There were five hundred German painters in Rome between 1800 and 1830. The Nazarenes were linked to the Rhine through contacts in Berlin and Düsseldorf (see chapter 5). Patrons of the Nazarenes in Rome, for example, included the Prussian Consul General Jacob Salomon Bartholdy (Mendelssohn's maternal uncle) and the Prussian ambassador to Rome and historian Barthold Georg Niebuhr (1776–1831). The

Nazarene painter and architect Johann Gottfried von Schadow (1764–1850) left Rome in 1787 to direct the Berlin Art Academy. His brother Wilhelm was appointed head of the state-financed Berlin Art Studio in 1819 and in 1825 succeeded Cornelius as director of the Düsseldorf Academy. Another brother, Rudolf, was a fellow Nazarene. See Le Bris, *Romantics*, 95–99, 104.

77. Hegel, "Of the Symbolic Form of Art," in *Philosophy of Hegel* 1:339.

78. Rethel, a native Rhinelander, had studied in Düsseldorf under Wilhelm von Schadow.

79. See *German Masters*, 263.

80. Ludwig I also championed the completion of the Rhenish Gothic Cologne Cathedral. See chapter 2.

81. See also Cecelia H. Porter, "Wagner and His Publics" (unpublished paper, 1969), which examines symbolist elements in French lithographs depicting Wagnerian Rhine Maidens as Loreley figures. Circa 1848 Schwind also produced an oil, "In the Forest," based on Arnim and Brentano's Rhine-suffused *Des Knaben Wunderhorn*.

82. In 1856 Wagner wrote Franz Müller in Weimar, listing his sources for the *Ring* poem: Lachmann's edition of and commentary to the *Nibelungenlied*; the *Eddas*; Friedrich H. von der Hagen's versions of the *Volsunga-Saga*, von der Hagen's *Wilkina und Niflunga-Saga*, and *Das deutsche Heldenbuch*, reedited by Simrock; Jacob Grimm's *Deutsche Mythologie*; Wilhelm Grimm's *Die deutsche Heldensage*; Mone's writings on the German hero sagas; and Mohnike's translation of the *Heimskringla*. Wagner probably had also read the aesthetician Friedrich Theodor Vischer's elaborate, though pedestrian, five-act scenario for a *Nibelungenlied* opera. This scenario illustrated Vischer's premise that the epic offered genuinely German mythic heroes worthy of a national opera. See Newman, *Wagner* 2:24–28. Wagner probably read Louise Otto's review of Vischer's scenario, along with some scenes for her own proposed Nibelungen drama, published in *NZfM* in 1845.

83. Jacob Arlow, "Psychoanalysis, Myth, and Fairy Tale," paper presented at Smithsonian Institution Symposium, Washington, D.C., 4–5 December 1987.

84. Jakob and Wilhelm Grimm, foreword to *The German Legends of the Brothers Grimm*, vol. 1, ed. and trans. Donald Ward (Philadelphia: Institute for the Study of Human Issues, 1981), 3.

CHAPTER 4

1. Franz Samans, ed., *365 fröhliche Guitarrlieder*, vol. 3 (Wesel: J. Bagel, 1848), 21.

2. G. W. Fink, *AmZ* (3 March 1841): 191–92.

3. One is reminded of the tradition going back to K. F. Zelter, a member of the second Berlin lieder school and the main adherent of Goethe's basic lied aesthetic: that the poetry and music of a lied should be equal in importance and that consequently the strophic form should have primacy over through-composition. This

tenet was taken over, partly consciously and partly unconsciously, by numerous nineteenth-century composers largely as the result of folksong influence, as in the renowned case of Schubert's "Heidenröslein" (1815).

4. Among the schematic possibilities, various ternary structures (aabbcc, aabcc, etc.), as well as forms resembling the rondo or frequently having a da capo return, are the most common. The "longer" Rheinlieder often employ four to six phrases, greatly extended by repetition.

5. See example 4.2, which reproduces the actual size of the print.

6. "Zur Geschichte des Männergesanges," AmZ (24 January 1844): 52.

7. Eric Sams, The Songs of Robert Schumann (New York: Norton, 1969), 85, suggests that Schumann decided to set this poem because of a family connection, Oswald Lorenz, his friend and colleague on the NZfM (and a Rheinlied critic). Apparently the poet modeled her poem on Brentano's Loreley poem, which I discuss in chapter 3.

8. As noted earlier, German musical images of the Rhine often sound barcarole-like, as do musical depictions of idyllic streams of many other nationalities. For Clara Schumann's setting of Heine's "Lorelei," (example A.1) composed in 1843, see Pamela Susskind, "Clara Schumann," New Grove 16:829; also Nancy B. Reich, Clara Schumann: The Artist and the Woman (Ithaca: Cornell University Press, 1985), 303.

9. See F. Mendelssohn-Bartholdy: Werke: Kritische durchgesehene Ausgabe, vol. 19, ed. J. Rietz (Leipzig, 1874–77).

10. Considering this "consistency" with which a basic "descriptive" figure is elaborated in so many Romantic lieder, one is tempted to wonder whether the old Baroque doctrine of the affects did not survive into this era in some form.

11. See Heinz J. Dill, "Romantic Irony in the Works of Robert Schumann," Musical Quarterly 73/2 (1989): 172–95. Dill discusses Schumann's musical representation of Romantic irony in its function as the unexpected, the incongruous, the disruptive, and the conscious—all qualities producing a clear sense of distance in expression. See also "The Natural World and the 'Folklike Tone'" in Carl Dahlhaus, Realism in Nineteenth-Century Music, trans. Mary Whittall (Cambridge: Cambridge University Press, 1985), 114. Yet in his Poem and Music in the German Lied, 100, Jack M. Stein faults this lied as "probably Schumann's worst misreading of a Heine poem": "The heavy, solemn setting completely misses the bold, perhaps blasphemous idea that the eyes, lips, and cheeks of the Madonna in a painting in the Cologne cathedral are exactly like his beloved's. From the beginning the tone of the poem is ironic. . . . When Heine writes of the Rhine as a 'sacred river,' the reader should put up his guard. The deliberate awkwardness, the silly naïveté of the language (repetition of 'gross' and 'heilig'), the ridiculous rhymes ('Well'n'-'Köln,' later 'Englein'-'Wänglein') ought to have warned Schumann away from his

straight-faced, pompous, patriotic-religious treatment. The solemnity of the music to the first stanza is in fact so inconsistent that it could stand as the ironic beginning of a satirical setting, but the rest of the song proves Schumann's earnestness. In fact, he insists on it to the very end, with a 17-measure piano epilogue."

12. Ibid., 103.

13. Between measures 15 and 35, for example, the composer assigns to the piano an ever-mounting sequential figure—strengthened by octave doublings—that matches the poet's intensifying sarcasm, unleashed through a comparison with three historic Rhine landmarks: "the coffin must be still larger than the Heidelberger Fass"; "it must be yet longer than the bridge at Mainz"; and the dozen giants transporting it "must be stronger still than the strong Christopher in the cathedral at Cologne on the Rhine." From measure 35 to 43, moreover, quite literal tone painting, through ponderous chords depicting the heavy weight of the coffin, directly mirrors the poet's bitterness.

14. The poems of this cycle did not originate as a group. See Stein, *Poem*, 111.

15. Eichendorff's title was "Waldgespräch."

16. Sams, *Songs*, 95.

17. After its first note, this "leading motive" evolves in a melodic line remarkably resembling, in its structure and slow pace, the chief theme of Schumann's "Im Rhein."

18. Prince Lichnowsky, a leader of liberal forces in the Frankfurt National Parliament, was murdered in the revolutionary year 1848.

19. As his first line, Liszt uses "Im Rhein, im *schönen* [beautiful] Strome." According to Stein, *Poem*, 200, it was Heine himself who later changed *heiligen* (holy) to *schönen*.

20. Liszt offers an alternative, "more difficult" (*più difficile*) piano part of faster, descending, ornamented chords. In the second version, the meter is 6/8 instead of 3/4. The extremes of chromaticism are gone and the voice range is more conservative. While retaining a triplet motion to "express" waves, the piano part, with a motive of its own, is contrapuntally independent of the voice. The "wave" figures are interrupted for important ideas in the text: e.g., abrupt chords for *das grosse, das heil'ge Köln* ("the great, the holy Cologne"); and, at the famous likening of the loved one to the Virgin, the piano expressively alternates between measures of complete silence and agitated syncopated chords, as in the postlude.

21. The date of composition of the second version of "Die Lorelei" is uncertain.

22. At the dedication of the Beethoven memorial in Bonn on 13 August 1845, Liszt conducted his *Festkantate zur Enthüllung des Beethoven-Denkmals in Bonn* (Festival cantata for the unveiling of the Beethoven monument in Bonn), completed earlier that year. The cantata, based on a text by O. L. B. Wolff, requires a soloist group

of sopranos, tenors, and basses (two of each), chorus, and orchestra. See Hans Engel, "Franz von Liszt," *Die Musik in Geschichte und Gegenwart* 8:967–68. In 1874 Liszt also composed another work with Rhine associations, "Die Glocken des Strassburger Münsters" (The bells of the Strassburg Cathedral) for baritone, chorus, and orchestra, to a translation of Henry Wadsworth Longfellow's "Golden Legend," completed and published in 1851. First performed on 10 March 1875, it was published that same year. See Humphrey Searle, *The Music of Liszt*, 2d ed. (New York: Dover, 1966), 112–13.

23. The final strophe, with some textual variation, actually makes the form da capo.

24. See Albert Methfessel, *Sechs deutsche Kriegslieder für eine und mehrere Stimmen, mit Chören und willkührlicher Begleitung des Fortepiano, in Musik gesetzt und allen braven deutschen Kriegern gewidmet*, op. 35, 2d ed. (Rudolstadt: Hof-, Buch-, and Kunst-Handlung, 1814), 10.

25. The original setting, for male chorus, a cappella, appeared in *Greefs Männerliedern*, vol. 9 (Essen: n.p., n.d.). The version appearing here (Leipzig and Berlin, 1854) calls for solo voice and piano. See "Carl Wilhelm," *Hugo Riemanns Musik Lexikon*, 11th ed., rev. Alfred Einstein (Berlin: Max Hesses Verlag, 1929), 2028.

If durability is a true test of *Volkstümlichkeit*, this tune qualifies beautifully. Wilhelm's setting still survives at Yale, where it serves the alma mater as "Bright College Years."

26. See Malcolm Boyd, "National Anthems," *New Grove* 13:54–55. Regarding French invasions of the German Rhinelands in the later eighteenth century, see chapter 2.

27. Von Fallersleben adapted it from a poem by Walther von der Vogelweide (ca. 1170–ca. 1230).

28. The publisher, Campe, was also Heine's. The original German text, translated here, appears in Volkmann, *Um Einheit*, 148–49. It was restored to popularity during 1870 and again during World War I. In 1922 it was declared the official German national anthem. The German of the third verse: "Einigkeit und Recht und Freiheit / Für das deutsche Vaterland! / Danach lässt uns alle streben / Brüderlich mit Herz und Hand! / Einigkeit und Recht und Freiheit / Sind des Glückes Unterpfand, / Glüh' im Glanze dieses Glückes, / Glüh', deutsche Vaterland!"

29. In 1933 the National Socialist "Horst-Wessel-Lied" ("Ich lebte einst im deutschen Vaterland" [Once I dwelt in the German fatherland]) had soared to equal status with the older German national anthem, the two lieder sharing equal popularity until the conclusion of World War II.

30. For a detailed explanation of Austro-German national anthems, see Alexander Sydow, *Das Lied: Ursprung, Wesen und Wandel* (Göttingen: Vandenhoeck & Ruprecht, 1962), 453–57.

CHAPTER 5

1. Adolf Bernhard Marx, "Standpunkt der Zeitung," *Berlin allgemeine musikalische Zeitung* 3 (1826): 422, cited in Sanna Pederson, "A. B. Marx, Berlin Concert Life, and German National Identity," *19th-Century Music* 18/2 (Fall 1994): 96.

2. Christa Bürger has observed that "the middle class saw its legitimation in the course of the nineteenth century in the consciousness of being bearers of cultural progress and at the same time keepers of national tradition"; quoted in Pederson, "A. B. Marx," 105.

An immense population explosion throughout Europe between the mid-eighteenth and mid-nineteenth centuries, with increases in some countries reaching two- and threefold, disrupted the very foundation of society. Germany and Britain tripled their populations; Prussia and its Rhineland expanded from three to six million. This demographic event, coupled with urbanization and industrialization, contributed to the reordering of the old social structure of Europe.

3. Richard Parker, *The Myth of the Middle Class* (New York: Liveright, 1972), 33, describes this alliance as the "homogenization" of society. See also William Weber, *Music and the Middle Class* (New York: Holmes & Meier, 1975), 29, 40.

4. Julius Bautz, *Geschichte des deutschen Männergesangs in übersichtlicher Darstellung* (Frankfurt am Main: Steyl & Thomas, 1890), 37ff.; Otto Elben, *Der volkstümliche deutsche Männergesang*, 2d ed. (Tübingen: H. Laupp'schen Buchhandlung, 1887), 91.

5. Bautz, *Geschichte*, 11.

6. Elben, *Volkstümliche*, 91–92.

7. See ibid., 75. Elben noted that seven Rhenish music festivals, organized to promulgate German unification through music (the oratorio above all) and the education of public taste, were given in Mannheim between 1816 and 1822.

8. This chapter is a revised version of an article published in *Musical Quarterly* 73/4 (1989): 476–512, and of a paper presented to the American Musicological Society, Ann Arbor, Mich., November 1982. Düsseldorf, the birthplace of Heinrich Heine, had long sustained influential intellectual endeavors. Goethe sojourned in the city during 1774 and 1814, consorting with its philosopher-literati and visiting its famous art gallery. His close friends the philosopher-poet Johann Gottfried von Herder and the poet Christoph Martin Wieland frequently traveled to the Rhine Province capital. See *Goethe und das Rheinland*, Ed. Rheinischer Verein für Denkmalpflege und Heimatschutz 27 (Düsseldorf, 1932), 102ff. et passim.

9. See Robert W. Gutman, *Richard Wagner: The Man, His Mind, and His Music* (New York: Time, 1968), 349–50.

10. In *The Emergence of the Past: A Theory of Historical Explanation* (Chicago: University of Chicago Press, 1981), Dale H. Porter cautions against convenient oversimplification in explaining a historical phenomenon as the sole, predictable result of a prior event. The period represented in this study, for example, was one of widespread

turbulent change and instability clouding the perception of precise conclusions as to cause and effect.

11. Cyril Ehrlich ascribes the tremendous growth of English piano manufacturing, from the late eighteenth century, to the affluent middle classes' shrewd marketing mentality and emphasis on sheer entertainment and materialistic prestige. See *The Piano: A History* (London: Ingram Price, 1976), 16–19.

12. See Arnold Hauser, *The Social History of Art*, vol. 3 (New York: Vintage Books, 1951), 224–25.

13. See Weber, *Music*, 57.

14. See Gerhard Pietsch, "Musiker an rheinischen Höfen" in *Zur mittelrheinischen und niederrheinischen Musikgeschichte: Beiträge zur Musikgeschichte der Stadt Düsseldorf* 118, ed. Julius Alf (Cologne: Arno Volk-Verlag, 1977), 20. Music and art flourished handsomely at the court of Duke Wilhelm der Reiche (1539–92). See too Alfred Einstein, "Italienischer Musiker am Hofe der Neuburger Wittelsbacher," *Sammelbände der internationalen Musikgesellschaft* 9:406; also Friedrich Walter, *Geschichte des Theaters und der Musik am kurpfälzschen Hofe* (Leipzig: Breitkopf & Härtel, 1898), 69–70. Johann Wilhelm's tastes were also influenced by his second wife, Maria Anna Louise Aloisia de Medici. His court favored Italian composers and operas.

15. Among other factors resulting in this move, the Thirty Years' War had debilitated German commerce, destroying cities economically and politically.

16. The Austro-Bavarian Treaty of Ried had dissolved Napoleon's Rhenish Confederation on 8 October 1813. See Roland Würtz, "Düsseldorfer Musiker in der Mannheim Hofkapelle," in *Beiträge zur Musikgeschichte der Stadt Düsseldorf*, vol. 118 (Cologne: Arno Volk-Verlag, 1977), 30–31, and Richard Fellner, *Geschichte einer deutschen Musterbühne: Karl Immermanns Leitung des Stadttheaters zu Düsseldorf* (Stuttgart: J. G. Cotta'schen Buchhandlung, 1888), 47ff. For the involved relationships between Düsseldorf and the other Rhine cities Heidelberg and Mannheim, see Friedrich Lau, "Die Regierungskollegien zu Düsseldorf und der Hofstaat zur Zeit Johann Wilhelms II," *Düsseldorfer Jahrbuch* 40 (1938): 270ff.

17. Prussia, in addition, transformed the chief old commercial roads into major highways between 1815 and 1825. A proliferation of industrial exhibitions further stimulated the Düsseldorf economy from 1811 on. The city's first Trade Exhibition was held in 1852, during Schumann's music directorship. See Otto Most, *Düsseldorf als Handels-Industrie, Kunst- und Gartenstadt* (Düsseldorf: August Bagel, 1912), 12ff.; also Herbert Drux, *Studien zur Entwicklung des öffentlichen Musiklebens in Ostniederberg*, Beiträge zur rheinischen Musikgeschichte 11 (Cologne: Arno Volk-Verlag, 1956), 7–41; and Bernd Balkenhol, *Armut und Arbeitslosigkeit in der Industrialisierung dargestellt am Beispiel Düsseldorfs, 1850–1900* (Düsseldorf: Droste, 1976), 12–27.

18. Legal equality, e.g., now replaced aristocratic hereditary privilege.

19. Balkenhol, *Armut*, 84–86, 111, 127. Prussia's coal production, in fact, expanded from 1.5 million tons in 1825 to 20.5 million in 1865.

20. For the Vienna-Rome-Berlin-Düsseldorf connection, see chapter 3.

21. Schadow's Düsseldorf circle included the artists Carl Friedrich Lessing, Julius Hübner, Theodor Hildebrandt, Carl Sohn, and Johann Wilhelm Schirmer (Mendelssohn's mentor); see Fellner, *Geschichte*, 53. Schadow had left Berlin in 1811 for Rome to join the Nazarenes, returning to the Prussian capital in 1819 as an Academy instructor there. He transformed the Düsseldorf school into one of Europe's most progressive and influential art centers, training, e.g., many members of the Hudson River School. See Schiff, *German Masters*, 16. The nineteenth-century German art academies strongly influenced cultural life and politics in general; the Düsseldorf Academy, the faculty of which included many Nazarenes, also answered to the Prussian Ministry of Culture in Berlin.

22. See Fritz Goldkühle, *Rheinische Landschaften und Städtebilder, 1600–1850*, exhibition catalogue, Rheinisches Landesmuseum, Bonn, 1960–61 (Cologne: Rheinisches Landesmuseum, 1960), 9–21; and Fellner, *Geschichte*, 54.

23. *Verfassung der Musik-Academie*, Düsseldorf statute, 26 August 1807, in Otto Most, *Geschichte der Stadt Düsseldorf*, vol. 2 (Düsseldorf: August Bagel, 1921), 231. The members of the academy included the Counts von Spee and von Nesselrode, the city notary Schorn, city commissioner of accounts Zilger, and the merchant Winkelmann.

24. *Stadtmusiker* did exist in Düsseldorf but received no official duties, income, or even uniforms, although they often performed at church festivals and processions, for which the city paid them; see Peter Darius, *Die Musik in den Elementarschulen und Kirchen Düsseldorfs im 19. Jahrhundert*, Beiträge zur rheinischen Musikgeschichte 77 (Cologne: Arno Volk-Verlag, 1969), 1–51. For the musical associations, the establishment of oratorio societies, and the politics of the Napoleonic Wars, see Würtz, "Düsseldorfer Musiker," 38–41. Occasionally Düsseldorf's musical amateurs paid professional musicians for assistance. See also Eberhard Preussner, *Die bürgerliche Musikkultur* (Kassel and Basel: Bärenreiter, 1950), 62ff. These earliest steps by Düsseldorf's upper middle classes toward establishing public music societies reflected the accelerating development of urban concert organizations over much of Europe; see Leo Balet and E. Gerhard, *Die Verbürgerlichung der deutschen Kunst, Literatur, und Musik im 18. Jahrhundert* (Strassburg: Heitz, 1936), 403.

25. J. F. A. Burgmüller, letter of 16 March 1820, in Most, *Geschichte*, 232.

26. John Kenneth Galbraith, *The Affluent Society* (Boston: Houghton-Mifflin, 1969), 239.

27. *Protokoll*, Düsseldorf City Council, 19 January 1828, in Darius, *Die Musik*, 26. This statement clearly attests to the middle classes' competitive spirit and status consciousness, characteristic of a developing market economy.

28. Burgmüller's son Norbert (1810–36), a highly regarded composer, was

known in Düsseldorf not only for his compositions but also for his unorthodox lifestyle. See Eric Frederick Jensen, "Norbert Burgmüller and Robert Schumann," *Musical Quarterly* 74/4 (1990): 550–65. Norbert Burgmüller unsuccessfully applied to fill his father's post. In 1835, when Mendelssohn resigned as city music director, Norbert Burgmüller again was rejected as his successor. During the interim of 1824–33 the Music Society was conducted by one of its members, Friedrich Wetschky, who led both the organization's subscription concerts and the city's church music performances. See W. H. Fischer, *Festschrift zur hundertjährigen Jubelfeier des städtischen Musikvereins Düsseldorf und zum hundertjährigen Bestehen der Niederrheinischen Musikfeste* (Düsseldorf: Forberg, 1918), 18–19.

29. The offer of the contract to Mendelssohn fulfilled an earlier dream, expressed in a letter from Paris to his father, 21 February 1832: "Your injunction, too, to make a choice of the country that I preferred to live in, I have carried out. . . . That country is Germany." See Mendelssohn, *Letters*, ed. G. Selden-Goth, 194. The festival program included his Trumpet Overture in C Major, op. 101, Handel's oratorio *Israel in Egypt* (with added obbligato organ accompaniments and woodwinds to grace the newly constructed concert hall), Beethoven's Sixth Symphony and third *Leonore* Overture, E. W. Wolf's *Easter Cantata*, Peter von Winter's cantata *Die Macht der Töne*, and arias from C. M. von Weber's *Der Freischütz*, Mozart's *The Marriage of Figaro*, and Beethoven's *Fidelio*; see Julius Alf, "Geschichte und Bedeutung der Niederrheinischen Musikfeste in der ersten Hälfte des neunzehnten Jahrhunderts," *Düsseldorfer Jahrbuch* 42–43 (1940–41): 42. Other members of the festival committee included Schadow, Wetschky, and a host of others: Count von Hacke, Sybel, von Pelser, Wolters, Hövel, Schumacher, Schreiber, Schmitz, Schramm, Schöller, Umpfenbach, Menkhoff, and Friedrichs; see Eric Werner, *Mendelssohn: A New Image of the Composer and His Age*, trans. Dika Newlin (London: Free Press of Glenco [Collier-Macmillan], 1963), 249; and Mendelssohn's letter to Karl Klingemann, 20 February 1833, in the Whittall Foundation Collection, Library of Congress, Music Division, Washington, D.C. Mendelssohn already was familiar with Düsseldorf, having visited it many times, occasionally staying with Schadow. See Mendelssohn's letter from Paris to the Düsseldorf painter Eduard Bendemann, 12 January 1832, in Mendelssohn, *Briefe aus Leipziger Archiven*, ed. Hans-Joachim Rothe and Reinhard Szeskus (Leipzig: VEB Deutscher Verlag für Musik, 1972), 21; also Heinrich Eduard Jacob, *Felix Mendelssohn und seine Zeit* (Frankfurt am Main: S. Fischer, 1959), 239ff.

30. Letter from Coblenz of 6 September 1833 to pastor Julius Schubring, in *Letters*, ed. Selden-Goth, 214.

31. Letter to Ignaz Moscheles, 7 February 1834, in ibid., 222. Regarding Mendelssohn's salary and contract, see Wilhelm Adolf Lampadius, *The Life of Felix Mendelssohn-Bartholdy*, trans W. L. Gage (Boston, 1887), 202; and *Die Rheinprovinz, 1815–1915:*

Hundert Jahre preussischer Herrschaft am Rhein, vol. 2, ed. Joseph Hansen (Bonn: A. Marcus & E. Webers Verlag, 1917), 364.

32. Letter to his colleague and Düsseldorf successor Ferdinand Hiller, in Hiller, *Mendelssohn: Letters and Recollections*, trans. M. E. von Glehn (London: Macmillan, 1874; reprint, 1972), 46.

33. Mendelssohn's letter to his sister Rebecca, 26 October 1833, in *Letters*, ed. Selden-Goth, 215.

34. Ibid. See also Peter Sutermeister, *Felix Mendelssohn-Bartholdy* (Zürich: Ex Libris, 1949), 79.

35. *AmZ* (1838): 328.

36. Ibid.

37. August Reissmann, *Felix Mendelssohn-Bartholdy: Sein Leben und seine Werke* (Berlin: L. Guttentag, 1867), 143. In June 1835 he wrote, "I owe it much too much to myself to remain in the [German] fatherland as long as I can." Letter from Cologne, 1 June 1835, in the Heinemann Collection, Library of Congress, Music Division, Washington, D.C.

38. For Rietz's salary, see Mendelssohn's letter to him of 7 June 1834, in the Whittall Foundation Collection. The Prussian government's permission was still necessary for a salary decision.

39. This merger occurred 1 July 1845. The *Gesangmusikverein* (Choral Society), however, the chief such group in Düsseldorf, remained untouched by Rietz's reforms; see Fischer, *Festschrift*, 32. The *AmZ* (1838): 328, reported that, under both Mendelssohn and Rietz, the totally amateur Choral Society differed much from the orchestra, a disparate conglomeration of dilettantes, a few professionals, and even oboists from the local military regiment.

40. Fellner, *Geschichte*, 260, 463.

41. Society for the Advancement of Music, *Denkschrift*, 15 July 1847, in Most, *Geschichte*, 235; also Alf, "Geschichte," 229.

42. Letter to Kistner, 10 May 1843, in Zimmer, *Rietz*, 56. Mendelssohn had promised Schirmer, his watercolor instructor, that the artist would receive cello lessons from Rietz; see Mendelssohn's letter to Rietz, 2 August 1834, in the Whittall Foundation Collection.

43. Stadtarchiv Düsseldorf, *Akten und Belage des Vereins für Tonkunst*, 1833–39, in Alf, "Geschichte," 235–37.

44. Zimmer, *Rietz*, 58.

45. Letter of 12 June 1847 in *Aus Ferdinand Hillers Briefwechsel*, Beiträge zur Rheinischen Musikgeschichte 7/92 (Cologne: Arno Volk-Verlag, 1970), 72–74. The city council and Prussian government, however, would ultimately determine these stipulations.

46. Ibid., 7/92:73, 76.

47. Ibid., 7/91:74–81.

48. Ibid., 7/92:78. On 17 October 1847 Euler himself explained to an irritated Hiller that the General Music Society's finances and the great expense of the Lower Rhine Music Festival restricted his salary but that he could conduct the festival of 1848 and receive an ample additional subsidy. The festival of 1848, though, never materialized because of the revolution that year. The contract stipulated no yearly holiday, one of Hiller's chief demands. In a letter of 16 October 1847 Hiller named Eduard Bendemann as his main supporter in the Düsseldorf art colony; see ibid., 6/70:10.

49. Letter of 3 February 1848, ibid., 6/50:11–12.

50. E. A. Hauchecorne, *Niederrheinisches Musikfest: Blätter der Erinnerung an die fünfzig-jährige Dauer der Niederrheinischen Musikfeste* (Cologne: Commissions-Verlag der M. Du Mont-Schauberg'schen Buchhandlung, 1868), *Verzeichnisse*, 48. Hiller also aided the capital's General Music Society executive committee in selecting Schumann as the next city music director.

51. Berthold Litzmann, ed., *Clara Schumann: Ein Künstlerleben, nach Tagebüchern und Briefe*, vol. 2, *Ehejahre, 1840–1856* (Hildesheim: Georg Olms, 1971), 225. The executive Committee—consisting of H. von Heister, Dr. Ernest von Heister II, the artist Hildebrandt, notary Euler (whom Clara called "the musical factotum here"), von Lezaak, Schleger, Hertz, R. Nielo, and Bloem—arrived in dresscoats to welcome the Schumanns.

52. In Dresden, Schumann had conducted a mixed chorus and had succeeded Hiller in directing a male chorus there. But Schumann had "tired of the eternal 6/4 chord"; Sutermeister, *Mendelssohn*, 220. Primarily through Hiller's influence, Schumann had first been approached by the General Music Society executive committee in November 1849. The pianist Tausch, in Düsseldorf since 1846, directed the *Künstlerliedertafel* (Artists' Song Society) and the *Männergesangverein*. See also Peter Sutermeister, *Robert Schumann: Sein Leben nach Briefen, Tagebüchern und Erinnerungen des Meisters und seiner Gattin* (Zürich: Ex Libris, 1949), 222; and Litzmann, *Clara Schumann*, 224–25.

53. See the copy of the subsidy grant awarded by the city council on 9 April 1850 in the Stadtarchiv Düsseldorf, in Paul Kast, ed., *Schumanns rheinische Jahre* (Düsseldorf: Droste, 1981), 50–52. Dr. Kast, the former director of the Universitätsbibliothek Düsseldorf, has been very helpful to me in providing much information about music in nineteenth-century Düsseldorf. See also Joseph Neyses, "Robert Schumann als Musikdirektor in Düsseldorf," *Düsseldorfer Almanach* 71 (1927): 73–74.

54. Sutermeister, *Schumann*, 225. For the 1851–52 season Schumann had brought the distinguished Leipzig violinist Wilhelm Joseph von Wasielewski (1822–96) to Düsseldorf as the City Orchestra concertmaster. For Schumann's reservations about accepting the Rhine post, see Peter Ostwald, *Schumann: The Inner Voices of a Musical Genius* (Boston: Northeastern University Press, 1985), 230.

55. Entries, 17 and 22 September 1850, in Litzmann, *Clara Schumann*, 226–28.

Düsseldorf soon brought opportunities for Clara, too, such as the establishment of close associations with Joseph Joachim and Johannes Brahms, as well as a renewal of her concert career. See also Reich, *Clara Schumann*, 134–35. In contrast to his Düsseldorf predecessors, Schumann at least had professed that his "greatest desire" was to conduct, happily anticipating that the city's musical forces could perform such major works as J. S. Bach's *St. John Passion* and B Minor Mass. But see Kast, *Rheinische Jahre*, 11, describing the meager orchestra of only about forty players. See also *Robert Schumanns Briefe, Neue Folge*, ed. F. Gustav Jansen, 2d ed. (Leipzig: Breitkopf & Härtel, 1904), 333–34.

56. See Kast, *Rheinische Jahre*, 62–63. Hasenclever was also Immermann's close friend, an important Music Society member, husband of Schadow's only daughter, and possibly a relative of the Düsseldorf artist Johann Peter Hasenclever (1810–53); see Hölscher, *Buch*, 64. Von Königswinter prescribed river bath treatments in the Rhine for the ailing composer; see Ostwald, *Schumann*, 249.

57. Schumann's *Der Rose Pilgerfahrt* had been premiered on 6 July 1851 by just such a group, twenty-four selected singers, in a private performance held at the composer's residence; see Litzmann, *Clara Schumann*, 229–35. Mendelssohn, too, had included choral music from the Renaissance, as well as that of J. S. Bach.

58. *Düsseldorfer Journal* 147 (21 June 1851), in Most, *Geschichte*, 236.

59. See Hermann Pongs, *Das kleine Lexikon der Weltliteratur*, 2d ed. (Stuttgart: Union Deutsche Verlagsgesellschaft, 1956), 661–62.

60. With the Dresden Choral Society, Schumann had grown to depend on Clara's interpretation of his conducting for the singers from her position at the piano. "Schumann," Nancy Reich emphasizes, "had never been an effective conductor, should never have been offered the position, and should not have accepted it"; see Reich, *Clara Schumann*, 137.

61. Diary entry, 30 March 1852, in Sutermeister, *Schumann*, 226. As Ostwald, *Schumann*, 246, observes, "It was becoming increasingly obvious during [Schumann's] second season [in Düsseldorf] that someone with medical authority would have to step in." Wortmann also was an influential member of the General Music Society's executive committee and board of the Choral Society.

62. Schumann nevertheless optimistically organized a *Verein für Kammermusik* (Chamber Music Society) among local musicians to perform both "older, also all newer important works." See Jansen, *Briefe*, 345–57. The ailing Schumann conducted very little in the *Männergesangfest* held in Düsseldorf in August 1852.

63. Becker's diary in Most, *Geschichte*, 237.

64. Ibid.

65. Neyses, "Schumann," 78.

66. See Jansen, *Briefe*, 365.

67. A city council member personally offered to cover the unexpected city budget deficit incurred by a mixup in ordering choral music on the part of the festival

committee; see Jansen, *Briefe*, 260, 377. At this same festival, Schumann conducted Handel's *Messiah*, his own Symphony No. 4 in D Minor, op. 120, and the Festival Overture and Chorus on the "Rheinweinlied," composed for this event. See also Heinrich Reimann, *Robert Schumanns Leben und Werke* (Leipzig: Peters, 1887), 54.

68. See Kast, *Rheinische Jahre*, 71.

69. Neyses, "Schumann," 78.

70. Ibid., 79–80, and Sutermeister, *Schumann*, 228.

71. *Niederrheinische Musikzeitung* 1 (Cologne, 1853): 15.

72. Letter to Stern, 12 February 1854, Jansen, *Briefe*, 392–93.

73. Clara's diary, 9 November 1853, in Litzmann, *Clara Schumann*, 245–46, and 6 June 1854, 319. Schumann's hospital expenses amounted to his entire income as city music director, but Clara's earnings from concertizing far exceeded Robert's Düsseldorf salary.

74. *Niederrheinische Musikzeitung* 3 (1855): 47. The anonymous author of "Die Musikzustände des Niederrheins," in the *NZfM* (23 March 1855): 138, reported that the Rhineland cities nevertheless were always seeking prestige at any cost, for they "strove to win . . . the participation of the most significant celebrities in the various artistic areas, a circumstance that soon led to an unpleasant rivalry among the participating cities. . . . It happened not infrequently."

75. Hauser, *Social History*, 154.

76. See chapters 1–3 and Weber, *Music*, 106.

77. William Weber, "Music," *19th-Century Music* 1/2 (November 1977): 176.

78. This section of the chapter is a revised version of an article published in *19th-Century Music* 3/3 (March 1980): 211–24. I have restricted this study to the first half-century of the festivals, the critical years of German musical Romanticism extending from the post-Napoleonic era to the eve of the Franco-German War and the period recorded in detail by Hauchecorne in his *Blätter der Erinnerung*. Hauchecorne's chronicle is an invaluable contemporary source of information on the festivals. The term *bourgeoisie* as used here encompasses a broad spectrum of varied middle-class interest groups including merchants, industrialists, members of the professions, and civil servants. This particular assortment of affluent social groups had developed primarily from the increasingly prominent forces of industry, urbanization, and civil bureaucracy present in nineteenth-century Germany. William Weber, "The Muddle of the Middle Classes," *19th-Century Music* 3 (1979): 175–85, explains the confusion resulting from the imprecise application of the terms *bourgeoisie* and *middle class* to music.

79. *Kölner Zeitung* (16 May 1841). See also Friedrich Lützenkirchen, "Über das jüngste rheinische Pfingstconcert, 1842," *NZfM* (12 July 1842): 13–15; and Preussner, *Musikkultur*, 114–19.

80. See Herbert Drux, *Studien zur Entwicklung des öffentlichen Musiklebens in Ostniederberg*, Beiträge zur rheinischen Musikgeschichte 11 (Cologne: Arno Volk-Verlag,

1956), 37, who notes that instrumental music societies were already flourishing among the middle classes in eighteenth-century Aachen, Cologne, Düsseldorf, and elsewhere in the Prussian Rhine Province.

81. An excellent examination of these academic and scientific conferences in Germany before and during this period is presented by R. Hinton Thomas, *Liberalism, Nationalism, and the German Intellectuals, 1822–1847* (Cambridge: W. Heffer, 1951).

82. Peter Kaufmann, *Nationalfeste des deutschen Volkes: Eine Forderung der Zeit* (Bonn, 1843), 17–24, cited in Faber, *Rheinlande*, 405.

83. Alf, "Geschichte," 24.

84. Ibid., 18.

85. Ibid., 188.

86. Hauchecorne, *Blätter*, 71–72.

87. See the *AmZ* (29 June 1825): 444.

88. Hauchecorne, *Blätter*, 72.

89. In 1929 Elberfeld was incorporated into Wuppertal.

90. Hans Hartmann, *Festschrift zur 100jährigen Jubelfeier des Elberfelder Gesangvereins* (Elberfeld, 1911), 8–59.

91. See Reinhold Zimmermann, "Zur Musikgeschichte des Aachener Raums im 19. und 20. Jahrhundert," in *Beiträge zur Musikgeschichte der Stadt Aachen*, vol. 6, ed. C. M. Brand and K. G. Fellerer (Cologne: Arno Volk-Verlag, 1954), 48–55; also Zdenka Kapko-Foretić, *Carl von Turányi, 1805–1873* (Cologne: Arno Volk-Verlag, 1973), 54–69.

92. Klaus Körner, *Das Musikleben in Köln um die Mitte des 19. Jahrhunderts* (Cologne: Arno Volk-Verlag, 1969), 87, explains that the orchestra of the Akademie was made up of amateur violinists and flutists, many cathedral musicians, and wind players from the city militia. See also Heinz Oepen, *Beiträge zur Geschichte des Kölner Musiklebens, 1760–1840*, Beiträge zur rheinischen Musikgeschichte 10 (Cologne: Arno Volk-Verlag, 1955), 4–15.

93. See Hölscher, *Buch*, 360–62.

94. See Karl Gustav Fellerer, "Der Kölner Singverein, 1820–1840," in *106. Niederrheinisches Musikfest in Düsseldorf, Jahrbuch 1951* (Düsseldorf: J. B. Gerlach, 1951), 50.

95. See H. J. Zingel, *Das Kölner Gürzenichorchester: Werden und Sein* (Cologne: Arno Volk-Verlag, 1963), 50.

96. See Oepen, *Beiträge*, 65–118; and Klaus Körner, *Das Musikleben in Köln*, 89–94.

97. Oepen, *Beiträge*, 65–118 et passim.

98. Cologne hoped to profit from the intensified musical activity being experienced by nearby Aachen and Düsseldorf after their establishment of city music directorships.

99. O. Klauwell, *Das Konservatorium der Musik in Köln: Festschrift zur Feier seines 50jährigen Bestehens* (Cologne: Arno Volk-Verlag, 1900), 1–6, and Paul Mies, "Aus der Vorgeschichte der Hochschule," in *Festschrift zur Feier der Gründung des Kölner*

Konservatoriums im Jahre 1850 und der Staatliche Hochschule für Musik Köln im Jahre 1925 (Cologne: Arno Volk-Verlag, 1950), 11–15.

100. Hauchecorne, *Blätter*, 1.

101. E. L. Gerber, "Etwas über grosse Singstücke, zum Behufe ausserordentlicher Musikfeste," *AmZ* (2 December 1818), 829–33.

102. These all-male boards numbered from five to twenty participants, the larger figure being fairly consistent in the later years of this half-century.

103. The oratorio composers represented during the rest of this period were Haydn, Handel, Maximilian Stadler, and Friedrich Schneider. The repertoire also included instrumental works by Beethoven, Ries, and Spohr.

104. There were no festivals in 1831, 1848, 1849, 1850, 1852, and 1859.

105. Jahn, *Aufsätze*, 173.

106. Other factors determined the remaining two periods of this first half-century. As table 5.2 shows, the period 1835–47 marked the end of the *Vormärz* and the first time dilettante and professional vocal soloists were roughly equal in numbers. The festivals resumed in 1851, the beginning of professional predominance. See Ernst Wolff, "Das musikalische Leben," in *Die Rheinprovinz, 1815–1915*, 2d ed., ed. Joseph Hansen (Bonn, 1917), 377–78.

107. See Hauchecorne, *Blätter*, 24. Ries (1784–1838), a composer-pianist, was the author of *Biographische Notizen über L. van Beethoven* (1838). Schornstein, Johann August Burgmüller (1766–1824), and Friedrich Schneider, music director in Dessau, had conducted during the 1818–24 epoch. Schornstein returned to conduct a festival in 1827. The *AmZ* (25 June 1834): 439 reported that at the 1834 celebration eminent visitors included Mendelssohn, Chopin, Hiller, and Fétis.

108. Hauchecorne, *Blätter*, 29, citing a letter written by Ries in 1829.

109. *AmZ* (29 June 1825): 448.

110. The complete oratorios heard during these years were Handel's *Alexander's Feast, Judas Maccabaeus, Samson, Israel in Egypt,* and *Deborah;* Beethoven's *Christus am Ölberge;* Spohr's *Die letzten Dinge;* F. Schneider's *Das verlorene Paradis;* Haydn's *The Creation;* Bernard Klein's *Jephta;* and Ries's *Der Sieg des Glaubens.*

111. The complete masses performed in this era were Beethoven's Mass in D Major; Mozart's Requiem; and Cherubini's *Messe solenelle* no. 4. The symphonies performed were Ries's nos. 4, 5, and 6; Beethoven's nos. 3, 4, 5, 6, 7, and 9; and Mozart's "Jupiter" Symphony.

112. Dorn was Cologne's music director at this time. Schornstein, still music director at Elberfeld, returned once again as choral conductor for the 1836 and 1839 festivals.

113. Clara Novello (b. 1818) was the daughter of Vincent Novello, the founder of the famous London music publishing house. The Cologne Quartet consisted of Franz Hartmann and Franz Derckum, violins, Franz Weber, viola, and Bernhard Breuer, cello.

114. It should nevertheless be noted that half of these soloists were still dilettantes.

115. The oratorio composers represented in this era were Handel, Mendelssohn, Ries, Bernard Klein, and Haydn. The symphonies played were those by Beethoven, Ries, Mozart, Mendelssohn, and Onslow.

116. The concerto was Beethoven's Piano Concerto No. 5 in E-flat Major (performed and conducted by Mendelssohn in 1842). The quartet, the only one performed during the first fifty years of these festivals, was Mendelssohn's op. 44, no. 5, in E-flat Major, played by the Cologne Quartet.

117. There were no festivals from 1848 to 1850 because of the unsettling conditions accompanying the 1848 Revolution, and no festival took place in 1852 or 1859.

118. Jahn, *Aufsätze*, 214.

119. Unlike the immediately preceding stage, when a maximum of two to four lieder and as many arias were heard in a single festival, now as many as ten lieder and about as many arias were commonly scheduled at each celebration. In 1856 Beethoven's lied cycle *An die ferne Geliebte* was first given at the festivals. The symphonic poem was Liszt's *Festklänge*, conducted in 1857 by the composer. The oratorios performed were those of Handel, Haydn, Schumann, Mendelssohn, Berlioz, and Ferdinand Hiller. The symphonists represented were Beethoven, Schumann, Hiller, Schubert, Mozart, and Haydn. The composers of the fourteen concertos presented were Schumann, Beethoven, Henri Vieuxtemps, J. Rietz, Mendelssohn, Liszt, Joachim, Mozart, Spohr, Bernhard Molique, and Paganini.

120. The tensions preceding the Franco-German War of 1870 no doubt help explain the dramatic drop to 538 performers at the 1867 festival.

121. Jahn, *Aufsätze*, 178.

122. Ludwig Bischoff, Vorwort to the *Textbuch* of the 1862 Lower Rhine Music Festival (Cologne, 1862), given in Hauchecorne, *Blätter*, 59, n. 14.

123. Jahn, *Aufsätze*, 201, reported that the chorus also comprised 168 tenors, 185 sopranos, and 140 altos.

124. Hauchecorne, *Blätter*, 17. Jahn, *Aufsätze*, 202, noted that at the 1856 festival the 164-member orchestra contained 16 double basses and 27 cellos.

125. Bischoff, Vorwort, 61, n. 14.

126. See Wolff, "Leben," 365; also Zimmermann, "Musikgeschichte," 51.

127. W. Jackson Bate, *Samuel Johnson* (New York: Harcourt Brace Jovanovich 1975, 1977), 167.

128. Alf, "Geschichte," 26, citing the *Deutsche Musikzeitung* (23 May 1839).

129. Alf, "Geschichte," 232–33.

130. In 1842 the two most important Rhenish choral societies, those in Cologne and Düsseldorf, were established.

131. Alf, "Geschichte," 233, 238.

BIBLIOGRAPHY

Albrecht-Carrié, René. *A Diplomatic History of Europe since the Congress of Vienna*. New York: Harper & Row, 1958.

Alexander, Frank G., and Sheldon T. Selesnick. *The History of Psychiatry*. New York: Harper & Row, 1966.

Alf, Julius. "Geschichte und Bedeutung der Niederrheinischen Musikfeste in der ersten Hälfte des Neunzehnten Jahrhunderts." *Düsseldorfer Jahrbuch* 42/43 (1940–41): 1–243.

———. "Schumanns Düsseldorfer Zeit: Kreuzungspunkt eines musikalischen Jahrhunderts." In *Robert und Clara Schumann: Dokumente zum Düsseldorfer Musikleben*, 10–15. Düsseldorf: Heinrich-Heine-Institut, 1977.

Allgemeine deutsche Biographie. 56 vols. Historische Kommission bei der Bayerischen Akademie der Wissenschaft. Munich: Duncker & Humbolt, 1875–1912.

Allgemeine musikalische Zeitung (28 September 1831): 52–53; (4 July 1838): 64–66; (9 December 1840): 1030–31; (3 March 1841): 205; (22 February 1843): 149–51; (4 October 1843): 711–14; (27 August 1845): 23–25; (18 December 1848): 859–63. Leipzig.

Allison, John M. S. *Thiers and the French Monarchy*. London: Archon, 1968.

Arndt, Ernst Moritz. *Die Frage über die Niederlande und die Rheinlande*. Leipzig: Weidmann'sche Buchhandlung, 1831.

Arnim, Ludwig Achim Freiherr von, and Clemens Brentano, eds. *Des Knaben Wunderhorn* (Heidelberg: 1806–8). Edited by Friedrich Bremer. Leipzig: Philipp Reclam jun., 1878.

Athenäum: Zeitschrift für des gebildete Deutschland (19 June 1841): 375; (26 June 1841): 397–98; (10 July 1843): 430. Berlin.

Augsburger allgemeine Zeitung (1 August 1840): 27–28; (2 August 1840): 18–19.

Baedeker, Karl. *The Rhine from Rotterdam to Constance: Handbook for Travellers*, 16th rev. Eng. ed. Leipzig: Karl Baedeker, 1906.

Balet, Leo, and E. Gerhard. *Die Verbürgerlichung der deutschen Kunst, Literatur, und Musik im 18. Jahrhundert.* Strassburg: Heitz, 1936.

Balkenhol, Bernd. *Armut und Arbeitslosigkeit in der Industrialisierung dargestellt am Beispiel Düsseldorfs, 1850–1900.* Düsseldorf: Droste, 1976.

Batts, Michael S., ed. *Das Nibelungenlied: Paralleldruck der Handschriften A, B, und C nebst Lesarten der übrigen Handschriften.* Tübingen: Niemeyer, 1971.

Baume, Peter la. *The Romans on the Rhine.* Translated by Barry Jones. Chicago: Argonaut, 1969.

Bautz, Julius. *Geschichte des deutschen Männergesangs in übersichtlicher Darstellung.* Frankfurt am Main: Steyl & Thomas, 1890.

Becker, Julius. "Liederschau." *Neue Zeitschrift für Musik* (26 October 1841): 134–36; "Liederschau (Gesänge für Männerstimmen)" (8 March 1842): 79; "Mehrstimmige Gesänge" (6 August 1841): 43–44; (10 August 1841): 135; (2 November 1841): 143.

———. "Über die hohe Bedeutung der Musik in der Gegenwart." *Neue Zeitschrift für Musik* (27 May 1842): 169–70.

Becker, Karl, ed. *Rheinischer Volksliederborn: Auswahl der edelsten und schönsten Volkslieder mit ihren Melodien der verschiedenen Gegenden der Rheinlande; aus dem Munde des Volkes und aus geschriebenen Liederbüchern gesammelt und herausgegeben.* Neuwied: Heuser, 1892.

———. *Volkslieder-Album für vierstimmigen Männerchor: Eine reichhaltige Sammlung wirklicher Volkslieder, volkstümlicher Lieder und Lieder im Volkstone nach den neusten Forschungen auf dem Gebiete des Volksgesanges bearbeitet.* 2d ed. Neuwied: Heuser, 1892.

Berenbruch, Brigitte, and Helmut Hellberg. *Robert Schumann und Bonn.* Bonn: Ed. im Auftrag der Stadt Bonn, 1981.

Berland, Prim. *Le Rhin allemand de Nicolas Becker.* Paris: Jean Flory, 1942.

Berlioz, Hector. *Memoirs of Hector Berlioz from 1803 to 1865, Comprising His Travels in Germany, Italy, Russia, and England.* Translated by Ernest Newman. Rev. ed. New York: Dover, 1966.

Berryer, Pierre Antoine, ed. *Oeuvres de Berryer: Discours parlementaires.* 2 vols. (1835–45). Paris: Didier, 1870–74.

Bigenwald, Martha. "Die Anfänge der *Leipziger allgemeinen musikalischen Zeitung.*" Diss., University of Freiburg, 1938.

Black, Eugene C., ed. *European Political History, 1815–1870: Aspects of Liberalism.* New York: Harper & Row, 1967.

Blommen, Heinz. *Anfänge und Entwicklung des Männerchorwesens am Niederrhein: Beiträge zur rheinischen Musikgeschichte.* Ed. Arbeitsgemeinschaft für rheinische Musikgeschichte 42. Cologne: Arno Volk-Verlag, 1960.

Blume, Friedrich. *Classic and Romantic Music.* Translated by M. D. Herter Norton. New York: Norton, 1970.

Blumner, Martin. *Geschichte der Sing-Akademie zu Berlin.* Berlin: Horn & Raasch, 1891.

Boehn, Max von. *Biedermeier: Deutschland von 1815 bis 1847.* Berlin: Bruno Cassirer, 1918.

Boetticher, Wolfgang. "Karl Kossmaly." In *Die Musik in Geschichte und Gegenwart,* edited by Friedrich Blume, 7:1643–44. Kassel and Basel: Bärenreiter, 1949–73.

Boor, Helmut de, ed. *Das Nibelungenlied.* Wiesbaden: Brockhaus, 1979.

Bornemann, Wilhelm. *Die Zeltersche Liedertafel in Berlin.* Berlin: Verlag der Decker-schen Geheimen Ober-Hofbuchdruckerei, 1851.

Bosanquet, Bernard. *A History of Aesthetic.* Cleveland: World, 1932.

Boyd, Malcolm. "National Anthems." *New Grove* 13:54–55.

Brand, Carl Maria, ed. *Beiträge zur Musikgeschichte der Stadt Aachen.* Beiträge zur rheinischen Musikgeschichte 24. Cologne: Arno Volk-Verlag, 1959.

Brand, Carl Maria, and Karl Gustav Fellerer, eds. *Beiträge zur Musik im Rhein-Maas-Raum.* Beiträge zur rheinischen Musikgeschichte 19. Cologne: Arno Volk-Verlag, 1957.

Brendel, Franz. "Fragen der Zeit II." *Neue Zeitschrift für Musik* (22 April 1848): 193–96; "Romantik in der Musik" (1 July 1848): 1–6 and (4 July 1848): 9–11; "Über die Anordnung des Inhaltes von Liederheften auf Grund eines leitenden Gedankens" (2 December 1848): 261–63 and (5 December 1848): 265–67.

Brinton, Crane. *Ideas and Men: The Story of Western Thought.* New York: Prentice-Hall, 1950.

The British and Continental Examiner. Leipzig: Robert Binder, 15 August 1840.

Bruns, Friedrich, ed. *Die Lese der deutschen Lyrik von Klopstock bis Rilke.* New York: Appleton-Century-Crofts, n.d.

Bruun, Geoffrey. *Europe and the French Imperium, 1799–1814.* New York: Harper & Row, 1938.

Bücken, Ernst. *Das deutsche Lied: Probleme und Gestalten.* Hamburg: Hanseatische Verlagsanstalt, 1939.

Butterfield, Herbert. *The Origins of Modern Science.* New York: Macmillan, 1956.

Byron, George Gordon, Lord. *Childe Harold's Pilgrimage and Other Romantic Poems.* Edited by Samuel C. Chew. New York: Odyssey Press, 1936.

Cäcilia: Eine Zeitschrift für die musikalische Welt. Edited by Gottfried Weber and Siegfried Wilhelm Dehn. Mainz: B. Schott, 1824–48.

Campbell, Joseph. *The Masks of God: Primitive Mythology.* New York: Viking Press, 1959.

Carli, Enzo. *The Landscape in Art.* Edited by Mia Cinotti. New York: Morrow, 1980.

Carlyle, Thomas. "The Hero As Divinity." Lecture I (5 May 1840). In *On Heroes, Hero-Worship, and the Heroic in History.* Vol. 1 of *The Complete Works of Thomas Carlyle,* 235–73. New York: Kelmscott Society, n.d.

Carné, L. de. "De la popularité de Napoléon." *Revue des deux mondes* 4/22 (1 April 1840): 857–69.

Challier, Ernst. *Ernst Challier's grosser Lieder-Katalog.* 15 vols. and supplement. Berlin: Ernst Challier's Selbstverlag, 1885–1914.

———. *Ernst Challier's grosser Männergesang-Katalog.* 6 vols. and supplement. Giessen: Challier's Selbstverlag, 1900–1912.

Charles-Roux, François. *Thiers et Méhémet-Ali.* Paris: Librairie Plon, 1951.

Cheval, René. *Heinrich Heine zwischen Deutschland und Frankreich.* Schriften der Heinrich Heine-Gesellschaft Düsseldorf 4. Düsseldorf: Heinrich Heine-Gesellschaft, 1969.

"Chronique de la quinzaine." *Revue des deux mondes* 4/23 (31 July 1840): 487–98; (14 August 1840): 647–53; (31 August 1840): 793–807; (14 September 1840): 943–50; (30 September 1840): 147–54; 4/24 (14 October 1840): 280–90; (31 October 1840): 446–53; (30 November 1840): 742–49; (14 December 1840): 865–72.

Clapham. J. H. *The Economic Development of France and Germany, 1815–1914.* 4th ed. Cambridge: Cambridge University Press, 1963.

Collins, Irene. "Liberalism in Nineteenth-Century Europe." In *European Political History, 1815–1870: Aspects of Liberalism,* edited by Eugene C. Black, 103–27. New York: Harper & Row, 1967.

Croce, Benedetto. *Aesthetic.* 2d ed. Translated by Douglas Ainslie. London: Macmillan, 1922.

Dahlhaus, Carl. *Realism in Nineteenth-Century Music.* Translated by Mary Whittall. Cambridge: Cambridge University Press, 1985.

Dampier, W. C. *A History of Science and Its Relations with Philosophy and Religion.* 4th ed. Cambridge: Cambridge University Press, 1961.

Darius, Peter. *Die Musik in den Elementarschulen und Kirchen Düsseldorfs im 19. Jahrhundert.* Beiträge zur rheinischen Musikgeschichte 77. Cologne: Arno Volk-Verlag, 1969.

Darwin, Charles. *The Darwin Reader.* Edited by Marston Bates and Philip S. Humphrey. New York: Scribner's, 1956.

Deetjen, W. *Sie sollen ihn nicht haben! Tatsachen und Stimmen aus dem Jahre 1840.* Weimar: n.p., 1920.

Dehn, S. W. Review. *Caecilia* 81 (1842): 52–54.

Devrient, Eduard. *My Recollections of Felix Mendelssohn-Bartholdy and His Letters to Me.* Translated by Natalia MacFarren. London: Richard Bentley, 1869. Reprint. New York: Vienna House, 1972.

Diamond, S. "Niederrheinisches Musikfest." *Neue Zeitschrift für Musik* (25 June 1841): 205–6; (28 June 1841): 209–10; (16 April 1842): 121–22; "Aus Köln (Kirchen- und Concertmusik)" (4 November 1842): 153–54; "Aus Köln (Das Theater-Fremde Künstler)" (11 Nov. 1842): 160–62; "Aus Köln (Fremde Künstler)" (15 November 1842): 165–66; "Das Musiktreiben am Rheine" (11 March 1842): 82–83; (15 March 1842): 86–88; (25 March 1842): 99–100; (29 March 1842): 103–4; (8 April 1842): 115–16; (12 April 1842): 119–20; (19 April 1842): 125–27; "Das rheinische Musikfest von 1842" (7 June 1842): 181–82; (29 November 1842): 179–80.

Dill, Heinz J. "Romantic Irony in the Works of Robert Schumann." *Musical Quarterly* 73/2 (1989): 172–95.

Dohmke, J., ed. *Brentanos Werke.* Leipzig: Bibliographisches Institut, 1930.

Droz, Jacques. *Europe between Revolutions, 1815–1848.* Edited by J. H. Plumb. Translated by Robert Baldick. New York: Harper & Row, 1968.

————. *Le libéralisme rhénan, 1815–1848: Contribution à l'histoire du libéralisme allemand.* Paris: F. Sorlot, 1949.

Drux, Herbert. *Studien zur Entwicklung des öffentlichen Musiklebens in Ostniederberg.* Beiträge zur rheinischen Musikgeschichte 11. Cologne: Arno Volk-Verlag, 1956.

"Düsseldorf." *Allgemeine musikalische Zeitung* (12 June 1839): 463–64; (4 June 1845): 393–94; (18 June 1845): 429–30.

Düsseldorf: Wandlungen einer Westdeutschen Residenz. Düsseldorf: August Bagel, 1938.

Düsseldorfer Almanach 71 (Düsseldorf: 1927).

Eberhardt, Hans. *Die ersten deutschen Musikfeste in Frankenhausen am Kyffh. und Erfurt 1810, 1811, 1812 und 1815.* Jena: Walter Biedermann, 1934.

Eichendorff, Joseph von. *Werke,* vol. 1. Edited by Ansgar Hillach. Munich: Winkler, 1970.

Einstein, Alfred. "Italienische Musiker am Hofe der Neuburger Wittelsbacher." *Sammelbände der Internationalen Musikgesellschaft* 9 (1907–8): 336–424.

Eismann, Georg. *Robert Schumann: Ein Quellenwerk über sein Leben und Schaffen,* vol. 1. Leipzig: Breitkopf & Härtel, 1956.

Eitner, Robert. *Biographisch-bibliographisches Quellen-Lexikon der Musiker und Musikgelehrten der christlichen Zeitrechnung bis zur Mitte des 19. Jahrhunderts.* 10 vols. Leipzig: Breitkopf & Härtel, 1898–1904.

Elben, Otto. *Der volkstümliche deutsche Männergesang.* 2d ed. Tübingen: H. Laupp'schen Buchhandlung, 1887.

Engel, Hans. "Franz von Liszt." *Die Musik in Geschichte und Gegenwart* 8:964–88.

Engels, Heinz, ed. *Die Handschrift C des Nibelungenlieds und der Klage: Handschrift C der F. F. Hofbibliothek Donaueschingen.* Stuttgart: Müller & Schindler, 1968.

Erk, Ludwig. *Die deutschen Freiheitskriege in Liedern und Gedichten.* Leipzig: Rudolf Winklers Verlag, 1913.

————, ed. *Erk's deutscher Liederschatz.* Revised by Max Friedlaender. Leipzig: C. F. Peters, 1890.

————, ed. *Mehrstimmige Gesänge für Männerstimme von verschiedenen Componisten: Für Seminarien, Gymnasien und kleinere Singvereine.* 2 vols. Essen: G. Bädeker, 1833–35.

————, ed. *Neue Sammlung deutscher Volkslieder mit ihren eigenthümlichen Melodien.* 2 vols. Berlin, 1841–45. Reprint. Edited by J. Koepp. Potsdam: Voggenreiter, 1939.

————, ed. *Volkslieder, alte und neue, für Männerstimme gesetzt und herausgegeben.* 2 vols. Essen: G. Bädeker, 1845–47.

Erk, Ludwig, and Franz M. Böhme, eds. *Deutscher Liederhort: Auswahl der vorzüglicheren deutschen Volkslieder nach Wort und Weise aus der Vorzeit und Gegenwart gesammelt und erläutert: Im Auftrage und mit Unterstützung der königlichen preussischen Regierung nach Erks handschriftlichem Nachlasse und auf Grund eigener Sammlung neu bearbeitet und fortgesetzt von Franz M. Böhme.* 3 vols. Leipzig: Breitkopf & Härtel, 1893–94.

Faber, Karl-Georg. *Die Rheinlande zwischen Restauration und Revolution: Probleme der rheinischen Geschichte von 1814 bis 1848 im Spiegel der zeitgenössischen Publizistik.* Wiesbaden: Franz Steiner, 1966.

Fellerer, Karl Gustav. "Der Kölner Singverein, 1820–1840." In *106. Niederrheinisches Musikfest in Düsseldorf.* Düsseldorf: J. B. Gerlach, 1951.

———, ed. *Beiträge zur Geschichte der Musik am Niederrhein.* Beiträge zur rheinischen Musikgeschichte 14. Cologne: Arno Volk-Verlag, 1956.

———, ed. *Musik im Niederländisch-niederdeutschen Raum.* Beiträge zur rheinischen Musikgeschichte 36. Cologne: Arno Volk-Verlag, 1960.

———, ed. *Rheinische Musiker.* Beiträge zur rheinischen Musikgeschichte 43. Cologne: Arno Volk-Verlag, 1960.

Fellinger, Imogen. *Verzeichnis der Musikzeitschriften des 19. Jahrhunderts.* Studien zur Musikgeschichte des 19. Jahrhunderts 10. Regensburg: Gustav Bosse Verlag, 1968.

———. "Zeitschriften." *Die Musik in Geschichte und Gegenwart* 14:1041–1188.

Fellner, Richard. *Geschichte einer deutschen Musterbühne: Karl Immermanns Leitung des Stadttheaters zu Düsseldorf.* Stuttgart: J. G. Cotta'schen Buchhandlung, 1888.

Fels, Joachim. "Kunst und Natur." *Neue Zeitschrift für Musik* (10 September 1842): 71.

Fétis, François J. *Biographie universelle des musiciens et bibliographie générale de la musique.* 2d ed. 8 vols. Paris: Firmin Didot Frères, 1866–75.

"Feuilleton." *Allgemeine musikalische Zeitung* (3 March 1841): 205; (23 June 1841): 503; (10 May 1843): 350; (14 June 1843): 446; (2 April 1845): 246.

Fink, Gottfried W. "Carl Banck." *Allgemeine musikalische Zeitung* (3 July 1839): 509–15.

———. "Die Begründung der deutschen Musikfeste in einer biographischen Skizze (über G. F. Bischoff)." *Allgemeine musikalische Zeitung* (20 March 1836): 265–70.

———. "Heerschau der Lieder und Gesänge für eine Singstimme mit Begleitung des Pianoforte." *Allgemeine musikalische Zeitung* (24 November 1830): 771–72; (9 November 1831): 746–47; (17 May 1837): 319–20; (18 April 1838): 252–53; (8 August 1838): 524–25; (26 September 1838): 637–38; (14 August 1839): 644–46; (3 March 1841): 275; (23 June 1841): 495; (25 August 1841): 430; (28 August 1844): 581–82.

———. "Nachtrag zur Geschichte der deutschen und schweizerischen Musikfeste." *Allgemeine musikalische Zeitung* (14 May 1840): 543–45.

———, ed. *Musikalischer Hausschatz der Deutschen.* 2d ed. Leipzig: Breitkopf & Härtel, 1845.

Fischer, W. H. *Festschrift zur hundertjährigen Jubelfeier des städtischen Musikvereins Düsseldorf und zum hundertjährigen Bestehen der niederrheinischen Musikfeste.* Düsseldorf: Forberg, 1918.

Fleming, Carrol B. "Maidens of the Sea." *Smithsonian* 14/3 (June 1983): 86–92.

Föppl, C. A. "Über den gegenwärtigen Zustand der teutschen Tonkunst, wie er ist und sein sollte." *Caecilia: Eine Zeitschrift für die musikalische Welt, herausgegeben von einem Vereine von Gelehrten, Kunstverständigen und Künstlern* 89 (1844): 1–25; 90 (1844): 73–94; 91 (1844): 141–67; 92 (1844): 213–32.

Forster, Leonard, ed. *The Penguin Book of German Verse*. Baltimore: Penguin Books, 1957.

Freiligrath, Ferdinand. *Gedichte von Ferdinand Freiligrath*. Edited by Max Mendheim. Leipzig: Philipp Reclam jun., 1907.

Friedlaender, Max, ed. *Commers-Buch für den deutschen Studenten*. 3d ed. Magdeburg and Leipzig: Gebrüder Baensch, 1858.

———, ed. *Das deutsche Lied im 18. Jahrhundert*. 3 vols. Stuttgart: J. G. Cotta, 1902. Reprint. Hildesheim: Georg Olms, 1962.

———, ed. *Volksliederbuch für Männerchor*, vols. 1 and 2. Leipzig: C. F. Peters, 1907.

Gathy, August. "Die Phantastik der Zeit." *Neue Zeitschrift für Musik* (29 April 1848): 209–12.

Gay, Peter. *Freud for Historians*. New York: Oxford University Press, 1985.

Gelbcke, F. A. "Classisch und romantisch." *Neue Zeitschrift für Musik* (11 June 1841): 187–89; (14 June 1841): 191–92; (19 June 1841): 195–96; (21 June 1841): 199–200; (25 June 1841): 203–5.

Gericke, Hermann Peter, Hugo Moser, and Alfred Quellmalz, eds. *Lieder unseres Volkes*. Reichsdeutsche edition. Kassel: Bärenreiter, 1941.

Gervinus, Georg Gottfried. *Geschichte der poetischen National-Literatur der Deutschen*. 3d ed. 5 vols. Leipzig: W. Engelmann, 1843–48.

Geschichte des Rheinlandes von der ältesten Zeit bis zur Gegenwart. Ed. Gesellschaft für rheinische Geschichtskunde. Essen (Ruhr): Baedeker, 1922.

Girardin, Madame Émile (Delphine Gay) de. *Lettres parisiennes, 1840–1848*. Vol. 5 of *Oeuvres complètes*. Paris: Plon, 1860–61.

Girardin, Saint-Marc. "Méhémet-Ali." Review of Clot-Bey's *Aperçu général sur l'Égypte*. *Revue des deux mondes* 4/23 (14 September 1840): 905–20.

Gish, Theodore. "*Wanderlust* and *Wanderleid*: The Motif of the Wandering Hero in German Romanticism." *Studies in Romanticism* 3/4 (Boston University Graduate School, summer 1964): 225–39.

Goethe und das Rheinland: Rheinische Landschaft, Rheinische Sitten, Rheinische Kunstdenkmäler. Ed. Rheinischer Verein für Denkmalpflege und Heimatschutz 27. Düsseldorf, 1932.

Goldkühle, Fritz. *Rheinische Landschaften und Städtebilder, 1600–1850*. Cologne and Graz: Böhlau Verlag, 1960. (Exhibition at Rheinisches Landesmuseum, Bonn; 1960–61.)

Gollmick, C. "Aus Frankfurt." *Neue Zeitschrift für Musik* (15 March 1842): 88; "Musikfest im Mainz" (4 October 1842): 115–16.

Gredy, F. M. "Über Liedertafeln im allgemeinen und die von Mainz ins besondere." *Caecilia* 95 (1845): 158–63.

————. "Wettgesang in Mainz und Sängerfest in Cöln im Juni 1846." *Caecilia* 100 (1846): 254–62.

Grimm, Jacob and Wilhelm. *The Complete Fairy Tales of the Brothers Grimm*. Translated by Jack Zipes. New York: Bantam Books, 1987.

————. "Foreword." In *The German Legends of the Brothers Grimm*, vol. 1. Edited and translated by Donald Ward. Philadelphia: Institute for the Study of Human Issues, 1981.

"Grosses Sängerfest in Frankfurt a.M." *Allgemeine musikalische Zeitung* (4 April 1838): 231–32.

Gutman, Robert W. *Richard Wagner: The Man, His Mind, and His Music*. New York: Time, 1968.

Haagen, Friedrich. *Geschichte Aachens*. Aachen: n.p., 1873.

Hansen, Joseph, ed. *Die Rheinprovinz, 1815–1915: Hundert Jahre preussischer Herrschaft am Rhein*, vol. 2. Bonn: A. Marcus & E. Webers Verlag, 1917.

Härtel, August, ed. *Deutsches Liederlexikon*. 9th ed. Leipzig: Breitkopf & Härtel, 1865, 1900.

Hartmann, Hans. *Festschrift zur 100jährigen Jubelfeier des Elberfelder Gesangvereins*. Elberfeld, 1911.

Hase, Carl, Felix Dahn, and Carl Reinecke, eds. *Liederbuch des deutschen Volkes*. 1843. 2d ed. Leipzig: Breitkopf & Härtel, 1883.

Hatto, A. T., trans. and ed. *The Nibelungenlied*. Harmondsworth, Middlesex: Penguin Books, 1965.

Hauchecorne, E. A. *Niederrheinisches Musikfest: Blätter der Erinnerung an die fünfzigjährige Dauer der Niederrheinischen Musikfeste*. Cologne: Commissions-Verlag der M. Du Mont-Schauberg'schen Buchhandlung, 1868.

Haug, Walter. "Höfische Idealität und heroische Tradition im Nibelungenlied." In *Atti dei convegni lincei*, 35–50. Rome: Accademia Nazionale dei Lincei, 1974.

Hauser, Arnold. *The Social History of Art*, vol. 3. New York: Vintage Books, 1951.

Häuser, Helmut. *Ansichten vom Rhein: Stahlstichbücher des 19. Jahrhunderts: Darstellung und Bibliographie*. Cologne: Greven, 1963.

Haymes, Edward R. *The Nibelungenlied: History and Interpretation*. Urbana: University of Illinois Press, 1986.

Hegel, Georg Wilhelm Friedrich. "Of the Symbolic Form of Art." In *Lectures on Aesthetics*, vol. 1, *Philosophy of Hegel*. Edited by Karl J. Friedrich. New York: Modern Library, 1954.

Heine, Heinrich. *Briefe*, vol. 1. Edited by Friedrich Hirth. Mainz: Kupferberg, 1950.

————. *Buch der Lieder*. Munich: Wilhelm Goldman, 1957.

————. "Deutschland, ein Wintermärchen." Edited by Klaus Briegleb. In *Heinrich Heine: Sämtliche Schriften*, vols. 1 and 4:571–646. Munich: Carl Hanser, 1968–71.

————. "Über Polen." In *Vermischte Schriften*, vol. 5/1 of *Heinrich Heine's Sämmtliche Werke*. Philadelphia: n.p., 1856.

Hessel, K. "Die Echtheit der Loreleisage." *Zeitschrift für den deutschen Unterricht* 19 (1905): 481ff.

Hiller, Ferdinand. *Aus Ferdinand Hillers Briefwechsel*. Beiträge zur rheinischen Musikgeschichte 6/50 and 70, 7/91 and 92. Cologne: Arno Volk-Verlag, 1970.

————. *Mendelssohn: Letters and Recollections*. Translated by M. E. von Glehn. 1874. Reprint. London: Macmillan, 1972.

Himmel, Friedrich Heinrich, ed. *Kriegslieder der teutschen*. Breslau: Joseph Max, 1813.

Himmelfarb, Gertrude. *The New History and the Old*. Cambridge, Mass.: Harvard University Press, 1987.

Hirschbach, H. "Mehrstimmige Gesänge." *Neue Zeitschrift für Musik* (13 December 1842): 195–96.

Hoffmann von Fallersleben, August Heinrich, ed. *Deutsches Volksgesangbuch*. Leipzig: Wilhelm Engelmann, 1848.

————. *Gedichte*. Leipzig: Weidmann'sche Buchhandlung, 1843.

————, ed. *Unsere volksthümlichen Lieder*. 2d ed. Leipzig: Wilhelm Engelmann, 1859.

Hofmeister, Adolph. *C. F. Whistling's Handbuch der musikalischen Literatur, oder allgemeines systematisch geordnetes Verzeichniss der in Deutschland und in den angrenzenden Ländern gedruckten Musikalien, auch musikalischen Schriften und Abbildungen, mit Anzeige des Verleger und Preise*. 3d ed. (to the beginning of 1844). 3 vols. Edited by Adolph Hofmeister. Leipzig: Friedrich Hofmeister, 1845; supplementary volume (from January 1844 to the end of 1851), 1852.

Holborn, Hajo. *A History of Modern Germany*. 3 vols. New York: Knopf, 1964–71.

Hölscher, Georg. *Das Buch vom Rhein*. 7th ed. Cologne: Hoursch & Bechstedt, 1927.

Honour, Hugh. *Romanticism*. New York: Harper & Row, 1979.

Hugo, Victor. *Le Rhin: Lettres à un ami*. 2 vols. Brussels: n.p., 1842.

"Intelligenzblatt." *Neue Zeitschrift für Musik* (November 1840); (January 1841); (February 1841).

Jacob, Heinrich Eduard. *Felix Mendelssohn und seine Zeit*. Frankfurt am Main: S. Fischer, 1959.

Jahn, Otto. *Gesammelte Aufsätze über Musik*. Leipzig: Breitkopf & Härtel, 1866.

Jensen, Eric Frederick. "Norbert Burgmüller and Robert Schumann." *Musical Quarterly* 74/4 (1990): 550–65.

Kahl, Willi. *Bilder und Gestalten aus der Musikgeschichte des Rheinlands*. Beiträge zur rheinischen Musikgeschichte 59. Cologne: Arno Volk-Verlag, 1964.

Kahlert, August. "Das Concertwesen der Gegenwart." *Neue Zeitschrift für Musik* (25 March 1842): 97–98; (29 March 1842): 101–2; (1 April 1842): 105–6; (5 April 1842): 109–10.

————. "Lieder für vier Männerstimmen." *Allgemeine musikalische Zeitung* (27 March 1844): 224–25.

Kapko-Foretić, Zdenka. *Carl von Turányi, 1805–1873*. Cologne: Arno Volk-Verlag, 1973.

Kast, Paul, ed. *Schumanns rheinische Jahre*. Düsseldorf: Droste, 1981.

Kaufmann, Henning. *Die Dichtung der Rheinlande: Eine landschaftliche und örtliche Bibliographie nebst einem Abriss ihrer Entwicklung*. Bonn: Kurt Schroeder, 1923.

Kayser, Wolfgang. *The Grotesque: Its Configuration in Painting and Literature*. English trans. Bloomington: Indiana University Press, 1963.

Kerman, Joseph. *Contemplating Music: Challenges to Musicology*. Cambridge, Mass.: Harvard University Press, 1985.

Klapheck, Richard. *Goethe und das Rheinland: Rheinische Landschaft, rheinische Sitten, rheinische Kunstdenkmäler*. Rheinischer Verein für Denkmalpflege und Heimatschutz 27. Düsseldorf: L. Schwann, 1932.

Klauwell, O. *Das Konservatorium der Musik in Köln: Festschrift zur Feier seines 50jährigen Bestehens*. Cologne: Arno Volk-Verlag, 1900.

Klävemann, D. "An die Liedertafeln in Norddeutschland." *Neue Zeitschrift für Musik* (18 July 1844): 23–24.

Klietzsch, Emanuel. "Beziehungen zwischen Kunst und Politik." *Neue Zeitschrift für Musik* (29 July 1848): 45–47.

Kohn, Hans. *The Idea of Nationalism: A Study in Its Origins and Background*. New York: Macmillan, 1944.

——. *The Mind of Germany: The Education of a Nation*. New York: Harper & Row, 1960.

Körner, Klaus. *Das Musikleben in Köln um die Mitte des 19. Jahrhunderts*. Cologne: Arno Volk-Verlag, 1969.

Kossmaly, Carl. "Musikalische Charakteristiken von C. Kossmaly." *Neue Zeitschrift für Musik*: "Über das 'Lied' im allgemeinen" (19 February 1841): 59–60; (22 February 1841): 63–64; "Das 'Volkslied': Über das N. Becker'sche Gedicht und die Compositionen desselben" (26 February 1841): 67–69; "Über die Compositionen des N. Becker'schen Gedichts" (1 March 1841): 71–72; "Über das Lied im allgemeinen mit besonderer Bezugnahme auf die verschiedenen Compositionen des 'Rheinliedes' von N. Becker" (13 August 1841): 49–50; "Über das Lied im allgemeinen usw" (17 August 1841): 53–54.

Kötzschke, Richard. *Geschichte des deutschen Männergesanges*. Dresden: Wilhelm Limpert, 1927.

Krehan, Arno, ed. *Ausgewählte Lieder für die ausziehenden Krieger*. 4th ed. Weimar: R. Borkmann, 1917.

Kretschmer, Konrad. *Historische Geographie von Mitteleuropa*. Osnabrück: Otto Zeller, 1964.

Krome, Hermann, ed. *Am Rhein beim Wein!* Leipzig: C. G. Röder, 1925.

Kruger, Eduard. "Übersicht der sämmtlichen Musik-Aufführungen in Breslau für den Winter 1840–1841, bis ultimo April." *Allgemeine musikalische Zeitung* (2 June 1841): 442–44.

Lamartine, Alphonse de. *Cours familier de littérature: Un entretien par mois 19.* 14 vols. Paris: Chez l'auteur, 1856–62.

———. *Oeuvres poétiques complètes.* Edited by Marius-François Guyard. Paris: Gallimard, 1963.

Lampadius, Wilhelm Adolf. *The Life of Felix Mendelssohn-Bartholdy.* Translated by W. L. Gage. Boston: Oliver Ditson, 1887.

Lau, Friedrich. "Die Regierungskollegien zu Düsseldorf und der Hofstaat zur Zeit Johann Wilhelms II." *Düsseldorfer Jahrbuch* 40 (1938): 270ff.

Le Bris, Michel. *Romantics and Romanticism.* New York: Rizzoli, 1981.

Ledebur, Carl F. H. P. J. *Tonkünstler-Lexikon Berlins von den ältesten Zeiten bis auf die Gegenwart.* Berlin: Ludwig Rauh, 1861.

"Leipzig." *Allgemeine musikalische Zeitung* (13 December 1837): 817–18; (20 December 1837): 835.

Lichtenstein. *Zur Geschichte der Sing-Akademie in Berlin.* Berlin: Trautwein, 1843.

Lieder-Album für eine Singstimme mit Pianoforte und Violin Begleitung. Leipzig: C. F. Peters, n.d.

Lieder aus der Fremde. Hannover: C. Rümpler, 1857.

Lieder der Heimat. Berlin: P. Schaeffer, 1940.

Lieder der Zeit. Stuttgart: A. Krabbe, 1841.

Lieder-Schatz: Eine Auswahl der beliebtesten Volks-, Vaterlands-, Soldaten-, Jäger-, Studenten- und Liebes-Lieder für eine Singstimme mit Pianoforte-Begleitung. Leipzig and Berlin: C. F. Peters, 1870.

Lieder teutscher Jugend. Stuttgart: I. B. Metzler, 1822.

Litzmann, Berthold, ed. *Clara Schumann: Ein Künstlerleben, nach Tagebüchern und Briefe.* Vol. 2, *Ehejahre, 1840–1856.* Hildesheim: Georg Olms, 1971.

Lorelei: Sammlung von Volks-und volkstümlichen Liedern nebst einem Anhange für Männerchor. Compiled by the Musikkommission des Mittelrheinischen Sängerbundes. Wiesbaden: Selbstverlag des Mittelrheinischen Sängerbundes, 1904.

Lorentzen, Theodor. *Die Sage vom Rodensteiner: Eine historische-kritische Darstellung.* Heidelberg: Groos, 1903.

Lorenz, Oswald. "Mehrstimmiger Gesang." *Neue Zeitschrift für Musik* (29 March 1841): 103–4.

Lützenkirchen, Friedrich. "Über das jüngste rheinische Pfingstconcert, 1842." *Neue Zeitschrift für Musik* (12 July 1842): 13–15.

"Mainzer Liedertafel und Damen-Gesangverein." *Allgemeine musikalische Zeitung* (16 January 1839): 42.

"Mancherlei (Aachen)." *Allgemeine musikalische Zeitung* (1 March 1837): 149.

Marlowe, John. *Anglo-Egyptian Relations, 1800–1953.* London: Cresset Press, 1954.

Marquant, Robert. *Thiers et le Baron Cotta: Étude sur la collaboration de Thiers à la Gazette d'Augsbourg.* Travaux et mémoires des Instituts français en Allemagne 7. Paris: Presses Universitaires de France, 1959.

McManners, John. *European History, 1789–1914: Men, Machines, and Freedom.* New York: Harper & Row, 1969.

Meinardus, Wolfdieter. "Düsseldorf." *Die Musik in Geschichte und Gegenwart* 3:871.

Mendelssohn, Felix. *Briefe aus Leipziger Archiven.* Edited by Hans-Joachim Rothe and Reinhard Szeskus. Leipzig: VEB Deutscher Verlag für Musik, 1972.

———. Letters. Heinemann Collection. Library of Congress, Music Division, Washington, D.C.

———. Letters. Whittall Foundation Collection, Library of Congress, Music Division, Washington, D.C.

———. *Letters.* Edited by G. Selden-Goth. Translated by Marion Soerchinger. New York: Pantheon Books, 1945. Reprint. New York: Vienna House, 1973.

———. *Letters of Felix Mendelssohn Bartholdy, from 1833 to 1847.* Edited by Paul Mendelssohn Bartholdy and Carl Mendelssohn Bartholdy. Translated by Lady Wallace. London: Longman, Green/Longman, Roberts, and Green, 1863.

———. *Werke: Kritisch durchgesehene Ausgabe.* 19 vols. Edited by Julius Rietz. Leipzig: Breitkopf & Härtel, 1874–77.

Methfessel, Albert. "Vorwort." In *Sechs deutsche Kriegslieder für eine und mehrere Stimmen, mit Chören und willkührlicher Begleitung des Fortepiano, in Musik gesetzt und allen braven deutschen Kriegern gewidmet,* Op. 35. 1813. 2d ed. Rudolstadt: Hof- Buch- und Kunst-Handlung, 1814.

Mies, Paul. "Aus der Vorgeschichte der Hochschule." In *Festschrift zur Feier der Gründung des kölner Konservatoriums im Jahre 1850 und der Staatliche Hochschule für Musik Köln im Jahre 1925.* Cologne: Arno Volk-Verlag, 1950.

Moser, Hans Joachim. *Das deutsche Lied seit Mozart.* Berlin: Atlantis, 1937.

Moss, Lawrence. "Text and Context in *Dichterliebe.*" *Ars Lyrica* 2 (Fall–Winter 1983): 23–38.

Most, Otto. *Düsseldorf als Handels-Industrie, Kunst- und Gartenstadt.* Düsseldorf: August Bagel, 1912.

———. *Geschichte der Stadt Düsseldorf.* 2 vols. Düsseldorf: August Bagel, 1921.

Müller, Nikolaus, ed. *Deutschland und Frankreich am Neujahr 1841: Worte zur Zeit, mit deutschen Vaterlandsgesängen.* Mainz: Seifert'sche Buchdruckerei, 1841.

"Die Musikzustände des Niederrheins." *Neue Zeitschrift für Musik* (23 March 1855): 76–77; (20 April 1855): 182–83.

Musset, Alfred de. *Poésies complètes.* Vol. 1 of *Oeuvres.* Edited by Maurice Allem. Paris: Librairie Gallimard, 1957.

"Nachrichten: Strassburg." *Allgemeine musikalische Zeitung* (28 September 1831): 644–48; "Nachrichten: Niederrheinisches Musikfest" (21 June 1837): 409–10; "Nachrichten: Jena" (27 December 1837): 855–56; "Nachrichten: Musikfest in Köln" (4 July 1838): 438–39; "Nachrichten" (9 December 1840): 1030–31; "Nachrichten" (27 January 1841): 80–81; "Nachrichten" (5 May 1841): 361–66; "Nachrichten: Enthüllung des Denkmals für Beethoven zu Bonn" (27 August 1845): 599–600.

Namier, Lewis B. "Nationality and Liberty." In *European Political History, 1815–1870: Aspects of Liberalism*, vol. 6, edited by Eugene C. Black, 128–54. New York: Harper & Row, 1967.

Newman, Ernest. *The Life of Richard Wagner*. New York: Knopf, 1937. Reprint. 1969.

Neyses, Joseph. "Robert Schumann als Musikdirektor in Düsseldorf." In *Düsseldorfer Almanach 71*. Düsseldorf, 1927.

Nouvelle biographie général depuis les temps les plus reculés jusqu'a nos jours. Paris: Didot Frères, 1857.

Novotny, Fritz. *Painting and Sculpture in Europe, 1780–1880*. 2d ed. Translated by R. H. Boothroyd. Baltimore: Pelican, 1971.

Oepen, Heinz. *Beiträge zur Geschichte des Kölner Musiklebens, 1760–1840*. Beiträge zur rheinischen Musikgeschichte 10. Cologne: Arno Volk-Verlag, 1955.

Ostwald, Peter. *Schumann: The Inner Voices of a Musical Genius*. Boston: Northeastern University Press, 1985.

"Panny, Joseph." "Nekrolog. *Allgemeine musikalische Zeitung* (28 December 1838). 883.

Parker, Richard. *The Myth of the Middle Class*. New York: Liveright, 1972.

Paulsen, Wolfgang, ed. *Der Dichter und seine Zeit: Politik im Spiegel der Literatur*. Heidelberg: Lothar Stiehm, 1970.

Pederson, Sanna. "A. B. Marx, Berlin Concert Life, and German National Identity." *19th-Century Music* 18/2 (Fall 1994): 96.

Pietzsch, Gerhard. "Musiker an rheinischen Höfen." In *Zur mittelrheinischen und niederrheinischen Musikgeschichte: Beiträge zur Musikgeschichte der Stadt Düsseldorf*, edited by Julius Alf. Cologne: Arno Volk-Verlag, 1977.

Plantinga, Leon B. *Schumann As Critic*. New Haven, Conn.: Yale University Press, 1967.

Plesske, Hans-Martin. "Friedrich Hofmeister." *New Grove* 8:636–37.

———. "Karl Friedrich Whistling." *New Grove* 20:382.

Politis, Athanase G. *Le Conflit turco-égyptien de 1838–1841 et les dernières années du règne de Mohamed Aly d'après les documents diplomatiques grecs*. Cairo: l'Imprimerie de l'Institut français d'Archéologie orientale du Caire, 1931.

"Die politische Bedeutung des Rheinliedes von Nicolas Becker: Ein Resumé von einem Norddeutschen." *Deutsche Jahrbücher für Wissenschaft und Kunst* 214, edited by Arnold Ruge (Dresden, 19 February 1841): 294–300.

Poll, B. "Preussen und die Rheinlande." *Zeitschrift des Aachener Geschichtsvereins* 76 (1964): 5–44.

Porter, Cecelia Hopkins. "The New Public and the Reordering of the Musical Establishment: The Lower Rhine Music Festivals, 1818–1867." *19th-Century Music* 3/3 (March 1980): 211–24.

———. "The Reign of the *Dilettanti*: Düsseldorf from Mendelssohn to Schumann." *Musical Quarterly* 73/4 (1989): 476–512.

———. "The *Rheinlieder* Critics: A Case of Musical Nationalism." *Musical Quarterly* 63/1 (January 1977): 74–98.

———. "The Rhenish Manifesto: 'The Free German Rhine' As an Expression of German National Consciousness in the Romantic Lied." Ph.D. diss., University of Maryland, 1975.

Porter, Dale H. *The Emergence of the Past: A Theory of Historical Explanation*. Chicago: University of Chicago Press, 1981.

Preussner, Eberhard. *Die bürgerliche Musikkultur*. 2d ed. Kassel and Basel: Bärenreiter, 1950.

Pulvermacher, Gunter. "Biedermeier." *New Grove* 2:695–97.

Raabe, Peter. *Liszts Schaffen*. 2d ed. Tutzing: Hans Schneider, 1968.

Rehberg, Paula, and Walter Rehberg. *Robert Schumann: Sein Leben und sein Werk*. Zürich: Artemis, 1954.

Rehm, Wolfgang. "Konrad Kreutzer." *Die Musik in Geschichte und Gegenwart* 7:1774–80.

Reich, Nancy B. *Clara Schumann: The Artist and the Woman*. Ithaca, N.Y.: Cornell University Press, 1985.

Reimann, Heinrich. *Robert Schumanns Leben und Werke*. Leipzig: C. F. Peters, 1887.

Reissmann, August. *Das deutsche Lied in seiner historischen Entwicklung*. Cassel: Oswald Bertram, 1861.

———. *Felix Mendelssohn-Bartholdy: Sein Leben und seine Werke*. Berlin: L. Guttentag, 1867.

———. *Geschichte des deutschen Liedes*. Berlin: J. Guttentag (D. Collin), 1874.

Rellstab, Ludwig. *Iris im Gebiete der Tonkunst* 3 (15 January 1841): 11–12; 4 (22 January 1841): 15; 7 (12 February 1841): 27–28; 8 (19 February 1841): 29–30; 12 (19 March 1841): 47–48; 15 (9 April 1841): 59–60; 31 (30 July 1841): 123–24; 39 (24 September 1841): 155–56.

Renouvin, Pierre, ed. *Le XIXe siècle, part I (de 1815 à 1871): L'Europe des nationalités et l'éveil des nouveaux mondes*. Histoire des relations internationales 5. Paris: Librairie Hachette, 1954.

"Rheinische Chronik: Aus Mainz, Strassburg." *Allgemeine musikalische Zeitung* (22 August 1838): 561–66.

Rheinisches Jahrbuch für Kunst und Poesie 2 (Cologne, 1841): 365–66.

Riemann, Hugo, ed. *Hugo Riemanns Musik Lexikon*. 11th ed. Revised by Alfred Einstein. Berlin: Max Hesses Verlag, 1929.

Robertson, J. G. *A History of German Literature*. 5th ed. Revised by Edna Purdie. Edinburgh: William Blackwood, 1966.

Röhrich, Lutz, and Rolf Wilhelm Biednich, eds. *Deutsche Volkslieder: Texte und Melodien*. Düsseldorf: Pädagogischer Verlag Schwann, 1965–67.

Rosenblum, Robert. *Modern Painting and the Northern Romantic Tradition.* New York: Harper & Row, 1975.

Rosenwald, Hans Hermann. *Geschichte des deutschen Liedes zwischen Schubert und Schumann.* Berlin: Benno Balan, 1930.

Rosenwald, Victor. "Nicolas Becker." *Nouvelle biographie générale depuis les temps les plus reculés jusqu'à nos jours, avec les renseignments bibliographiques et l'indication des sources à consulter,* vol. 5, edited by Hoefer, 99–100. (Paris: Didot Frères, 1855.)

Rudé, George. *Revolutionary Europe, 1783–1815.* New York: Harper, 1964.

Rudnytsky, Peter L. *Freud and Oedipus.* New York: Columbia University Press, 1987.

Sabry, M. *L'Empire égyptien sous Mohamed-Ali et la question d'Orient (1811–1849): Égypte, Arabie, Soudan, Morée, Crète, Syrie, Palestine: Histoire diplomatique d'après des sources privées et des documents inédits recueillis aux archives du Caire, de Paris, de Londres et de Vienne.* Paris: Librairie Orientaliste Paul Geuthner, 1930.

Samans, Franz, ed. *365 fröhliche Guitarrlieder.* Wesel: J. Bagel, 1848.

Sams, Eric. *The Songs of Robert Schumann.* New York: Norton, 1969.

Schaal, Richard. "Feste und Festspiele." *Die Musik in Geschichte und Gegenwart* 4:104–28.

Schauffler, Robert Haven. *Florestan: the Life and Work of Robert Schumann.* New York: Holt, 1945. Reprint. New York: Dover, 1963.

Scheffel, Joseph Viktor von. *Der Trompeter von Säkkingen: Ein Sang vom Oberrhein.* Edited and translated by Mary A. Frost. New York: Holt, 1895.

Schenk, H. G. *The Mind of the European Romantics.* Garden City, N.Y.: Doubleday, 1969.

Scherr, Johannes. *Menschliche Tragikomödie: Gesammelte Studien, Skizzen und Bilder.* Vol. 12, 3d ed. Leipzig: Otto Wigand, 1884.

Schiff, Gert. "An Epoch of Longing: An Introduction to German Painting of the Nineteenth Century." In *German Masters of the Nineteenth Century.* New York: Metropolitan Museum of Art, 1981.

Schiller, Friedrich von. *Naive and Sentimental Poetry and On the Sublime.* 1795–1801. Translated by Julius Elias. New York: Unger, 1966.

Schilling, Gustav, ed. *Das musikalische Europa, oder Sammlung von durchgehends authentischen Lebens-Nachrichten über jetzt in Europa lebende ausgezeichnete Tonkünstler, Musikgelehrte, Componisten, Virtuosen, Sänger.* Speyer: F. C. Neidhard's Buchhandlung, 1842.

Schlegel, August Wilhelm. *A Course of Lectures on Dramatic Art and Literature.* Translated by J. Black. London, 1846.

Schlegel, Johann Elias. "Hermann, ein Trauerspiel." In *Werke,* vol. 1, edited by Johann Heinrich Schlegel, 283–384. Copenhagen and Leipzig: Christian Gottlob Proft and Rothens Erben, 1764–73. Facsimile reprint. Frankfurt am Main: Athenaum, 1971.

Schmidt, August, ed. *Orpheus: Musikalisches Album für das Jahr 1842.* Vienna: Friedrich Volke, 1840–42.

Schmidt, Julian. "Das vierunddreissigste niederrheinische Musikfest in Düsseldorf den 11., 12. und 13. Mai 1856." *Grenzboten* 2 (1856): 481ff.

Schmidt, Paul Ferdinand. *Deutsche Landschaftsmalerei von 1750 bis 1830.* Deutsche Malerei um 1800 1. Munich: R. Piper, 1922.

Schubring, Julius, ed. *Briefwechsel zwischen Felix Mendelssohn Bartholdy und Julius Schubring.* Leipzig: Duncker & Humblot, 1892.

Schumann, Robert. *Briefe: Neue Folge.* 2d ed. Edited by F. Gustav Jansen. Leipzig: Breitkopf & Härtel, 1904.

————. *Gesammelte Schriften über Musik und Musiker.* Leipzig: Wigand, 1854. 5th ed. Leipzig: M. Kreisig, 1914.

Searle, Humphrey. *The Music of Liszt.* 2d ed. New York: Dover, 1966.

Seeliger, H. *Die Loreleysage in Dichtung und Musik.* Leipzig-Reudnitz: Hoffmann, 1898.

Shafer, Boyd C. *Nationalism: Myth and Reality.* New York: Harcourt, Brace and World, 1955.

Shaw, George Bernard. *The Perfect Wagnerite: A Commentary on the Niblung's Ring.* London, 1898. Reprint. New York: Time, 1972.

Silcher, Friedrich, ed. *XII deutsche Volkslieder mit Melodien, gesammelt und für eine oder zwei Singstimmen mit Begleitung des Pianoforte oder der Gitarre gesetzt.* Tübingen: L. F. Fues, 1840.

Silcher, Friedrich, and Friedrich Erk, eds. *Allgemeines deutsches Commersbuch.* 27th ed. Lahr: Moritz Schauenburg, 1886.

Simrock, Karl J. *Das malerische und romantische Rheinland.* 4th ed. Bonn: Cohen, 1865.

Sitwell, Sacheverell. *Liszt.* New York: Dover, 1967.

Spence, Donald P. *Narrative Truth and Historical Truth: Meaning and Interpretation in Psychoanalysis.* New York: Norton, 1982.

Stearns, Peter N. *European Society in Upheaval: Social History since 1750.* 2d ed. New York: Macmillan, 1975.

Stegemann, Hermann. *Der Kampf um den Rhein: Das Stromgebiet des Rheins im Rahmen der grossen Politik und im Wandel der Kriegsgeschichte.* Stuttgart: Deutsche Verlags-Anstalt, 1924.

Stein, Jack M. *Poem and Music in the German Lied from Gluck to Hugo Wolf.* Cambridge Mass.: Harvard University Press, 1971.

Steiner, Irwin H., ed. *Auswahl deutscher Lieder.* 6th ed. Leipzig: Serig'sche Buchhandlung, 1844.

Stephan, Heinz. *Die Entstehung der Rheinromantik.* Rheinische Sammlung 2 and 3, edited by C. Enders and P. Bourfeind. Cologne: Rheinland-Verlag, 1922.

Stockmann, Erich, ed. *Des Knaben Wunderhorn in den Weisen seiner Zeit.* Veröffentlichungen des Instituts für deutsche Volkskunde, Deutsche Akademie der Wissenschaften zu Berlin 16. Berlin: Akademie-Verlag, 1958.

Suppan, Wolfgang. "Volksgesang, Volksmusik und Volkstanz." *Die Musik in Geschichte und Gegenwart* 13:1923–56.

Susskind, Pamela. "Clara Schumann." *New Grove* 16:829.

Sutermeister, Peter. *Felix Mendelssohn-Bartholdy.* Zürich: Ex-Libris-Verlag, 1949

———. *Robert Schumann: Sein Leben nach Briefen, Tagebüchern und Erinnerungen des Meisters und seiner Gattin.* Zürich: Ex-Libris-Verlag, 1949.

Tacitus. *The "Agricola" and the "Germania."* Translated and edited by H. Mattingly and S. A. Handford. New York: Penguin Books, 1983.

Taton, René. *Science in the Nineteenth Century.* Translated by A. J. Pomerans. New York: Basic Books, 1965.

Tetzner, Franz, ed. *Deutsche Geschichte in Liedern deutscher Dichter.* Leipzig: Philipp Reclam jun., 1892–93.

Thiers, L. Adolphe. *Discours parlementaires (1837–1841),* vols. 4 and 5. Paris: Calmann Lévy, 1879–89.

Thomas, R. Hinton. *Liberalism, Nationalism, and the German Intellectuals, 1822–1847.* Cambridge: Heffer, 1951.

Tschirch, Wilhelm, ed. *Liederquell: 247 Volks-, Vaterlands-, Soldaten-Gesänge.* Leipzig: Steingräber, 1885.

Tuchman, Barbara W. *Practicing History: Selected Essays.* New York: Knopf, 1981.

Unger, Hermann, ed. *Festbuch zur Hundertjahrfeier der Concert-Gesellschaft in Köln, 1827–1927.* Cologne: Die Direktion der Concert-Gesellschaft, 1927.

Valsecchi, Marco. *Landscape Painting of the 19th Century.* Translated by Arthur A. Coppotelli. Greenwich, Conn.: New York Graphic Society, 1971.

Venedey, Jakob. *La France, l'Allemagne et les Provinces Rhénanes.* Paris: Auguste le Gallois, 1840.

———. *Der Rhein.* 2d ed. Bellevue bei Konstanz: Buchdruckerei der deutschen Volkshalle, 1841.

Virneisel, Wilhelm. "Friedrich Hofmeister." *Die Musik in Geschichte und Gegenwart* 6:574–77.

Volkmann, Ernst, ed. *Um Einheit und Freiheit, 1815–1848: Vom Wiener Kongress bis zur Märzrevolution.* Deutsche Literatur: Politische Dichtung 3. Leipzig: Philipp Reclam jun., 1936.

Walzel, Oskar. *German Romanticism.* Translated by Alma Elise Lussky. New York: Putnam, 1932. Reprint. New York: Capricorn Books, 1966.

Ward, Donald, ed. and trans. *The German Legends of the Brothers Grimm,* vol. 1. Philadelphia: Institute for the Study of Human Issues, 1981.

Wasielewski, Joseph Wilhelm von. *Life of Robert Schumann.* Translated by A. L. Alger. Boston: Oliver Ditson, 1871.

Weber, Gottfried. *Das Nibelungenlied: Problem und Idee.* Stuttgart: Metzler, 1964.

Weber, William. "The Muddle of the Middle Classes." *19th-Century Music* 3 (1979): 175–85.

———. "Music." *19th-Century Music* 1/2 (November 1977): 176.

———. *Music and the Middle Class.* New York: Holmes & Meier, 1975.

Wedel, Gottschalk [W. von Zuccalmaglio]. "Das deutsche Lied." *Neue Zeitschrift für Musik* (29 February 1844): 69–71; "Deutsches Volkslied" (13 May 1842): 153–54; (17 May 1842): 157–59; (7 June 1842): 162–63; "Vierstimmiger Gesang" (15 April 1842): 121–24.

——, ed. *Deutsche Liederhalle: Sammlung der ausgezeichnetsten Volkslieder*. Elberfeld and Leipzig: J. Rietz, 1846.

Wedel, Gottschalk, A. Kretzschmer, Massmann, and E. Baumstark, eds. *Deutsche Volkslieder mit ihren Original-Weisen*. Berlin: Vereins-Buchhandlung, 1840.

Wellek, René. "German and English Romanticism: A Confrontation." *Studies in Romanticism* 4/1 (Boston University Graduate School, autumn 1964): 35–56.

——. "Romanticism Re-examined." In *Concepts of Criticism*, 220–34. New Haven, Conn.: Yale University Press, 1963.

Wenzel, E. "Aus der baierischen Pfalz (das bevorstehende Musikfest)." *Neue Zeitschrift für Musik* (18 November 1842): 168.

Werner, Eric. *Mendelssohn: A New Image of the Composer and His Age*. Translated by Dika Newlin. London: Free Press of Glencoe (Collier-Macmillan), 1963.

Whistling, C. F. *C. F. Whistling's Handbuch der musikalischen Literatur, oder allgemeines systematisch geordnetes Verzeichniss der in Deutschland und in den angrenzenden Ländern gedruckten Musikalien, auch musikalischen Schriften und Abbildungen, mit Anzeige des Verleger und Preise*. 3d ed. 3 vols. and supplementary vol. (1839 to the beginning of 1844 and January 1844 to the end of 1851). Edited by Adolph Hofmeister. Leipzig: Friedrich Hofmeister, 1845, 1852.

White, Hayden. "The Value of Narrativity in the Representation of Reality." In *On Narrative*, edited by W. J. T. Mitchell, 1–23. Chicago: University of Chicago Press, 1981.

Whyte, Lancelot Lew. *The Unconscious before Freud*. New York: Doubleday, 1962.

Widmann, Benedikt. *Die kunsthistorische Entwickelung des Männerchors in drei Vorlesungen dargestellt*. Leipzig: C. Merseburger, 1884.

Wiora, Walter. *Das deutsche Lied: Zur Geschichte und Ästhetik einer musikalischen Gattung*. Wolfenbüttel: Möseler Verlag, 1971.

——. "Die Romantisierung alter Mollmelodik im Liede von Schubert bis Wolf." *Deutsches Jahrbuch der Musikwissenschaft für 1966*, edited by Rudolf Eller, 11:61–71. Reprinted in *Jahrbuch der Musikbibliothek Peters* 58. Leipzig: Peters, 1967.

Wolff, Ernst. "Das musikalische Leben." In *Die Rheinprovinz, 1815–1915*, edited by Joseph Hansen. 2d ed. Bonn: A. Marcus & E. Webers Verlag, 1917.

Würtz, Roland. "Düsseldorfer Musiker in der Mannheim Hofkapelle." In *Beiträge zur Musikgeschichte der Stadt Düsseldorf* 118:30–34. Cologne: Arno Volk-Verlag, 1977.

Zeitung für die elegante Welt 214 (Leipzig, 31 October 1840): 31.

Zeuner, Charles (1795–1857), comp. *German Songs*. Unpublished holograph, Library of Congress, Music Division, Washington, D.C.

Zimmer, Herbert. "Julius Rietz." Diss., Humboldt University, Berlin, 1943.

Zimmermann, Reinhold. "Zur Musikgeschichte des Aachener Raums im 19. und 20. Jahrhundert." In *Beiträge zur Musikgeschichte der Stadt Aachen* 6, edited by C. M. Brand and K. G. Fellerer. Cologne: Arno Volk-Verlag, 1954.

Zingel, H. J. *Das Kölner Gürzenichorchester: Werden und Sein.* Cologne: Arno Volk-Verlag, 1963.

"Zur Geschichte des Männergesanges." *Allgemeine musikalische Zeitung* (24 January 1844): 49–53; (31 January 1844): 65–68.

INDEX